Debating nationhood and governance in Britain, 1885–1945

MANCHESTER
1824

Manchester University Press

DEVOLUTION series
series editor Charlie Jeffery

Devolution has established new political institutions in Scotland, Wales, Northern Ireland, London and the other English regions since 1997. These devolution reforms have far-reaching implications for the politics, policy and society of the UK. Radical institutional change, combined with a fuller capacity to express the UK's distinctive territorial identities, is reshaping the way the UK is governed and opening up new directions of public policy. These are the biggest changes to UK politics for at least 150 years.

The *Devolution* series brings together the best research in the UK on devolution and its implications. It draws together the best analysis from the Economic and Social Research Council's research programme on Devolution and Constitutional Change. The series will have three central themes, each of which are vital components in understanding the changes devolution has set in train.

1 **Delivering public policy after devolution: diverging from Westminster**: Does devolution result in the provision of different standards of public service in health or education, or in widening economic disparities from one part of the UK to another? If so, does it matter?

2 **The political institutions of devolution**: How well do the new devolved institutions work? How effectively are devolved and UK-level matters coordinated? How have political organisations which have traditionally operated UK-wide – political parties, interest groups – responded to multi-level politics?

3 **Public attitudes, devolution and national identity**: How do people in different parts of the UK assess the performance of the new devolved institutions? Do people identify themselves differently as a result of devolution? Does a common sense of Britishness still unite people from different parts of the UK?

Debating nationhood and governance in Britain, 1885–1945

Perspectives from the 'four nations'

Edited by Duncan Tanner, Chris Williams, Wil Griffith and Andrew Edwards

Manchester University Press

Manchester and New York

distributed exclusively in the USA by Palgrave

Published by Manchester University Press
Oxford Road, Manchester M13 9NR, UK
and Room 400, 175 Fifth Avenue, New York, NY 10010, USA
www.manchesteruniversitypress.co.uk

Distributed exclusively in the USA by
Palgrave, 175 Fifth Avenue, New York,
NY 10010, USA

Distributed exclusively in Canada by
UBC Press, University of British Columbia, 2029 West Mall,
Vancouver, BC, Canada V6T 1Z2

British Library Cataloguing-in-Publication Data
A catalogue record for this book is available from the British Library

Library of Congress Cataloging-in-Publication Data applied for

ISBN   0 7190 7166 6 *hardback*
EAN   978 0 7190 7166 9

First published 2006

15 14 13 12 11 10 09 08 07 06   10 9 8 7 6 5 4 3 2 1

Typeset in 10/13 Galliard
by Servis Filmsetting Ltd, Manchester
Printed in Great Britain
by CPI, Bath

Contents

Contributors

D. George Boyce is Professor in the Department of Politics, University of Wales Swansea. His many books include *The Irish Question and British Politics, 1868–1996* (Palgrave/Macmillan, 1996); *The Making of Modern Irish History* (Routledge, 1996) edited with Alan O'Day and *Decolonization and the British Empire, 1775–1997* (Macmillan, 1999).

Matthew Cragoe is Professor of Modern British History at the University of Hertfordshire. He is the author of *An Anglican Aristocracy: The Moral Economy of the Landed Estate in Carmarthenshire, 1832–95* (Oxford University Press, 1996), and *Culture, Politics and National Identity in Wales, 1832–86* (OUP, 2004). Other works include edited collections on *Anticlericalism in Britain 1500–1900* (Sutton, 2000) with Nigel Aston; *London Politics, 1760–1914* (Macmillan, 2005) with Antony Taylor; and *Wales and War: Politics, Society and Religion in the Nineteenth and Twentieth Centuries* (University of Wales Press, 2006) with Chris Williams.

Dr John Davis has been Fellow in Modern History and Politics at The Queen's College, Oxford since 1989. Major publications include *Reforming London: the London Government Problem, 1855–1900* (Oxford University Press, 1988) and *A History of Britain, 1885–1939* (Macmillan/Palgrave, 1999). He was a Research Associate on the *Oxford Dictionary of National Biography*, contributing more than 50,000 words of biographical entries. He is currently working on a study of London in the 1960s and 1970s, and in the process has written on Rackmanism, road protests and other issues.

Dr Andrew Edwards is lecturer in the Department of History and Welsh History, University of Wales Bangor, and was formerly research assistant on the ESRC-funded History of Welsh Devolution project. He has published in *Welsh History Review*, *Llafur* (the Journal of the Welsh People's History Society) and in *Contemporary Wales*. He is currently writing a book on the fortunes of the Labour Party in north-west Wales from the 1960s to 1979 and the political and ideological challenge which it faced from Plaid Cymru and the Conservative Party.

Richard J. Finlay is Professor of Scottish History at the University of Strathclyde. His many books include *Independent and Free: Scottish Politics and the Origins of the SNP* (John Donald, 1994) and *A Partnership for Good: Scottish Politics and the Union Since*

1800 (John Donald, 1997). His latest book is *Modern Scotland, 1914–2000* (Profile Books, 2005).

Dr Wil Griffith is Head of the Department of History and Welsh History, University of Wales Bangor, and was a member of the ESRC-funded History of Welsh Devolution project. His most recent work concerns local government in Wales, and includes a book, *Power, Politics and Local Government in Wales: Anglesey 1780–1914* (Anglesey Antiquarian Society, Studies in Anglesey History, vol. 11, 2006).

Dr Matthew Kelly is British Academy Postdoctoral Research Fellow at Hertford College, University of Oxford. His first book, *The Fenian Ideal and Irish Nationalism, 1882–1914* (Boydell & Brewer, 2006). He is currently working on a study of Irish attitudes towards international affairs during the time of the French Second Empire.

Dr James McConnel is research associate at the Institute of Ulster Scots Studies, University of Ulster, and was research assistant on the ESRC-funded History of Welsh devolution project. His original research was on the Irish Parliamentary Party 1900–14. He has published articles on Irish politics in *Irish Historical Studies, Historical Journal, Past and Present*, and on Wales in the *Welsh History Review*. He is currently working on the commemoration of 5 November in nineteenth-century Ireland and a biographical study of the Ulster nationalist politician Joe Devlin.

Dr Deirdre McMahon is lecturer in History, Mary Immaculate College, University of Limerick. Recent publications include a chapter in Kevin Kenny (ed.), *Ireland and the British Empire* (OUP, 2004) and an edited volume of letters *The Moynihan Brothers in Peace and War 1908–18* (Irish Academic Press, 2004). She is currently completing an oral history project on Irish Catholic missionaries in India.

Duncan Tanner is Professor of History at the University of Wales Bangor and Director of the Welsh Institute for Social and Cultural Affairs. He organised the ESRC-funded History of Welsh Devolution project, 2002–05. His publications on British Labour politics include *Political change and the Labour party 1900–18* (Cambridge University Press, 2000) and *Labour's First Century* (CUP, 2000), edited with Nick Tiratsoo and Pat Thane. His publications on Wales include *The Labour Party in Wales, 1900–2000* (University of Wales Press, 2000), edited with Chris Williams and Deian Hopkin.

Chris Williams is Professor of Welsh History at the University of Wales Swansea. He is the author of *Democratic Rhondda: Politics and Society, 1885–1951* (University of Wales Press, 1996), *Capitalism, Community and Conflict: The South Wales Coalfield, 1898–1947* (UWP, 1998), and a series of works relating to the writer and miner B. L. Coombes, with Bill Jones. He is the editor of *A Companion to Nineteenth Century Britain* (Blackwell, 2004), of *The Labour Party in Wales, 1900–2000* (UWP, 2000) with Duncan Tanner and Deian Hopkin, of *Postcolonial Wales* (UWP, 2005) with Jane Aaron, and of *Wales and War: Politics, Society and Religion in the Nineteenth and Twentieth Centuries* (UWP, 2006) with Matthew Cragoe.

Acknowledgements

Five of the contributors to this book were part of an ESRC-funded project on Welsh devolution (grant award L219252120) which was part of the ESRC Devolution and Constitutional Change Research Programme. The editors are especially grateful to Professor Charlie Jeffery, director of the programme, for his assistance and support. Four of the essays in this volume are derived directly from that project. We are also grateful to Stephanie Dolben from the University of Wales Bangor for her administrative support with the manuscript and with the ESRC project more generally.

Abbreviations

AOH	Ancient Order of Hibernians
CA	*Cape Argus*
CF	*Cymru Fydd*
CT	*Cape Times*
CUL	Cambridge University Library
CWB	Central Welsh Board
DC	*Daily Chronicle*
DD	Dáil Debates
DWB	*Dictionary of Welsh Biography*
EHR	*English Historical Review*
EPH	*Eastern Province Herald*
ESRC	Economic and Social Research Council
FJ	*Freeman's Journal*
GJ	*Grahamstown Journal*
GLC	Greater London Council
HC	House of Commons Debates
HDC	*Huddersfield Daily Chronicle*
HWJ	*History Workshop Journal*
IF	*Imperial Federation*
IFL	Imperial Federation League
IRA	Irish Republican Army
ISDL	Irish Self-Determination League
JBS	*Journal of British Studies*
JHG	*Journal of Historical Geography*
LCC	London County Council
LGB	Local Government Board
LLP	London Labour Party
LMA	London Metropolitan Archives
NAI	National Archives of Ireland
NAVSR	National Association for the Vindication of Scottish Rights
NEC	National Executive Committee
NLF	National Liberal Federation
NLS	National Library of Scotland
NLW	National Library of Wales
NLWJ	*National Library of Wales Journal*

NM	*Natal Mercury*
NPH	*Natal Province Herald*
NPS	National Party of Scotland
NW	*Natal Witness*
NWC	*North Wales Chronicle*
ODNB	*Oxford Dictionary of National Biography*
PET	*Port Elizabeth Telegraph*
PLA	Port of London Authority
PN	*Pretoria News*
SHR	*Scottish Historical Review*
SNP	Scottish Nationalist Party
SWGCTPA	South Wales Garden Cities and Town Planning Association
SWMF	South Wales Miners Federation
TD	Teachta Dála
THSC	*Transactions of the Honourable Society of Cymmrodorion*
TN	*Times of Natal*
TNA	The National Archives
TP	*The Press*
TRHS	*Transactions of the Royal Historical Society*
TUC	Trades Union Congress
UIL	United Irish League
UWB	University of Wales Bangor
WEA	Workers' Educational Association
WHDA	Welsh Housing and Development Association
WHDYB	*Welsh Housing and Development Year Book*
WHYB	*Welsh Housing Year Book*
WHR	*Welsh History Review*
WM	*Western Mail*
WO	*Welsh Outlook*
YSS	Young Scots Society
YW	*Young Wales*

Introduction: devolution, identity and British politics

Duncan Tanner

Devolution has attracted considerable attention from scholars of governance, policy and the law – much of it from within the Economic and Social Research Council's (ESRC's) Devolution and Constitutional Change Research Programme or from the Leverhulme-funded Constitution Unit. This has created a major concentration of research activity on the unprecedented constitutional changes of the last decade, which have embraced far more than devolution itself.[1] Nonetheless, a large proportion of the research has focused on the new political landscape created in Ireland, Scotland and Wales as a result of the asymmetrical devolution settlement constructed by New Labour. Scholars from a range of disciplines have understandably examined the ways in which this huge shift has influenced UK policy and the way that it continues to evolve. Whilst this book is unashamedly historical, it also highlights trends in the process of devolution which are of continuing significance to those who wish to explain the nature of the recent constitutional changes and to appreciate the problems of creating legitimate and popular devolved governance.

Devolution and the constitutional agenda

Current research programmes, with their interest in English regional devolution, freedom of information and other constitutional changes, have rightly relocated devolution within British constitutional history, rather than portraying it as a purely 'Celtic' issue. From the time when John Smith became leader of the Labour Party onwards, party documents openly portrayed devolution as just one part of an attempt to modernise the 'machinery of British governance'.[2] The creation of the Department for Constitutional Affairs in June 2003 demonstrated institutionally that devolution was part of a British programme of reforms.[3] Yet studies which examine devolution as just one part of Labour's constitutional agenda (both in the past and even in the 1990s) are still unusual.[4]

At the same time, devolution is undoubtedly the cornerstone of the programme. Its significance has been widely recognised. It could have serious ramifications for the unity of the United Kingdom because of its capacity to intensify 'Celtic' identities. Separate Assemblies could gradually act more independently of the UK Government and come into conflict with Parliament. It seems highly likely that devolved governance will lead to calls for more devolved powers, both from those who want to make things 'happen' when in power and those in opposition who seek a ready made alternative approach which is difficult to attack or refute. The call for more powers can also be invested with populist overtones. The relegation of the Secretaries of State for Wales and Scotland to bit parts within the Department of Constitutional Affairs was perceived as a national 'slight' by sections of the media. Wales had been 'sold out' according to one newspaper.[5] At least one Welsh Labour figure called for greater Assembly powers as a result. Such events feed the altogether more rational case for change made by bodies like the Richard Commission, set up to discuss further changes in the Welsh devolution settlement.[6] However, other developments may also promote the extension of devolved powers. Empirical analysis shows how all forms of national identity (including Englishness) have grown in strength since 1997. If the majority feel that devolution has made little difference (itself a disturbing fact) fewer people now oppose devolution and many wish to extend the powers of devolved Assemblies.[7] Such studies therefore unsurprisingly indicate that the political and constitutional structures established immediately after 1997 are unlikely to survive in this form, with greater devolved powers and increasingly separate political structures as the most plausible development.[8] Yet old institutional structures die hard. Many Labour MPs have argued that the relegation of the Secretary of State has reduced their capacity to influence the British government, since it is now harder to lobby for Wales and Scotland.[9] Parliamentary figures – especially those in the Labour Party – have already shown their hostility to further changes.

None of this should surprise the historian. The British Labour Party has seen devolution as just one aspect of its concern with the 'machinery of government' since 1918, when a policy committee bearing this title was formed under the chairmanship of Ramsay MacDonald. Similarly named committees have been formed throughout the party's history, and have also been formed in the Conservative Party.[10] During these detailed discussions it was always recognised that creating fresh Welsh and Scottish institutional frameworks could diminish the role (and number) of Scottish and Welsh MPs at Westminster. Predictions to this effect when devolution was debated in the 1970s have seemingly born fruit.[11]

Devolution and popular opinion

An historical approach to these and other recurrent issues is an important check on the tendency to see what has been achieved – and what is likely to develop – as an inevitable outcome of popular sentiment. We need to recognise that support for devolved governance still has to be built, that it is not the natural product of powerful national sentiments. Enthusiasm for devolution remains partial because, for a century, support has been limited. Identities remain unclear because, for a century, identities have been strongly contested. These historic realities – evident from the 1880s onwards – came to fruition in the 1979 referendum. Devolution obtained a narrow majority in Scotland in 1979 and was overwhelmingly rejected in Wales. Nor had the longstanding obstacles and problems entirely disappeared by the time of the 1997 referendum. If in Scotland there was a further increase in support by 1997, in Wales a large increase still resulted in a majority in favour of devolution of just 7,000. Regional devolution in England has proved even less popular. This does not necessarily indicate weak national or sub-national identities. Many people who saw themselves as 'Welsh' or 'Scottish' opposed devolution, especially in 1979.[12] There was no explosion in the proportion of people who claimed a Welsh or Scottish identity between 1979 and 1997.[13] Rather, more of those who identified themselves as Welsh or Scottish supported devolution – a development which has continued since the first elections for the devolved bodies. Although some writers identified a crisis of identity in the rejection of nationhood in 1979, work on Anglo-Welsh, Anglo-Scottish and Black-British literature has done much more to explain how hybrid or overlapping identities are not part of a 'crisis' but a 'normal' feature of many lives. This may help us to explain how identity politics do not necessarily lead to support for separate governing bodies.[14] Certainly at the moment neither historians nor political scientists have done much to explain the relationship between identity and voting over the twentieth century by embracing a cross-disciplinary, cross-period, cross-border perspective on the evolving nature of popular opinion.

If study of the present – and of the future – is in good hands, the history of devolution and the explanation of the limited historical (and limited current) enthusiasm for devolved governance has been less well-served. There has been some excellent but limited academic analysis of changes in popular opinion between 1979 and 1997, much of it emanating from specialist research units and sophisticated electoral and attitudinal surveys. There has been still more on the period since 1997.[15] The process by which devolution returned to the political agenda even in the 1990s has been less well-treated. Studies of the 1997 referendum campaigns (like earlier studies of the 1979 campaigns) once again placed devolution within a Celtic context, focusing on politics within Wales and Scotland and telling us little about the way in which devolution might be seen as part of a broader (British) concern with the modernisation of governance.[16]

Hence there is still much to explain even about the recent past. The nature and scale of the partial shift of opinion between the two referenda is more dramatic seen in the context of devolution's historic problems as a mass movement. Opposition to devolution was not a product of 'weak' pro-devolution campaigns in 1979 or 1997. It was far more deeply rooted. Nor was that opposition confined to Scotland, Ireland and Wales. 'Celtic' opinion was not just determined exclusively by 'Celtic' campaigners, and the nature of devolved governance was not determined by narrowly Welsh, Scottish or Irish concerns. In the end, the extent of devolved governance was not decided in Cardiff, Edinburgh or Belfast at all. It was decided in London. Yet whatever the gaps in our knowledge of events in Scotland, Ireland and Wales, they are as nothing compared to our ignorance of the British dimension.

Devolution, identity and Britishness

Research on the role of British politicians in the history of devolution is remarkably limited. Some episodes have received detailed attention, although largely from scholars based outside the UK, where interest in Britain's odd but internationally significant constitution remains substantial.[17] Within Britain, Vernon Bogdanor has fought, almost alone, a battle to present devolution as an historic issue which is also part of British constitutional history.[18] Historically-minded political scientists apart, Miles Taylor's study of the Labour leadership's varying attitude to constitutional issues across the century is almost unique, since most historians of the party have generally argued that it was indifferent to such concerns.[19] Rather, (and even before devolution) the culturally minded were stressing the historic separateness of 'Celtic' Britain in the past, and looked less at British unity than at actual and imagined literary and cultural distinctiveness. Scholars have demonstrated how Scottish identity in particular had been reinforced and reconstructed from medieval times to the present day.[20] Literary imaginings and political discourse have been seen as significant elements in the construction of identities, alongside ceremonies, material culture, visual cultures, the heritage industry and a host of other influences.[21] In this respect, events in the 'Celtic fringe' were part of a broader cultural process of nation building, since national identities were being constructed across Europe from the eighteenth century onwards.[22]

Whilst Britishness was once a significant area of interest,[23] that focus also seems to be shifting. Paralleling the growing volume of work on Celtic culture and identities, there has been considerable new research on regional separateness within England – especially on 'the North' and Cornwall[24] – and some work on the extent to which strongly developed local identities meshed with and sustained a sense of Englishness.[25] Similarly, a great deal has been written on early twentieth-century depictions of an English national character.[26] For some writers, it is no coincidence that public expressions of a British identity coincided with Victorian imperial expansion and later imperial problems. They draw clear parallels between English/ British cultural domination of the Empire and a comparable attempt to dominate the 'Celtic fringe'. To be English was to be part of a great Empire and to espouse a host of confident English values, represented as Britishness.[27] Post-colonial writers argue that the formation of more sharply defined national and separate Celtic identities was stifled by this dominant, and government sustained, sense of Englishness. At home and abroad, 'Englishness' (rebranded as Britishness) dominated institutional policy and public discourse. A colonial mindset was created, in which peoples' capacities to think independently and outside of this English/British framework of values became increasingly constrained.[28]

Such theories are a vital source of new ideas and approaches. Whilst there may be legitimate doubts about the historical credibility of some postcolonial analysis, the approach itself cannot be ignored. There were certainly people who wrote of 'the English' and the superiority of an English culture to the 'peasant' cultures of Scotland, Ireland and Wales. There were different cultural emphases (and different languages) in the Celtic countries which declined as the English language and its attendant values permeated the Celtic fringe.[29] However, that does not mean there was a single English discourse which replaced a single Welsh, Scottish or Irish discourse as a result of an imperialistic intellectual ascendancy. Moreover, if 'Celtic' peoples changed their views, there were other possible explanations of their behaviour, including contact with 'English' organisations – churches, voluntary organisations, trade unions and other groups – which expressed similar aims to their own. The demise or limited appeal of an indigenous discourse could also reflect its weaknesses as an expression of local sentiments. To explain this, we need to go beyond post-colonial analysis. One common distinction in the theoretical writing on constructed national identities (of the kind which might have rivalled an English/British discourse) is between an essentialist perspective – which stresses the way in which identities are constructed around a common core of ethnic, linguistic or cultural values – and manufactured identities built through a discourse of civic nationhood, expressed in literature, symbolism or even national institutions.[30] Whilst 'ethnic' emphases were much in evidence in nineteenth-century nationalist writing, most writing since the 1980s has highlighted the ways in which identities have been manufactured around either civic institutions or depictions of an assumed national character.[31] This varying conceptual literature could be used to explain the absence of support for devolved governance in ways which go beyond post-colonial ideas. It is possible, for example, that 'colonial' English 'invaders' were insufficiently resented in Scotland and Wales to be seen as an alien 'other', and hence to inflame a more politicised sense of Welsh and Scottish separateness. The very fact that the Irish, Scottish and Welsh nations were not constructed institutionally – and had to be imagined – could be significant because research on other countries has indicated that national sentiment is often much enhanced *after* nations came into being.[32] However, we should also ask whether there was a colonial 'domination' of Scottish, Irish and Welsh thinking, or a simple – and 'rational' – rejection of the discourse of identity and nationhood developed within the Celtic countries was a significant element of this relationship.

When looking at the purchase of either ethnic or civic conceptions of identity within the Celtic countries, we have to recognise that these were not united countries with a single outlook. All the Celtic nations had their own languages, although only Wales had a language which was still widely spoken at the start of this period, and even then English was spreading.[33] As important as language has been in constructing identities and nations – and in feeding national resentment where repressed by a dominant force – it could also be an internally divisive factor. As Anthony Smith in particular has argued, identities built on linguistic or religious cohesion can easily alienate those outside these 'ethnic' cultures. Identities based on civic inclusion, whilst less easy to mobilise, have generally been more securely based in the longer term. Ethnic nationalisms which adopt civic clothes may still be perceived as narrowly cultural or anti-modernist, making it harder to gain mass support in periods where 'modernisation' was an attractive if intangible sentiment.[34] Given the division of Ireland on religious lines, Wales by language, and the division of all three Celtic nations into discrete geographical areas, the construction of a cohesive and persuasive national discourse, whether ethnic or civic, was hardly easy.

The literature on countries which have needed (or need) to integrate a variety of distinct national groups into a multinational state also helps to explain how Britishness may have remained strong, for it suggests that states may appropriate sub-national identities into an attractive and cross-national discourse.[35] The British monarchy's approach to Scotland and Wales could be seen in this light, since it tried to present the monarchy as an institution which had roots and sympathies across the United Kingdom. Of course, we should not assume that this automatically works. States that are constructed from diverse sub-national ingredients are subject to varying internal tensions. All recent work recognises the existence of fluid, complex, overlapping, hybrid, multi-layered and other forms of identity within such units.[36] Success in turning this complex mix into support for the central state in the absence of a more strident sense of conflict (such as war or invasion) is not common. Even in famously centralised countries like France, where peasants were allegedly turned into Frenchmen at the end of the nineteenth century, a sense of identity based on a constructed sense of nationhood did not necessarily develop into a vehement political nationalism.[37] Nor was Britishness so powerful, even in 1914, that people rallied to King and country as fervently as the propagandists would have liked. Rather, motives were mixed, and in the Celtic areas were as much a consequence of martial traditions as of British patriotism.[38]

The literature on constructed identities – whether relating to states or their constituent sub-national elements – has one shared and major defect. Few such studies look at how these creative imaginings were received and understood by ordinary people. This is understandable, in that hard empirical evidence is difficult to find for the period before 1945. Even thereafter, seemingly neutral measures, like opinion polls, were often tools in the construction of national expectations rather than value-free measures of national sentiment.[39] Yet obsessively examining those who imagined their nation compounds an existing imbalance in the literature. Advocates of devolution have always received considerable attention. For the pre-1918 period, there are shelves of books on the 'Irish Question.' Historians have shown how Scotland, Wales and England were swept into debates on Irish Home Rule as opponents of Home Rule tried to avoid the break up of Britain by developing a federal solution.[40] Scottish and Welsh historians have examined their countrymen's own interests in 'Home Rule All Round.'[41]

The literature on the period after 1918 is little different. There are numerous references to campaigns to secure a Secretary of State for Wales.[42] The formation and development of nationalist parties between the wars has also produced a series of monographs.[43] In Wales, far more has been written about the Nationalist Party before 1945 (when it was a small organisation which failed to contest more than a few seats) than has been written about the Welsh Conservatives and Welsh Liberals. Both of these parties vastly outpolled the nationalist party, not just between the wars but until the first National Assembly elections in 1999. Their continued popularity after 1945 remains neglected, whilst post-war nationalism has received considerable attention. There are also few studies of what was achieved or undertaken by the Welsh Office, perhaps because for many it was a halfway house on the way to 'real' devolved governance.[44] Studies of the Welsh Office's precursors, the devolved administrative boards, or of what was achieved through Westminster, are almost unknown.[45] Much Welsh history has thus been the history of a nation in the making and the makers of the nation. Myths of betrayal surround figures once associated with Home Rule – notably Lloyd George – whose reputation was sullied within Wales for his 'failure' to support devolution when it became a serious issue in 1919–21.[46] Those who supported the small 'Parliament for Wales' movement in the 1950s have been held up as heroes.[47] In such an intellectual climate, it is perhaps unsurprising that 'Labour nationalists' in Wales – as in Scotland and Ireland – have received more attention than a host of politicians who worked for Wales at Westminster.[48] It is a remarkably unbalanced historical record.

The literature on Ireland is (understandably) fuller on Unionist opponents of devolution both before and after 1918.[49] In Scotland too there are some excellent works on the Conservatives and their support for the Union,[50] and good work has been done on the Scottish Office, both in general[51] and at particular moments in time.[52] However, even here the 'good Scotsman' would seem to be a supporter of the national solution and the preservation of a rural culture which some saw as the heart of Scottish identity.[53] In all the Celtic countries, the emphasis on nationhood and identity in academic texts is nothing compared to the images created by popular histories and school text books, with their lurid tales of oppression by invading English forces and cultures.[54] Popular culture, museums and the heritage industry continue to sustain their own 'national' assessments of past events, even when academics portray them very differently.[55]

Nor have historians in England used the archives on their doorstep to counter these developments and study how the 'peripheral' parts of the United Kingdom were governed and rendered part of Britain. Whilst the mammoth archives at Kew have spawned many histories of British social and economic policy, and almost as many studies of colonial administration, few have used their holdings to study the governance of Wales and Scotland or to compare policy across the territories of the UK. The activities of the separate administrative Boards constructed to administer Welsh policy after 1900 are seldom mentioned in studies of British agricultural, educational or health policy. Scotland's governance before 1945 has been similarly marginalised within texts on British policy.[56] Even when some professed students of Britishness look at the twentieth century, their references to Scotland, Ireland and Wales invariably focus on nationalist parties or on nationalist imaginings and writings.[57] Despite some excellent recent historical works,[58] the construction of Britain through the political process remains under-researched.

Devolution 1885–1945: governing structures and opportunities for change

The aim of this volume on the period before 1945 is not to go to the other extreme, to identify and study the most strident defenders of class above nation, of British unity and internationalism over Celtic separateness. These people – who were especially prominent in opposing devolution when it was debated – have been the subject of much research already.[59] Nor is this a complete history of devolution between 1885 and the end of the war. That task is too large and current research too limited to sustain such an ambition. Rather, the volume seeks to explain why those who supported devolution were not stronger, focusing on how a system of decentralisation through local government (and moderate advances on that in Ireland, Scotland and Wales) came to be seen as the final stopping point, not just by Labour's most vehement class warriors or by rabid defenders of the Union but by the majority of politicians outside the nationalist parties. The book builds on conceptual approaches and comparative studies which highlight the obstacles to the development of sub-national governance and identities, combining this with fresh archival material in order to point research in new directions. In doing so, we implicitly reassert the importance of various bodies of scholarship – that which emphasises the role of the 'Celtic countries' as part of the UK,[60] which examines Britishness[61] or addresses local/regional governance within the UK as 'Britain's' form of decentralisation.[62] The essays also provide a context for fuller studies of devolution since 1945, and provide an antidote to analysis which sees the current position as the 'natural' end point of a long journey.

We are aware that this work might be portrayed as a preference for a particular constitutional settlement, as scepticism about post-colonialism or post-modernism, or as 'ethno-centric' – as other works on the limitations of national unity have been.[63] This would be both an inaccurate rendition of the contributors' (diverse) constitutional views (which includes much enthusiastic support for devolution) and a misunderstanding of the volume's contents. Several of the essays examine the relationship between imperial attitudes and debates over devolution.[64] Several identify colonial ways of thinking about Celts generally and especially about Wales.[65] It is more plausible to see the volume as an assertion of the value of historicism, of reading sources within a contemporary framework informed but not dominated by any particular theory. This is not a retreat into empiricism. We have demonstrated elsewhere that apparently robust empirical measures of national identity may themselves be contested representations of 'facts'.[66] We are aware that everyday life may develop a banal but implicit nationalism which often goes unstudied, and which may suggest the capacity to develop a national perspective. We appreciate that the ritualistic turn which followed the linguistic turn allows us to see how events like rugby matches and political demonstrations carry implicit messages about national identities – which again could have a political capacity. [67] Indeed, we hope that research building on such ideas will show how separateness *and* Britishness have been sustained in the past by features of everyday life and by public ritual.[68] We offer a volume which is influenced by the conceptual ideas and approaches outlined above, but more mindful than most theoretical works to historical sources.

If much of the past history of devolution remains to be researched, we at least know how it looked in terms of concrete governing structures. Before 1914, Ireland was governed from Dublin, in a unit which embraced the activities of forty Whitehall departments. War and civil war terminated that arrangement. The post-war conflict in Ireland was ended when the Anglo-Irish Treaty established an Irish Free State. Formed from twenty-six counties (i.e. excluding six counties in the north), the new Irish Republic was initially a self-governing dominion within the Empire. However, following the Irish civil war the remaining constitutional links with Britain were gradually severed. Largely symbolic changes diminished the formal role of the Crown and in 1936 reduced it to almost nothing when Ireland left the Commonwealth. Northern Ireland was very different. An act of 1920 devolved considerable powers to the Northern Ireland Parliament, although a tight financial relationship, and the retention of British laws, taxes and the power of veto, meant freedom within certain limits. The parliament did little to integrate the nationalist minority. Leading state officials were largely drawn from the old elite, together with new junior appointments, who (like the police) were often Protestant ex-servicemen. The parliament's education and housing policies were particular sources of internal tension, as well as being an embarrassment to the British Government. Both policy and administration discriminated against Catholics. The devolved parliament – from 1932 based at Stormont – also always needed additional financial support from Westminster over and above its allocation.

Scotland had retained a variety of separate laws and institutions after the Act of Union. Whilst supporters of Home Rule could not assume mass support, further administrative independence was more popular. The creation of a Secretary of State for Scotland by Lord Rosebery in 1885 made little initial impact on governance. However, the Secretary of State was made a Cabinet post in 1892, and over the next decades the scale of activity – and status and size of the staff – increased substantially. The Scottish Office – not formally located in Edinburgh until 1936–37 – was responsible for health, education, justice, agriculture, fisheries and farming. It sustained and improved a distinctive and successful Scottish educational system and lobbied hard for the consideration of Scottish interests in agriculture and other areas. In various policy areas it was necessary to pass separate legislation at Westminster because of distinctive Scottish and Irish practices.

Wales – more fully integrated with England in legal and institutional terms – nonetheless had its own widely spoken language, a distinctive religious position and had started to develop 'national' institutions by the 1880s. Initially, Wales was treated separately only on religious issues – if one also sees education and temperance as religious issues. A separate Welsh Board of Education was established in 1906 and a Welsh Insurance Commission in 1911. Thereafter Welsh Boards were set up to deal with agriculture and health (some of the issues devolved to Scotland). There was a notable expansion of these devolved responsibilities during the First World War and its aftermath. The devolved boards acquired responsibility for the treatment of tuberculosis, venereal disease, maternity and child welfare and other issues. There were attempts to downgrade the chairmanship of the Welsh Board of Health in 1926, to regularise the appointments system and make posts accessible to people from outside Wales. These developments were resisted within Wales as a 'national insult'. Eventually, the 'insult' was withdrawn and some posts were effectively reserved for Welsh-speaking staff. In the 1930s, the monitoring of Poor Law functions, notably in relation to health, were devolved to the Boards, alongside further responsibility for nursing and midwifery. During the Second World War, town planning functions were temporarily added to the list. If the Welsh Boards are now seldom studied, at the time they were defended against incursions from central government as Welsh rule of Welsh concerns, and defended by some as a bulwark against the centralisation of authority which would result if power was focused in the hands of a Secretary of State for Wales based in London. County councils supported the Boards, concerned that the alternative was the creation of a distant and new bureaucracy.

Local councils were the final piece of the jigsaw. The complex and overlapping system of elected county councils, borough and county boroughs, and smaller urban, rural and parish councils created numerous hierarchies and divided responsibilities. Despite this, the status quo had many defenders. Locally based – and not overly large – administrative units improved accountability and helped develop a sense of civic commitment. Historic towns and counties in particular could claim genuine popular legitimacy. People in all parties supported changes in the way that local councils were organised so that they could cope with increased administrative responsibilities. A variety of developments – from suburbanisation through to the development of greater state planning – made it evident that the smaller units could no longer cope. Mass unemployment and the government's desire to expand health and maternity provision were not easily addressed by small local authorities with limited incomes and staff. Whilst

the capacity to fund local services through the rates meant councils were theoretically able to develop a degree of policy flexibility, the economic crisis of the
1930s meant that core services could only be delivered to a reasonably uniform
standard if they were paid for by central grants in aid. The larger bodies gained
powers at the expense of smaller administrative units, seemingly addressing
national problems in their own ways and (generally) in alliance with central government or its agencies.[69] These powers and the councils' remaining independent powers were highly valued. Although local authority independence was
further curtailed by war and by post-war central planning, councillors wished to
retain as much power in their own hands as was possible.

By 1945, an asymmetrical pattern of devolved administration had been
established, albeit one which stopped substantially short of the asymmetrical
position established after 1997. This was not more widely challenged in part
because Scottish and Welsh interests and concerns were at least being
addressed.[70] Alongside this, there was widespread, indeed passionate, support
for 'British' features of the post-war Labour government's policy agenda. The
National Health Service, the nationalised industries and the larger trade
unions were British institutions which addressed Scottish and Welsh problems
through looking at issues in a UK context. Wartime events may also have
helped to bring Britain together as a multinational state. Propaganda films
had tried to create the impression of a nation fighting as one, in which all
classes and parts of the UK pulled together. Labour leaders seemed to believe
their own rhetoric, both on class and on national unity.[71] They felt that
nationalism (meaning national separatism) should be vehemently opposed as
a destructive and corrosive force, whether it occurred abroad (as in the 1930s)
or at home (in the form of fascist or nationalist parties).[72] Moreover, reconstruction seemed to require not the fragmentation of the wartime national
effort but its continuation, the maintenance of control not its dilution.

The belief in Britishness and in economic planning was not a simple
product of wartime patriotism. The experience of devolved governance and
administration in the decades before 1945 was itself an influence. The creation of an Irish republic had not been a smooth and easy process for Britain.
On the contrary, it had incited rebellion and independent thinking in the
Empire between 1916 and 1922 and again in the 1930s.[73] If the existing
Scottish devolved system was accepted in London, since it removed difficult
issues from the agenda of the Imperial Parliament, and because Ireland and
Scotland were historically 'different', there was no desire to repeat the
problems that this process at times created for central government.[74]
Northern Ireland was felt to be a particularly poor precedent. Devolution had
worked – in the sense that it created an expert group which was able to deliver
policies and a political structure which deflected blame and controversy from

Westminster. However, the British Government felt the pre-war administration was a very partial success, and that its wartime government was lethargic and inept.[75] In 1945, Labour's General Secretary also reported that the experience of wartime administration suggested that devolved powers for Scotland had produced 'an unnecessary delay' in decision-making, notably in education.[76] As a result, at the end of the war the centralised governing system seemed stronger than ever, with Northern Ireland a recognised blot on the record and Scottish education an admired exception (for some) rather than a reason for taking things further.

The small nationalist parties and supporters of devolution within the British political parties were in no position to challenge this. Nationalist parties gained little support in 1945 from within existing elites or from the electorate. They had struggled to provide relevant thoughts on the economic problems of the 1930s. Both the Welsh and Scottish parties were internally divided over tone and tactics, and were dismissed as cranks by observers.[77] In Wales, leading nationalist figures were opposed to the war effort. As a result they were watched by the police during the war and faced much hostility during the 1945 election.[78] Whilst pacifism had been an accepted part of a Welsh elite culture between the wars, especially when combined with religious values, this was hardly the basis for a mass appeal.[79]

In fact, the views of nationalist parties were less significant than the reactions within the British-wide political parties and within civil society. The way in which Welsh and Scottish concerns were at times received in England – the negative attitudes to Wales, Scotland and Ireland which were periodically expressed by the English political establishment   still had the capacity to inflame national sentiments at the end of the period covered, contributing to a sense of national 'difference'.[80] Support for a Secretary of State for Wales had also grown within the Labour Party from the later 1930s. Although there were largely pragmatic reasons for this, dismissive English reactions to Welsh representations on this issue caused some disquiet.[81]

This political friction was in part a consequence of some little-studied developments, including increased concern with the preservation of Welsh life in the face of depopulation, economic decline, large scale social change and substantial in-migration.[82] There was certainly support for a stronger Welsh voice in planning and regional policy amongst rural councils in particular during the latter stages of the war.[83] In 1944, the Labour Party's national conference rejected Attlee's mechanism for dealing with these problems (regional governance) following a rebellion led by people wedded to existing local government structures.

Nor did these tensions disappear during the post-war Labour government. The Scottish wartime administration – first under Walter Elliot and then Thomas Johnston – was favourably received in Scotland at least. Many Scots were very positive about the Scottish devolved system and there was some support – even within the Conservative Party – for the Secretary of State to play an enhanced role. Although the poor performance of Labour's Scottish Office between 1945 and 1951 was seen as a problem, the answer was felt to be new faces or new powers.[84] In Wales, several new Labour supporters of devolution and of Welsh culture were elected to Parliament for the first time between 1945 and 1951. There were also tensions within the Welsh Parliamentary Labour group because the Labour leadership refused to appoint a Secretary of State for Wales (and hence at long last treat Wales like Scotland). The centralised nature of post-war reconstruction helped fuel aspects of this unease. Those who favoured decentralisation – whether in the Health Service or in local government – soon became disillusioned with the policy thrust of the post-war Labour government.[85] A Home Rule petition in Scotland attracted millions of signatures. There was, in short, no complete identification of the 'Celts' with Britain. The capacity to revive devolution remained, but within a system which nonetheless seemed broadly stable.

Devolution and constitutional change: rewriting the story

Our desire to explain the strength of opposition to devolution does much to justify the unusual balance and emphases of the volume. The first section of the book deals with Scotland and Ireland. It shows that the experience of having a Secretary of State (as discussed in Chapter 1 by Richard Finlay), of setting up an Irish Free State (as discussed in Chapter 13 by Deirdre McMahon) and of developing Stormont (as discussed in Chapter 2 by George Boyce) were unlikely to encourage governments either to support the extension of devolved governance to England and Wales or to support Home Rule for Scotland. We examine Irish Home Rule not to repeat the familiar story of those who supported change, but to understand the attitudes of those (in England) who resisted it. We also puncture the myth of Celtic unity on the Home Rule issue to explain the absence of stronger and more united pressure for change across Ireland, Scotland and Wales.

Wales – where devolution was least pronounced – forms the second part of the volume. The often unspoken concerns and silent prejudices generated in British minds by the 'lessons' of devolution in Scotland and Ireland were concentrated on proposals that devolved governance should be applied more fully in Wales. This helps to explain why British governments were happy to continue with the oddly asymmetrical constitutional relationship established after 1918, which gave Wales much less control of its affairs than had been awarded to Scotland. Welsh advocates of devolution were unable to create an inclusive, practical and popular response. Pre-war calls for change (discussed in Chapter 4 by Wil Griffith) reveal that many of the themes which have dogged the progress of Welsh devolution across a century were apparent even before 1914. The position became worse after the war, as pre-war supporters of 'Wales' moved in politically different directions. The cultural – and elitist – sense of Welsh identity adopted by many nationalists was not confined to members of the new nationalist party. Cultural elitism ensured that even some Liberal nationalists were distant from the mass electorate (even though we should not underestimate their roots in a substantial section of traditional Welsh society). Advocates of a 'national solution' involving devolution did little to maximise their support across parties, languages and cultures (as is revealed in Chapter 5 by Andrew Edwards and Wil Griffith). Many 'social radicals' outside the Labour Party might agree with them on the preservation of Welsh culture and traditions, but they held varying views on devolved administration (as noted in Chapter 6 by Chris Williams). Pressures for change from within Wales were thus an ineffective challenge to the established parties' rather different emphases. Whilst there was certainly some emulation of and support for English/British values within Wales (as post-colonialists would expect) at least part of the problem was the limited appeal of 'Welsh' solutions to the problems faced by the mass electorate.

The third part of the book shows how across the period British political parties were influenced by ideas and priorities which pushed them further away from devolution. They mounted a strong defence of existing constitutional structures. Imperial concerns were one such factor (discussed in the chapter by James McConnel and Matthew Kelly). We also show how the Conservatives promoted a sense of English/British identity (considered in Chapter 8 by Matthew Cragoe). Likewise, Labour politicians developed an agenda which they felt was more relevant than devolution to the needs of Wales and Scotland. Like regionalism, devolution was rejected in favour of other constitutional reforms and methods of territorial management (as discussed in Chapter 10 by Duncan Tanner). Efficient central and local government were best promoted through an integrated system (an issue explained in Chapter 9 by John Davis) which could mean larger local government units, rather than more substantive forms of devolution. The National Government helped in this respect by making symbolic concessions to the devolved administrations in Wales and Scotland which were meant to make the existing system more 'Celtic'.[86]

As a result of these emphases, this section of the book does not deal directly with the Celtic fringe at all, a major shift of emphasis within the literature. By looking at central government attitudes to territorial management, we examine the views of the decision-makers, unearthing their explanations of why devolved governance should go no further. Relocating the study of devolution within a British context – as students of contemporary devolution have done – has positive implications for our understanding of the past. A concern with the machinery of government is shown to have been an aspect of Labour's interest in constitutional affairs for more than a century. A series of other sub-themes within the book also help to identify how the Westminster system was reinforced. Objections to devolution from within local government and the Civil Service have always provided powerful institutional opposition to proponents of change. The difficulties of finding a devolution settlement which reflected the different circumstances in Ireland, Scotland and Wales, but also satisfied desires for equality between nations, has been a recurrent problem. Even within a particular part of the UK, discussions over the powers which devolved assemblies should have and the methods by which people should be elected divided advocates of change. Neither a 'civic' nor an 'ethnic' approach created unity. Whilst our analysis is confined to the period before 1945 in this volume, the same themes are apparent in our research on the period from 1945 to 1979 and reoccur as problems which were (partially) addressed between 1979 and 1997.

The cumulative impact of the book is to demonstrate that before 1945 the forces which pulled Britain together were more potent than those which might pull it apart. Those who argued against devolution had considerable influence and power, and a good degree of support within the Celtic fringe itself. Yet this cannot be explained solely by a 'post-colonial' domination of the 'Celtic' mind. Anti-devolutionists were materially assisted by the limitations of 'Celtic' thinking, by divisions amongst advocates of change – and by the mixing of families, peoples and economic livelihoods, all of which (like the success of some British institutions) made Britishness if not an enthusiasm at least a functional identity. That is not to say that tensions had been eradicated, whether through the persistence of (resented) colonial attitudes or the purchase of varying 'Celtic' identities. However, these tensions were politically manageable. By putting devolution back into British history, albeit as something which was hardly central to most British politicians, the book offers an approach which fits more comfortably with the long, difficult and resisted process by which Britain has achieved devolution. Putting Britain back into Welsh, Irish and Scottish politics adds to our understanding of events within those countries. Devolution was not central in the past because it did not relate sufficiently to the core concerns of British decision-makers or the diverse peoples of Scotland, Ireland and Wales. Advocates of devolution did not rise to a challenge which remains as significant today as it was in the past.

Notes

1 For details of projects see www.devolution.ac.uk and www.ucl.ac.uk/constitution-unit.
2 Labour Party, *Meet the Challenge, Make the Change: A New Agenda for Britain* (London, 1989) and *A New Agenda for Democracy: Labour's Proposals for Constitutional Reform* (London, 1993).
3 Alan Trench (ed.), *Has Devolution made a Difference? The State of the Nations* (Exeter, 2004), pp. 183–6.
4 For an exception, e.g. Mark Evans, *Constitution-making and the Labour Party* (Basingstoke, 2003).
5 *WM*, 13 June 2003.
6 See the discussion in e.g. Laura McAllister, 'The Richard Commission – Wales's alternative constitutional convention?', *Contemporary Wales*, 17 (2005).
7 Anthony Heath, James Tilley and Sonia Exley, 'The decline of Britishness', EPOP conference 2004; Richard Wyn Jones and Roger Scully, 'Turnout, participation and legitimacy in post-devolution Wales', *British Journal of Political Science*, 34 (2004).
8 Richard Rawlings, *Delineating Wales: Constitutional, Legal and Administrative Aspects of National Devolution* (Cardiff, 2003); Martin Laffin, Eric Shaw and Gerald R. Taylor, 'The role of the party in governmental relations after devolution', ESRC report (2004); Roger Scully and Richard Wyn Jones, 'Politics and national identity', EPOP conference 2004. For Scotland, see e.g. Michael Keating, *The Government of Scotland: Public Policy Making after Devolution* (Edinburgh, 2005) and for Ireland, Jonathan Tonge, *The New Northern Ireland Politics* (Basingstoke, 2004).
9 The Newport East AM, John Griffiths, *WM*, 14 June 2003.
10 R. I. McKibbin, *The Evolution of the Labour Party* (Oxford, 1974), pp. 216, 219. The NEC had a Machinery of Government Sub-Committee from the 1960s to the 1980s, during which time it became increasingly preoccupied with the House of Lords and the monarchy. In the 1970s the Conservatives' Machinery of Government committee dealt largely with the need to break up government departments and reform the Civil Service.
11 See for example predictions in the Parliamentary Labour Party Minutes by Leo Abse, Tam Dalyell and others , 2 December 1975.
12 Geoffrey Evans and Dafydd Trystan, 'Why was 1997 different?' in Bridget Taylor and Katrina Thomson (eds), *Scotland and Wales: Nations Again?* (Cardiff, 1999).
13 The 2001 census put the number of Welsh identifiers at 67%, just a fraction higher than in the 1960s and 1970s, when the figures fluctuated but generally stood in the low to mid 60s.
14 See e.g. Colin Kidd, *Subverting Scotland's Past: Scottish Whig Historians and the Creation of an Anglo-British Identity 1698-c.1830* (Cambridge, 1993) and Roderick Watson, 'Maps of desire: Scottish literature in the twentieth century', in Tom Devine and Richard Finlay (eds), *Scotland in the Twentieth Century* (Edinburgh, 1996). For Anglo-Welsh writing, Kirsti Bohata, *Postcolonialism Revisited* (Cardiff, 2004).
15 See essays in Taylor and Thomson, *Scotland and Wales: Nations Again?* and e.g. Richard Wyn Jones and Roger Scully, 'A settling will? Wales and devolution, five

years on', *British Parties and Elections Review*, 13 (2003). For Scotland, see e.g. John Curtice et al. (eds), *New Scotland, New Society?* (Edinburgh, 2001). More generally, see the programmes of work detailed by the Constitution Unit, the National Centre for Social Research and the Centre for Research into Social Trends (CREST) at Oxford.

16 J. Barry Jones and Dennis Balsom (eds), *The Road to the National Assembly for Wales* (Cardiff, 2000); Kevin Morgan and Geoff Mungham, *Redesigning Democracy: The Making of the Welsh Assembly* (Bridgend, 2000); Leighton Andrews, *Wales Says Yes: The Inside Story of the Yes for Wales Referendum Campaign* (Bridgend, 1999); Kenyon Wright, *The People Say Yes: The Making of Scotland's Parliament* (Argyll, 1997). For 1979, John Bochel et al. (eds), *The Referendum Experience: Scotland, 1979* (1981); David Foulkes et al. (eds), *The Welsh Veto: The Wales Act 1978 and the Referendum* (Cardiff, 1983).

17 E.g. John D. Fair, *British Interparty Conferences: A Study of the Procedure of Conciliation in British Party Politics 1867–1921* (Oxford, 1980).

18 Vernon Bogdanor, *Devolution in the United Kingdom* (Oxford, 1999) and Vernon Bogdanor (ed.), *The British Constitution in the Twentieth Century* (Oxford, 2003).

19 Miles Taylor, 'Labour and the constitution', in Duncan Tanner et al. (eds), *Labour's First Century* (Cambridge, 2000).

20 Dauvit Braun, Richard Finlay and Michael Lynch (eds), *Image and Identity: The Making and Remaking of Scotland through the Ages* (Edinburgh, 1998); Ian Donnachie and Chris Whatley (eds), *The Manufacture of Scottish History* (Edinburgh, 1992); Murray G. H. Pittock, *Scottish Nationality* (Basingstoke, 2001).

21 This reflects a decade of shifts in scholarship. For applications, John S. Ellis, 'Reconciling the Celt: British national identity, empire, and the 1911 I investiture of the Prince of Wales', *Journal of British Studies*, 37 (1998); Peter Lord, *Imaging the Nation* (Cardiff, 2000); S. Jones, 'Making place, resisting displacement: conflicting national and local identities in Scotland', in Jo Littler and Roshi Naidoo (eds), *The Politics of Heritage: Commemoration, Hybridity and National Stories* (London, 2005).

22 This has been especially apparent in work on Ireland. See e.g. Roy Foster, 'History and the Irish question', *Transactions of the Royal Historical Society*, 33 (1983), Brendon Bradshaw, 'Nationalism and historical scholarship in modern Ireland', *Irish Historical Studies*, 26 (1989), Lionel P. Curtis Jr., 'The greening of Irish history', *Eire/Ireland* (1994). For a comparable process in Wales, Huw Pryce, 'Modern nationality and the medieval past: the Wales of John Edward Lloyd', in Rees Davies and Geraint Jenkins (eds), *From Medieval to Modern Wales: Historical Essays in Honour of Kenneth O. Morgan and Ralph A. Griffiths* (Cardiff, 2004) and for Scotland, Kidd, *Subverting Scotland's Past*. More generally, Jim MacLaughlin, *Reimagining the Nation State* (London, 2001). The construction of national histories is the focus of a major European Social Foundation research programme entitled 'Representations of the Past: The Writing of National Histories in Europe.' (www.uni-leipzig.de/zhs/esf-nhist and www.esf.org/nhist).

23 The most cited work is Linda Colley, *Britons: Forging the Nation 1707–1837* (New Haven, 1992). Suggestive work on the nineteenth century includes Keith

Robbins, *Nineteenth-century Britain: Integration and Diversity* (Oxford, 1988) and his *Great Britain: Identities, Institutions, and the Idea of Britishness* (London, 1998). For the period since 1940, R. Weight, *Patriots. National Identity in Britain 1940–2000* (London, 2002).

24 Neville Kirk (ed.), *Northern Identities: Historical Interpretations of 'The North' and 'Northernness'* (Aldershot, 2000); David Russell, *Looking North: The North in the National Imagination* (Manchester, 2004); and Philip Payton, *A. L. Rowse and Cornwall: A Paradoxical Patriot* (Exeter, 2004).

25 Paul Readman, 'The place of the past in English culture', *Past and Present*, 186 (2005).

26 Robert Colls, *Identity of England* (Oxford, 2002); David Matless, *Landscape and Englishness* (London, 1998); Julia Stapleton, *Political Intellectuals and Public Identities in Britain since 1850* (Manchester, 2001).

27 Ben Wellings, 'Empire-nation: national and imperial discourses in England', *Nations and Nationalism*, 8 (2002).

28 Jane Aaron, 'Postcolonial change', *New Welsh Review*, 67 (2005); Stephen Knight, *A Hundred Years of Fiction: Writing Wales in English* (Cardiff, 2004); Liam Connell, 'Scottish nationalism and the colonial vision of Scotland', *Interventions: International Journal of Postcolonial Studies*, 6 (2004).

29 Wil Griffith, ' "Preaching second to no other under the sun": Edward Matthews, the Nonconformist pulpit and Welsh identity during the mid nineteenth century', in Robert Pope (ed.), *Religion and National Identity: Wales and Scotland c.1700–2000* (Cardiff, 2001), pp. 61–83.

30 Miroslav Hroch, *Social Preconditions of National Revival in Europe: A Comparative Analysis of Patriotic Groups among the Smaller European Nations*, trs Ben Fowkes (Cambridge, 1995).

31 Notably following Benedict Anderson, *Imagined Communities* (New York, 1983).

32 Ernest Gellner, *Nations and Nationalism* (Oxford, 1983), p. 85; Eugen Weber, *Peasants into Frenchmen: The Modernization of Rural France, 1870–1914* (London, 1979); Timothy Baycroft, *Culture, Identity and Nationalism: French Flanders in the Nineteenth and Twentieth centuries* (Woodbridge, 2004).

33 Gwenfair Parry and Mari A. Williams, *The Welsh Language and the 1891 Census* (Cardiff, 1999).

34 Anthony D. Smith, *Nationalism and Modernism: A Critical Survey of Recent Theories of Nations and Nationalism* (London, 1998); Jeremy Webber, 'Just how civic is civic nationalism in Quebec?', in Alan C. Cairns (ed.), *Citizenship, Diversity and Pluralism* (Montreal, 1999).

35 Karen Barkey and Mark von Hagen, *After Empire: Multi-ethnic Societies and Nation-building* (Boulder, USA, 1997). For a modern example, Helene Perrin Wagner, 'Social and political collective identities in central Asia', *Harvard Asia Quarterly*, 27 September 1999.

36 This is usefully summarised in Smith, *Nationalism and Modernism*.

37 The classic text is Weber, *Peasants into Frenchmen*. For more complex and, in the British context, more helpful pictures of State building see Robert Tombs (ed.), *Nations and Nationalism in France from Boulangism to the Great War, 1889–1918* (London, 1991), p. 3; Baycroft, *Culture, Identity and Nationalism*; Caroline Ford, *Creating the Nation in Provincial France: Religion and Political Identity in Brittany* (Princeton, 1993).

38 Peter Dewey, 'Military recruitment and the British labour force during the First
    World War', *Historical Journal*, 27 (1984).
39 Duncan Tanner and Andrew Edwards, 'Defining or dividing the nation? Opinion
    polls, Welsh identity and devolution 1966–1979', *Contemporary Wales*, 18
    (2006)
40 Pat Jalland, 'United Kingdom devolution 1910–14: political panacea or tactical
    diversion', *EHR*, 94 (1979); Gary Peatling, 'Home rule for England, English
    nationalism and Edwardian debates about constitutional reform', *Albion*, 35
    (2003).
41 See e.g. J. Graham Jones, 'E. T. John and Home Rule, 1910–14', *WHR*, 13
    (1987), and 'E. T. John, devolution and democracy, 1917–24', *WHR*, 14 (1989).
    For Scotland see e.g. H. J. Hanham, *Scottish Nationalism* (London, 1969).
42 See e.g. J. Graham Jones, 'Early attempts to secure a Secretary of State for Wales,
    1890–1939', *THSC* (1988) and James McConnel, ' "Sympathy without relief is
    rather like mustard without beef": devolution, Plaid Cymru, and the campaign
    for a Secretary of State for Wales, 1937–38', *WHR*, 22 (2005).
43 Examples include, Richard Finlay, *Independent and Free: Scottish Politics and the
    Origin of the SNP* (1994); Peter Lynch, *SNP: The History of the Scottish
    Nationalist Party* (Cardiff, 2002); D. Hywel Davies, *The Welsh Nationalist Party,
    1925–1945: A Call to Nationhood* (Cardiff, 1983); John Davies, *Plaid Cymru:
    The History of the Welsh Nationalist Party* (Cardiff, 2003); Laura McAllister,
    Plaid Cymru: The Emergence of a Political Party (Bridgend, 2001); Martin
    Laffan, *The Resurrection of Ireland: The Sinn Fein Party, 1916–23* (Cambridge,
    1999); Brendan O'Brien, *The Long War: The IRA and Sinn Fein* (3rd edn,
    Dublin 1999).
44 Exceptions include Russell Deacon, *The Governance of Wales: The Welsh Office
    and the Policy Process 1964–99* (Cardiff, 2002) and Dylan Griffiths, *Thatcherism
    and Territorial Politics: A Welsh Case Study* (Aldershot, 1996). Neither study util-
    ises manuscript collections to assess the way in which the Welsh Office functioned.
45 For one of the few such studies, Ted Rowlands, *'Something Must Be Done': South
    Wales v. Whitehall 1921–51* (Merthyr, 2000).
46 See McMahon below, p. 79.
47 Robert Griffiths, *S. O. Davies: A Socialist Faith* (Llandysul, 1983). For the cam-
    paign and its supporters, J. Graham Jones, 'The Parliament for Wales campaign
    1950–1956', *WHR*, 16 (1992).
48 David Howell, *A Lost Left? Three Studies in Socialism and Nationalism*
    (Manchester, 1986); Deian Hopkin, 'Y werin a'i theyrnas: ymateb sosialiaeth i
    genedaetholdeb, 1880–1920', *Cof Cenedl*, 6 (1991).
49 See e.g. Paul Bew, *Ideology and the Irish Question: Ulster Unionism and Irish
    Nationalism 1912–16* (Oxford, 1994); James Loughlin, *Ulster Unionism and
    British National Identity since 1885* (London, 1995); Alvin Jackson, 'Unionist
    myths 1912–1985', *Past and Present*, 136 (1992).
50 Examples include James Mitchell, *Conservatives and the Union: A Study of
    Conservative Party Attitudes to Scotland* (Edinburgh, 1990); Catriona M. M.
    MacDonald (ed.), *Unionist Scotland 1800–1997* (Edinburgh, 1998).
51 Ian Levitt (ed.), *The Scottish Office: Depression and Reconstruction, 1919–59*
    (Edinburgh, 1996); John S. Gibson, *The Thistle and the Crown: A History of the
    Scottish Office* (Edinburgh, 1988).

52 R. H. Campbell, 'The Scottish Office and the Special Areas in the 1930s', *Historical Journal*, 22 (1979); Graham Walker, *Thomas Johnston* (Manchester, 1988).

53 Christopher Harvie, 'The folk and the *gwerin:* the myth and reality of popular culture in 19th century Scotland and Wales', *Proceedings of the British Academy*, 80 (1994).

54 Helen Brocklehurst and Robert Phillips (eds), *History, Nationhood and the Question of Britain* (Basingstoke, 2003).

55 See the extensive literature summarised in Fiona McLean, 'Guest editorial', *Museum and Society*, 3 (2005); Anwen Jones, *The National Theatre Debate in Wales 1880–2002* (Cardiff, 2006).

56 Most of the research on these themes is concentrated in volumes dealing exclusively with Wales or Scotland. See e.g. Charles Webster, 'Devolution and the health service in Wales, 1919–1969', in Pamela Michael and Charles Webster (eds), *Health and Society in Twentieth Century Wales* (Cardiff, 2006); Gareth Elwyn Jones, 'Policy-making in Welsh education: a historical perspective, 1889–1988', in Richard Daugherty et al. (eds), *Education Policy Making in Wales: Explorations in Devolved Governance* (Cardiff, 2000) and for health and the devolved Scottish administration, Jacqueline Jenkinson, *Scotland's Health 1919–48* (Oxford, 2002).

57 E.g. David Powell, *Nationhood and Identity: The British State since 1800* (London, 2002).

58 Steve Caunce et al. (eds), *Relocating Britishness* (Manchester, 2004); Paul Ward, *Britishness since 1870* (London, 2004).

59 There was a good deal of virulent anti-nationalism in Wales and Scotland between the wars and thereafter. Some studies stress the role of the marxisant National Council of Labour Colleges and its Scottish variant in developing such attitudes. See Dai Smith, *Aneurin Bevan and the World of South Wales* (Cardiff, 1993) and the summary of the Scottish position in I. G. C. Hutchinson, *Scottish Politics in the Twentieth Century* (Basingstoke, 2001), pp. 61–3.

60 See e.g. Kenneth O. Morgan, *Wales in British Politics 1868–1922* (Cardiff, 2nd edition, 1970).

61 Colley, *Britons*; Robbins, *Idea of Britishness*. Suggestive essays can also be found in Laurence Brockliss and David Eastwood (eds), *A Union of Multiple Identities: The British Isles c. 1750–1850* (Manchester, 1997) and Raphael Samuel, *Island Stories: Unravelling Britain* (London, 1998), pp. 21–73.

62 Janet Mather, 'English regional policy', unpublished paper; Michael Tichelar, 'The Scott Report and the Labour Party: the protection of the countryside during the Second World War', *Rural History*, 15 (2004) and 'Central-local relations: the case of the Labour Party, regional government and land-use reform during the Second World War', *Labour History Review*, 66 (2001).

63 See Aaron, 'Postcolonial change'. For the accusations of 'ethno-centric' attitudes, see review symposium on Graham Day's *Making Sense of Wales* in *Contemporary Wales*, 17 (2004). The potential of a post-colonial perspective is put less abrasively in Stephen Howe, 'Internal decolonization? British politics since Thatcher as post-colonial trauma', *Twentieth Century British History*, 14 (2003).

64 Chapters by McMahon and McConnel and Kelly below. For other discussions by contributors, Jane Aaron and Chris Williams (eds), *Postcolonial Wales* (Cardiff,

2005) and Richard Finlay, ' "For or against?": Scottish nationalists and the British Empire, 1918–39', *SHR*, 71 (1992).

65 See Tanner, below, pp. 238–9, 250.

66 Tanner and Edwards, 'Defining or dividing the nation'.

67 Michael Bilig, *Banal Nationalism* (London, 1995). For the 'ritualistic turn', Peter Burke, 'Performing history: the importance of occasions', *Rethinking History*, 9 (2005).

68 See Mari Elin Wiliam, 'Hunaniaeth a moderneiddio yng Nghymru c. 1950–1970: yr ymadwaith diwylliannol rhwng 'Prydeinod' a 'Chymreictod' (Identity and modernisation in Wales c. 1950–70: the cultural engagement between 'British-ness' and 'Welshness'), University of Wales Bangor PhD thesis in progress.

69 In south Wales health experts regularly proposed that county councils should take the responsibilities of urban district councils. See Glamorgan County Council, Public Health and Housing Committee Minutes, 14 October 1931, 28 November 1933, 27 November 1934.

70 See below, pp. 40–1, 141, 254–5.

71 Richard Weight and Abigail Beach (eds), *The Right to Belong: Citizenship and National Identity in Britain, 1930–60* (London, 1998); Sonya O. Rose, *Which People's War? National Identity and Citizenship in Wartime Britain 1939–45* (Oxford, 2003); Steven Fielding, Paul Thompson and Nick Tiratsoo, *'England arise!' The Labour Party and Popular Politics in 1940s Britain* (Manchester, 1995).

72 See below, pp. 253–4.

73 Duncan Tanner, 'Electing the governors / the governance of the elect', in Keith Robbins (ed.), *Short Oxford History of the British Isles: The British Isles 1901–51* (Oxford, 2002), pp. 54–8, 63–5.

74 The problems included coping with different legal and educational systems, different land laws and hence housing conditions and different agricultural interests – all of which could be used to delay actions and protect Scottish interests.

75 See Patrick Buckland, *The Factory of Grievances: Devolved Government in Northern Ireland 1921–39* (Dublin, 1979), p. 278.

76 Morgan Phillips to Miss E. M. Jones (Bangor), 15 June 1945, Labour Party archive, Morgan Phillips MSS, GS/WAL/4.

77 Hutchison, *Scottish Politics*, pp. 83–7; Kenneth O. Morgan, *Rebirth of a Nation: Wales 1880–1980* (Oxford and Cardiff, 1981), pp. 253–8.

78 WM, 21 and 24 April 1945. I am grateful to Matthew Cragoe for this reference. For surveillance, e.g. 'History of F3', 21 June 1945, TNA KV 4/58/105231

79 Plaid Cymru gained 16,000 votes in the 1945 election. Its leader, Gwynfor Evans was a pacifist. Its main ideologue, Saunders Lewis, was pointedly 'neutral' during the war. The neutrality of the Republic of Ireland was also much resented.

80 For the enduring significance of this, D. Tanner, 'Richard Grossman, Harold Wilson and devolution, 1966–70: the making of government policy', *Twentieth Century British History*, 17 (2006).

81 See Edwards and Griffith below, pp. 140–1.

82 J. Graham Jones, 'The national petition on the legal status of the Welsh language, 1938–1942', *WHR*, 18 (1996); Andrew Edwards, 'Answering the challenge of nationalism: Goronwy Roberts and the appeal of the Labour Party in North-West Wales during the 1950s', *WHR*, 22 (2004), 128–30.

83 Kenneth O. Morgan, 'Power and glory: war and reconstruction, 1939–51', in

Duncan Tanner et al. (eds), *The Labour Party in Wales 1900–2000* (Cardiff, 2000), pp. 179–81.

84 Mitchell, *Conservatives and the Union*, pp. 27–30; Christopher Harvie, 'The recovery of Scottish Labour, 1939–51', in Ian Donnachie et al. (eds), *Forward! Labour Politics in Scotland 1888–1988* (Edinburgh, 1999), pp. 78–9.

85 John Stewart, *The Battle for Health: A Political History of the Socialist Medical Association, 1930–51* (Aldershot, 1999), pp. 188–98. For Cole, Robson and other authorities on local government, Abigail Beach, 'Forging a nation of participants: political and economic planning in Labour's Britain', in Weight and Beach, *The Right to Belong*, pp. 96–7.

86 See below, pp. 36–7, 204.

Part I
IMPERFECT EXAMPLES: IRELAND, SCOTLAND AND DEVOLVED GOVERNANCE

1
Scotland and devolution, 1880–1945

Richard Finlay

The advent of the Scottish Parliament and the Welsh Assembly in the latter part of the twentieth century might be expected to cast a long shadow over the history of modern Scotland and Wales. Yet the historian is hard put to find evidence that devolution was the dominant historical theme in either nation in the period from the mid-nineteenth century.[1] Indeed, nationalism is somewhat episodic in its appearance and only rarely managed to move onto the mainstream political agenda. As such, it should always be borne in mind when discussing the history of devolution, that it was the concern only of a minority and discussion was often confined within the walls of the self-interested and the self-appointed. This chapter will examine the issue in a chronological manner as each of the three periods under review was subject to different characteristics. The period from the 1880s to 1914 will be examined first and engage with how devolution was largely part of a wider debate as to the evolution of British government. The second period will cover the inter-war era and assess the significance of moving the debate into an era of mass democracy in which social and economic priorities dominated the political agenda. The third period under review will examine how the structure of Scottish government was radically affected by the demands of the Second World War and arguably laid the template for much of the post-war administration of Scotland. The issue of the campaign for greater Scottish self-government had a chequered career in the period from 1880 to 1945. At various times the debate has been fuelled by changes in administrative functioning, increased national sentiment and changes affecting the government of other parts of the British Isles. Contrary to what might be expected, national sentiment was not always the most important factor in driving the demand for greater devolution and any attempt to portray it as such is guilty of historical misrepresentation. Furthermore, the issue of devolution in Scotland in this period cannot be divorced from politics within Britain and it cannot be represented as an autonomous development. To understand the debate about devolution in Scotland, it is necessary to examine perspectives from both the core and the periphery.

In the 1880s the campaign for the re-establishment of the Scottish Secretary was driven by a combination of unease at the limited amount of governmental attention the Scots received, increasing demands placed on the legislative process and the perception that Ireland was being accorded preferential treatment, in spite of the troublesome activities of Irish nationalist MPs in the House of Commons. Furthermore, the campaign was given an extra impetus by an appeal to national sentiment in the sense that Scotland as a partner in the Union was not given its due recognition and certainly not as much attention as the Irish. The establishment of the Scottish Secretary and the Scottish Office was followed by Gladstone's conversion to Irish Home Rule, which once more demonstrated that Ireland was accorded more importance in terms of government reform, much to the Scots chagrin. Keen not to be upstaged, some protagonists began a campaign for the establishment of a Scottish Parliament. In this period, Scottish Home Rule was driven more by Celtic one-upmanship than Celtic solidarity. In the period before the First World War, the Scots used a variety of arguments to make the case for Scottish devolution, ranging from the idea of 'Home Rule All Round', which would reform the government of the United Kingdom, to the establishment of a parliament in Edinburgh as a means for the implementation of advanced social and welfare policies. As much as anything, this debate was driven by ideas about the future government of the British Empire and British State. Another way of looking at the Scottish Home Rule debate at this time is to see it as a manifestation in Scotland of a bigger debate that was taking place in the United Kingdom concerning the future development of the role of the state.

The debate in the period between the wars was conditioned by two key factors. Firstly, some saw greater autonomy as a way to rectify the endemic social and economic problems that dogged Scottish society in this period. Others would use the same problems as their principal defence of the political status quo in the sense that the dire economic and social conditions could only be tackled by the full resources of the British State and that Scottish problems were of such a magnitude that the Scots could not solve them by themselves. Secondly, the demands of government administration increased the presence of the state north of the border and the consolidation and organisation of the departments of the expanding Scottish Office gave rise to notions of devolution as a means to democratise the administration of Scotland. Others made the case that administrative devolution as opposed to political devolution would make for better government north of the border. In terms of the postwar period, the wide ranging expansion of government responsibility during the Second World War set the template for the expansion of state activity in the era after 1945. It is the objective of this chapter to examine the evolution of Scottish government in the period between 1880 and 1945 and relate this to the wider issue of devolution in British politics. In particular, this chapter will focus more on political discourse, rather than the mechanics of government as this has already been charted by other historians.[2]

Home Rule in the era of Empire, 1880–1914

Scottish resentment at the amount of attention government lavished on Ireland in the 1880s was one of the key driving forces behind the campaign for the re-establishment of the office of Scottish Secretary. The position had been abolished in 1746 following the Jacobite rising. In 1853, the National Association for the Vindication of Scottish Rights (NAVSR) was established to act as a pressure group that would press the claim that Scotland's position within the Union was being undermined by indifference from Westminster.[3] It was argued that more self-government and self-administration were not incompatible with the Union and that 'Scotland will never be improved by being transformed into an inferior imitation of England but by being made a better and truer Scotland'.[4] What this would entail was never clearly spelled out. The National Association was not a coherent political grouping as it contained Tories, Whigs and radical Liberals and the issues that it took to heart ranged from anger at a trust established by the bishop of Orkney being misused to fund street lighting in London to inappropriate use of heraldic devices. The NAVSR died off in the mid-1850s, largely because attention was diverted by the impact of the Crimean War. Yet, even so, the Association faced widespread condemnation from many who argued that the benefits of the Union far outweighed any disadvantages and the trivial nature of much of the grievances were subject to ridicule in the Scottish press.[5] The campaign to establish a national monument to Sir William Wallace absorbed much of the energy of mid-Victorian Scottish patriots after the collapse of the NAVSR.[6] In spite of the fact that Wallace had been a champion of Scottish independence in the late thirteenth and early fourteenth centuries, few of those involved in the campaign to build a monument believed that this constituted a threat to the Union. Quite the contrary, most believed that the pivotal role played by Wallace in the Wars of Independence was essential to the maintenance of a separate Scottish identity that would find its historic destiny in the Union of 1707. What this episode demonstrates is that the Scottish conception of the Union was one in which the separate national identities, characters and institutions of Scotland and England each contributed a distinctive function within the British State and Empire.[7] The Union was not believed to be a process of amalgamation and assimilation.

Scotland attained a high profile in British politics following Gladstone's Midlothian Campaign in 1879 when the Grand Old Man returned to lead the Liberal Party.[8] Undoubtedly, this helped to propel Scotland higher up the British political agenda and a number of prominent Scottish politicians were willing to use this increased attention to highlight the role that Scotland played in the advance of the Liberal Party. Writing to Gladstone in April 1880, Lord Rosebery claimed that: 'the stimulus and inspiration that Liberalism required must come from you and that the proper tripod for you was Scotland . . . Our little country has answered its purpose, and has been the pivot on which you have turned the country'.[9] By the mid-1880s it was argued that the Scots needed their own man in the Cabinet to oversee Scottish legislation and guard the interests of Scotland. The position was also believed to be an important symbolic acknowledgement of Scotland's unique position within the Union.[10] For many, the attention given to Ireland was unwarranted. The disestablishment of the Irish church, the obstructionist tactics employed by nationalist MPs, the amount of parliamentary time absorbed by the Irish and the recurrent threat of terrorism occupied much space in the Scottish press.[11] Unlike the Scots, whom they believed had acted as model citizens, the increasing amount of time given to troublesome Ireland meant that Scotland was denied parliamentary attention. A common complaint was that Scottish parliamentary time was condensed into one afternoon's work, which was described as wholly inadequate.[12] For many Scottish politicians, the elevation of Irish grievances up the political agenda was believed to be a reward for engaging in terrorist activities and parliamentary obstructionism. Rosebery argued that Irish preferential attention was having an adverse effect on the Scots:

> The words Home Rule have begun to be distinctly and loudly mentioned in Scotland . . . I believe that the late Lord Beaconsfield, on one occasion in Scotland, implored the people of Scotland to give up 'munching the dry bones of political economy, and munching the remainder biscuit of effete Liberalism'. I believe the people of Scotland, at the present moment, are mumbling the dry bones of political neglect, and munching the remainder biscuit of Irish legislation.[13]

A further factor in garnering support for the position of Scottish Secretary among Liberals was the fact that it avoided the awkward issue of Scottish Church disestablishment, which all senior figures agreed was a political minefield.[14]

The campaign for the re-establishment of the Scottish Secretary commanded a cross spectrum of political support. Perhaps the most influential was Archibald Primrose, Lord Rosebery, who had taken a leading role in Gladstone's Midlothian Campaign of 1879 and whose radical politics mixed with an aristocratic background made him the dashing figure of Scottish politics. Central to the demands for the re-establishment of the Scottish Secretary was the fact that parliament devoted so very little time to Scottish legislation and that with growing demands for a range of legal reforms, the six hours set aside for Scottish affairs was inadequate. Writing to Gladstone in May 1882, Rosebery claimed:

> Though I do not in any sense pretend to represent Scotland or to assert that Scotland will be seriously outraged if you do not appoint a Scottish Lord of the Treasury. Yet, I would venture to remind you . . . that Scotland is the backbone of the Liberal Party, and that, if I am rightly informed, there is some discontent as to her treatment.[15]

Rosebery was also suffering a fit of pique on account of Gladstone's refusal to reward him with a sufficiently high enough position in the Cabinet after his efforts during the Midlothian Campaign.[16] Rosebery had a significant power base in the Scottish Liberal organisation and it is difficult to avoid the conclusion that as he felt personally overlooked by the British Government; he transposed this sense of injustice onto the Scottish political nation. Campaigners pointed out that much of the legislation designed for Scotland was based on English Acts that did not take into account the peculiarities of the Scottish legal system. It was argued that the Scottish Secretary was necessary to oversee a system where Scottish legislation could be vetted in advance and have its faults ironed out before being passed to the House of Commons.[17] This role was currently filled by the Lord Advocate; an individual who was not answerable to the political parties and whose role was limited to one of a technical adviser on legal issues. As such, the political dimension of Scottish legislation received no attention and could produce quite unintended political consequences. At this juncture, it is important to emphasise that the impetus for the campaign was based on the pragmatic need for more effective administration and that while national sentiment was an important factor in mobilising support, it could in no sense be described as being driven by nationalist demands. Indeed, central to the claims in favour of re-establishing the Secretaryship was the claim that greater administrative attention would strengthen the Union. One radical, Duncan McLaren, even went so far as to claim that the reform of Scottish government could be done in such a way as to make it cheaper.[18] A key factor worth emphasising is the growing power of radical Liberals in Scotland and an important aspect of their ideology was a belief in the virtue of minimal government.[19] Few advocated the reform of Scottish government in order to increase the presence of the state as that would have been anathema to them.

Yet, Scottish delight that their special position within the Union had finally received acknowledgement in 1885 with the re-establishment of the Scottish Secretary (the first being a Tory, the Duke of Richmond and Gordon, as the Liberal government fell before it could appoint a candidate) was soon overshadowed by the fact the Irish had once again apparently upstaged them with Gladstone's conversion to Home Rule in 1886. For many Scots, this was once again evidence that the Irish received preferential treatment. The issue divided the Scottish Liberal Party with one segment refusing to countenance support for their leader's policy.[20] Both pro Home Rulers and those against the policy recounted Gladstone's words, spoken in Aberdeen in 1871, that he could not countenance a scheme of Home Rule for Ireland if were not also applied to Scotland and Wales:

> If the doctrine of home rule is to be established in Ireland, I protest on your behalf, that you will be entitled to it in Scotland, moreover, I protest on behalf of Wales, that it will be entitled to home rule also.[21]

A key aspect in opposition to Irish home rule was the prevalent belief that Irish nationalism, unlike the nationalism of Italy and Hungary, was conservative and backward-looking. It was argued that if the Irish nationalists controlled a Dublin parliament, it would lead to the expropriation of property and a breakdown in law and order.[22] Unlike European nationalism which sought to establish liberal regimes in the face of aristocratic and Catholic opposition, Ireland's demand for Home Rule was portrayed as being led by landowners and priests; two of the most potent adversaries in the demonology of Scottish liberalism. The establishment of the Scottish Home Rule Association in 1886 had Ireland firmly in its sights. It was claimed that to give Ireland Home Rule but to deny it to the Scots was to reward terrorism while being a slight on the most loyal part of the kingdom: 'The proposal to grant a legislature and Executive Government to Ireland, and withhold them from Scotland is *unjust to a loyal, industrious and intelligent people, and appears to set a premium upon disorder.*'[23] Other contrasts were made between how much the Scots paid into the Exchequer compared with Ireland. Parnell's quip that the Scots had ceased to be a nation did not help matters.[24]

Yet, pique at Ireland's preferential treatment was not the only reason for the espousal of Home Rule. In the period between 1886 and 1914, a variety of arguments were put forward to strengthen the Scots' claim for self-government. Central to the claims of Scottish Home Rulers was the fact that the present system of government could not cope with the increasing demands placed on the Scottish Office and the Scottish Secretary. As the Scottish Liberal Party increasingly came to espouse a programme of social reform, it was believed that some new governmental mechanism would be required to implement policy. The fact that land reform, temperance, education reform and housing increasingly climbed up the political agenda meant that there was increasing frustration at the fact that there was perceived

English parliamentary and House of Lords obstructionism in the face of attempts to promote Scottish social welfare reform. This was especially the case after the 1906 Liberal landslide when endeavour to pass social reform was sabotaged by the Conservative dominated House of Lords. Furthermore, the fact that the Liberal Party held up well in Scotland during the two general elections of 1910, in contrast to England where the Conservative Party was able to almost equal the Liberal Party, led many to claim that Scotland's radicalism was being held back by England's conservatism. According to one Liberal parliamentarian 'there is not one single item in the whole programme of radicalism or social reform today, which, if Scotland had powers to pass laws, would not have been carried out a quarter of a century ago.'[25] Also, the fact that Irish Home Rulers held the balance of power in the House of Commons helped to elevate Scottish home rule further up the political agenda as many Scots believed that an Irish secession would leave them in a more English dominated and anti-devolutionist House of Commons.[26]

Scottish Home Rulers argued the case that far from being a priority, Ireland should not have precedence over Scotland when it came to Home Rule. The case was put that devolution could only come as a British-wide policy and for some, the fact that it was so would take away some of the criticism against Irish Home Rule in the sense that as it was to be applied to the whole of the United Kingdom, there was nothing singular about Ireland. For some, the issue of 'Home Rule All Round' was one way to postpone the issue of Irish Home Rule in the sense that it tied the success of the Irish case to the rest of the United Kingdom and it was expected that inertia in other parts of Britain would stall the programme indefinitely. For some historians, this was the fundamental reason behind Winston Churchill's unexpected proclamation of United Kingdom devolution in Dundee in 1911.[27] For some radicals in the Liberal Party, Home Rule would become a device to implement social welfare. The creation of a Scottish Parliament, it was argued, would further free up time at Westminster as there would be no need to discuss Scottish domestic legislation, and as such, it would make the Imperial Parliament more efficient.[28] The extent to which the issue of home rule had climbed up the political agenda can be demonstrated by the activities of the Young Scots Society (YSS). Often described as a Liberal 'ginger group', the Young Scots came to occupy a significant position within the Liberal electoral machine north of the border and by 1911 was actively vetting prospective parliamentary candidates on the basis of their commitment to Home Rule. The extent to which Home Rule had become a key objective of the Scottish Liberal Party can be demonstrated by a confidential memorandum written by the Conservative Party chairman, Sir George Younger, who in anticipation of a possible general election held in 1915, claimed that a Liberal victory would mean a mandate for Scottish Home Rule.[29] Events seemed to bear him out when Sir Henry Cowan's Scottish Home Rule Bill passed its second reading in 1913. Liberal leaders, such as Asquith and Lloyd George, publicly at least, affirmed their support for a Scottish Parliament.[30] The outbreak of war in 1914 put the brake on the Bill's parliamentary passage.

Home Rule in the era of dislocation, 1918–39

At the end of the First World War, a Speaker's Conference at Westminster demonstrated that interest in the issue had effectively died away. According to one Scottish Tory MP, Scotland had effectively ceased to be a nation having been 'absorbed into a wider area'.[31] Pre-war Home Rule Liberals such as the Coalition Scottish Secretary, Robert Munro, had abandoned their previous enthusiasm for a parliament in Edinburgh.[32] The war had compromised the Liberal Party; Irish Home Rule had ended in revolution and developments in the Empire tended towards separation rather than imperial unity. All of this helped undermine much of the previous rationale for the creation of a Scottish Parliament.[33] The Labour Party emerged as the main proponents of the Home Rule cause in the immediate aftermath of the First World War. To a large extent, this was simply acquired as part and parcel of the radical baggage that was inherited from the Liberal Party. Much of Labour's rhetoric on the subject was regurgitated without much thought or development. Home rule was an effective way to unite the disparate wings of the party as it was one of the few things that both left and right could agree on. Furthermore, the 'blame it on the English' theme of many of the Home Rule rallies struck a chord among the crowd.[34] Increased state presence during the war boosted the perception that there was too much control from London and a keen advocate of the cause was the Co-operative Movement which wanted both to maintain its independence from its British counterpart and at the same time was resentful at the way government control of supplies blatantly discrim-inated against it.[35] The Scottish Trade Union Congress (STUC) was also a keen supporter of Home Rule as a means to protect smaller unions from absorption into larger British ones.[36] Furthermore, the fact that Labour made a spectacular electoral breakthrough in Scotland at the general election of 1922 helped to reinforce the idea that the Scots were a more radical people than their southern counterparts.[37] This sense of cultural difference was cer-tainly reinforced among the first contingent of Scottish Labour MPs in London who initially kept themselves apart from the decadence of parlia-mentary life and instead chose to live a teetotal life in dingy digs.[38]

In 1924, a private member's bill was talked out and led to uproar among the Scottish Labour MPs, resulting in a number of parliamentary suspensions.[39] Yet, by the mid-1920s, doubts were beginning to emerge as the centrality of Home Rule to Labour's Scottish plans. Problems in the economy continued and the trade unions had been comprehensively defeated in the General Strike of 1926. This did much to undermine the confidence of the Labour movement in the efficacy of home rule and increasingly, the party came to believe that the solution of Scotland's endemic social and economic problems could only be achieved by using the combined resources of the British state. The Scottish trade unions believed that amalgamation into bigger British unions would afford the best protection from aggressive employers by providing safety in numbers. The key thinker in this process was John Wheatley, a former pre-war Irish Home Ruler, who believed that in a world dominated by capitalism, socialism could only survive in one country if it took protective economic measures against hostile capitalist states.[40] This meant centralised control of state resources which would be used to effect redistributive policies. Wheatley believed that socialism in Britain could also be extended to the Empire and thus ensure that a significant chunk of the globe was red for political as well as imperial reasons. In such a scheme of things, Scottish Home Rule was irrelevant. A key reason for the promotion of a Scottish Parliament in the past was to promote social welfare policies, but according to Wheatley, this could now only be achieved by the centralised British State. Although Labour Scottish parliamentarians had only a smattering of Wheatley's ideas, increasingly they emphasised the primacy of economic interests over the establishment of a Scottish Parliament. According to James Maxton, one of the party's leading public figures, 'The general social problem always takes premier place in my mind, before the nationalist or political changes, and I do not think that I am likely to change in that respect'.[41] This was further reinforced by a speech by Labour leader Ramsay MacDonald who claimed that the United Kingdom could not be broken up into separate economic units and if this were to happen it would be to the Scots' detriment.[42] Unlike 1924, a private member's bill in 1927 was allowed to fail with out too much fuss. The bill's sponsor, Reverend James Barr, later admitted that there was only lukewarm support for his proposal. Labour's commitment to Scottish Home Rule effectively died on its feet.[43]

Labour's *volte face* on Home Rule was the principal catalyst in the creation of the National Party of Scotland (NPS) in April 1928.[44] Frustrated by the lack of progress that the pressure group tactics of the Scottish National Convention and the Scottish Home Rule Association had made, nationalists decided that it was time to set up their own political party in order to secure an electoral mandate for home rule. A key factor in the establishment of the

NPS was a belief among former Labour supporters that a demonstration of the electoral power of Home Rule would soon bring Labour back to the fold. For some there was a belief that the issue was so popular that the National Party would be able to secure a Scottish electoral mandate. This expectation proved forlorn as the party was unable to present more than a handful of candidates at elections and even then it was lucky to save most of its deposits. A key element in NPS strategy was a decision to make interventions in by elections that worked against Labour and in 1932 such tactics helped to keep Tom Johnston out of parliament. Needless to say, rather than convince Labour about the efficacy of Home Rule, it simply hardened attitudes against it. Yet the NPS, due to a combination of ideological differences and disputes about electoral strategy within its membership, was an impotent electoral force. Nationalist endeavours to present a more moderate image by purging fundamentalists and a fusion of the NPS with the devolutionist Scottish Party to create the Scottish National Party in 1934, likewise, failed to bear electoral fruit.[45] By the second half of the 1930s, nationalism no longer appeared to pose any serious political threat and Labour politicians could once again discuss the issue of Home Rule without fear of giving succour to political opponents.

Yet it was not just the demise of political nationalism that instigated Labour's cautious flirtation with the prospect of a parliament in Edinburgh in the late 1930s. Although the party had recovered much of its lost vote in the 1935 general election, the first past the post electoral system held back progress in the number of seats won. Furthermore, Labour was confined to opposition at a time when the National Government began to instigate reform of the system of government in Scotland. Following the Gilmour Report of 1935, the Scottish Office had its powers extended and streamlined and according to Labour politicians, this meant that that the Scottish Secretary of State had the kind of authority associated with a colonial governor general. Home Rule was mooted as a possible democratic antidote to the increasing consolidation of state power in the hands of one man.[46] The second half of the 1930s witnessed increasing forms of corporatist government intervention in Scotland with semi-official bodies such as the Scottish Economic Committee and the Scottish Council (Industry and Development) springing up to offer advice on policy.[47] Labour and the Scottish Trade Union Congress were left out of such developments and many believed that the increasing association between government and big business was both undemocratic and anti-working class.

The decision to move the Scottish Office to Edinburgh was in part motivated by what might be called nationalist grumblings that were increasingly coming from stalwart Unionist allies, such as various chambers of commerce and the press.[48] In particular, the fact that the depression had been deeper in Scotland with a greater rate of industrial closures and higher rates of unemployment, together with the fact that recovery was much slower, added to public disquiet that the Scots were not receiving a fair deal. Even Unionist politicians such as Walter Elliot and Bob Boothby aired widely shared views that the Scots were being hard done by. While Unionist politicians were quick to claim that nationalism was not a cure for the endemic social and economic problems, they nevertheless acknowledged the legitimacy of the national mood of unease.[49] Administrative devolution was conceived as a way in which the decisions affecting Scotland could be taken in Scotland by 'men on the spot' and thus increase government efficiency. It had the added bonus that while appearing to bring government closer to the people, it did not concede any political authority from Westminster. Furthermore, it was believed that the creation of a custom built Scottish Office in Edinburgh would act as an emblem of Scotland's national status within the Union. The fact that the design of the building went to an English architectural firm did much to undermine the National Government's endeavours to quieten nationalist discontent.[50] A further reason for the dispersal of the Scottish Office to Edinburgh was the fear that too much government apparatus was concentrated in London and vulnerable to enemy attack.[51]

Labour polemics on the government of Scotland in the late 1930s concentrated on the power held by a small number of industrialists and their close association with Conservative politicians.[52] For good measure, large landowners came in for stringent criticism as well, with much being made of the emotive issue of the Highland Clearances. A key Labour organisation that emerged in the late 1930s to promote the issue of Home Rule was the London Scots Self-Government Committee, which contained a number of high profile parliamentarians.[53] The creation of a parliament in Edinburgh was mooted as a way to circumvent the increasing power of the Scottish Secretary of State and democratise the economy by breaking the stronghold of capitalism. It was argued that increasing government intervention was being used to prop up the stranglehold of capitalism in Scotland. The extensive use of public subsidies for the shipbuilding industry was a particular source of grievance for Labour as the principal beneficiary was Sir James Lithgow, the head of the Federation of British Industry and a vociferous opponent of working-class state benefits. In particular, Lithgow was a proponent of the idea that workers had overpriced themselves in the international market and the solution to unemployment was for lower wages.[54] Labour Home Rulers believed that a directly elected Scottish Parliament ought to take responsibility for the offices of state in Scotland and there was an expectation that Labour would have a better chance of forming a government north of the border than in the United Kingdom.

Labour Home Rulers did display some inconsistencies in their advocacy of a Scottish Parliament. Firstly, there was little promotion of the idea of devolution as a better system of government per se in that it would be more democratic and accountable to the people. Nor was there any real discussion of the wider implications of a policy of Scottish devolution for the rest of the United Kingdom. Political pragmatism and a desire to have access to the levers of Scottish government were the key determinants of Labour's growing sympathy with Home Rule. Furthermore, economic issues dominated the debate and the analysis of the faults of the Scottish economy focused on both the dominance of an over-powerful industrial hierarchy and the subsidies that this group received as a result of rearmament. It was argued that rather than use state funds to build weapons, money should be directed towards housing and social welfare. This was the position that was advocated as late as 1938.[55] This was in spite of the fact that rearmament was inflating the Scottish economy and bringing work to some of the most depressed industries and areas. Economics were at the heart of Labour concerns. In essence nothing had changed from the late 1920s when politicians recognised the primacy of economics as it was vital to the regeneration of Scottish economy and society. Labour's flirtation with Home Rule in the late 1930s was more than anything motivated by a desire to get their hands on the government levers of economic power and, at the time, a parliament in Edinburgh was seen by many as the best way to achieve this.

Home rule in the era of total war, 1939–45

The Second World War revolutionised the climate in which the debate about Scottish Home Rule would take place. During the war, two seemingly contradictory developments took place. On the one hand, nationalist sentiment and support for a Scottish Parliament appeared to be on the increase, while on the other, there was increasing faith in the ability of the centralised British State to provide a solution to the endemic social and economic problems that had plagued Scottish society between the wars. Central to both these developments the figure of Churchill's Scottish Secretary of State, Thomas Johnston, looms large.[56] Appointed in February 1941 as part of the wartime coalition, Johnston was the most senior figure in the Scottish Labour Party. Although he had a reputation as a radical in his earlier days, Johnston was first and foremost a pragmatist. While much is made of how there was a revolution in the role of government during the Second World War, which paved the way for the post-war consensus, less attention has been paid to the lines of continuity. The corporatist tendencies that had emerged in the 1930s were

extended to include Labour and the trade unions within the realm of decision-making and Johnston's Committee of the Ex-Secretaries of State was
similar to previous non-governmental advisory boards such as the Scottish
Economic Committee.[57] Although the role of the state had increased as a
result of the wartime emergency, the mechanisms of planning and control
were increasingly used to devote time and attention to the issue of post-war
reconstruction. One example of this is to be found in the way that the emergency hospital system in Scotland was used as a de facto 'National Health
Service' during the war. The hospital and medical services had been mobilised
in expectation to deal with mass bombing, but the fact that Scotland largely
escaped the attentions of the Luftwaffe meant that these resources were
under-utilised. Johnston, under the guise of increasing wartime industrial
production, made medical services free to workers.[58] In effect, the wartime
emergency powers were used to lay down the blueprint of the post-war
National Health Service in Scotland.

Of greater interest to the post-war planners, however, were the structural
problems that had plagued the Scottish economy. The prognosis of the
experts was the same of those in the 1930s; the Scottish economy was over-
reliant on a narrow range of industries and the solution lay in a greater degree
of industrial and economic diversity.[59] Johnston frequently made the case for
greater industrial development in Scotland during the war, in particular the
claim for more light industries, and was not slow in promoting his success to
the Scottish public. The effect of this was to demonstrate that a 'strong man
in the Cabinet' could effectively put forward the Scottish case and ensure that
more British resources went north.[60] In doing so, Johnston demonstrated
that the existing system of government, albeit during wartime conditions,
could be made to work to Scottish advantage and breathed new life into the
Union after the disappointing inaction of politicians during the 1930s. In
short, it was the poor quality of Scottish Secretaries of State, and not the
system, that had been the difficulty in the past. A further problem identified
by planners was that there was a population imbalance, in that there were too
many people in the Glasgow conurbation and that a more even distribution
of population would help the economy. It was soon established that the political priority of the post-war era for Scotland would be to achieve these objectives. This development was aided and abetted by the publication of the
Beveridge Report and, along with other parts of the United Kingdom, the
Scots endorsed the principle that post-war Britain would be a more equitable
place where the state played a more active role in safeguarding the wellbeing
of its citizens. Indeed, the fact that there was much for the state to do in terms
of social and economic restructuring in Scotland made the Beveridge Report
especially welcome.

It is doubtful that Johnston seriously entertained the belief that the gargantuan tasks of social and economic restructuring would be achieved by home rule. The enormity of the task of reconstruction could only be done by the mobilisation of the resources of the centralised British State.[61] Scottish resources would not be equal to the task on their own. Furthermore, a parliament in Edinburgh would, it was believed, be a bureaucratic impediment in the process of British-wide reconstruction. Although Johnston was particularly adept at using the existing system to ensure that Scotland received its fair share of state resources, a critical aspect of his strategy was the ability to whip up nationalist sentiment as a tool to exert greater leverage in his dealings with the Cabinet. Tokenism was an essential element in this ploy. The Scottish Grand Committee was reconvened to meet in Edinburgh, protests were issued regarding the manufacture of Scottish military uniforms in England and Johnston kept publicly demanding that Scotland be given its fair share of war work.[62] So while appearing to encourage nationalist sentiment and greater self-government, Johnston was in fact using it as a means to back up his case for greater state intervention in Scotland, which of course, would come from central government. There was no mention of the seeming contradictions in the strategy of on the one hand, calling for more self-government, while at the same time, promoting a greater role for centralised British state planning. Even as late as the May general election in 1945, Scottish Labour was still promoting the creation of a parliament in Edinburgh as its most important priority after the defeat of Japan.

The trend towards greater central government control was accentuated by the fact of wartime administration. Given the enormity of the tasks that government was expected to perform during the war, there was an expansion of the Civil Service in Scotland, and the Scottish Office was the prime beneficiary.[63] The demands of war fell on the pre-war structure of the Scottish Office. This was the only framework available and it is one of the peculiarities of history that in an era that witnessed the expansion of the centralised British state committed to universal welfare provision, the form it took in Scotland was one that was simply grafted on to the existing structure. This unusual state of affairs (after all, it would have been more logical to have British-wide agencies) can be explained by two reasons. Firstly, the exigencies of war meant that the existing apparatus had to implement wartime demands. Therefore, even before the establishment of the post-war consensus regarding state intervention, much of the machinery of government that would have the task of implementing policy had already been earmarked to the Scottish Office. Secondly, Johnston jealously guarded his powers. He actively promoted a loyalty among his civil servants to the Scottish Office and fought off any encroachments by other government departments.[64] Furthermore, the evolution of the Scottish

Office came to reflect the priorities of government in Scotland with the Boards of Agriculture, Education and Health (the latter because it dealt with housing) occupying a much larger role in Scottish administration than their British equivalents did south of the border. Large scale projects regarding recon-struction, such as Patrick Abercrombie's *Clyde Valley Plan* (1947), were kept firmly within the Scottish Office's sphere of influence. One other point must also be noted. The Scottish Office relocated to Edinburgh at the beginning of the war and in so doing, physically removed Scottish civil servants from their colleagues in London, which could have only accentuated their sense of separateness.

At the end of the Second World War the number of civil servants in Edinburgh had doubled to 5,000. Furthermore, the Scottish Office emerged with a firmer sense of its own identity and, with plans for reconstruction in the offing, a clear sense of purpose in the post-war world. The experience of 'total war' and the opportunities for economic and social regeneration that the command economy seemed to promise clearly defined the role that the Scottish Office would play in post-war reconstruction. The prospect of nationalisation of key industries, the pivotal role that the Treasury would play through the allocation of wartime Board of Trade factories and the import-ance of the Ministry of Works in the allocation of scarce resources would mean that the British state would remain absolutely crucial to the social and eco-nomic wellbeing of the Scottish citizen in the post-war period. In other words, the template that Johnston had created during the war of securing the maximum amount of resources from the British State would remain the key objective of Scottish politicians for the rest of the century. Although Home Rule could attract public sympathy, it could not compete against the fruits of centralised British state planning.[65]

Notes

1 I. G. C. Hutchison, *Scottish Politics in the Twentieth Century* (Basingstoke, 2001), p. xii.

2 See in particular James Mitchell, *Governing Scotland: The Invention of Administrative Devolution* (Basingstoke, 2003); Ian Levitt, *Government and Social Conditions in Scotland, 1845–1919* (Edinburgh, 1988); Ian Levitt, *The Scottish Office: Depression and Reconstruction, 1919–1959* (Edinburgh, 1996); J. S. Gibson, *The Thistle and the Crown: A History of the Scottish Office* (Edinburgh, 1988); L. Paterson, *The Autonomy of Modern Scotland* (Edinburgh, 1994); and H. J. Hanham, 'The development of the Scottish Office' in J. N. Wolfe (ed.), *Government and Nationalism in Scotland: An Enquiry by Members of the University of Edinburgh* (Edinburgh, 1969), pp. 51–71.

3 H. J. Hanham, *Scottish Nationalism* (London, 1969), pp. 77–82.

4 NLS, The Scottish rights association, NE20, 13–14, book 1, 3.
5 *Glasgow Sentinel*, 19 November 1853.
6 Graeme Morton, 'The most efficacious patriot: the heritage of William Wallace in nineteeth-century Scotland', *SHR*, 77 (1998).
7 Some of these issues are discussed in E. J. Cowan (ed.), *William Wallace: The Man and Myth* (East Linton, 2005).
8 J. Kellas, 'The Liberal Party in Scotland, 1876–95', *SHR*, 44 (1965).
9 Quoted in Lord Crewe, *Lord Rosebery* (1931), vol. I, p. 132.
10 A collection of the documents pertaining to the issue were published by the Convention of the Royal Burghs of Scotland as *The National Meeting in Favour of the Creation of a Separate Department of State for Scotland* (Edinburgh, 1900).
11 See for example the *Scotsman*, 1 April, 16 July and 20 August 1868 on the Irish Church Act and 18 August and 16 November 1883 for matters dealing with land reform.
12 Richard J. Finlay, *A Partnership for Good? Scottish Politics and the Union Since 1880* (Edinburgh, 1997), p. 47.
13 Quoted in Crewe, *Rosebery*, vol. I, p. 142.
14 I. G. C. Hutchison, *A Political History of Scotland: Parties, Elections and Issues, 1832–1924* (Edinburgh, 1986), pp. 160–2.
15 Quoted in Crewe, *Rosebery*, vol. I, p. 153.
16 Ibid., p. 158.
17 H. J. Hanham, 'The creation of the Scottish Office, 1881–87', *Juridical Review*, 10 (1965).
18 J. B. Mackie, *Life and Work of Duncan McLaren*, vol. II (Edinburgh, 1888), p. 127.
19 Graeme Morton, 'Scottish rights and "centralisation" in the mid-nineteenth century', *Nations and Nationalism*, 2 (1996).
20 J. F. McCaffrey, 'The origins of Liberal Unionism in the west of Scotland', *SHR*, 50 (1971).
21 Quoted in *Scottish Home Rule: The Case in 60 Points* (Glasgow, 1912), p. 12.
22 This was the view taken by Duncan McLaren writing to the *Scotsman*. Quoted in Mackie, *Duncan McLaren*, vol. II, pp. 352–4.
23 *Protest of the Scottish Home Rule Association Against the Denial or Delay of Scottish Home Rule* (Edinburgh, 1890).
24 Finlay, *Partnership for Good*, pp. 44–5.
25 Robert Munro Ferguson, *House of Commons Debates* [*H.C. Debs.*], vol. CLXX IX, 26 May 1908, 967.
26 Dr. Chapple, HC, vol. XXXIV, 28 February 1912, col. 1446.
27 Pat Jalland, 'United Kingdom devolution, 1910–14: political panacea or tactical diversion', *EHR*, 94 (1979).
28 T. Shaw, *Patriotism and the Empire* (Edinburgh, 1903).
29 NLS, Acc. 10424, *Younger Memorandum: Scots Home Rule*, 19 May 1914.
30 *Young Scots Handbook 1911* (Edinburgh, 1911), pp. 1–2.
31 HC, 5th ser. vol. 127, 16 April 1919, col. 2044.
32 Mitchell Library Glasgow, Muirhead papers, Robert Munro to R. E. Muirhead, 11 January 1922.
33 Richard J. Finlay, *Independent and Free: Scottish Politics and the Origins of the Scottish National Party, 1918–1945* (Edinburgh, 1994), pp. 3–24.

34 For example, James Maxton's speech at St Andrews Hall, Glasgow reported in
    Scottish Home Rule, April 1924, 74–5.
35 *Self Determination for Scotland* (Glasgow, 1919), p. 3.
36 Scottish Trade Union Congress, *STUC Annual Report, 1918.*
37 David Kirkwood quoted in *Scottish Home Rule*, September 1924, 8.
38 See W. W. Knox (ed.), *Scottish Labour Leaders, 1918–39* (Edinburgh, 1984),
    pp. 15–26.
39 *Scottish Home Rule*, June 1924.
40 David Howell, *A Lost Left: Three Studies in Socialism and Nationalism*
    (Manchester, 1986), pp. 229–65.
41 NLS, Acc. 6058, Maxton to R. Scott, 2 May 1928.
42 *Daily Record*, 9 January 1929.
43 T. Johnston, *Memories* (1952), p. 66.
44 Finlay, *Independent and Free*, pp. 71–80.
45 Ibid., pp. 162–90.
46 For Labour criticisms see Thomas Burns, *A Plan for Scotland* (Perth, 1937) and
    The Real Rulers of Scotland (Glasgow, 1939).
47 R. H. Campbell, 'The Scottish Office and the Special Areas in the 1930s',
    Historical Journal, 22 (1979).
48 R. J. Finlay, 'National identity in crisis: politicians, intellectuals and the "end of
    Scotland", 1920–39', *History*, 79 (1994).
49 A parliamentary debate was held on the state of Scotland on 22 November 1932.
50 Open letter by the Council of the Royal Incorporation of Architects in Scotland,
    quoted in the *Scots Independent*, April 1930, 64.
51 James Mitchell, *Conservatives and the Union: A Study of Conservative Party
    Attitudes to Scotland* (Edinburgh, 1990), p. 25.
52 Burns, *The Real Rulers of Scotland.*
53 Eleven Scottish Labour MPs held positions within the Committtee; Tom
    Johnston, James Barr, Robert Gibson, J. R. Leslie, Andrew Maclaren, Neil
    Maclean, Malcolm MacMillan, L. MacNeil Weir, George Mathers, H. G. McHee
    and J. C. Welsh.
54 *Address to the International Engineering Congress* (Glasgow, 1938).
55 Burns, *Plan for Scotland*, p. 9.
56 Graham Walker, *Thomas Johnston* (Manchester, 1988).
57 R. H. Campbell, 'The committee of ex-Secretaries of State for Scotland and
    industrial policy', *Scottish Industrial History*, 2 (1981).
58 Johnston, *Memories*, p. 153.
59 Scottish Office, *Industry and Employment in Scotland*, Cmd. 7125 (Edinburgh,
    1947).
60 Chris Harvie, 'Labour and Scottish government: the age of Tom Johnston', *The
    Bulletin of Scottish Politics* (Spring 1981), 1–20.
61 R. Saville, 'The industrial background to the post-war Scottish economy' in
    R. Saville (ed.), *The Economic Development of Modern Scotland, 1950–1980*
    (Edinburgh, 1985).
62 Johnston, *Memories*, pp. 150–73.
63 I. G. C. Hutchison, 'Government' in T. M. Devine and R. J. Finlay (eds),
    Scotland in the Twentieth Century (Edinburgh, 1996), pp. 49–50.
64 Johnston, *Memories*, pp. 160, 168.

65 Although the Scottish Covenant of 1948 was able to gain about two million sig-
    natures in support of a Scottish Parliament, the movement fizzled out when dared
    to compete in the area of party politics by the Labour Secretary of State, Hector
    McNeil. As a *Scotsman* editorial put it (9 August 1950): 'They [the main parties]
    imply that the desire for self-government should be demonstrated by voters at an
    election. When an election takes place, however, they claim that larger issues are
    at stake, which overshadow the minor domestic problems of Scotland and urge
    the electors to ignore the latter'. This is what the Scottish electorate did.

2

A place apart? Ulster, Britain and devolution, 1886–1939

D. George Boyce

There can be fewer modifications to the British constitution that were so neglected by its makers as the devolved system of government in Northern Ireland; fewer that have attracted so much attention since its collapse in 1972. The lack of understanding – and indeed knowledge – of the 1920 Government of Ireland Act which established the state helps explain the confusion about its status in the United Kingdom in the last years of its existence. And even in the 1970s, when devolved government for Scotland and Wales was on the political agenda, Northern Ireland was seen as exceptional: its history, sectarian politics, and above all political violence marked it out as so different from the rest of the United Kingdom that it could offer little or no illustration of how devolved government might work elsewhere, and what impact it might have on the state and the sense of British nationality that underpinned the state.

Ulster in the shadow of Home Rule

The Home Rule controversy lasted for some forty years, and although the essential issues remained the same – satisfying Irish Nationalists and safeguarding Irish Unionists, and reconciling both these aspirations with the unity of the United Kingdom – yet the debate shifted its ground during this long controversy. When Gladstone introduced his first Home Rule Bill in 1886 he insisted that Ireland was a special, even a moral, case; and while he acknowledged Irish and especially Ulster Unionist apprehensions about being placed under a Dublin parliament, he held that these could be considered without any special treatment of Ulster, such as that proposed by Joseph Chamberlain for a special Ulster assembly.[1] But the organised and determined opposition of Ulster Unionists to the third Home Rule Bill of 1912, strongly supported by the British Conservative and Unionist Party, provoked two important developments in the debate. One was that it might be necessary to consider some special arrangements that would disarm Ulster Unionists' threatened rebellion against the Liberal government's imposition of Home Rule upon them; the other, and closely connected, was that a federal reorganisation of the United Kingdom, with 'Home Rule all Round' for England, Scotland and Wales, would enable British Unionists to accept Irish Home Rule, since they objected to Home Rule as recognising that the Irish constituted a distinct nation; would meet Ulster Unionists' objections, since the whole United Kingdom was being accorded the same treatment; and would resolve the practical problems created by the ever-growing burden of legislation that was falling upon the Westminster Parliament. Thus the whole ground of the Home Rule controversy would be shifted and set in a different perspective: it would no longer be driven by a conflict of nationality, but would sit in the context of a sensible, all-British, rational reorganisation of the whole Kingdom.

This wider view was never lost sight of between 1914 and the end of the First World War. The entry of the Conservative and Unionist Party into the Coalition government in 1915, and the continuation of the Coalition under the premiership of Lloyd George in the December 1918 general election, made it seem all the more imperative. In April 1918 Lloyd George was told that a 'considerable number of the younger generation of Conservatives are by no means disinclined for a measure of Home Rule, as a war measure, provided that it would fit in hereafter with a Federal plan for the United Kingdom'.[2] Austen Chamberlain wrote to Lloyd George in April 1918 that an Irish settlement must not be 'inconsistent with the extension of the same system of Government to England, Scotland and Wales. . . .'[3] An Irish Committee set up on 11 April to find a way to implement self-government acceptable to the Coalition had strong federalist inclinations, and worked to preserve the Union, grant Irish Home Rule and yet safeguard Ulster Unionists. Walter Long, its chairman, mused on the chances of devising a scheme 'which would if necessary be adopted as a basis for Federation of United Kingdom'.[4] There was encouragement from Conservative Central Office, which took a sample of opinion in sixteen different districts, and found that only three were definitely hostile to federalism.[5] Long reported on 23 April that he was receiving 'many representations daily in favour of a Federal solution from Liberals and from Unionists'.[6] Austen Chamberlain drew attention to what he called the 'British Problem': that many of the questions upon which the political parties concentrated on before the war had now lost their interest: 'A new order of questions has taken their place'. How was it possible for one government and parliament to deal adequately with all those matters and at the same time perform their functions as the 'great central organs of government of the Empire'?[7] But this optimism was dashed with the government's increasing concern about disaffection in Ireland and the rise of Sinn Fein, fuelled, it must be said, by its own determination to impose military conscription on Ireland. Long drafted a federal scheme by the end of June 1918, but he admitted that Sinn Fein was by now dominant in the south of Ireland and estimated that it would capture 90% of the seats outside Ulster in both parliamentary and local elections. But equally important was a sign that the federal high tide, if not past, was beginning to flow more sluggishly. Lord Curzon voiced the objection that Lloyd George for his part also harboured: that federalism would 'pull up the British Constitution by the roots'.[8]

With the end of the war, the Coalition Government found that it must again face the question of Irish self-government. Federalism was still in the air. It was debated in the House of Lords in March 1919, and on 7 October the Cabinet agreed to make an early statement of its Irish intentions, and was also charged with drafting a bill on federal lines; at the same time a Parliamentary Inquiry chaired by the Speaker was set up to look at the possibility of federating the whole United Kingdom.[9] But there were signs that Ireland was still a special case. The Speaker's Conference on devolution was excluded from considering Ireland; and when Long's Irish Committee presented its first report, on 4 November it addressed the old familiar issues: how to reconcile a measure of Irish self-government with the needs of British and imperial security and fiscal organisation, and what to do about Unionist Ulster. The Committee explained that the background to its deliberations was that the government was committed against any solution which would break up the unity of the empire; but also committed that 'Ulster must not be forced under the rule of an Irish Parliament against its will'. The first condition excluded any possibility of an Irish republic; the second the establishment of a single parliament for all Ireland 'on the lines of the Home Rule Acts [sic] of 1886, 1893 and 1914'. Three alternative courses were debated: a single parliament with the people of Ulster voting themselves out by county option or a plebiscite; a special Ulster Committee within a single parliament with veto powers, or the 'artificial over-representation of Ulster in the Irish parliament; and a parliament for the three southern provinces and a second parliament for Ulster, together with a Council of Ireland composed of members of the two Irish parliaments, to discharge certain immediate functions, but 'mainly to promote as rapidly as possible, and without further reference to the Imperial Parliament, the union of the whole of Ireland under a single legislature'. The Committee decided in favour of the last alternative, which would avoid the coercion of Ulster, but also enabled Irish unity to come from within. If the 'withdrawal of British rule' and the establishment of a local legislature in Ulster 'is necessary to heal the feud which has estranged Ireland and Great

Britain for so many decades, and which is now seriously imperilling the relations of Great Britain both with the rest of the Empire and with the United States of America, the sacrifice which Ulster will be called upon to make in assuming control of its own local affairs is one which the Imperial Government and Parliament is clearly entitled to ask its people to make'. The committee revealed a brief flash of federalism in proposing that the historic province of Ulster (nine counties) be the unit for the northern parliament since 'reasons of administrative convenience ought to be a principal consideration in drawing the line between them, [the two parts of Ireland] as it was in the federal constitutions of the United States and the Dominions'. Each unit would enjoy 'state rights', and it was up to Ulster to persuade nationalist Ireland to its views, and thus it 'will be able to secure that Ireland forms part of a United Kingdom federation at the price of agreeing to Irish unity themselves'.[10] When the Cabinet met on 10 December there were still vestiges of United Kingdom federalism, especially in its agreement to insist on a nine county Northern Ireland: the bill 'in its present form possessed the advantage of fitting into any scheme for the establishment of a federal system in the United Kingdom'. But there was a declining note in the next phrase: 'should such a scheme ever be adopted'.[11] Walter Long took soundings from the Ulster Unionists in January 1920. They accepted the principle of Home Rule for Ulster, fearing that a different Westminster parliament, in which the Labour Party would have stronger representation would offer them lesser terms. But they demanded that the area of the northern parliament be confined to six, not nine counties (Antrim, Armagh, Down, Londonderry, Fermanagh and Tyrone) as the price of their acceptance of the government's plan.[12]

The creation and character of 'Northern Ireland'

The debate on Irish Home Rule generally since the 1870s raised key issues about how a legitimate desire for self-government could be reconciled – if at all – with the unity of the United Kingdom. It also provoked reflections on how best the rights of the minority in Ireland, the Protestant and Unionist people, could be secured in a state governed by a permanent Roman Catholic and nationalist majority. The outcome of this double conundrum – the unity of the Kingdom and the rights of minorities – ended with a paradox: the partition of Ireland, the granting (after a bitter guerilla and terrorist war between the Irish Republican Army (IRA) and the Crown Forces) of Dominion status to 26 counties known as the 'Irish Free State', and the creation of the six county Northern Ireland devolved government which the local majority in that area, the Ulster Unionists, had always opposed. Northern Ireland lasted fifty years, but it was not initially intended to last so long, for the 1920 Government of Ireland Act which created Northern Ireland embodied a kind of double bar-relled Home Rule, with parliaments for 'Northern' and 'Southern' Ireland, and a Council of Ireland to facilitate the voluntary reunification of the country. If such an outcome seems, in retrospect (and indeed, given the violence that accompanied this attempted settlement by the British Government, at the time) unlikely, yet this was a central part of the plan, and a whole section of the Act was devoted to setting out the procedure to be followed if the parliaments of Northern and Southern Ireland, by identical acts, agreed to by an absolute majority of members of the House of Commons of each parliament established a parliament for the whole of Ireland; the date at which this parliament was established would be referred to as the 'date of Irish union'.[13]

The Government of Ireland Act had an impact on Ireland and Great Britain, for it was intended to satisfy Irish Nationalism, Ulster Unionism, and the broader needs of the United Kingdom. Irish nationalists, represented from 1918 by Sinn Fein, protested vehemently against the partition of Ireland; and subsequent Irish parties and governments would not let the issue die: as the first Prime Minister of Northern Ireland, Sir James Craig, put it in 1938, 'So long as we live there will always be the danger of Home Rule [sic] or merging into the Free State. We will never get rid of it'.[14] Ulster Unionists were obliged to work a political and administrative system that they had always opposed, and one which existed in a region with a large (one third of the population) Catholic and nationalist minority that was left stranded and embittered in a partitional Ireland. But Unionists had a lively awareness that the British, who had imposed Home Rule upon them, had hoped when nego-tiating a treaty with Sinn Fein in 1921 to persuade Sir James Craig to enter an all-Ireland Dominion. The British Prime Minister Lloyd George impressed upon Craig the 'kind of difficulties which must arise from the grant of Dominion powers to a part of Ireland only', to which Craig replied that if Ulster were to be thrust out of the United Kingdom 'she desires to be left in a position to make her own fiscal and international policy conform as nearly as possible with the policy of the Mother Country, and to retain British trad-itions, British currency, British ideals, and the British language, and in this way render the disadvantages entailed by her separation from Great Britain as slight as possible'. Craig insisted that equality between North and South in Ireland was the principle of the 1920 Government of Ireland Act, and that if Ulster must leave the United Kingdom, she should do so with the status of a Dominion. But it had always been the desire of Northern Ireland to remain in the closest possible union with Great Britain and the Empire, 'which Ulstermen have helped to build up, and to which they are proud to belong'.[15]

The British Government would have none of this, and to persuade Sinn Fein to accept partition Lloyd George and his colleagues offered them a boundary commission, which would be implemented if Northern Ireland refused to accept the subordination of its devolved government to a Dublin parliament; this commission would rectify the border between north and south in accordance with the wishes of the population, but also in the light of geographical and economic conditions. Nationalists on both sides of the border hoped, or believed, that sufficient territory would be transferred to the Free State to make Northern Ireland unviable as a state. They were mistaken. But the Anglo-Irish treaty negotiations of October to December 1921 revealed British exasperation with Ulster Unionists, a dislike of their intransigent attitude to what the British perceived as the best interests of the United Kingdom and the Empire, and no great love of the devolved state that was in the process of taking shape as a political and administrative reality.[16] The 1921 treaty placed Northern Ireland in the new Irish Free State, and although this was but a formality, since Craig's government could, and did, vote itself out of the state that it was never actually in, yet symbols were, and are, of vital importance in Irish politics, and Craig protested indignantly against what he called the 'complete reversal' of the declared policy that 'Ulster should remain out until she chose of her free will to enter an all-Ireland Parliament'. In years to come, he added, 'the British nation will realise the advantage in having in Northern Ireland a population which is determined to remain loyal to British traditions and citizenship'.[17]

The constitution of Northern Ireland revealed the characteristics that had shaped the debate on Irish Home Rule in the late nineteenth century. The 1920 Government of Ireland Act was one of many bills for devolved government in Ireland, the chief of which were those of 1886, 1893 and 1912.[18] There were various motives behind these bills and the 1920 Act. The desire to satisfy Irish nationalist aspirations persuaded the British to seek to give as wide a measure of devolved government compatible with British fiscal and security needs. This was because one of the key arguments for Home Rule was that, as the Unionist A. V. Dicey rightly discerned, Home Rulers held that 'under all politics, and especially under the system of popular government, institutions derive their life, and laws their constraining power, not from the will of the law-giver, or from the strength of the army, but from their correspondence with the permanent wishes and habits of the people'. Thus Home Rule meant the 'application to Ireland of the very principle on which the English constitution rests – that a people must be ruled in accordance with their own permanent ideas of right and justice, and that unless this be done, law, because it commands no loyalty, ensures no obedience'.[19] In the debates on the third Home Rule Bill of 1912 speakers from the Government Front

Bench used the same language: Winston Churchill claimed that the bill was 'the acceptance of a measure which implements, amplifies, and carries out the union of the two countries under forms which for the first time will receive the assent of the Irish people'.[20] Asquith said that he desired a 'real union', with local freedom, local elasticity, local flexibility and local power of adaptation enabling separate communities to 'mould each its domestic fortunes in accordance with its own ideals'.[21] The 1920 Act was based on this principle: each of the two main Irish religious/political communities (Ulster Unionists and the nationalists of 'Southern Ireland') would be able to mould their own destiny, based on extensive law-making powers. The Act, like its predecessors, gave the two parliaments the power to make laws for the 'peace, order and good government' of the country, subject to certain express limitations. These limitations were the 'excepted' powers (matters concerning the Crown, making war and peace, the armed forces, treaties with foreign states, dignities and titles of honour, treason, naturalisation, aliens and domicile, trade with any places outside Northern (and Southern) Ireland, submarine cables and wireless facilities); and the 'Reserved Powers', that is, those which would eventually be transferred to an all-Ireland government and parliament, and which included the postal service, post office and savings banks and trustee savings banks, and designs for stamps. The Act also precluded the Irish parliaments from passing laws that would discriminate against religious minorities.[22] Thus the 1920 Act did give the six counties the powers to ensure that their laws would be in conformity with the wishes of the majority of the people; the problem was that the nationalists would not enjoy that experience, but, on the contrary, would find themselves living under laws which they played little or no part in making. This would have applied to the previous Home Rule bills, with the difference that had they become law the Protestants would have been the minority people. However, it seems safe to suggest that in the nineteenth century, Westminster would have continued to exercise a more determined supervisory role in Ireland. By 1919 the British Government wanted to escape from the burden of the Irish Question, and indeed a main purpose of the devolution of power to Northern Ireland, instead of its retention under direct rule, was that it would prevent the criticism in Ireland and overseas that the British were seeking to retain power in any part of Ireland , for 'If it is retained anywhere in Ireland the opponents of Great Britain will be able to say either that Great Britain is ruling nationalist majorities against their will, or that it is giving its active support to Ulster in its refusal to unite with the rest of Ireland'.[23]

This was a considerable measure of devolved government, one whose limitations belied its extensive concessions: as the constitutional and legal expert, Professor Newark, wrote in 1953, 'the proper way to use the Government of

Ireland Act 1920, is not to read it to see what the Stormont Parliament can do, but to assume it can do everything and then read the Act to see what it cannot do'.[24] Apart from the excluded and reserved matters, he argued, the Northern Ireland Parliament was a 'Sovereign Parliament'. This raised another question from the nineteenth century debates: if there were express limitations on what was an otherwise 'sovereign parliament', would not those who voted for, served in that parliament, and the executive derived from it, press for full national sovereignty? Would Home Rule really be, as its supporters claimed, a final settlement of the Irish difficulty? The 1920 Act, like the previous bills, asserted the sovereignty of the Westminster Parliament over the devolved state; but this could be challenged politically, and in 1886 and 1893 Unionists in Britain and Ireland claimed that it would be thus challenged: Irish nationalists were separatists at heart, enemies of Britain and the Empire. This cannot be proved one way or the other; and the establishment of Northern Ireland was likewise inconclusive. For the government of Northern Ireland was a Unionist one, and seemed likely to remain so. The 1920 Act introduced proportional representation (PR) in order to protect the rights of minorities in both parts of Ireland. Unionists complained that this might result in an electoral mishap, producing a parliament that would take Northern Ireland into the Irish Free State. However unlikely this may have seemed, its possibility haunted Ulster Unionists: in 1925 the Northern Ireland Labour Party fielded three candidates in Belfast, all of whom were elected (including one in the Unionist heartland of East Belfast). Something must be done. In 1922 the Northern Ireland Government abolished PR in local government elections, followed in 1929 by its abolition in elections for the Northern Ireland Parliament. This was not aimed against the Nationalist Party in Northern Ireland, but rather to ensure its identification as the prime enemy of Unionism; the abolition of PR would eliminate small minority MPs and parties, thus leaving a straight fight between 'loyal' and 'disloyal' men.[25] This was a fight that Unionists felt they could and must win.

Unionists hoped that the substitution of PR by the first past the post voting system and single member constituencies would safeguard Northern Ireland. Some wondered if they would not be safer still under direct Westminster rule. But the British response to the Northern Ireland Government's decision to abolish PR for local elections in 1922 was a timely warning. Pressure from the Irish Free State persuaded the British Government to delay the royal assent to the bill, which occasioned cries of outrage from Unionists. Sir James Craig warned that 'No government could carry on in Northern Ireland if it knew that the powers of the Parliament . . . were to be abrogated' and to succumb to Westminster's withholding of the royal assent would set a precedent, warranting 'the interference by the Imperial Government in almost every Act introduced in Northern Ireland'. As Craig anticipated, the British backed down rather than risk 'complete disorganisation in Ulster at the moment'; he knew that if he resigned then the British would have to take up what they feared most: the burden of governing Northern Ireland directly.[26] But Craig knew that he must not push matters beyond this point, for Northern Ireland depended upon Great Britain for financial and security assistance. The cry of 'back to Westminster', the Ulster Unionist Council warned in 1936, was 'fraught with danger'.[27]

It suited Ulster Unionists to work their parliament, rather than seek a return to direct rule from Westminster; it suited the British Government to allow much latitude in how Unionists worked their parliament, rather than interfere in ways vexatious to the Northern Ireland Government. There was another respect in which the 1920 Government of Ireland Act was now acknowledged to suit both parties. The original plan of two parliaments in Ireland would have meant that Ireland would have 63 representatives in the British House of Commons, but with no right to vote on any bill not affecting Ireland. This figure was reduced on 10 December 1919 to 46: the Irish Members were given the right to vote on all issues raised in the House of Commons, but with their number reduced to prevent the Irish Members from exercising 'a decisive voice in our domestic policy'.[28] Now that 'Southern Ireland' was a stillborn political entity, Irish representation was confined to Northern Ireland, and consisted of only twelve MPs. This reduced Ulster Unionist representation in the House and was followed by a almost terminal decline in their occupation of significant government offices; but it also meant that the Ulster Unionist Members could safely tuck themselves in behind the British Conservative Party. They could not hope to play any significant role in its politics; but neither would their presence prove troublesome to the British party system (at least not until 1964 when Harold Wilson was frustrated at their reduction of his majority to a handful of seats) and thus bring down on their heads the anger of British parliamentarians about the troublesome behaviour of Members from across the Irish Sea. The fact that there was no 'Minister for Northern Ireland' meant that it became the convention that Northern Irish affairs were not discussed in the House of Commons: the Speaker ruled in 1923 that questions 'must be asked of Ministers in Northern Ireland, and not in this House'.[29] The Speaker of the Northern Ireland Parliament ruled that it could not debate on matters outside its own jurisdiction. This desire to steer clear of confrontation or controversy was reflected in the British Government's gradual acceptance that one of the key principles of devolution – fiscal responsibility – must be compromised. Northern Ireland was never a self-sufficient economy, because it was, as a survey published in 1955 noted, 'economically so woven with Great Britain that, looked at broadly, it is not a separate economy at all but an undifferentiated part of a single economic system embracing the whole of the United Kingdom'. Thus the main policy decisions affecting economic conditions in Northern Ireland 'are made by the central government and apply indiscriminately to the whole of the United Kingdom; and likewise, the main economic and financial institutions are common to the whole'.[30]

This meant that the government of Northern Ireland was severely constrained in what it could do to manage its own economy. British Governments were not keen to bail it out when after 1929 the great economic depression threatened Northern Ireland's viability as a state. But Northern Ireland had the advantage that, if it were to fail, then again Irish affairs would be the direct responsibility of the British Government. In November 1932 the Northern Ireland Minister of Finance, reviewing the annual report on the government's work schemes to provide employment, complained that the debts thus incurred were 'throttling the power of government to effect real improvements in the condition of the province'.[31] J. M. Andrews, Minister of Labour, and a future Prime Minister of Northern Ireland, believed that it was fair for the British to subsidise Northern Ireland: 'We are a very subordinate parliament, and our financial position, as well as our social conditions, are from time to time really in practice fixed not by ourselves but by actions of His Majesty's Imperial Government'.[32] Andrews pointed out that the 1920 Act made no proper financial provision for unemployment benefit; Ulster, no more than the 'Clyde or Sheffield' should be made to bear the cost of its own unemployed.[33] The British Government responded in 1926 with an arrangement by which the British Exchequer gave grants to defray three-quarters of the excess cost of the Northern Ireland unemployment costs. In 1933 the Northern Ireland Government campaigned that its 'Imperial Contribution' (fixed under the 1920 Act to cover services provided by the United Kingdom that were common to all British citizens, such as defence) should be made a 'minus' contribution. The devolved state's budget was only balanced by means of what one senior Treasury official described as 'fudges' and' wangles', 'dodges and devices' giving gifts and subventions 'within the ambit of the Government of Ireland Act so as to save the Northern Ireland Government from coming openly on the dole as Newfoundland did'.[34] Under the 1936 Employment (Agreement) Act (Northern Ireland) the per capita payments to Northern Ireland were assessed, not on the basis of total population, but of the insured population. In Northern Ireland fewer people were in insurable employment and this offered a way out of the immediate crisis.[35]

In the first decade of Northern Ireland's existence Treasury officials in Britain held no favourable opinion of its government, believing that Ulster

Unionists wanted to enjoy local autonomy at the expense of the British tax-payer, and although this attitude softened in the 1930s, the Treasury still believed that Britain should avoid any long-term financial commitments to Northern Ireland.[36] Yet Home Rule had been intended, as Asquith put it in 1912, quoting from a contemporary of James VI of Scotland and I of England, to ensure that England, Scotland and Ireland united 'will be such a trefoil as no prince except yourself weareth in his crown'. The 'hand of man' would join with the 'hand of Nature to bring about for the first time in deed as well as in name a United Kingdom'.[37] This highlighted the importance of insisting between 1886 and 1912 that Home Rule should apply to the whole of Ireland, for it was intended that it should conciliate Irish nationalism – if necessary, at the expense of Irish and Ulster Unionism. Now that it was the prerogative of Ulster Unionists, it must have a very different effect. It might be said that the imposition of Home Rule on the Ulster Unionists was the singing of one song to the tune of another. The resulting discord might be expected to provoke a crisis in relations between Northern Ireland and the British Government, but it did not: Ulster Unionists were aware of the need to avoid any serious confrontation. Indeed, they were highly susceptible, not always in their own interests, to appeals from British Ministers. In 1931 Snowden imposed higher taxation in his September budget. In 1932 Northern Ireland agreed to an increase of £150,000 following the new Chancellor, Neville Chamberlain's appeal that the increase was of 'paramount importance to every part of the United Kingdom'. Craig agreed 'without hes-itation that the interests of the Imperial Budget are paramount in the present crisis'.[38] Nevertheless the Government of Ireland Act did change Ulster Unionists' and Nationalists' relationship with the broader themes of British Unionism/Conservatism and Irish nationalism respectively.

The isolation of Ulster politics

Ulster Nationalists found themselves in an unenviable position. Their strongest supporter in the formative years of the two states in Ireland was Michael Collins; his death in 1922 was followed by the disaster of the Boundary Commission which in 1926 recommended, not the considerable changes in the territory of Northern Ireland that had, perhaps naively, been anticipated, but only minor alterations, including the transfer of some terri-tory to the North. The Irish Free State, preoccupied with establishing its authority and indeed its legitimacy, withdrew from any real concern for Ulster Nationalists, contenting itself with irredentist rhetoric, particularly under the leadership of Eamon de Valera, whose 1937 Constitution claimed the whole island of Ireland as the 'national territory'. Sir James Craig replied that if the south was a 'Catholic state' then Northern Ireland was a 'Protestant Parliament and a Protestant state'.[39] Ulster Nationalists found themselves being included in the Irish nation in the abstract, but left to their own devices when it came to real political life. They remained, throughout Northern Ireland's existence, a disaffected minority, complaining that they were subject to discrimination by the state, and particularly aggrieved at the Northern Ireland Government's resolution in 1930 of a long running dispute over state education, which, they alleged, amounted to the effective endowment of Protestantism.[40] They felt unable to turn to the British Government for support, even though, the nationalist *Irish News* pointed out, Catholics should be given equal rights as their Protestant fellow-citizens, since they were not 'rebels' but 'loyal citizens'.[41] But following serious riots in Belfast in July 1935 a Catholic demand for a British inquiry was refused by the Prime Minister, Stanley Baldwin, because responsibility for law and order rested with the Northern Ireland Government. An inquiry by the British based National Council for Civil Liberties found strongly against the Unionists, and especially their Special Powers Act which was introduced by the Unionist Government in 1922, renewed annually until 1929, then for four years, and then made permanent in 1933, and which gave extensive powers of arrest and detention to the Minister for Home Affairs.[42]

Devolution also affected the identity of Ulster Unionists. When they began their long crusade against Home Rule in the 1880s, Ulster Protestants insisted that their fight was to keep the whole of Ireland within the United Kingdom and the British nation. In a great Ulster Unionist Convention in Belfast in 1892, the Reverend Dr Kane, Grand Master of the Orange Order (whose headquarters was and is in Dublin) warned that it was 'quite possible to write the word Ulster too large in this controversy. This Convention is assembled to protest most solemnly against any kind of dismemberment of the United Kingdom; the people of Cork and Middlesex should be subjected to the same laws.[43] His reference to Middlesex emphasised another key aspect of the Ulster Unionist cause: that they were thoroughly British by blood and descent, but also Irish by birth. The Duke of Abercorn told the Convention that Ulster Unionists were 'descendants of English puritans' and of Scottish Presbyterians, members of a great empire, and also 'Irishmen' whom England must not desert.[44] Another delegate insisted that the empire was not made by Englishmen, nor by Scotsmen or Irishmen, but by the union of English pluck, Scottish prudence and Irish enthusiasm.[45]

But the creation of Northern Ireland altered these sentiments, slowly but inexorably. Ulster Unionists, believing themselves under siege, and with much justification given the IRA's determined efforts to bring down the state from its inception, built up barricades of the mind as well as of the map. The coming to power of de Valera enhanced their sense of difference from the rest of Ireland, for his efforts to consolidate a Gaelic and Catholic state, and especially his 1937 Constitution, provoked Sir James Craig to emphasise even more the Britishness and un-Irishness of Ulster. There was not a man born who could produce the 'miracle union' of north and south. It was better for the Northern Ireland people to be left 'absolutely free to be able to shake hands' with those who were 'English-born, Scottish-born, Welsh-born, or born of that stock in other parts of the world in all equality under British citizenship, saying to each-other: "How can we help to develop the Empire?".'[46] Craig's British agenda, it must be noted, was given power and authenticity by the Ulster Nationalist Cahir Healy's claim that the only 'true Irishman' was one who wanted an 'Irish-Ireland not an anglicised Ireland'.[47] It was not hard for Unionist leaders to define as 'disloyal' those who, as a future Prime Minister of Northern Ireland Sir Basil Brooke put it in 1932, were scheming and plotting to destroy the country in which they lived: 'any man who is out to break up the constitution, which has been established by Great Britain, is to my mind disloyal'.[48]

Devolution both acknowledged and increased the differences between nationalist and Unionist in Ireland, helping to solidify a narrower kind of Ulster Unionist patriotism. But Ulster Unionists claimed they were not narrowly focused, but self-conscious members of the wider British nation. They recognised that this British nation was itself varied in its identities: as Craig said, it consisted of the English, the Scots and the Welsh as well as the Ulstermen. His province, he emphasised, was also part of that wider conglomeration of peoples that comprised the British Empire (by which he meant the 'white' dominions). The Unionists' determination to remain part of the Kingdom and the Empire was given a powerful and striking physical presence in the completion of the new Northern Ireland Parliament buildings at Stormont, on the outskirts of Belfast in November 1932. The visitor was confronted on the drive up to the buildings with a larger than life statue of Sir Edward Carson in defiant pose: a curiosity, admittedly, since Carson fought to keep all Ireland in the Union; now he graced a regional Home Rule edifice. But Stormont was a message to those who would look and learn: that the Protestant State of Northern Ireland was here to stay, and would not fall prey to its enemies.

But who were its enemies? Some were easily identified: southern Irish nationalists and Northern Ireland Catholics. The most dangerous foe, as always, was not the declared opponent, but the false or unreliable friend. The question that troubled Northern Ireland's Unionists from – and including – the state's beginnings in 1921–22 was that which vexed all Irish Protestants since, and indeed before, 1886: could Britain, or as they more accurately put it, England, be depended upon? Ulster Unionists stressed their awareness of the great British (not English) Empire. This was by no means a weak card to play, since the Empire was between 1919 and 1939 at its zenith; and it did indeed encompass loyal Britons in Canada, Australia, New Zealand and South Africa. In the crucial elections in Northern Ireland in May 1921 Craig stressed that the eyes of Unionists' friends in the Empire were on Ulster.[49] The problem was that the Irish Free State was also in the Empire, and indeed was more privy to its deliberations as a Dominion with the same status as the mighty Canada. If Ulster was an Imperial Province, then the Free State was a Commonwealth Dominion, and able to play a role not only in that organisation, but in international politics generally. The superior grip of the south upon Britain was felt in the Anglo-Irish negotiations of 1938, which were intended to end an 'economic war' between Great Britain and Ireland over de Valera's decision to cease paying annuities to the British (monies owed to the Treasury from sums advanced to Irish tenant-farmers in the period 1887–1904 to enable them to purchase their holdings). Sir James Craig could only watch and wait while Neville Chamberlain bargained with de Valera, in particular making a trade agreement which allowed goods from Ireland almost free entry into the United Kingdom but still restricted United Kingdom exports to the south, thus damaging Northern Ireland's already ailing economy. When Craig protested, Chamberlain called upon his British patriotism to show that 'peace by negotiation' was possible on the international scene, and urged Craig not to undermine the 'impression of solidarity' here and in Berlin. Craig, to the fury of some members of his Cabinet, succumbed.[50]

Ulster Unionist unease at the safety of their devolved state, their anxiety that their 'half way house' might be seen as some kind of lean-to merely, was expressed by Henry Maxwell in his book, *Ulster was Right*, published in 1934. Maxwell described the opening of the Northern Ireland Parliament buildings at Stormont as having 'constituted the final harvesting of the long-tended promise': the establishment of Northern Ireland. But he noted that, since the foundation of the state, 'much had happened to impair the confidence of the Ulster people in the durability of the original charter, and even, it must be said, in the good faith of English politicians'. Yet the bond of union between the Ulster and British people was 'the breath of their living', for there existed a 'sympathy of race and sentiment' which was 'deep and abiding'. Ulster was, he admitted, dependent on Great Britain 'for her very existence'; but Britain was dependent on Ulster, which had fought her battles in the past, 'often without assistance and without recognition'. Hence the visit of the Prince of Wales to open Stormont was 'greatly treasured'.[51]

The fear that the treasuring of this visit, and what it stood for, was a one-way process was, Maxwell contended, epitomised in an interview given by Sir Edward Carson, who complained that in the 'vast British electorate there is a large percentage of young people who naturally have little or no knowledge of the difficulties and dangers that Ulster men and women had to overcome ten or more years ago'. The Ulster people regarded themselves as 'a branch of the British oak. Cut off the branch, and not only will the branch itself wither, but the tree will be left mutilated and weakened'. Maxwell warned that unless the younger generations were familiar with these events they could not give Ulster the full support and sympathy to which she was entitled: Englishmen were 'too willing to shut their eyes to hostility'.[52] Ulster as much as England would like to forget the past but neither could afford to do so. As an outpost of Great Britain, the imperial province of Northern Ireland had her enemies within and without her gates. With the 'help and hand' of Great Britain she would emerge triumphant in the end, but 'he that guardeth Israel must neither slumber nor sleep'.[53]

Maxwell's reference to the younger generation reflected that change in British attitudes towards Ireland, and Northern Ireland, since the heady days of the battle against Home Rule. Before the Great War the Conservatives, who had called themselves Unionists since Gladstone's first Home Rule adventure in 1886, stood for the constitutional union with Ireland. But they changed with the times, abandoned their Unionist title and acknowledged that the battle was lost, and that the Government of Ireland Act of 1920 must be implemented. They were as anxious as the Liberals to put pressure on Craig to enter an all-Ireland Parliament in the treaty negotiations of 1921, for the sake of a settlement, and in the wider interests of England and the empire. When, in the 1920s and 1930s, Stanley Baldwin redefined Conservatism he did so in terms not altogether familiar to Northern Ireland political culture: he stressed inclusive politics, shared humanity, community, love of nature, Christian faith and patriotism.[54] Christian faith was a common link between Ulster and Baldwin's Conservatism; but Austen Chamberlain's reference in 1920 to the 'bitterness of religious strife' in Ulster was not what Baldwin had in mind.[55] When sectarian tension erupted in civil strife in Belfast in the high tide of the annual Orange Order demonstrations in July 1935, *The Times*, once a staunch defender of the Union and the Unionists, referred loftily to the riots 'of the type which is called communal in India, religious in Ireland, and irreligious by impartial persons everywhere'. It criticised the Northern Ireland Government for not seeing the danger signs sooner, and for revoking an earlier ban on all parades except funerals in any part of Belfast. The responsibility for preventing future riots, it concluded, lay with Stormont and 'they will no doubt devise means which will prevent the next "Twelfth" from being an occasion for scandal'.[56]

Patriotism was another common ground between Ulster Unionism and Britain. But devolution had altered its character: Lady Londonderry lectured on 'The meaning of Union', despite the fact that the original idea had 'gone beyond recall'.[57] This was strange, since after 1920 the Union of England, Scotland, Wales and Northern Ireland still existed under the sovereign Westminster Parliament. But its moral foundation, the idea that, as A. V. Dicey put it, the British were 'morally a nation' with the right to insist that the 'supreme authority belonged to the majority of its citizens' (as the federal government in the United States of America believed when it went to war to preserve the Union in 1861) was gone.[58] The 'original idea' was to preserve the unity of the United Kingdom and the empire, not to rope off Ulster Protestants in their own six county state; indeed, the government originally intended in 1919 to create a nine county Northern Ireland in order the better to facilitate re-unification, but conceded the Ulster Unionists' demand that the state be confined to six counties only as the area they could control.[59] Ulster Unionists' insistence on a six county state was strongly criticised by some of their former Conservative allies,[60] and Unionists were always sensitive to the ground that they had to make up in keeping in with the British. J. M. Andrews asserted in 1936 that 'we should never have a boundary between ourselves and Great Britain'.[61] But devolution created two boundaries: one between the north and south of Ireland, and one – less obvious but no less important – between Northern Ireland and the rest of the United Kingdom. How far this sense of difference was justified is debatable. Scotland had long experienced sectarianism, especially in Glasgow and Lanarkshire, but the Orange Order in Scotland, now that the battle for the Union with Ireland was lost, became increasingly a social institution, offering the possibility of securing employment through membership; most Lodge members voted Labour.[62] Wales was firmly locked into British politics, especially Liberal and Labour politics, and although it had a nascent nationalist movement, with strong cultural aspirations, it made no electoral headway.[63] But the notion took root, that 'Ulster' was 'a place apart'; and this perception helped turn Northern Ireland into what was regarded as peripheral to the identity of the British United Kingdom.

The concept of Britishness, which Ulster Unionists celebrated and upon which they in large measure depended for their political creed and cultural identity, was itself hard to define. Yet its very lack of clarity might be expected to suit Ulster Unionists: as John Walton points out, divisions in Britain based on culture, class, language, landscape, settlement, architecture and consumer preferences 'undermined any attempt at presenting a unified British identity in other respects, and where such claims were made they almost invariably assumed that Englishness (and certain kinds of southern Englishness at that) could stand in for Britishness'.[64] But here again Northern Ireland did not quite fit the concept, however elastic, precisely because its assertion of Britishness was too monolithic and too strident. Devolution hemmed its patriotism in, in ways that current notions of Britishness could not comfortably accommodate: what were held to be British – or perhaps more accurately English – values such as decency and fair play were at odds with Ulster political life and thought. But, above all, devolution encompassed and intensified a very different kind of politics that did obviously and clearly separate Northern Ireland from the rest of the United Kingdom. Whatever the divisions of class or creed in Great Britain, there existed consensual politics, based on the possibility of agreement; but not on the absence of conflict. The difference between Northern Ireland and Britain was that in England, Scotland and Wales conflict could be 'resolved in a consensual context because all parties accepted the rules of the political game, giving their consent to outcomes which they might vote against – for example a general election or the devolution referendum in Scotland'.[65]

In the devolved state of Northern Ireland, Unionists could not give their consent to outcomes they might vote against. Devolution cemented a strong and inseparable link between the state, the Unionist people, and the Unionist Party which meant that a crisis for the party would be a crisis for the state and for the people, as events after 1968 demonstrated. It is arguable, therefore, that the chief beneficiary of devolved government in Northern Ireland was not Unionist Ulster, whose victory in 1921 proved in the end a pyrrhic one, but Great Britain, which after 1921 could intensify its development as a union state with a highly centralised form of governance.

The long history of Ulster Unionism and Home Rule is part of the struggle between British Liberals and British Conservatives over the reorganisation of the United Kingdom to meet the problems of the modern world, notably the revival of nationalism in Ireland, and its triumph in Germany and Italy. The kind of Home Rule that was proposed and opposed between 1886 and 1921 was manufactured in Great Britain: its 'Irish' input was minimal; its 'Ulster' input even more marginal. And although British supporters and opponents of Home Rule fought a bitterly contested struggle, their ideas were based upon the same principles: their difference in means must not obscure their common ends, that of strengthening the United Kingdom in an increasingly troublesome and indeed dangerous age, and making its multinational character more, not less, British. Ulster Unionists were the uneasy beneficiaries of this desire to maintain the integrity of the British state; and it is this that makes the origins of their Northern Ireland, and its subsequent history, a central, and not a marginal part of the history of devolved government in the United Kingdom.

Notes

1 Alan O'Day, *Irish Home Rule, 1867–1921* (Manchester, 1998), pp. 110–13.
2 Ian Malcolm to Lloyd George, 15 April 1918, House of Lords Library, Lloyd George papers, F/3/3/8.
3 Chamberlain to Lloyd George, 10 April 1918, House of Lords Library, Lloyd George papers, F/7/2/8.
4 O'Day, *Irish Home Rule*, p. 291.
5 Sir George Younger to J. C. C. Davidson, 3 May 1918, House of Lords Library, Bonar Law papers, 83/3/11; O'Day, *Irish Home Rule*, p. 292.
6 War Cabinet, Minutes of meeting on 23 April 1918, TNA, Cab. 23/6.
7 Austen Chamberlain, 'The Irish Question and federalism', paper prepared for the War Cabinet, 17 June 1918, Cabinet papers, G-212, TNA, Cab. 24/5.
8 War Cabinet, Minutes of meeting on 29 July 1918, TNA, Cab. 23/7.
9 O'Day, *Irish Home Rule*, p. 294.
10 First Report of the Cabinet Committee on the Irish Question, 4 November, TNA, Cab. 27/68.
11 Cabinet Minutes, Meeting of 10 December 1919, TNA, Cab. 23/18.
12 O'Day, *Irish Home Rule*, pp. 296–7.
13 10 and 11 Geo. V,c. 67, section 3; 'Power to establish a Parliament for the whole of Ireland'.
14 Thomas Hennessey, *A History of Northern Ireland, 1920–96* (London, 1997), p. 77.
15 Correspondence between His Majesty's Government and the Prime Minister of Northern Ireland relating to proposals for an Irish settlement, Cmd. 1561, 1921.
16 D. G. Boyce, *Englishmen and Irish Troubles: British Public Opinion and the Making of Irish Policy, 1918–1922* (London, 1971), pp. 161–4.
17 Patrick Buckland, *A History of Northern Ireland* (Dublin, 1981), p. 38.
18 For a thorough account of these and other attempts to solve the question of Irish Home Rule see O'Day, *Irish Home Rule*, chs. 4, 6 and 9.
19 A. V. Dicey, *England's Case against Home Rule* (London, 1886), pp. 70–1.
20 *Home Rule from the Treasury Bench: Speeches during the First and Second Reading Debates: with an Introduction by H. H. Asquith* (London, 1912), p. 113.
21 Ibid., pp. 318–19.
22 Brigid Hadfield, *The Constitution of Northern Ireland* (Belfast, 1989), pp. 71–8.
23 Cabinet Committee on Ireland, 1st report, 4 November 1919, TNA, Cabinet Papers, C.P. 56, Cab. 27/68.
24 Hadfield, *Constitution of Northern Ireland*, p. 70.
25 Buckland, *History of Northern Ireland*, pp. 57, 62.
26 Ibid., pp. 53–4.
27 Hadfield, *Constitution of Northern Ireland*, p. 47.
28 Cabinet Minutes, 10 December 1919, TNA, Cab. 23/18.
29 Hadfield, *Constitution of Northern Ireland*, p. 81.
30 David Harkness, *A History of Northern Ireland* (Dublin, 1983), p. 48.
31 Ibid., p. 51.
32 Ibid., p. 53.
33 Ibid.
34 Buckland, *History of Northern Ireland*, p. 80.

35 Harkness, *History of Northern Ireland*, p. 56.
36 Patrick Buckland, *The Factory of Grievances: Devolved Government in Northern Ireland, 1921–39* (Dublin, 1979), pp. 91–2.
37 *Home Rule from the Treasury Bench*, pp. 319–20.
38 Buckland, *Factory of Grievances*, pp. 95–6.
39 Northern Ireland House of Commons Debates, Vol. XVI, 24 April 1934, Col. 1095.
40 Buckland, *Factory of Grievances*, ch. 11.
41 Hennessey, *History of Northern Ireland*, pp. 68–9.
42 Buckland, *History of Northern Ireland*, pp. 71–2.
43 The Ulster Unionist Convention, 17 June 1892. Belfast, n.d., p. 36.
44 Ibid., p. 23.
45 Ibid., p. 90.
46 Hennessey, *History of Northern Ireland*, p. 76.
47 Ibid., p. 74.
48 Ibid., p. 65.
49 Patrick Buckland, *James Craig* (Dublin, 1980), p. 59.
50 Ibid., pp. 102–3.
51 Henry Maxwell, *Ulster was Right* (London, 1934), pp. 8–9.
52 Ibid., pp. 13–14.
53 Ibid., pp. 15–16.
54 Philip Williamson, 'The Conservative Party, 1900–1939: from crisis to ascendancy', in Chris Wrigley (ed.), *A Companion to Early Twentieth Century Britain* (Oxford, 2003), p. 11.
55 Hadfield, *Constitution of Northern Ireland*, p. 79.
56 *The Times*, 27 July 1935.
57 Martin Pugh, *The Tories and the People, 1880–1935* (Oxford, 1985), p. 185.
58 A. V. Dicey, *A Leap in the Dark* (London, 1893: 1911 edition), p. 181.
59 D. G. Boyce, 'British Conservative opinion, the Ulster Question, and the partition of Ireland, 1912–1921', *Irish Historical Studies*, 17 (1970), 99–100.
60 Ibid., 100–1.
61 John F. Harbinson, *The Ulster Unionist Party, 1882–1973* (Belfast, 1973), p. 55.
62 I. G. C. Hutchinson, 'Scottish issues in British politics, 1900–39', in Wrigley, *Companion*, p. 81.
63 R. Merfyn Jones, 'Wales and British politics, 1900–1939', in Wrigley, *Companion*, pp. 96–8.
64 John K. Walton, 'Britishness', in Wrigley, *Companion*, pp. 518–19.
65 Brian Girvan, 'The making of Irish nationalism: between integration and independence', in Patrick J. Roche and Brian Barton (eds), *The Northern Ireland Question: Nationalism, Unionism and Partition* (Aldershot, 1999), p. 23.

3

Irish Home Rule as devolutionary paradigm, 1914–39

Deirdre McMahon

It has often been assumed that Scottish, Irish and Welsh 'home rulers' operated as part of a self-supporting group within the 'Celtic fringe'. Whilst there were certainly overlaps and influences, Irish land campaigns inspired Welsh movements and the Irish Parliamentary Party was regarded by some as a model for the Welsh equivalent. Movements like the Pan-Celtic League promoted notions of a united tradition and shared aim. Yet there were also tensions and differences, which could lead to quite substantial difficulties in applying the 'Irish model' to other parts of the UK. If the Easter Rising inspired nationalists in the Empire, it caused concern to many constitutional nationalists in Wales. Moreover, some Irish and Welsh nationalists clearly had very different conceptions of national identity and of nationhood. As Irish Home Rule came to monopolise government attention after 1918, so these tensions came to the fore. This chapter indicates how the 'Home Rule movement' could fragment and divide under pressure. The Irish situation was thus hardly a model for Wales to adopt, whilst the evident tensions and differences meant that opponents of devolution all round were put under very little pressure from a unified 'Celtic' movement.

Home Rule All Round?

In the two years after the introduction of the third Irish Home Rule Bill in 1912, Home Rule Bills were introduced for Scotland in 1913 and 1914 and Wales in 1914. The Welsh debate, which took place in the momentous spring of 1914, just as Irish Home Rule was starting its last parliamentary session, illustrated how the incomprehension and downright hostility which the Irish bill had evoked affected Welsh aspirations.

The sponsor of the bill, E. T. John, Liberal MP for Denbighshire and a committed federalist, asserted that 'no portion of the United Kingdom is more frequently governed in direct defiance of its desires than the Principality':

> During the last three years . . . the Welsh National Liberal Council, the official mouthpiece of Welsh Liberalism, has with complete unanimity declared in favour autonomy on lines somewhat similar to those proposed in the case of Ireland, but naturally approximating more closely to those desired for Scotland.[1]

The bill that John was about to introduce was, like the Scottish Home Rule Bill of the previous year, based on the Irish Home Rule Bill but with the following differences: (1) control of the Post Office, Customs & Excise was reserved to the Imperial Parliament; (2) a single chamber legislature of 90 members elected by proportional representation; (3) women would get the vote on the same basis as men; (4) services listed as reserved under the Irish bill, such as pensions, national insurance and labour exchanges 'are from the outset placed under the control of the Welsh Legislature, and the devolution of domestic affairs generally is made absolute, effecting thereby a rational division of labour as between the Welsh Legislature and Imperial Parliament'.[2] The provisions for proportional representation and women's suffrage were significant advances on the Irish template.

In finance the Welsh bill followed the 'somewhat complicated and cumbersome' provisions of the Irish bill, although John believed that simpler arrangements would meet Welsh and Scottish needs, nor would the financial relations of Wales to the United Kingdom involve any disparity comparable with the present position. As in the Irish bill, there would be reduced Welsh representation, twenty-seven MPs in the Imperial Parliament, compared to 42 for the Irish.

'In submitting this Bill', John declared, 'we are profoundly convinced that while effectively advancing the interests of Wales, we are also facilitating the early adoption of a happier solution of the perils and troubles which today confront the body politic'. If autonomy were granted to Scotland and to Wales during the present parliament, there would be achieved in large measure 'that similarity and simultaneity of treatment by which we understand the right hon. and learned Gentleman the Member for Trinity College [Sir Edward Carson], and Unionist opinion generally, would be almost, if not wholly, persuaded to be reconciled to Irish self-government'.[3]

William Ormsby-Gore, another Denbigh (but Conservative) MP supported the thrust of John's arguments: 'There does remain a sentiment which has got to be recognised, a sentiment which is growing in Wales, in Scotland, and in England too'. He devoutly hoped that the sentiment could be diverted from a separatist sentiment to a unionist sentiment. 'I say frankly that in Wales . . . unless there is some devolution of Welsh business, especially private business, from this House, you will have an increasing tendency to see national tradition and racial feeling fomented against England'.[4]

John's bill got nowhere, as did the Government of Scotland Bill in May. But there was more success for another long contentious measure, the bill to disestablish the Welsh Anglican church, which entered its last parliamentary session. Like the Irish Home Rule Act, it would pass automatically under the terms of the Parliament Act which had overridden the House of Lords' veto. The debate demonstrated the close relationship between Irish Nationalist and Welsh Liberal MPs as legislation which they had demanded for several decades was now on the verge of fulfilment. The Attorney-General, Sir John Simon, argued that disestablishment had been good for the Church of Ireland. Walter Long, a former Chief Secretary and prominent Conservative supporter of the Southern Irish Unionists, disputed this and remarked scornfully that the bill 'could not have secured a majority except by the Irish vote'. The Conservative leader, Andrew Bonar Law, echoed this: 'This Bill would have been dead today but for the votes of men who, in the words of the Irish Leader [John Redmond], have given their votes without any regard to the merits of the question'.[5] But the Welsh Liberal MP, William Llewelyn Williams (MP for Carmarthen District), expressed his gratitude to the Irish Party for their 'unflinching support . . . I am not ashamed to accept the help of the hon. Gentlemen from Ireland, who know what benefits Disestablishment will bring'. He expressed surprise that 'we have not heard from Ulster some Presbyterian voices thanking us Welsh Members for what we did for them in 1869, and promising to help us to get the boon which they craved equally with their Catholic brethren in Ireland at that time'.[6]

The ideological parameters, implicit and explicit, in these debates are revealing. The endless refrain about the integrity of the Union obscured fundamental contradictions in the Conservative position. There had never been full legislative and executive union since 1801 as the Irish executive had remained at Dublin Castle. Under legislative union, Ireland was represented by 103 MPs at Westminster but once pro-Home Rule MPs became the dominant wing after 1885, Conservatives consistently, like Long and Law during the disestablishment debate just cited, attacked their votes as being somehow unconstitutional and less valid, thus undermining the very *raison d'être* of the 1801 Union. Federalism, devolution, Home Rule All Round had been the subject of intense discussion among Conservative and Liberal elites since 1910 but it was a risky strategy for the Conservatives to propose as it accepted a form of Home Rule, however limited, for Ireland. It also had limited popular appeal. To Irish Nationalist MPs, it was a Trojan horse to destroy Irish home rule, and John's optimistic comment that his Welsh bill might help make home rule more palatable to unionists only intensified their suspicions.

As Llewellyn Williams had reminded the Commons, the close parliamentary alliance between Welsh Liberal and Irish Nationalist MPs went back to the 1880s. Although there had been disagreements over aspects of Welsh disestablishment, particularly denominational education and temperance, Welsh Liberals had been staunch in their support of Home Rule since 1886. Ironically, however, just as Irish Home Rule now finally looked like being a reality, relations between Irish and Welsh MPs would never be as close again.

War and Rising

After war broke out in August 1914, Irishness and Welshness were used to recruit men but, as John Turner has observed, were not encouraged as expressions of assertiveness.[7] Just as Kitchener refused to allow the Irish Volunteers to form their own battalions, as had happened with the Ulster Volunteers, so did he forbid the appointment of Welsh nonconformist chaplains and the use of the Welsh language. Among the Irish communities in Wales, which were now almost completely assimilated, there was, as with other Irish communities elsewhere in the Empire, strong support for the war. The famous boxer, 'Peerless' Jim Driscoll, took part in recruiting campaigns and in Merthyr Tydfil alone 200 members of the local Ancient Order of Hibernians (AOH) joined up.[8] The 1916 Easter rebellion in Dublin was a most unwelcome thunder clap.

Two of the rebellion's executed leaders, James Connolly and Patrick Pearse, were known in Wales. Connolly had addressed meetings there and his writings were familiar in Labour Party circles. Pearse, a great admirer of Welsh bilingualism, had attended the Eisteddfod and other pan-Celtic gatherings in Wales. The rebellion was vigorously condemned by branches of the United Irish League (UIL) throughout Wales. In his memoir *The Story of a Toiler's Life* (1921), Dr James Mullin, who was chairman of the Cardiff UIL for twenty-five years, painted a particularly acid portrait of Pearse whom he had first met in 1899. He was, Mullin recalled:

> completely obsessed with one idea, and that was the cult of the Irish language, which he considered to be a panacea for all the ills that Ireland suffered from. In fact, I sat beside him at a lecture in which he told his Irish audience that if they only learned Irish it would save them from pauperism, lunacy, and crime.

As for his political ideas:

> Pearse's political views seemed to me to be quite mediaeval . . . Like many others of his unfortunate countrymen he was unable to differentiate between facts and fancies, and fondly imagined that the hard realities of the actual world would cease to exist in the presence of his highly coloured imaginings, and that one bird in the bush was worth two in the hand. As with so many Irish idealists whom I have met his political and historical horizon was limited to his own country. As far as

> I could learn he had never travelled and was unable to estimate the drawbacks under which Ireland laboured in comparison with other nations. He was a man of one idea, and such a man is always dangerous, if not to others, to himself, even though their motives are most pure and patriotic.

For the Irish in Wales, as elsewhere in the Empire, the Rising led to divided loyalties at a time when they were trying to prove both their patriotic credentials and their status as an integrated community in support of the war effort. The Rising and its aftermath left organisations like the UIL and the AOH stranded as the Irish political landscape began its seismic shift towards Sinn Fein. Mullin was not impressed and considered that Sinn Fein was infinitely inferior to the Fenians: 'its voice sounds like autumnal winds moaning through leafless woods'.[9]

No Welsh MP, Liberal or Conservative, made any direct statement in the Commons about the Rising although E. T. John, when questioning the prime minister, H. H. Asquith, on 25 May, asked him to reconsider the advisability of federal devolution for Ireland. Asquith replied laconically: 'I cannot say more than that we shall not fail to keep in mind all considerations which are relevant to this problem'.[10] F. S. Oliver, the *éminence grise* of federalism, was more trenchant about the rebellion and the efficacy of grapeshot not just in Ireland but elsewhere in the United Kingdom. The executions were necessary 'because if we had not, we should have had the uprising which was planned over the whole of Ireland, we should have had another on the Clyde, another in South Wales, and probably industrial trouble in all sorts of quarters'.[11]

During the summer of 1916 Asquith deputed Lloyd George (now Minister of Munitions) to find a settlement based on the immediate introduction of the Home Rule Act. The negotiations collapsed when the incompatible promises which Lloyd George had been making to nationalists and unionists were revealed; for nationalists it was a foretaste of his devious negotiating methods. Lloyd George had promised to resign if the negotiations failed but did not, for which his secretary (and mistress) Frances Stevenson faulted him: 'The Irish are angry with him . . . & I think they have reason to be angry . . . Now, however, he upholds the P.M. and says the Irish are unreasonable . . . it would be a pity if it were spoilt by this wretched Irish business'.[12]

'Wretched Irish business' was to loom over much of Lloyd George's premiership from December 1916 to 1922. A certain amount of mythology hovers over Lloyd George's record on Ireland. In both sets of his memoirs he scarcely mentioned Ireland,[13] although colleagues like Winston Churchill and Austen Chamberlain were not as reticent. When Frank Pakenham was researching his study of the 1921 Treaty negotiations, *Peace by Ordeal* (1935), he visited Lloyd George but found him very reluctant to discuss Ireland.[14]

After 1922, apart from a brief intervention on the Boundary Commission debate in 1924, he never again referred to Ireland in parliamentary debates. The 1921 Treaty was widely hailed as a triumph for Lloyd George's statesmanship but clearly it was one he did not care to dwell on.

The assumption that Lloyd George had some mysterious Celtic affinity with Irish nationalism needs to be qualified.[15] The first major qualification concerns religion which had often figured in his disagreements with Irish MPs, notably funding for Catholic schools and a Catholic university in Ireland. Lloyd George's biographers have described the importance of his fundamentalist nonconformist background.[16] Although early on he realised the 'sham and mockery' of religion,[17] he retained from this background a strong vein of anti-Catholicism which often emerged in his dealings with Ireland, particularly during the 1918 conscription crisis which he blamed on the machinations of the Catholic hierarchy. This was discussed by W. G. S. Adams, who had worked on Ireland at the cabinet secretariat in 1917–18. In January 1948 he wrote to Thomas Jones, the former deputy cabinet secretary, who was writing a book about Lloyd George. Like Adams, Jones had been recruited to the cabinet staff at the start of Lloyd George's premiership. 'The real crux – genuinely and deeply for him – was Ulster as you say. I remember feeling as I talked with him that when I got below the surface of his mind there was this deep primitive "No Pope here" of Ulster – something that stirred depths in his makeup'.[18]

He only visited Ireland once, in 1907. True, he had read A. M. Sullivan's best seller, *The Story of Ireland*, and, according to his brother William, was powerfully affected by it.[19] He admired the Irish MP Michael Davitt, the great campaigner for Irish land reform and, like him, a prominent opponent of the Boer War. But he never understood the fundamental difference between Irish and Welsh nationalism: the Irish was centripetal, the Welsh centrifugal. This emerged early in his political career in two speeches he made in 1889 and 1890. In the first, in February 1889, he commented that of the constituent parts of the United Kingdom, Wales always came in third, 'highly commended' after Ireland and Scotland; the Welsh people had to organise, as the Irish had, to end this state of affairs. A year later in Cardiff, he made the case for Welsh Home Rule. All the arguments for Irish Home Rule applied to Wales: the Imperial Parliament had neither the time nor the knowledge to deal with Welsh affairs; Wales was a distinct nationality, even more so than Ireland because the Irish had lost the title deeds to their language; the religious barriers which poisoned the Irish Home Rule debate did not apply to Wales; nor would Home Rule be the first step to complete separation in Wales. Finally, Home Rule in Wales could not be seen as a surrender to outrage and murder, as Conservatives had argued about Ireland since 1886.[20]

The symbiotic relationship between language and nationality was one that Lloyd George constantly returned to down the years. If Wales was more nationalist than Ireland because it had retained its language, then it followed that the Irish should be content with any measure of self-government which satisfied Wales. Lloyd George's wariness of Irish Home Rule possibly intensified after the disintegration of the Cymru Fydd movement in the 1890s which not only underlined Welsh dependence on the Liberal leadership but also 'cruelly emphasised how shallow was the Welsh demand for separation'.[21] In 1920, at the height of the Anglo-Irish war, George Davies, the Welsh director of the Fellowship of Reconciliation, reported to Thomas Jones that 'the constructive side of Sinn Fein is full of idealism, enthusiasm for cooperation & the burial of the religious feud. It has just that boyish romance & fervour that Lloyd George helped to create in the Cymru Fydd. Can it be possible that he will bludgeon the child that he was himself twenty years ago'.[22] W. G. S. Adams, in the letter quoted above to Thomas Jones, doubted whether Lloyd George was ever a real Home Ruler: 'he didn't feel the crusader for it in him as the old man [Gladstone] had done for his H.R.'. Adams also wondered about his commitment to federal home rule, recalling a meeting in 1918 when he was being urged to bring in a big measure of devolution all round: 'What was his answer? "Gentlemen I have always been a Home Ruler. You don't need to convince me. But what will the men of Sheffield think about it. They won't have it". Some such words and I felt what a chance lost. What a failure in real brave leadership. No, he wasn't in real heart and soul a Federal Home Ruler – at least his faith had grown dim and the cares of the world were too heavy for this extra fight'.

Once the Liberals returned to power in 1906, Lloyd George became increasingly sympathetic to Ulster, which he visited in 1907 on his one and only visit to Ireland. In a speech in Belfast he declared that 'Ireland has a great and distinguished part to play in maintaining in peace that great commonwealth of nations which we refer to as the British empire . . . To sever the bonds – why, it would be a loss to Ireland. The greatest loss would be to humanity, that is if you confine the brilliant genius of Ireland within the bounds of an island, when you have hundreds of millions of the human race who would be benefited by your taking a full share in the direction of the British Empire'. Irish nationality, like Welsh nationality, had everything to gain from participation in the United Kingdom and the Empire.[23]

The First World War fostered Lloyd George's imperial consciousness. After he succeeded Asquith as Prime Minister in December 1916, he was surrounded by imperialist prophets such as the South African leader, J. C. Smuts, and Sir Alfred Milner, as well as leading members of the Round Table group including Philip Kerr, Edward Grigg and L. S. Amery who had joined the cabinet secretariat after 1916. Irish MPs had hoped that he would give a greater impetus to the search for a settlement and were heartened by a speech the Prime Minister made during the adjournment debate in March 1917 when he declared that the Tory policy of killing Home Rule by kindness had failed. Ireland 'is no more reconciled to British rule than she was in the days of Cromwell . . . It is something that has to do with the pride and self-respect of the people . . . It is a fact which must be grasped . . . by any Government which means to attempt a settlement of this question'.[24] But by 1918 Irish expectations of Lloyd George had turned to ashes. There is no evidence that he was forced by his Conservative colleagues in the coalition government to take a hard line on Ireland: this was his own clear preference.

John Redmond died suddenly in March 1918 and the Prime Minister's relations with his successor, John Dillon, had always been prickly. Lloyd George's only major initiative, the Irish Convention of 1917–18, which had been convened mainly to appease American and Dominion criticism, collapsed as he knew it would. This enabled him and the government to blame the Irish for not reaching a solution. Although Lloyd George had major reservations about imposing conscription on Ireland (the only part of the UK exempted from the 1916 Act) in spring 1918, he was nevertheless irritated by Irish objections. He told Dillon that it was 'illogical and unjust' to ask Scottish, Welsh and English men to fight when young Irishmen were staying at home.[25]

As the government thrashed around for yet another solution, interest in federalism was reignited in 1918. This was discussed in a pamphlet entitled *Enter the Celt* which featured articles from Welsh, Irish and Scottish contributors.[26] The Welsh contributor was E. T. John, who had introduced the Welsh Home Rule Bill in 1914, and was still a dedicated supporter of federalism. There was, John argued, 'a very salutary contrast' between Scottish and Welsh conceptions of autonomy, and those embodied in the Irish bill. The former were based upon 'the well-justified assumption that the Scottish and Welsh nations may safely be trusted to manage their own affairs wisely. On the other hand, the opposition of Ulster has filled the Irish Bill with limitations and restrictions which go far to deprive autonomy of much of its healing virtue'. Thus, while Ireland needed autonomy most, by reason of its internal divisions and the inefficiency of its educational system, it was 'least fitted for the responsibilities and the privileges of self-government' although John recognised that to withhold autonomy would only 'perpetuate existing deficiencies and difficulties'.

Warming to his theme, John claimed that 'left to work out its own salvation, Wales with its perfervid idealism, would probably prove the New Zealand of these islands – courageous and unconventional, fearlessly, perhaps audaciously, testing methods which promised increased comfort and happiness for its humbler sons and daughters'. Scotland would move 'more cautiously, but its intensely democratic instincts would not long tolerate much that exists today that is detrimental to the well-being of its thrifty and hard-working populace'. Ireland, in such large degree a Catholic peasant proprietorate, 'would almost certainly develop on relatively Conservative lines'.

John predicted that the limits of state intervention in the three Celtic countries would vary considerably, particularly in taxation. The greatest advances would come in the educational development of Scotland, Wales, and Ireland, 'the two latter strenuously striving to overtake their more highly privileged sister'. In Wales, people were determined that the educational system should take the 'fullest cognisance of, and be based upon, our Cymric language and literature, embodying traditions which for nearly ten centuries spread over the whole of Europe, and which alone explain our almost miraculous national persistence.' Scotland and Ireland had lost incalculably by the loss of their ancient languages, 'by the comparative neglect of their old world literature, resulting in some considerable measure of intellectual denationalisation'. Nations, John concluded, like individuals, 'best grow in mental and moral stature by fidelity to their own instincts and traditions, rather than by assimilation of the extraneous and incongruous qualities of other nationalities, however powerful, successful and aggressive'.

The Irish contributor, known only under the pseudonym 'Belfast', was unimpressed by John's arguments. While opinion in Ireland was favourable to the idea of Celtic entente, its contribution to any Celtic endeavour, given the present state of Ireland, would be 'inconsiderable . . . we would be only too glad to co-operate with our Celtic cousins of Wales and Scotland . . . if a practicable way could be found . . . I feel certain that most Irishmen would hail it with enthusiasm and act on it with vigour – as soon as the political situation and circumstances of our country admit it'. For 'Belfast', finance was a key issue in Irish autonomy and the financial provisions of the Welsh Home Rule Bill were 'far more advantageous' than the provisions of the Irish Act.

'Belfast' analysed the three main schools of Irish nationalist thought: (1) those who wanted complete national independence; (2) those who wanted to preserve the English connection under Home Rule; (3) Sinn Fein. He did not think John had proved that separatism was:

> wholly inapplicable to Ireland . . . I imagine that not only would this proof be very hard to find, but that those who seek it would get very little for their pains. Ireland existed, and did a deal more than 'existing' in the sense of merely vegetating, long before the British empire or the English connexion was born or thought of. And if both those supports were tomorrow withdrawn from her, presumably Ireland would have to do precisely as any other country would be required to do under parallel circumstances – that is to say make the best shift she

could to rub along without them. Theoretically, then, there is nothing that is 'absurd' or 'impossible' in the Separatist doctrine; nor is there anything 'wicked' or 'immoral' in it, as some would appear to imagine.

In 'Belfast's' opinion, separatists were not very numerous at present but were active and well organised particularly in the United States. As to Sinn Fein, there was much misunderstanding about the party and its role in the Rising as it had nothing to do with it. The Sinn Fein policies of abstention and passive resistance were 'simplicity itself, and *if* the nation as a whole makes up its mind to endorse it, English protests, however noisy and violent they might be for a time, would assuredly succumb to the dictates of reason and common sense – to say nothing of considerations derived from a sense of present-day zeal for "small nations" and national rights and liberties'. Would Irish electors endorse the Sinn Fein programme? 'Belfast' was uncertain but judged that events were tending in that direction as there was great dissatisfaction with John Redmond and 'Westminster methods'. There was a familiar adage to the effect that 'he who elects to sup with the devil should repair to the feast provided with a long spoon'. This Redmond had failed to do. He should have insisted on the delivery of Home Rule before pledging Irish support for the war. If that had happened the Irish would have fulfilled their side of the bargain 'and the world would have been spared one of the most sickening and ridiculous displays of English hypocrisy, cant and humbug'.

The government of Ireland Act

Although federalism had the support of several cabinet ministers, nothing came of these debates, hardly surprising when the war was entering its final gruelling stages. The Sinn Fein advance accelerated and culminated in the annihilation of the Irish Party at the December 1918 elections. In January 1919 the 73 Sinn Fein TDs [MPs] seceded from Westminster and set up their own assembly, Dáil Éireann, in Dublin. Within days the first shots of a two and a half year long guerilla war were fired. The government had decided to draft a new Government of Ireland Bill, to supersede the Home Rule Act which was due to come into force at the end of the war. Lloyd George had left the drafting of the bill to a cabinet committee chaired by Walter Long but his various statements in parliament over the next two years demonstrated clearly the negative way in which Wales influenced his thinking on Ireland. In July 1919 he gave the following disquisition on Irish nationality:

> To come to the real practical difficulty: it is that Ireland is not a nation . . . The mere fact that it is one island is no proof that it is one nation . . . It is a difference

in temperament, religion, tradition, and in everything that constitutes the fundamental essentials of nations. If they can bridge over that difficulty I do not believe
there is any other difficulty, but until you do that there is no use talking about the
principle of self-determination

This incensed T. J. Harbison, MP for Tyrone and one of the last remaining
Irish Party MPs in the Commons. 'I would tolerate that coming from an
Englishman, but not from a Welshman who belongs to my own race. I am a
Celt and so is he, and I would like him to get up and say that there are two
kings in Wales, because there is a Conservative opposition in Wales as there is
in Ireland'.[27]

When Lloyd George introduced the new Government of Ireland Bill in
March 1920, he developed the theme of self-determination, this time in
relation to the American Civil War. This was aimed squarely at opinion in
America where the President of the Dáil, Eamon de Valera, was on a major
fundraising tour. In a number of speeches de Valera had used the analogy of
the American Civil War to argue against partition and the exclusion of
Ulster. Self-determination, Lloyd George declared:

> does not mean that every part of a country which has been acting together for
> hundreds of years shall have a right to say 'We mean to set up a separate Republic'.
> That is the very thing which was fought for in the Civil War in America. If any
> section in Wales were to say, 'We want to set up a Welsh Republic', I should
> certainly resist it to the utmost of my power. Not only that, Britain in its own inter-
> ests, including the interests of Wales, would be absolutely right to resist it, and yet
> Wales has a definite and clear nationality. The same applies to Scotland . . . There
> must be that limitation to the application of any principle; otherwise you might
> carry it to every fragment or locality in every country throughout the world.

Lloyd George expressed irritation at the attention being focused on Ireland.
There were, after all, two other nationalities in the kingdom which were just
as Celtic as Ireland. Scotland and Wales were both as 'intensely patriotic as
the Irish, both as intensely national, both as proud of their nationality and the
traditions of their nationality'. Wales, above all, 'has conserved the Celtic language . . . I come from a country where probably the bulk of the people can
talk the language which their people talked two thousand years ago with a
living literature'. He referred contemptuously to the 'artificial attempt' to
revive the Irish language by putting up names at street corners 'to the confusion of every honest patriot'. Referring to Scotland, Lloyd George argued that
if the Scottish Highlands demanded exclusion, 'you would not get Scotsmen
insisting upon them having a Parliament that would put them under the heal
[sic] of Edinburgh if they objected. It is because they do not, and the fact that
they do not, is proof that they are a unit, and the fact that Ulster does not
agree is a proof that Ireland is not a unit'.

Lloyd George concluded with a warning to 'our American friends' that de Valera was putting forward the same claim as the Civil War Confederate leader Jefferson Davis. He criticised the US senators who just passed a motion of sympathy with Irish independence: 'The ancestors of some of the men who voted for that Motion in the Senate the other day fought to the death against conceding to the Southern States in the United States of America the very demand they were supporting for Ireland'. The British Government would never concede that demand. 'It is a demand which, if it be persisted in, will lead to exactly the same measures of repression as in the Southern States of America. We claim nothing more than the United States claimed for themselves. We will stand no less.' Lloyd George concluded with an angry but rather curious statement: 'Union – there is no union. There is union between Scotland and England and Wales. There is a union that bears the test of death. There is no union with Ireland. A grappling hook is not a union'.[28]

In a later stage of the debate in June 1920 Lloyd George praised the modesty of Scottish aims. 'Scotland', he observed approvingly, 'the most sensitive and proud nationality in the British Empire', asked for nothing more in recognition of its nationality or its powers of self-government; it wasn't asking for a measure as extensive as the Irish bill which was being treated as 'a sham and a farce' by Irish nationalists. When the Scottish Liberal MP Joseph Johnstone retorted that 'the disease is not so acute in Scotland', Lloyd George stated flatly that 'the remedy which would be adequate for Scotland and Wales would be equally adequate here'.[29]

Scottish MPs played a more active role than Welsh MPs in the debates on the Government of Ireland Bill. Lloyd George was the only Welsh MP, Liberal, Labour or Conservative, to speak during the second reading. During later stages there were minor contributions from two Coalition Liberal MPs, Lewis Haslam (Newport) and Sir Edgar Rees Jones (Merthyr). Haslam was strongly opposed to giving the Irish Parliament control of its own taxes as this might lead to similar demands in England, Scotland and Wales: 'just imagine the chaos that would exist if we had to have Customs houses between the different parts of the country'. For strategic and other reasons Haslam insisted that 'we ought to combat anything that will separate Great Britain from Ireland. The Irish people at the present time really do not know what they want. They are not in a position, quarrelling as they are now, to tell us what policy we should pursue'.[30] Lloyd George had been vitriolic on this point just the week before when he met with senior Liberal ministers, Christopher Addison, H. A. L. Fisher and Edwin Montagu, who were urging him to give greater financial autonomy to the Irish. He lashed out:

> The test to apply was whether you could give to other parts of the United
> Kingdom that which you were giving to Ireland, and it was obvious that it would

be impossible to do so. The retention of customs was always regarded as a sign of unity . . . We, who had control of income tax, were now talking of giving it up. That would be to let Ireland off financially. That was not the home rule on which he had been brought up . . . He was all for justice for Ireland but at the same time it must be remembered that justice was due to England, Scotland and Wales, who had made greater sacrifices in the war than Ireland. This country would have to bear the extra burden of the financial concessions proposed, and there would be in Ireland cheap whiskey, cheap tobacco – everything cheap; and here people would be staggering under their burdens . . . He was still a Gladstonian home ruler, and wished to keep Ireland as an integral part of the United Kingdom, and that was why he hoped that the present bill would be proceeded with.[31]

A month later, in possibly the worst week of the Anglo-Irish war, the Central Wales Federation of the Evangelical Free Churches passed a resolution deploring the murders of soldiers and police by the IRA but also condemning the policy of reprisals adopted by the government. The Prime Minister was unimpressed and assured MPs that he had recently addressed a meeting in Wales on the subject, and had 'every reason to believe my fellow-countrymen approve of the steps taken by the Government to stamp out murder in Ireland'.[32] His brother William did not agree and was opposed to the Black and Tans. 'My brother was mistaken in his public utterances at this time when he said that the trouble in Ireland was due to the machinations of a "murder gang" which was about to "meet its doom" '.[33]

If Welsh Liberals were silent as the Irish administration gradually disintegrated amidst a vicious guerrilla war, two Welsh Labour MPs, Vernon Hartshorn (Ogmore) and Thomas Griffiths (Pontypool) consistently questioned ministers about individual cases and outrages. Why were Welsh MPs so silent during the Irish Troubles? Both as a Welsh Prime Minister and victorious war leader, Lloyd George was the focus of immense pride and prestige in Wales. Whatever their private reservations, there was an understandable reluctance among Welsh MPs to break ranks and attack his Irish policy. The Welsh nationalist Saunders Lewis (later one of the founders of Plaid Cymru) noted cynically: 'see how grateful and obsequious and grateful we Welsh are because the English tolerate one of us as their prime minister'. Writing just after a Coalition Liberal won the Cardigan by-election in February 1921 Lewis commented: 'Ireland means nothing to these people, but a handshake from Mrs George and a word that you musn't stab Lloyd George in the back, – that has won the women and men . . . Isn't Lloyd George the grand Welshman and true Celt? I'm proud to sign myself his countryman – I suppose Cromwell must have been Welsh too'.[34]

In March 1919 Sinn Fein set up a front organisation in Britain, the Irish Self-Determination League (ISDL). By the end of 1921 it had 300 branches;

the extent of its membership is harder to gauge and seems to have ranged between 30,000 and 40,000. Although in Wales the League was most active in the south and established branches along the coastal belt and in the coal-fields, membership was small and the ISDL Cardiff branch complained that out of an estimated Irish population of 30,000, only 1,000 joined. This may have been due to the somewhat restrictive view it took of its terms of membership. In 1920 the South Wales District Committee of the ISDL proposed at the League's annual conference that membership be 'confined to those of Irish birth or descent and the wives of Irishmen resident in Great Britain who shall undertake to support the objects of the League'. The husbands of Irishwomen who married 'out' were excluded on the basis that a husband influenced his wife's political beliefs. However, as Paul O'Leary notes, the ISDL did reach sections of the Irish communities which had never been drawn into the UIL and AOH, particularly women, some of whom were active in both nationalist and labour organisations. The Welsh ISDL branches collected money for Irish prisoners, over £1,000 in 1921 alone, and branch meetings passed resolutions critical of government policy. Irish language classes were also popular and by March 1922 Aberavon Gaelic League had 240 students enrolled in its classes.[35] There was some IRA activity in south Wales in 1921 centred on efforts to smuggle arms and explosives to Ireland but the organisation was uncovered in October 1921 leading to arrests in Cardiff, Neath and Merthyr Tydfil. Saunders Lewis had a peripheral involvement in these stirring events as he confided to his fiancée: 'The Irish leader here in Cardiff was arrested last Friday after a raid on his house. He had thirty revolvers in his possession. Is it safe to tell you in a letter that I have one! I am keeping it for the Welsh Sinn Fein which is to start in Cardiff, this year – next year – sometime – never'.[36] At the subsequent trials long sentences were handed down ranging from four to fourteen years although those convicted were released shortly afterwards in spring 1922.

In South Wales there were close links betweeen the ISDL and the trade unions, and several ISDL branches affiliated to the Labour Party. However, the Labour Party was reluctant to get too involved in Irish affairs although, as we have seen, two of its Welsh MPs, Hartshorn and Griffiths, played a leading role in highlighting individual cases of injustice. Labour organised a series of protest meetings at the beginning of 1921, one of which was held in Cardiff and was addressed by J. H. Thomas, the railway union leader.[37]

As the year wore on, petulance and irritation marked Lloyd George's public utterances on Ireland. 'Every time this country has been in trouble after a great war', he told the Commons in March 1921, 'or when there were civil convulsions here, as in the days of Charles I, the great war, the Napoleonic war when England and Scotland and Wales had their hands

full . . . we have always had rebellions in Ireland, always had these disturb-
ances in Ireland'.[38] As late as June 1921 he was annoyed when J. C. Smuts,
the South African leader, suggested that the Irish be given Dominion Home
Rule. He told Smuts that 'the Br. Isles are a federation: you do not contemplate giving Dom. Home Rule to Natal, or the Orange States. Why then do
you suggest it for us?'[39]

In the event, of course, the Anglo-Irish Treaty signed in December 1921
was considerably in advance of Dominion Home Rule. Lloyd George hardly
spoke during the ratification debate in the Commons on the Irish Treaty.
However, Welsh MPs were more vocal on this occasion. Sir Robert Thomas,
Liberal MP for Wrexham, delivered a paean of praise to the Prime Minister:

> We have been Home Rulers in Wales for at least 30 years, and we are Home Rulers
> today . . . I think it requires a Celt from Wales or Scotland to appreciate the Irish
> point of view. We in our country feel very proud that a Welshman is at the head
> of the Administration which is today bringing a message of peace and goodwill
> to Ireland . . . By supporting the Prime Minister and the Government in this
> matter we are fulfilling the earnest and enthusiastic wish of practically the whole
> of the Welsh nation.

When Thomas suggested that 'if we were able to trust to the Dutch in South
Africa, surely we can trust men of our own blood across the water', a
Conservative MP interjected 'we cannot trust the Welsh'. Thomas retorted:
'We had civilisation in Wales when [the Hon. Member's] ancestors were
running in the backwoods with painted skins. Not trust a Welshman! I would
like to know what would have happened in the War if it had not been for a
Welshman'.[40]

A more thoughtful contribution to the Irish Treaty debate came from
Morgan Jones, the Labour MP for Caerphilly. He dismissed the apocalyptic
utterances being made about Ireland from the Conservative benches. Jones
thought that the real kernel of the opposition was reflected in the statement
by the Ulster Unionist MP, Ronald McNeill, when he said that 'the more
complete the democratic institution, the further are the people removed from
control over the country'. Jones considered that since 1914:

> we have stored up the idea of democracy. It is now penetrating into the mind of all
> the nations of the world, and not least into the mind of the Irish people. The trouble
> with the hon. Members opposite is that they live in pre-1914 days. We are living in
> days when new ideals, new aspirations, and a new outlook pervade the minds of the
> people of the world . . . In Ireland you have attempted a method of repression
> which has completely failed. I say, and my countrymen from the Principality say,
> God-speed to the Irish people in this new attempt at self-government.[41]

For Saunders Lewis the Treaty aroused mixed feelings, given the divisions
which it had opened up between the anti-Treaty side led by de Valera, and the

pro-Treaty party led by Michael Collins and Arthur Griffith. De Valera had lost the vote in the Dáil on 7 January 1922. 'So the Irish Free State exists', he wrote shortly after this, 'and the unbelievable is a fact'. He found de Valera's defeat 'rather tragic' although he understood the bitterness. He regarded the women of the anti-Treaty party with distaste, especially Countess Markievicz and Mary MacSwiney. 'They showed the qualities I dislike in the Celt, especially his love of martyrdom, which is to me detestable'.[42]

Ironically, there was considerably less goodwill towards Wales and Welshness during the Dáil debates on the Treaty. Lloyd George, the 'Welsh Wizard' who had imposed a Treaty on Ireland that now looked as if it might lead to civil war, was spoken of with detestation and abuse. The Welsh ancestry of Arthur Griffith, founder of Sinn Fein and now chairman of the Provisional Government, was mocked with several references to Welsh leeks. Seamus Robinson, the anti-Treaty TD for Tipperary and a prominent IRA commander, declared that 'we can, and will if necessary, strike the Empire where and how no other people could do it – except the Scotch and the Welsh if they should so choose'.[43]

As for the Irish in Wales, the ISDL was wound up after the signing of the Treaty in December 1921, though meetings were held to protest about the continued detention of political prisoners in Britain. As elsewhere among the Irish diaspora, there was a revulsion against the civil war which broke out in June 1922 and a disinclination to get further involved in Irish affairs. The *Welsh Catholic Herald* summed up the feelings of most Irish in Wales when it stated in October 1922 that the new Irish Free State could now settle its own affairs. As Paul O'Leary has observed, this was really the culmination of a change which had begun with the rejection of Fenianism in the 1870s and preference of the Irish communities in Wales, and elsewhere in the Empire, to embrace electoral politics in order to advance their political integration.[44]

In the wake of the Anglo-Irish Treaty

The Irish civil war ended in May 1923 and the last prisoners were released the following year. After the excitements of the previous decade, and with the founding of the new state, Irish-Welsh political relations were quiescent after 1922. However, when Saunders Lewis became president of Plaid Cymru in 1926 he invited Kevin O'Sheil to address several meetings in Wales. O'Sheil, a member of the Irish Land Commission, had been assistant legal adviser to the Provisional Government in 1922 and then became head of the North-East Boundary Bureau. The Bureau was set up in 1922 to prepare the Irish Government's case for the revision of the Ulster boundary under article 12 of the Treaty. O'Sheil, in Lewis's opinion, was 'a splendid help to the meetings and made a profound impression'.[45] There was more concern with cultural issues, particularly the respective condition of the Irish and Welsh languages. The Irish Government's efforts to revive the Irish language were encountering serious difficulties and Irish TDs looked enviously at the success of bilingualism in Wales. Frank Carney, a TD who represented a Gaeltacht [Irish-speaking] constituency in Donegal, wondered why Welsh people were so anxious to preserve their language when the people of the Gaeltacht were not. He thought it was a question of economics:

> In Wales, for some generations, the use of the Welsh language has never been prohibited, nor have the people ever been penalised for trying to preserve their national language. At their great national Eisteddfod of Wales, you have the most prominent people, politicians and others, taking an interest in and encouraging the use of the language, and native music. All this goes to show that the people were encouraged, as far as possible, to preserve their language and customs.[46]

Another TD argued that the Welsh language flourished because there was no government compulsion as in Ireland. Welsh lawyers and Welsh businessmen spoke the Welsh language because they wanted to. 'Wales accomplished all this thing, and it dealt with the same apathy amongst the people and had the same difficulties as confront this nation'.[47] One result of this admiration for the Welsh linguistic achievement was that in 1929 Irish radio broadcast weekly lessons in Welsh.

Ten years after the Anglo-Irish Treaty, the disengagement from Ireland was deemed a distinct success in British terms. The government got a settlement of the Ulster question, a relatively peaceful withdrawal from Southern Ireland and the preservation, for the moment, of the Empire. The results in Ireland were more problematical. By the wave of a constitutional wand which harked back to the first Home Rule debates in 1886, Ireland was given the same constitutional status as Canada. But as critics had pointed out then, Canada was too distant and too big to prevent it seceding from the Empire. The Canadian analogy was based on a profound misconception: Ireland, unlike Canada, was a dominion by revolution not evolution. Furthermore the dominion settlement suffered from fatal flaws: as a concept dominion status was still in the process of evolution; the Irish had never asked for it; it came too late; it was imposed; and it was accompanied by partition and civil war. The surprise is that it lasted as long as it did.

The 1930s

In March 1932 Eamon de Valera and his Fianna Fail party took office. It was only eight years since de Valera had been released from prison at the end of the

Irish civil war. Fianna Fail, the anti-Treaty party founded in 1926, had refused to take its seats in the Dáil but in August 1927 finally did so. It came to power pledged to remove the most objectionable features of the Treaty, most notably the oath of allegiance to the King. It also promised to withhold several financial payments to Britain. These election promises were speedily implemented and set in train a six-year dispute with Britain. When the British Government responded with economic sanctions on Irish cattle and other Irish exports to Britain, the Irish retaliated with punitive tariffs on the main British exports to Ireland: coal, cement, electrical machinery, iron and steel goods. The cabinet minister with responsibility for Ireland was the Dominions Secretary, J. H. Thomas, one of the National Labour MPs who had split so acrimoniously from the Labour Party the previous year. Thomas was MP for Derby but came from Newport in South Wales. He was taunted with this by the Labour MP for Gower, David Grenfell, who predicted that the people of Newport and south Wales would pay for 'this miserable dispute'.[48]

In a fiery speech Aneurin Bevan, MP for Ebbw Vale, ridiculed the hysterical atmosphere surrounding the dispute with de Valera: 'This evening I have heard taunts thrown across the Floor and I have heard jeers and gibes and laughter concerning our relations with Ireland which I have never heard when discussing our relations with any other Power. Not even the abhorred Russia has given occasion for such ribaldry as I have heard this evening'. Thomas was:

> so anxious to get Tory cheers that he has been incapable of dealing with this grave issue in the way it should be dealt with. He has out-heroded Herod, and he seems anxious to go down to history as the English Bismarck. There is nothing at all in the recent history of the dispute to warrant the high feeling which has been created . . . the Irish Sea is very narrow, and we have to live with this nation for many generations to come. The people of my generation have already suffered sufficiently from the bitterness, the prejudice and the myopia of past generations, not to want that sort of thing to happen again . . . The Dominions Secretary may win the applause of the House of Commons at the moment but he will win the contempt of generations to come by his failure to be a bigger man'.[49]

Over the next two years the trade war caused considerable hardship in the Welsh coalfields. The Irish duties on British coal led to accumulating stocks and short working hours in Wales, Scotland and Lancashire. George Hall, MP for Aberdare, outlined the serious effects in South Wales. In the first five months of 1932 nearly 1 million tons of coal were exported to Ireland. For the first five months of 1934 exports had dropped below 500,000 tons. Cement exports were also down from 24,000 tons to 5,000 tons.[50] Grenfell told the Commons in May 1933 that nearly 5,000 Welsh miners were out of work. The ports of Holyhead and Fishguard were also affected. The Irish

Government put pressure on private and state companies to buy German coal and this led to complaints from Welsh colliery owners to the Dominions Office and the Board of Trade. Grenfell made several attempts to mediate in 1933–34 and suggested to the Irish High Commissioner in London, J. W. Dulanty, and to J. H. Thomas the possibility of an exchange agreement on the retaliatory duties. After secret negotiations, the Coal-Cattle Pacts were concluded at the end of 1934 and were extended over the next two years. They mitigated the worst effects of the trade dispute by reducing and in some cases abolishing the punitive duties.[51]

The dispute finally concluded with the Anglo-Irish agreements in April 1938. When the Agreements bill came before the Commons the following month, Grenfell recalled 'the light-hearted way in which we entered into a trade war with Ireland' and condemned the inexcusable delay in reaching a settlement.[52] James Griffiths, MP for Llanelli, thought that the people of south Wales had paid the heaviest price:

> There has been no difference at all between the Welsh people and the Irish people. We recognised that the Irish people were entitled to get the rights of nationality . . . One thing we welcome in this Bill, which we hope will pass very quickly, is that it does restore something like a decent relationship between the Irish and the Welsh people commercially. The natural market for Welsh coal, which is the Irish market, was cut off overnight. Now it has been, for some time, restored, and in so far as it makes that an assured market, I want, as a Welshman, to welcome it'.[53]

After coming to power de Valera maintained friendly relations with Plaid Cymru and was regularly asked to write special messages in Irish and Welsh for St David's Day in their journal *Y Ddraig Doch* and for Plaid rallies and meetings. In 1936 the Fianna Fail newspaper, the *Irish Press*, reported on the trials which led to the imprisonment of Saunders Lewis, Lewis Valentine and D. J. Williams following an arson attack on the RAF bombing school at Penyberth.[54] After the Second World War, the organising secretary of Plaid Cymru, J. E. Jones, wrote to de Valera saying that he and Gwynfor Evans were planning a visit to Dublin as 'we would desire to bring back to Wales as much information as we can about the progress of Eire under self-government'. De Valera arranged for them to meet ministers and officials who could show them projects in industry, services, education and local government.[55] In a letter to the Scottish nationalist, Robert Blair Wilkie, de Valera wrote, 'I understand so well how the Scottish and Welsh nationalists feel'. Wilkie thought that any intervention by the Irish Government would be a mistake 'but the *support* moral and patriotic of Irish movements for Scottish and Welsh self-Government could not but be a source of strength and can be extended on a basis of Celtic Unity'. Unfortunately, the Irish in Britain were 'still voting Labour against all forms of Nationalism, Devolution or Separatist, yet are seething with discontent at Labour's shameless breaches of pledges to Scots and to Irish Anti-Partitionists'.[56]

The efforts made to rebuild a sense of 'Celtic' national affinity in the later 1930s may have been influenced by the fact that nationalists in the Republic and in Wales shared ideas – but were also similarly unpopular with the British Government. There was also perhaps a shared concern that a cultural Britishness was emerging from the war stronger even than it had been in the past. Both Welsh and Irish nationalists certainly shared a sense of Britain as an Imperial predator.[57] However, that had not helped create united action in the past, especially when calls for Home Rule All Round seemed to threaten the primacy of Ireland's claims. If much scholarship has focussed on the relationship between Ireland and Scotland, there was in fact a neglected and significant relationship between the new Irish republic and Wales.

Notes

1   HC, 59, 1235–38, 11 March 1914. For a discussion of E. T. John and federalism see John Kendle, *Ireland and the Federal Solution: The Debate over the United Kingdom Constitution, 1870–1921* (Kingston & Montreal, 1989), pp. 112–15, 129–30, 133–4.

2   Ibid.

3   Ibid.

4   HC, 60, 1417–19, 2 April 1914.

5   HC, 61, 636, 652, 673, 874, 20–1 April 1914.

6   HC, 62, 1832, 19 May 1914.

7   John Turner, 'Letting go: the Conservative Party and the end of the Union with Ulster', in Alexander Grant & Keith Stringer (eds), *Uniting the Kingdom? The making of British History* (London, 1995), p. 274.

8   Paul O'Leary, *Immigration and Integration: The Irish in Wales, 1798–1922* (Cardiff, 2000), p. 280.

9   James Mullin, *The Story of a Toiler's Life* (1921: new ed. Dublin, 1999 ed. Patrick Maume), pp. 77, 200–4.

10 HC, 82, 2264–5, 25 May 1916.

11 Turner, 'Letting go', p. 274.

12 Frances Stevenson (ed. A. J. P. Taylor), *Lloyd George: A Diary* (London, 1971), p. 109.

13 *War Memoirs* (London, 1933–6) and *The Truth about the Peace Treaties* (London, 1938). He wrote a short article on 'How the Irish Treaty was signed' which was published in the *Daily Telegraph* on 16 December 1922. This was later included in a collection of essays and articles, *Is It Peace?* (London, 1923). Understandably, one aspect of Irish history which did fascinate Lloyd George and which he discussed with Frances Stevenson was the career and fall of Parnell. Stevenson, *Diary*, pp. 92, 292, 322.

14 Frank Pakenham (Lord Longford), *Peace by Ordeal* (1972 ed.), p. 9.

15 This point is emphasised by Frances Stevenson, *The Years that are Past* (London, 1967), p. 189; John Grigg, *Lloyd George: From Peace to War 1912–16* (London, 1997), p. 109; and Thomas Jones, *Whitehall Diary: vol. III Ireland, 1918–25* ed. Keith Middlemas (Oxford, 1971), p. xvii.

16 John Grigg, *The Young Lloyd George* (London, 1973), pp. 26–35.

17 Stevenson, *Diary*, p. 77.

18 NLW, Thomas Jones Papers, A vol. 2, f.24, Adams to Jones, 31 January 1948.

19 William George, *My Brother and I* (London, 1958), pp. 128–9.

20 Grigg, *Young Lloyd George*, pp. 55–6.

21 Kenneth O. Morgan, *Wales in British Politics 1868–1922* (Cardiff, 1980 edition) pp. 120–1.

22 NLW, Thomas Jones Papers, G1, f.120, Davies to Jones, 9 August 1920.

23 Grigg, *Lloyd George: From Peace to War*, pp. 109–12.

24 HC, 91, 454–9, 7 March 1917.

25 HC, 104, 1361, 9 April 1918.

26 *Enter the Celt* (Perth, 1918). The articles were originally published in the *Scottish Review*. The Scottish contributor was the Duke of Marr. The identity of 'Belfast' isn't certain but was possibly Shane Leslie.

27 HC, 118, 1052–3, 1103, 21 July 1919. Lloyd George, whether deliberately or not, was borrowing directly from arguments made by Lord Salisbury in his famous anti-Home Rule speech of May 1886 (reported in *The Irish Times*, 19 May 1886).

28 HC, 127, 1323–35, 31 March 1920.

29 HC, 131, 169, 28 June 1920.

30 HC, 133, 2039–40, 28 October 1920.

31 TNA, CAB 23/23, meeting of Ministers, 28 October 1920.

32 HC, 135, 623–4, 25 November 1920.

33 George, *My Brother and I*, p. 266.

34 Mair Saunders Jones, Ned Thomas and Harri Pritchard Jones, *Saunders Lewis: Letters to Margaret Gilcriest* (Cardiff, 1993), pp. 431, 441, 465.

35 O'Leary, *Immigration and Integration*, pp. 283–94.

36 Jones et al., *Saunders Lewis: Letters*, pp. 471–2.

37 O'Leary, *Immigration and Integration*, pp. 291–3.

38 HC, 139, 2680–1, 23 March 1921.

39 Stevenson, *Diary*, pp. 221–2.

40 HC, 149, 114–17, 14 December 1921.

41 HC, 151, 1415–18, 8 March 1922.

42 Jones et al., *Saunders Lewis: Letters*, p. 479.

43 DD, 3, 290, 416, 6–10 January 1922. Saunders Lewis had been delighted to learn of Griffith's Welsh connections. Jones et al., *Saunders Lewis: Letters*, pp. 471–2.

44 O'Leary, *Immigration and Integration*, p. 294.

45 Jones et al., *Saunders Lewis: Letters*, p. 558.

46 DD, 23, 767, 2 May 1928.

47 DD, 28, 1356, 13 March 1929.

48 HC, 268, 720–22, 7 July 1932.

49 Ibid., 764–72, 7 July 1932.

50 HC, 291, 25–26, 18 June 1934.

51 Deirdre McMahon, *Republicans and Imperialists: Anglo-Irish Relations in the 1930s* (Yale, 1984), pp. 136–52.
52 HC, 335, 1079, 5 May 1938.
53 HC, 335, 1533–4, 10 May 1938.
54 *Irish Press*, 9, 17 September, 14 October 1936, 20 January 1937.
55 NAI TAOI/2001/6/377.
56 Ibid.
57 See Chapter 5 by Edwards and Griffith, pp. 130–1.

Part II
UNFINISHED BUSINESS: DEVOLUTION IN WALES 1885–1945

4
Devolutionist tendencies in Wales, 1885–1914

Wil Griffith

It can be argued that demands for devolutionary concessions to Wales in the late nineteenth and early twentieth centuries were a culmination of long-term trends and not merely accidental contemporary developments. The motivations for those demands either emphasised that devolved government was beneficial for the entire British imperial state or, increasingly, they became centred on a conviction that Wales was a distinctive entity and deserved separate treatment. The demands themselves varied from calling for a devolved representative institution with legislative powers to securing ministerial and departmental distinctiveness for Wales, to securing national bodies with special delegated powers.[1] We can see that this distinctiveness was wrought out of a conviction that there was a central core of identity which was linguistic and cultural and age old. This *essentialist* view was not however the sum total of this assertion of distinctiveness. Changes within modern Welsh society also produced features and characteristics which could be exploited and manipulated into enhancing the idea of being distinctive. In other words, there was also an element of *manufactured* (or imagined) identity promoted by aspirant or idealistic groups and individuals, responding to what were perceived as the requirements for establishing an effective national civil society in Wales.[2]

It can also be argued that the latter was a response, or indeed a reaction, to Wales's political and economic position within the United Kingdom. Politically, Wales had been absorbed into the English (and later British) political parliamentary system after the acts of union in 1536 and 1543 as a very marginal region indeed in terms of representation and thus with little voice. Economically, Wales became transformed by the growth of heavy industry and urbanisation and by Wales's increasing integration into a British and imperial economic system. The debate about political devolution thus was very much about identity and control, therefore, and of balancing the merits and demerits of being part of a wider whole. Since that balance was always unclear, different views and conclusions were reached concerning separate powers and at the end of the nineteenth century there was a spectrum of views and beliefs about Welshness and about Wales's status. Ultimately, that range of views, stemming from competing social, ideological and cultural interests, explains the failure to produce an effective consensus about devolution in Wales before the Great War. While there were some modest administrative and some singular cultural institutional achievements by 1914, there was no major constitutional shift.[3]

Background

Although ideas about a politically autonomous or semi-autonomous Wales appear principally in the late nineteenth century, it is important to note that there were passing precursors. In reviving the history of Owain Glyndŵr during the later eighteenth century, for example, Thomas Pennant was subscribing to a patriotic sense of national distinctiveness among some of the Welsh gentry and other educated Welshmen. Similarly, Sir William Jones, the Orientalist, viewed the Welsh as a distinctive people and this was a feature of the Welsh intelligentsia's response to the ideas of Britishness and the 'New Britain' of the Hanoverians. The Welsh were the original inhabitants of Britain, the 'ancient Britons.' Whilst they were loyal to the British crown and to being part of Great Britain, they were nevertheless a distinctive people possessing an inherent cultural and linguistic essence.[4] However, that distinctiveness was not marked in a substantial institutional sense. The regional structure of government under the ancient regime, of prerogative courts and councils, was gradually dissolved. The Council of Wales and the Marches had been finally abolished in the Glorious Revolution and without much fuss since, although it gave Wales a distinctive administrative and formerly also a judicial identity, it was too intrusive of local interests. Nonetheless, when it came to defending the separate system of assize courts in Wales, the courts of great sessions, there was significant resistance. When these courts were abolished in 1830 the Welsh political nation offered emphatic opposition. It was only achieved against the wishes of Welsh MPs.[5]

Asserting a political distinctiveness was a characteristic, albeit not a pronounced one, of the Tory gentry and the Anglican clergy in the 1830s and 1840s when they sought to enhance the Welsh character of the Established Church by demanding that appropriate Welsh appointees were made to Welsh benefices and that native Welshmen were appointed to the Welsh bishoprics. Similarly, expatriate Welsh clergymen were calling for separate treatment for Wales in cultural and educational matters. Indeed, this represented a theme which was to recur, namely the seeking of parity for Wales with the other nations of Britain.[6]

The cultural and educational issue was also taken up by the growing Nonconformist population and ministry by the mid-nineteenth century. In claiming civil rights as Nonconformists, Welsh campaigners such as Henry Richard not only deployed the arguments of their English counterparts but also began increasingly to emphasise distinctive Welsh national claims:

> By degrees, the writing, and speeches of these and others began to leaven the public mind, and to give rise to a vague feeling of dissatisfaction, among at least some of the leaders of the people, at the somewhat ignoble position which Wales occupied in our political system, coupled with a longing to do something to remove the reproach that rested upon us, a professed nation of Nonconformists.[7]

Thus, when the Liberation Society eventually saw the value of concentrating on Wales in its disestablishment campaign during the early 1860s, Welsh national aspirations formed an additional and increasingly more powerful motivation, which came to predominate as the English campaign waned after 1885.

The idea of separate legislation for Wales stemmed from the denominational rivalry between Nonconformity and Anglicanism in Wales, a rivalry that also contained ideological and class features. The idea that the Nonconformist people of Wales *were* the nation was diffused among the middle and working classes by a politically active combination of 'shopocracy' and chapel ministers exploiting a press and deploying a Welsh political language which became more and more inaccessible to the landed gentry and clergy. This assertion of difference had become pronounced from the 1840s. The reaction to the infamous education reports of 1847 (which castigated the morals of the Welsh people and the values of the Welsh language) though they drew condemnation from all quarters of Welsh life, contributed much more to a radical national agenda which Welsh Nonconformists intruded into Liberal politics.[8] The 1840s also saw ideas of Welsh political autonomy from the quasi-revolutionary end of the political spectrum with the Chartist Dr William Price of Pontypridd advocating the creation of a Silurian republic in south Wales and the Young Ireland movement advocating separate parliaments for all the four nations of the United Kingdom.[9]

Party political, patriotic and antiquarian influences

Although such ideas did not gain much currency there is no doubt that a sense of Welsh distinctiveness began to be played out more firmly within Liberal politics. It would have been difficult however to say that Welsh MPs, Liberal or Tory, were in any way overly assertive in their Welsh patriotism during the early 1880s, when they were regarded as a largely non-contentious and deferent group, not given to dissent from the main party machine:

> The Welsh members give no trouble to Ministers or 'Whips'. They never resort to the meretricious artifice of obstruction. They vote straight as a party on broad issues; and may be relied upon to obey the 'whips' of the rival leaders. They have nothing to do with 'caves', but proceed haughtily upon their way, unaffected by the intrigues of their neighbours, the English, the Scotch, and the Irish members.[10]

This behaviour did bring to Wales a modicum of concessions from Gladstone's second administration, such as the Welsh Sunday Closing Act of 1881 and support for the establishment of two university colleges maintained by government grants – concessions which in the short term satisfied the desires of the Welsh Nonconformists and the middle class.

Thereafter, Welsh politics became more nationalistically inclined due in part to the changing balance of forces in parliament after Gladstone's Irish policy. This gave Welsh MPs greater purchase within the Liberal Party. In addition, issues surrounding the tithe rent charge, Church disestablishment and land reform all assumed a greater significance in Welsh eyes. Ironically, both the gentry and clergy in Wales, the traditional elites which were already being increasingly subjected to political criticism, contributed to this growth of Welsh self-awareness by inculcating an interest in Welsh history and antiquarianism. The popular sense of past was largely contained in rather mythological 'histories', of which Theophilus Evans's *Drych y Prif Oesoedd* remained a core text.[11] But from the early and mid-nineteenth century the gentry and clergy had, under the influence of romanticism, turned to antiquarianism and recovery of the past and this established a tighter sense of history and identity. The Cambrian Archaeological Association and the revived Honourable Society of Cymmrodorion in London became vehicles for 'scientific' history and an assertion of Welsh historical distinctiveness. The Cymmrodorion also became a vehicle for analysing the needs of modern Wales by organising debates on Welsh educational and cultural issues.[12] Similarly, the creation of a National Eisteddfod from 1859 led to not only the promotion of Welsh literary competition but also to instituting a Social Science section. This initiative of (Sir) Hugh Owen, Chief Clerk at the Poor Law Board, was meant to review Wales's social and economic needs and propose policy solutions to modernise Welsh life. There was a sense in which the Welsh, along with the Highland Scots and the rural Irish, were depicted in metropolitan England as being backward or deficient in civility. Racial stereotypes derived from the writings of John Pinkerton in the early nineteenth century and reinforced later by the views of Matthew Arnold and others, distinguished between the rational Teutonic peoples and the less refined and less advanced Celts and (still more) Slavs. Thus, the modernising agenda featured heavily in Owen's approach.[13]

The Cymmrodorion were avowedly non-political, and in that respect were able to include Anglicans as well as Nonconformists, Tories as well as Liberals, aristocrats and the Welsh middle class. Their membership encompassed a broad range of Welsh opinion but, significantly, their governing Council was composed of expatriate and metropolitan Welshmen, including lawyers and especially some civil servants. Though the Cymmrodorion Society's prime function was to enhance an appreciation of the Welsh past – and in doing that it added to the sense of Welsh particularism – it too was committed to a Welsh reforming agenda insofar as it addressed non-partisan issues such as reforming intermediate education in Wales and establishing a national university system.[14] More controversially, however, in 1882, at its gatherings during the Denbigh National Eisteddfod, it heard a paper advocating in essence a system of federal Home Rule in Britain. This was the first tangible proposal for a devolved framework for Wales and was proposed by the Liberal activist and quarrymen's leader, W. J. Parry of Coetmor, Bethesda in rural/semi-industrial north Wales.

Parry's paper[15] was given short shrift at the time because it was regarded as being too political – that it offended 'unionist' feelings among the leadership. It remained unpublished in the Society's *Transactions* until 1918 by which time, of course, various schemes for Welsh Home Rule had been and gone, although the debate over devolution continued.[16] Parry's scheme however did see the light of day when he published it privately in late 1889 in the form of a draft bill, by which time a nationalist skein had become apparent in Welsh politics, largely as a result of the emergence of the Cymru Fydd Society[17] in London and subsequently among Welsh émigrés in some of the other large English conurbations, notably Liverpool. Significantly, societies were formed among Welsh students at Oxford, Cambridge and the Scottish universities, as well as among Welsh students at the new Welsh university colleges at Aberystwyth, Bangor and Cardiff which had been established with general all-party support. At Oxford, for example, Cymdeithas Dafydd ap Gwilym (the Dafydd ap Gwilym Society) held regular gatherings and heard papers on the distinctive cultural and intellectual traits of the Welsh nation while Cymdeithas Gomer at Cambridge held similar gatherings and discussed topics such a 'Y Deffroad Cymreig' – The Welsh Awakening. And it was from among these students that a cadre of Welsh leaders and social administrators emerged; a cadre which was very different from the traditional gentry and clergy. As was reported of the Oxford society:

y mae'r gymdeithas hon yn gwneud gwaith ardderchog drwy roddi gwybodaeth o hanes eu gwlad, a dyddordeb yn ei llenyddiaeth, i arweinwyr dyfodol Cymru.[18]

The Cymru Fydd Society's aims included explicitly the securing of a:

> 'National Legislature for Wales', dealing exclusively with Welsh affairs, while pre-
> serving relations with the British parliament upon all questions of Imperial interest.[19]

The more assertive momentum in Welsh politics since 1868, and the frustrations over the failures to get parliament's attention on Welsh issues, particularly on disestablishment, were a motivating influence. But, in addition, and
just as importantly, the (supposedly) broader interest in Home Rule all round
evinced by leading party figures such as Chamberlain, Dilke, Hartington and
even Derby after 1885 was a stimulus to the Welsh Home Rule cause.[20]

A Welsh Home Rule schema

Parry's draft bill, therefore, came out of this changing environment. It was significant in several ways. Firstly, it coincided with the increase in Welsh Liberal
efforts in parliament to raise Wales's profile in British politics during the later
1880s, as seen in the campaigns over, amongst other things, disestablishment,
tithe, land reform, magisterial reform and secondary (and higher) education
reform. This was much associated with the quasi-nationalist tendencies seen
within Welsh Liberalism, not only in the Cymru Fydd movement in which
Parry was a participant, but also in the formation of a Welsh Parliamentary
Party in 1888.

Secondly, it was a product not only of a general interest in devolution in
these years but of various published schemes for devolved government, such
as Digby Seymour's *Outline of a Federal Union League for the British Empire*
(1888) and *Statement of Scotland's Claim for Home Rule issued by the Scottish
Home Rule Association* (1888).[21] One proposal, *Historical Lessons of Home
Rule* published in 1887, drew the ire of J. E. Vincent, the Conservative commentator on Wales for *The Times*. It suggested a federal plan not dissimilar to
Parry's. It aimed to establish a Welsh legislative assembly, based at Caernarfon.
Vincent's Tory and Unionist inclinations made him view this proposal as too
exclusivist and too one-sided to be effective. In other words, it set Welsh and
English apart and instituted government by a domineering Nonconformist
and Liberal majority.[22] That sort of view was to be typical of Conservative
opposition to Welsh Home Rule and to any form of devolved power.

Parry's own scheme also met with critical comments from *The Times*, possibly by Vincent again. But it also won approbation in other quarters, as an
example of how 'brave little Wales' was producing a tangible federal legislative
proposal which was more imaginative than anything proposed by the Parnellites
and ahead of the better organised Scottish Home Rule movement.[23]

Thirdly, Parry's proposals were also a product of the democratisation of local government following the Local Government Act of 1888 which created the county councils. Associated with this, and as part of the sweeping Welsh Liberal and Nonconformist triumphs at the first county council elections, there was a desire to enhance this democratic trend both by reforming parish government but also by establishing a Welsh national *council* to address the national issues which formed the Welsh agenda. This was certainly the aspiration of the foremost Welsh Liberal advocate of devolution at the time, Thomas Edward Ellis MP. Clearly Parry's scheme fitted in with this aspiration.[24]

On the other hand, and finally, this scheme did not advocate autonomy in any way and in fact asserted that devolution was a means of strengthening the unity of the imperial state. Indeed, it was couched in terms which stressed the value of devolution as a means of improving administrative efficiency throughout the UK and not in making any inordinate claims for Wales on particularist grounds. Parry stressed the worth of provincial assemblies as a means of relieving the burden of work on the Imperial parliament by devolving responsibilities to the four home nations. This was not an untypical argument for Home Rule All Round by most advocates in these years.

What Parry sought in terms of an elected body, in fact appears to have become a pattern for subsequent calls for devolved administration and local legislative powers, some of which reiterated administrative efficiency as the aim while others played up more to the sense of national sentiment. Equally, some of the critical and antagonistic comments and rationales against establishing devolved bodies when Parry's plan came out in 1890 were repeated later.

Parry's scheme had originally addressed three levels of government – county, provincial and imperial. By 1889, the county level had been more or less addressed, with Parry himself becoming a councillor and vice-chairman of the new Caernarfonshire County Council. Parry had himself supported the idea of a democratically elected provincial parliament having taxation and legislative powers – to relieve the burdens on the Westminster parliament. A governor general would represent the crown and have the power to reject any measure not having a two-thirds majority. A triennially elected assembly, it would have remunerated members.

These ideas were far from winning universal approval. Critical and antagonistic responses were found in both the English and Welsh press and included ridicule of the idea of paid members. More fundamental objections centred on resistance to the idea of separation from England and the apprehension that autonomy would impoverish Wales because it would cause 'inward' investment from England to seize up. Grants in aid would be lost, the legal system would become more partial and subject to local politicking and jobbery. As one opinion put it:

> Let us be governed by those who are socially and educationally qualified and not by political carpet-baggers or the riff-raff of society.

The Welsh language would be a hindrance to progress and there could be no agreement about the location of such a provincial parliament.[25] Despite this, there was a head of steam for some devolved scheme, as became evident at a conference held by the South Wales Liberal Federation in February 1890.

Alternatives and priorities, competing interests

Parry was among just a few north Wales representatives who were invited to speak at that conference. His ideas were very well received. Yet, at the very time that some real enthusiasm was being expressed, there were also clear doubts too amongst Liberals. These were two-fold and, again, were to echo down the decades as Welsh Home Rule (or Welsh devolution) was debated. Firstly, it was asked, how far would achieving a degree of domestic autonomy deprive Wales of influence at the centre of government in London? Was it not better to secure Welsh interests in central government, as Scotland had with its Scottish Office and Secretary of State? Secondly, would some of the core Welsh issues currently being addressed be swept aside if the siren voices calling for devolved government were heeded? This applied in particular to the advocates of Welsh Church disestablishment, the core issue in Welsh politics for more than a generation. As one commentator put it:

> We want 'Home Rule' in Wales but let us make sure first of all what it is we want. Just now our hands are full with the working of the County Councils, the launching of the Intermediate Schools, and the Disestablishment of the Church. Festina lente – yn araf deg yr â gŵr ymhell.[26]

Welsh disestablishment was an issue which English Nonconformists especially wished to see pursued, since a successful Welsh bill would give them greater purchase to disestablish the state church in England. Thus, the *British Weekly* was one of several publications which raised the concern that the Welsh were being led astray.[27]

An alternative to establishing a separate Welsh legislature was the securing of a distinctive Welsh voice at the heart of government. Cymru Fydd, among others, had complained that British governments had been largely apathetic to Welsh national aspirations and that this was due to a lack of proper (Welsh) advocacy. Therefore, in 1890 Alfred Thomas MP moved the creation of a Welsh Department, headed by a Welsh minister. A year later he moved the appointment of a Secretary of State for Wales as part of his National Institutions (Wales) bill to co-ordinate the establishing and control over Welsh cultural and educational institutions.[28] Thomas's original proposal had met with no little annoyance on the part of members of the Welsh Party since he had not consulted them on his intentions.[29] Indeed, the Welsh Party's membership lacked the uniformity of outlook which its critics had anticipated from the start.[30] For example, Sir George Osborne Morgan, chairman of the Welsh Party after the death of the venerable Henry Richard, was sceptical about Home Rule of the sort which Parry had been advocating. It was impracticable, he argued, because of Wales's smallness and integration with England.[31]

Nevertheless, there was a whole raft of issues which had a particular resonance in Wales and they enabled the Welsh Party to draw up an agenda around which they could organise their parliamentary activity. In addition, these issues justified Morgan in arguing not for a wholly autonomous legislature but for an assembly of sorts, which would have some lawmaking powers over particular Welsh issues. Indeed, what may have annoyed many about Alfred Thomas's initiative was that he had ignored moves to bring about a national representative institution of this sort.

The idea of establishing a national council was in the making in 1889 and 1890. One of the prime movers was J. Herbert Lewis MP. Essentially, this came out of the reform of local government in England and Wales in 1888. The ensuing elections in March 1889 had resulted in the Liberals sweeping Wales, with strong performances in all the counties and county boroughs except for Breconshire and Radnorshire. The Tories and the landed oligarchies were effectively swept aside. Given such a homogeneous pattern, it gave every encouragement to Lewis, T. E. Ellis and others to consolidate this development. It was thought that the Local Government Act of 1888 itself offered the opportunity to do this, since section 82 (1) noted:

> Any county council or councils, and any court or courts of quarter sessions, may from time to time join in appointing out of their respective bodies a joint committee for any purpose in respect of which they are jointly interested.[32]

An added justification for attempting to use these powers was education and specifically the development of secondary or intermediate education in Wales. This was arguably the most debated issue after disestablishment and the one which won the most non-partisan support. The Liberals in 1885 and 1887 had attempted to introduce a bill. Eventually the Tory administration allowed parliamentary time for the Welsh Liberals to bring forth a bill which, with amendments, became law as the Welsh Intermediate Education Act 1889.[33] The main difference between the Act and the Liberals' previous proposals was the absence of a clause to establish an all-Wales representative body to administer intermediate education. Thus, with the democratisation of local government, an opportunity presented itself to rectify that absence by reference to the Local Government Act.

An attempt to justify a national council in general terms had been met with little sympathy from the Local Government Board (LGB) in 1889. Glamorgan County Council, among the main movers, was given short shrift. Sect. 81(1), they were told, was not intended for that purpose. There was no reason for uniting to establish such a 'committee'.[34] Presumably it was with a view to legitimising a national council initiative that Alfred Thomas introduced the idea of ministerial control over a devolved Welsh body. Indeed there were attempts in 1891–92 by Lewis and others to renovate the national council ideal. This again met with resistance from the LGB. When plans for a national council were raised yet again during the Welsh reaction to the 1902 Education Act and the subsequent Welsh 'revolt' of 1904, and again in 1906 and 1908, the notion of attaching such an administrative council to a Secretary-ship of State for Wales became well established. However, the Board of Education, which had by then taken over responsibility for education, was extremely sceptical and wanted a guarantee that the Welsh authorities were unanimously in favour of such a body.[35]

Part of the scepticism was to do with uncertainty over whether there was unanimity among Welsh local authorities and local education authorities (LEAs) in favour of a united all-Wales body. While there must certainly have been some party political considerations at work in some counties, especially where Tories were in a stronger position, it was also the case that there were tensions between the larger and smaller counties and educational authorities. These centred on the patterns of representation on these proposed national bodies. Inevitably, council membership would be based on population sizes which gave an unassailable majority to the industrialised counties of the south. As Radnorshire had made plain in 1892, the county was:

> declining to join any National Council of Wales and Monmouthshire which adopts the basis of population for representation on that Council.[36]

A decade later, in 1904, the issue of representation was raised yet again in relation to Lloyd George's campaign to establish a national council. Charles Shuker of Welshpool put forward the view of a rural county by observing that, under the proposals, Montgomeryshire would only have two representatives whereas Glamorgan and Monmouth, together, would have as many as twenty-six. He was also sceptical about the idea that most of the council's activities would be held at Cardiff, thus making it unlikely that many north Wales counties would be able to participate with any regularity. Moreover,

Shuker, as a Tory, had doubts about the ulterior motives behind setting up the council: 'Radicals are making most of this council as a first step towards Home Rule.' Again he noted the disparity in the proposed representation for north and south Wales.[37]

The possible distribution of government funds similarly caused concern. During the late 1880s and 1890s, when proposals for disendowing the Church in Wales were debated among Welsh Nonconformists and Liberals, there were significant cleavages over how the Church's wealth would be distributed by a national council, whether by allocating equally per county, or per head of population.[38]

Thus, rural-industrial and north-south divisions became more emphatic. It was ironic that in 1890 it had been south Wales which had headed the support for devolved government but that by 1895 it was the north, with David Lloyd George MP in the van, which made the running. There, a new Cymru Fydd League had merged with the local Liberal associations and with the North Wales Liberal Federation. This did not appeal to the south. As is well known, Lloyd George was rebuffed at the South Wales Liberal Federation conference at Newport in January 1896, notably by Liberals who were suspicious of the rural and Welsh language agenda supposedly being promoted.[39]

Notions of Welsh unity

The representative nature of the south Wales Liberal vote might be debated, but it did help weaken the devolution agenda in Wales for at least ten years. It was in part an outcome of an intraparty personality struggle between Lloyd George and D. A. Thomas, but it also highlighted the tensions within the Welsh Parliamentary Party. The attempt by T. E. Ellis, by then a junior whip in Gladstone's fourth administration, to proclaim the successes of the government in respect of Wales was not met favourably by all.[40] And as is well known, Lloyd George had led what threatened to be a fissiparous development, by attempting to establish an independent Welsh Liberal movement centred on the Cymru Fydd League. He argued that Welsh parliamentary representation was always liable to be outnumbered and that parliamentary concessions to Wales were always likely to be tame and unexceptionable. But, he added:

> . . . what England happened to have any particular prejudice against Wales was not allowed to get, however much she wanted it and how often and how emphatically soever she demanded it, even although it would cost England nothing to concede.[41]

What Lloyd George had wanted was Welsh unity, 'Cymru Gyfan' [All Wales], encompassing all parts both rural and urban, and the creation of a party organisation separate from the (English) National Liberal Federation with an independent line of action on the part of Welsh MPs.[42]

That was hardly practicable. Lloyd George's near neighbour as MP, Bryn Roberts, was a British Liberal Party man through and through. He was unwilling always to follow a Welsh Party line, let alone act entirely independently. Indeed, it was a moot point how far the Welsh MPs adhered to the full run of issues which had been set out as the agenda for Welsh reforms in 1892–93.[43] An admittedly rather idiosyncratic assessment of the thirty-four overwhelmingly middle class Welsh MPs in 1894 labelled only six as 'Welsh nationalists', eight as Home Rule supporters and only four as adherents of Cymru Fydd; about ten might be counted clear devolutionists. Seven MPs were marked down as avowedly 'not nationalist', of whom only one was a Tory and only two were Englishmen. Five were deemed to show no interest in Welsh matters at all; in all, about eleven who could be counted anti-Welsh Home Rule. The rest were straightforward party men or single issue advocates, notably for disestablishment or temperance. Indeed, efforts by Cymru Fydd adherents to broaden their appeal by introducing class and gender issues seem to have alienated the more cautious and conservative Liberals. It was intimated at the time that the momentum for devolution had been lost following T. E. Ellis's promotion to Gladstone's government in 1892.[44] Ellis's acceptance of a post had been a calculated risk. He was giving up the independence of a backbencher, and with it the ability to make penetrating criticisms of government policy in Wales – but gaining the power which might enable him to become an advocate for Wales, though having also to toe the party line.[45]

What had motivated Ellis during his backbench days in the 1880s had been his keenness to justify devolutionary changes and separate legislation for Wales, and his preparedness to compare Wales with Ireland and to a lesser extent with Scotland.[46] He was not, of course, alone in wanting Wales to emulate the other Celtic countries – indeed, it had been a strong motivation behind the Welsh university movement from the1850s. What marks Ellis out is his historicist approach, his preparedness to seize on the new developments in Welsh historiography to emphasise Welsh distinctiveness.[47] This carried over into the writings of other Cymru Fydd and Home Rule advocates. Ellis's historical emphasis in relation to justifying the existence of a distinct Welsh land question and hence separate Welsh land legislation, such as the Welsh land bill introduced by Bryn Roberts with the support of Ellis and others in 1887.[48] He was also a prominent figure in attempting to cull statistical information in order to justify separate attention to Wales. Unlike Scotland or Ireland, there was little separate statistical data for Wales; figures had to be disaggregated from English statistics. For those wishing to see a devolved system emerge in Wales, it was necessary to accumulate an army of Welsh facts. Although progress to Welsh Home Rule was tardy and unproductive, one of the more significant developments was the creation of the statistical information necessary to supplement Ellis', 'imagined' Wales.

Bureaucratic and administrative cross-currents

The establishment of a Royal Commission on Land in Wales and Monmouthshire 1893–96, reluctantly established by Gladstone's government to satisfy the Welsh MPs and the radical agrarian activists in the country, produced a wealth of new data.[49] The Commission's secretary, Daniel Lleufer Thomas, was himself a product of rural Wales and of Welsh-speaking Nonconformist Wales. He was also part of that new generation of Oxford Welshmen and his legal training enabled him to adopt a forensic approach to Welsh matters. His historical depiction of Wales reinforced the concept of Wales as an ancient nation. His interests were entirely modern and as secretary he was regarded by the landowners as a radical and biased against traditional aristocratic leadership. His contribution was significant in the mass of information he accumulated as appendices to the Commission's report and minutes of evidence. This data established a basis upon which future social investigations about Wales could build. Indeed, Thomas himself was one of a pioneering group of writers and investigators – social radicals – who were concerned with social and economic conditions in Wales who later helped create the Welsh School of Social Service. Thus, in the years immediately before the Great War ideas about welfare reform and economic regeneration began to be fed into the debate about Home Rule, to go beyond the issues of land reform or disestablishment.[50]

Thomas was an example of the sort of professional public servant emerging in Wales by the turn of the twentieth century, who aimed to create a broader civil society and leadership of the sort which Sir Hugh Owen had wanted. Well educated Welshmen were beginning to emerge within the ranks of the civil service in London, notably W. N. Bruce at the Charity Commission and later the Board of Education; and Howell Thomas and John Rowland at the Treasury, the latter being in attendance at the 1908 conference to discuss yet another attempt to establish a national council.[51]

Executive power was also delegated to Wales, and this too enabled the growth of an incipient bureaucracy. This included, for example, Owen Owen of the Central Welsh Board and James Evans of the Welsh Insurance Commission.[52] Welsh Party aspirations to see the Welsh university colleges organised into a federal university were fulfilled by the granting of a university charter in 1893 that led to the creation of a federal governing structure. This was followed by the creation in 1896 of the Central Welsh Board (CWB) which consisted of nominated representatives of the county governing bodies and educationists the secretary of which was Percy Watkins. They were to administer the curriculum and examinations of the new intermediate schools. This was essentially aimed at facilitating the smoother implementation of Whitehall policy in Wales, rather than providing room for local initiative. Indeed, this gave rise to vested interests which might oppose any further devolutionary change. The CWB, for example, was originally meant to be a solution to ad hoc co-operation between governing bodies in north and south Wales. The arrangement was meant to be reviewed, with the prospect of forming a comprehensive administrative system which would combine both the university and intermediate sectors into a Welsh national system. It failed to materialise because of the competing interests. As Watkins noted, there was a conflict between having a national system and preserving localism. Localism took precedence, especially since the 1902 Education Act had turned the counties and various boroughs and urban districts into inclusive local education authorities responsible for both intermediate and elementary education. With so many LEAs, it was difficult to establish a common national view, as was seen in the attempts to establish a Welsh National Education Council.[53]

The administrative devolution which followed after 1906 was in part recognition that the Liberal government could not fulfil anything more major because of the opposition of the House of Lords. The 1906 Education Bill had included a proposal to establish a Welsh National Education Council. This was specifically attacked by the Conservative opposition, particularly in the Lords where the Welsh bishops and Anglican peers were especially vocal in defending the Church schools in Wales from Radical and Nonconformist interference.[54] It was also the case that the Welsh Liberals themselves still gave priority to disestablishment, about which there was general unity. By contrast, a devolved assembly of some kind was counted a distraction and a possible hindrance. The result of all this was the creation of Welsh departments in several ministries and the creation of a Welsh Insurance Commission after the introduction of National Insurance in 1911. The most contentious development was the establishment of a Welsh Department in the Board of Education in 1907, which followed the failure to set up a Welsh national council. This soon resulted in a conflict of powers between the Department in London and the CWB in Cardiff. Both bodies claimed to be the most beneficial for education in Wales. The CWB was criticised by some of the more the nationalistically minded for merely administering an English curriculum in Wales. Nevertheless, as a body with delegated powers it was thought essential 'to preserve what is essentially a national organization, that has rendered great service to the country'.[55] The Welsh Department, on the other hand, was London based and very much the handmaiden of the Board's civil servants. Nonetheless, whilst it not only justified government education grants in Wales, it was also still able to make far reaching proposals under its chief inspector, O. M. Edwards, which would make education more attuned to Welsh society, particularly in regard to the use of the Welsh language. Edwards' report of 1910 gained particular notoriety for his criticism of the CWB examinations structure and fed concerns that the Department meant to extinguish the CWB entirely. On the other hand, the Department's work in trying to establish a clear and 'Welsh' educational structure met with no little favour, so that a common view began to emerge that both bodies could with profit be amalgamated to create a really powerful Board of Education for Wales.[56] Edwards, like Lleufer Thomas, a product of rural Wales, was increasingly influential in idealising the land and the Welsh speaking folk as the essences of Welsh national identity and his views prefigured an increasing trend among inter-war political nationalists to structure their ideology around these concepts.[57]

The national federal university stood apart from the school system and again came in for criticism for being less than engaged with Wales. This demonstrated the failure early on to have a national body to maintain a comprehensive oversight of education across the intermediate and higher levels. As a federal institution, the national university left much to be desired. During the decade before the Great War it seemed in danger of breaking up into competing collegiate interests. Within the University Court, there were tensions between those who were prepared to accept that the Senior Deputy Chancellor should be an absentee and those who wanted the post rotated annually among senior academics in Wales. Moreover, there were tensions between the lay members and the academic members of the Court over whose voices should have precedence in decision making, the 'amateurs' who were the democratic representatives of local authorities or the academic staff representatives. Tension also arose between Cardiff and the other university colleges, with Cardiff seeking autonomy, in line with the town's assertion of its primacy. Indeed, all the university colleges had separate interests which seemed to augur ill for the national institution.[58]

Language and culture and a devolutionary rationale

Criticisms of the national university and its constituent colleges centred on the fact that they were too anglicised and lacked any interest in teaching Welsh language, literature and history.[59] The importance of culture and language as fundamentals to devolved government was emphasised by several writers, who queried whether devolution was worth anything if it did not represent a distinctive nation. The rival view was that a cultural nationalism might be too narrow and become chauvinistic, especially towards England. The English businessman and erstwhile MP for Denbigh Boroughs, Sir Robert Cunliffe, warned against:

> a tendency in some of those who speak or write, and who may be presumed to lead or reflect Welsh opinion, to dwell with too much complacency on Welsh virtues, or too much severity on English shortcomings

and he stressed the merit of Wales cultivating 'that English inheritance which is lying ready for her to take up'.[60]

A more sympathetic English view, by the educationist Thomas Darlington, while acknowledging the worth of using the English language and of acquiring the most recent knowledge emanating from England, stressed that the Welsh political revival required a cultural justification. Echoing a reference to Darwin that the most adaptable survived, the Welsh language needed to justify itself as an essential element in Welsh nationalism. Welsh nationalism, he argued, was a 'community of feelings and of ideas, of memories and hopes, of culture and language'. Although Wales had woken up to the need for a broader culture this did not imply anglicisation. The language should be the medium. He had hopes that the chairs of Welsh in the university colleges and even the creation of a Welsh university would fulfil this; or, failing that, of achieving at least home rule (*ymlywodraeth*) in education.[61]

The language as a political issue within education had materialised in the 1880s as it became apparent that it had only a very limited part to play in the education system. The Revised Code had made little concession to its being taught as a subject let alone as a medium of instruction. Arguably, too, the dismissive attitude of the upper classes and of English press opinion contributed to making the language an issue at a time when Cymru Fydd was beginning to make an impact. More directly, the Society for the Utilization of the Welsh Language in 1885 was established by Dan Isaac Davies to campaign for a better status for the language. The Society's aim of ensuring a bilingual Wales met with general all-party support and it resulted in a revision of the Code in 1890 which sanctioned a greater role for the language within the system:

> Daeth yr iaith Gymraeg i fwy o fri yn 1890 nag erioed o'r blaen. Addawodd y Llywodraeth roddi tâl i'r ysgolfeistriaid am ei dysgu yn yr ysgolion dyddiol, argraffwyd adroddiad y ddirprwyaeth fu'n chwilio effeithiau Deddf Cau ar y Sul ynddi, ac argreffir ynddi hefyd raglenni'r pwyllgorau sir, er gwaethaf deddf Harri'r Wythfed.[62]

Whether it would achieve that was up to the local authorities; and attitudes were mixed on that.[63]

Although the debate about Welsh within education was an expression of the importance of language to national identity, it was not necessarily the primary concern of all Liberal nationalists and devolutionists. Their perspectives centred around resolving outstanding issues which bore on Wales's relation to the rest of the kingdom. But for some the language was paramount and an argument not for some devolution but for separatism. The most fully expressed advocacy for such a view can be found in the political ideas of Emrys ap Iwan (Robert Ambrose Jones), ideas which anticipated the founding ideas of twentieth-century Welsh nationalism. Familiarity with European society may well have influenced his language based nationalism. He stood out in his criticism of Welsh Liberalism, attacking its slavish adherence to English capitalism, and its infatuation with sectarian strife and the politics of disestablishment. What was needed was a real Welsh politics, a commitment to Wales and not to England and Wales. Even Cymru Fydd in his view was too temporising and wanted to please the English as well as the Welsh. Politics in Wales was overwhelmingly geared to English structures rather than being fully committed to Wales. The predominance of England and of anglicised values propounded by anglicised Celts prevented Wales and the other Celtic countries from fully being themselves. Thus, he argued, the call should not merely be 'Cymru Gyfan', as Lloyd George wanted, but 'Cymru Rydd, Cymru Gyfan a Chymru Gymreig' (Free Wales, All Wales, Welsh Wales).[64] He was advocating the creation of a strictly Welsh political party, committed to full self-government – something well outside the normal political spectrum in late nineteenth-century Wales. His ideas were not directly influential on any politician, though arguably there are hints of it contemporaneously in T. E. Ellis and in Lloyd George's actions. Certainly Lloyd George felt that the gains made by including the language in the curriculum of Welsh schools during the late 1880s were being offset by attitudes in other areas. This included the appointment of (non-Welsh speaking) county court judges[65] and the attitude of the London and North West Railway Company to the employment of Welsh speaking staff.[66] Later on, there were echoes in the concerns expressed about the philistine emphasis of some Home Rulers because they lacked a spiritual component, a sense of nationhood.

Devolution debates were largely associated with the reform agenda of Liberal Nonconformity, but an alternative vision emerged from the ranks of nationally minded Anglicans who were unable to subscribe to the devolutionary movement as long as disestablishment possessed such a high profile. Conservative nationalism gained some visibility through the writings of John Arthur Price, another of the Oxford Welsh generation. Price argued that

Welsh national identity and other nationalisms were less a product of the radical thought and behaviour which had emanated from the French Enlightenment and Revolution than from reaction against them. That reaction had stressed the continuity of national communities united by language, historical identity and custom, and had thereby revived or enhanced patriotic and national sentiment. This, he argued, had nurtured not only a British patriotism but also a Welsh national sentiment:

> Nationalism aided by the new historical movement, which has gradually developed during the last fifty years, and has reconstructed the past for us, could not help affecting Wales.

He suggested that Welsh national sentiment had been captured by radicalism largely because the natural leaders of Wales, the aristocracy and also the clergy, had become divorced from the mass of Welsh people and were out of sympathy with their culture and aspirations. If they could but re-engage with the Welsh people – and this they could do by reacquiring the Welsh language and by participating in a Welsh system of education – then they could once again lead and save Wales from being in thrall to English radicalism, which in reality had no real sympathy for Welsh aspirations or national identity:

> Wales cannot be for ever radical in the modern sense of the word. A people that is conscious of distinct and peculiar needs, and is proud of its past, cannot permanently accept the levelling doctrines of the English radical movement.

Re-engagement would necessarily involve accepting disestablishment and other reforms in Wales, including by implication devolution, but would allow a healthy Welsh nationalism to be coupled with a continuing loyalty to Britain. He therefore appealed to conservatives in Wales to:

> cease denouncing what they cannot resist; they must cease to stand in isolated reservation from the life of the people; and they must leave silly sneers at their countrymen's hopes and aspirations to English Philistines.[67]

In reality, there was little hope that the majority of the gentry and the great landowners of Wales would join Price in affirming to a Welsh conservatism and to a Welsh politics. They had been subject to too much vituperation in the Welsh press to contemplate sharing much if any common ground with Radicals.[68] On top of that, Gladstone's Irish policies, not only of Home Rule but also of land reform, had driven many erstwhile Liberal or Whig landowners into the Tory and Unionist ranks. This was seen in the support given to the Second Lord Penrhyn's North Wales Property Defence Association whose aims included:

> To use every constitutional means to oppose any special legislation affecting the rights of property, more particularly the creation of any different system of land

laws or land tenure in Wales from England, and to keep before the public the fact that the land tenure and customs are identical in England and Wales.[69]

This reluctance to acknowledge any distinction between England and Wales also marked the attitude of the Anglican hierarchy in the face of increasingly aggressive tactics aimed at securing Church disestablishment. There were some Church efforts to realign with the Welsh people in terms of appointing native and Welsh speaking bishops after 1870 and Welsh liturgical reforms, but Wales's remaining a part of the Establishment and of the Province of Canterbury remained the *sine qua non* for church leaders.[70] Thus, anti-national accusations could be directed at the Church by advocates of disestablishment. The idea of an alien church became part of Radical rhetoric, notably in Lloyd George's speeches during the 1890s.[71] Even so, there were Anglicans of a nationalist, or at least Welsh patriotic, hue, clerics as well as a few laymen such as Arthur Price, who saw some merit in disestablishment in order to Cymru-cise the Church, while there were others who sought to restore a distinctive linguistic and cultural character to the Church as a Welsh national institution to obviate the need for separation. Both these groups of nationalist clergy always amounted to a minority, but they based their ecclesiastical nationalism on historical foundations by reference as far back as to the early British (i.e. Welsh) Church.[72]

Reference back to early and medieval Welsh history applied in other areas of Welsh life also. Irrespective of whether Home Rule would come about, some wanted to make local government in Wales 'more Welsh' by emulating ancient medieval units of government rather than adhering to those imposed after English conquest or which reflected English hegemony. Ironically, this was also regarded as having the merit of recasting local government units to be more efficient for the modern age. One Robert Owen of Welshpool believed that local government reform of a 'particularist' kind, i.e. one which applied to Wales and Wales only, would provide the nation with sufficient distinctiveness that it would avoid the Home Rule question, i.e the need to establish an autonomous parliament. In anticipation of what was to occur some seventy years or more later, Owen proposed the reorganisation of the thirteen Welsh counties into six more substantial similar sized *provinces*, with, additionally, Welsh and early Welsh titles and names to re-emphasise their Welshness.[73] The counties would survive but as *cantons* of the provinces. Borough and parish units were also to be restructured in this fashion and the whole administration of the judicial system, policing and the Poor Law was to be altered accordingly. Even educational and cultural institutions would be organised provincially. Appropriate Welsh medieval labels were to be applied to lesser units and offices and overall administrative responsibility for local government in Wales was to be devolved from the LGB to a Welsh National

Bureau. The administrative link with central government in London was to be maintained by a Minister of State for Wales.[74]

This concern to establish a clear national and cultural identity expressed itself in the literature of the period, particularly of the kind which showed that Wales had an historical and intellectual status. O. M. Edwards was clearly foremost in this enterprise and this undoubtedly coloured his view about education in Wales and the failure as he saw it of the CWB. Edwards had made it clear as early as 1890 that 'race', language and distinctive Welsh thought should all be utilised in pressing for Welsh Home Rule.[75] In his anxiety to ensure that a sense of unity be preserved in Wales he wanted the non-Welsh speakers of Wales, particularly the lower orders of society, to appreciate a common body of literature. This could inculcate a shared spirit of Wales which could be distinctive.[76] Significantly perhaps, he steered clear of politics and appealed for non-partisanship. More distinctively political were the efforts of J. Hugh Edwards and others to produce magazines in the English language which would address devolution and other political questions, as well as the literary and historical material with which Edwards was concerned.[77]

The relationship of language and culture to nationhood (and possibly to justifying self-government) was emphasised in the years before the Great War. This was a reaction against the anglicisation of parts of Wales which seemed to jeopardise a sense of Welsh cultural identity. A notable spokesman for this point of view was the expatriate and non-Welsh speaking scholar, Idris Bell, who was also an espouser of socialist ideas. In a series of articles he stressed the centrality of language to a 'common national consciousness.' To lose a language was to lose a sense of self:

> It may acquire a new self better than the old, but just that old self, that something that is meant to the world, and which no other nation could mean, has ceased to be forever.[78]

The language cause had to be put in a wider context of enhancing the commitment of nationalists:

> We must seek to promote the study of Welsh history, so that to the rising generation the triumphs and sorrows of their forefathers shall be as familiar as the story of England to Englishmen. To arouse a love of literature, of Welsh songs and Welsh traditions, to revive, as far as possible, Welsh customs, to preserve the national love of poetry and music against the inroads of English exaggerated athleticism, to kindle amid wider and yet wider circles the pride of nationality and the enthusiasm for the national cause, to allay the mutual jealousies which have so often proved fatal to Welsh unity, to work for a more liberal recognition of Welsh nationality in matters of government – all these things are tasks which the Nationalist should set before himself.[79]

He saw modern Welsh nationalism as being always self-critical and enlightened, as a middle way between anglicisation and narrow provincial patriotism.[80] He rejected the criticisms of socialists like H. G. Wells, who advocated a universal language, and imperialists like J. E. Vincent, who believed the future lay in integrated Empires.[81] Indeed, as a subscriber to racial stereotypes, Bell – echoing Arnold, Renan and others – believed that Celtic traits of spirituality and imagination could modify the 'coarse Teutonic mind' of the Philistine English.[82]

Mixed into all this were expressions of anti-commercialism, anti-urbanism and of cultural and linguistic survivalism, perennially intruding on an idealised self-contained, historically aware community and nation:

> We all know, and too well, what gifts we receive from England – football, the betting fever, commercialism, the 'Daily Mail'. Too often it is for these things that the Anglicized parts of Wales exchange the harp, the englyn, the eisteddfod. Doubtless they have penetrated into the Welsh-speaking districts also, but they have not there destroyed the national life of the people. It cannot be too often insisted upon that in pleading the cause of the Welsh language we are defending, not the nationality only, precious as that is, [but] the soul of Wales.[83]

Such expressions were not new nor were they to disappear after the Great War. The sense of a coherent community fracturing was a concern for many social thinkers and reformers.[84]

Symbolism and federalism

Some institutional credibility was given to the language and culture of Wales, notably through the foundation of a national museum, a national library and a records commission. All these were not secured without some effort from the Welsh Parliamentary Party, or parts of it. But these gains were mixed blessings, since there was little unanimity about which was the proper location for these national symbols and there was no little jockeying on the part of aspirant middle class Welshmen to acquire posts and offices. The transfer of the semi-official Welsh National Memorial Association from its original location in Newtown, Montgomeryshire, to Cardiff, reawakened north-south differences, but also raised the question of providing the aspirant nation with a proper capital city:

> the desirability of the creation of a capital for Wales which shall not only serve to symbolise the national entity of Wales, after the manner of England, Scotland and Ireland, but shall also give place and hospitality to such of our institutions and movements as affect the interests and welfare of our people as a whole.[85]

Although there were views about re-centring some functions other than in Cardiff – Aberystwyth was favoured[86] – the place, in spite of its ambiguous 'cosmopolitan' character, had made strides in capturing aspects of national sentiment which were indicative of its determination to lead Wales. It elevated itself as a venue for modern sport and for commemorating in pageant the heroism of the Welsh past in Owen Rhoscomyl's productions. It organised the competition to name the ten greatest Welshmen in order to tender for statutes of those Welsh heroes, paid for by D. A. Thomas, to be set in City Hall. It successfully beat back Swansea's challenge to locate the national museum there, and had pretensions to be the leading centre for science in Wales. Its aspiration to be an imperial capital was also marked by Cardiff Corporation having led the campaign to include a Welsh symbol on the royal standard in 1897.[87]

Indeed, it had been at Cardiff in 1897 that Lord Rosebery had offered hope to Welsh nationalists in the Liberal Party by his comments to the National Liberal Federation on the imperial ideal. He argued that although there were issues that were regarded as central by the Welsh, Scots or Irish, they did not necessarily meet with much interest among an English audience. The solution was to have a system of devolved government such as in the Empire.[88] Admittedly, this was electioneering but it was the exact opposite of what Arthur Balfour had been saying to a Tory audience in Manchester, i.e. that devolution would destroy the Empire, betray Ulster and 'destroy English policies, English finances and the English Constitution'.[89]

Rosebery's comments implied that there could be a future in Home Rule All Round. This idea had fired the first Cymru Fydd effort in the later 1880s. It had inspired both Welsh Liberal Federations to hold talks with the Scottish Home Rule Association in 1890. While this led to some common ground it had no real long-term implications. Many Welsh Liberals were still committed to the Newcastle Programme which put Irish Home Rule and Welsh disestablishment as priorities. Even so, there was some interest in how the Scots would proceed, if only so Wales could plead for comparable treatment. In 1893–94 the Welsh Parliamentary Party supported and sought to imitate Scottish demands for a grand committee and there were efforts to secure support for Sir Henry Dalziel's motion on Scottish Home Rule.[90] In 1895, Lloyd George was attracted to the prospect of Home Rule All Round, but found that indicative Welsh opinion was still strongly in favour of Welsh disestablishment as a priority. There was some sympathy from Scots and English Liberals, but the Irish Nationalists were distinctly cool on the idea if it meant diluting Ireland's primacy.[91]

Home Rule All Round remained an aim of Lloyd George and some of his allies during the period of Tory governments of 1895–1905, but he failed to convince British Liberal leaders, and some Welsh Liberals objected to it as well. The logic of securing local parliaments in order to enact disestablishment and other desiderata and of not giving unnecessary precedence to Ireland was insufficiently convincing.[92]

The federal solution continued to raise its head among some Welsh politicians and writers even as the disestablishment question and its attendant educational issue led Welsh politics to look for specific Welsh solutions. The failure to secure a Welsh National Education Council after 1903, and the growing frustrations over the delays in promoting disestablishment after 1906, led to an interest in bodies such as the Federal Union Committee[93] and in attempts by the Scots to formulate a measure of Home Rule All Round. Although many Welsh MPs were still more devoted to single issue campaigns to make a federal initiative a real prospect,[94] it seemed a positive sign that about half the Welsh MPs, Liberal and Labour, supported various Scottish and federal home rule bills after 1906.[95]

Policy motivations and limitations

Indeed, Home Rule sentiments were still very evident, encouraged by the institutional developments and the elements of devolved administration or executive responsibility which had been given to Wales. Moreover, such sentiments were not merely driven by language and cultural considerations or by the symbolic recognition of Wales in the royal firmament,[96] but by attempts to define policy and identify what a future Wales might want. The Welsh Parliamentary Party was busily engaged in organising sub-committees to investigate select aspects of Welsh life, notably concerning itself with the regeneration of Welsh rural society.[97] Other writers produced proposals concerning health, transport reforms, radical changes in the agrarian economy and educational restructuring, with the idea of a national council still being broached.[98] Where there were limitations was in conducting investigations into Welsh industry or even regarding industrial Wales as one entity. The north-south distinction came out quite clearly and was indicative of a broader bifurcation. There was also a generational question. It was pointed out that political leadership in Wales was inaccessible to a younger generation. The dynamic young Cymru Fydd stalwarts of T. E. Ellis's day had become middle aged and establishmentarian. They were shutting out the youthful dynamism of a succeeding generation.[99]

Although E. T. John's Government of Wales Bill in 1914 set out to establish a comprehensive structure of domestic self-government based on powers which had been devolved already, he was not fully supported by Welsh MPs.[100] In part this was because they did not want to jeopardise the disestablishment legislation which was proceeding through Parliament,[101] but also because they felt that Irish Home Rule (which was similarly threatened by Tory opposition) took precedence. In part, as well, it was a question of determining the appropriate course to take in negotiating between local and Welsh national interests. The devolved legislature would have a preponderance of members from Glamorgan and Monmouthshire and cultural nationalists from the north feared this would not deliver the type of nation they wanted. An alternative was to have a cabinet representative at the heart of imperial government as some, including a few Conservatives for anti-home rule purposes, now thought more preferable.[102]

The critique of John's proposals also suggested that there were inherent deficiencies in Welsh society and in the Welsh character which made the adoption of home rule unwise. The smallness of the nation, the implied racial characteristics of narrowness and cliquishness and unsteady temperament all implied an unfitness for full self-government. This was all the more so given the emergent threats from socialism and industrial conflict and the 'baser' democracy of the industrial south.[103] The political nationalists of the inter-war period were to perceive the same threats but come to a different conclusion.

In the meantime, the Liberal E. T. John remained the principal Welsh campaigner for Welsh devolution during and immediately after the Great War. In that war, Wales again gained some institutional credibility with the creation of the Welsh Army Corps (Lloyd George's Army) and of the Welsh Guards. Politically, the majority of Welsh MPs concentrated on ensuring that the Welsh Church Disestablishment Act, suspended for the duration of the war, would be implemented thereafter. Appropriately, those Welsh politicians who showed any interest at all concentrated on rationalising education by means of a Welsh National Education Council, but it was observed that little thought had been given to funding issues or to working out the relationship between such a council and the Board of Education.

Such lapses thus did not augur well for the more ambitious devolutionary ideas which were to emerge after 1918, but much had taken place in the nature of Welsh nationalism by 1918. On the positive side, a concern to identify what was precious in Welsh life had developed and was given some institutional representation. Education, religion, language, history had to be developed and valued, for without this devolution would develop a nation with representative institutions but no soul. At the same time, devolved administration of these key areas was creating a cadre of Welsh public servants who believed that these key issues were being developed through their efforts. A more active anti-Englishness, like a positive engagement with the experiences of English-speaking Welshmen in the south, were minority trends within nationalism before 1914. However, and in the longer term, parties grew which could exploit or see the need to address these aspects of Welsh life.

Notes

1 For a narrative, see Edgar L. Chappell, *Wake Up Wales! A Survey of Welsh Home Rule Activities* (London, 1943).

2 Miroslav Hroch, *Social Preconditions of National Revival in Europe: A Comparative Analysis of Patriotic Groups among the Smaller European Nations*, tr. Ben Fowkes (Cambridge, 1985); Edward Shils, 'Nation, nationality, nationalism and civil society', *Nations and Nationalism*, 1 (1995). One might add that in addition to an essentialist character there were perennialist traits too which hinted at bio-ethnicity derived possibly from the writings of Iolo Morganwg (Edward Williams) in the late eighteenth century. Cf . Anthony D. Smith, *The Nation in History: Historical Debates About Ethnicity and Nationalism* (London, 2000) and Geraint H. Jenkins (ed.), *A Rattleskull Genius: The Many Faces of Iolo Morganwg* (Cardiff, 2005).

3 Cf. Emyr W. Williams, 'Liberalism in Wales and the politics of Welsh Home Rule 1886–1910', *Bulletin of the Board of Celtic Studies*, 37 (1990).

4 R. Paul Evans, 'Thomas Pennant (1726–1798): the "father of Cambrian tourists" ', *WHR*, 13 (1987), esp. 412ff.; Caryl Davies, ' "Romantic Jones": the picturesque and politics on the south Wales circuit, 1775–1781', *NLWJ*, 28 (1994).

5 Mark Ellis Jones, ' "An invidious attempt to accelerate the extinction of our language": the abolition of the Court of Great Sessions and the Welsh language', *WHR*, 19 (1998), esp. 242ff.

6 Matthew Cragoe, 'A question of culture: the Welsh Church and the bishopric of St Asaph', *WHR*, 18 (1996).

7 Henry Richard, 'Cymru Fu: a retrospect', *CF*, 1:1 (1888), 67.

8 Prys Morgan (ed.), *Brad y Llyfrau Gleision* (Llandysul, 1991); Gwyneth Tyson Roberts, *The Language of the Blue Books: The Perfect Instrument of Empire* (Cardiff, 1998); Jodie Kreider, ' "Degraded and Benighted": gendered constructions of Wales in the Empire, ca. 1847', *North American Journal of Welsh Studies*, 2 (2002) [www2.bc.edu/~ellisjg/Kreider.html].

9 Ivor Wilks, *South Wales and the Rising of 1839* (London, 1984), chs. 12–13.

10 A. Pendragon, 'Our "red dragons" at Westminster', *Red Dragon*, 1 (1882), 454.

11 Bedwyr Lewis Jones, 'Theophilus Evans' in Dyfnallt Morgan (ed.), *Gwŷr Llên y Ddeunawfed Ganrif a'u Cefndir* (Llandybïe, 1966).

12 Prys Morgan, *The Eighteenth Century Enlightenment* (Llandybïe, 1981), ch. 5.

13 Gwyn A. Williams, 'Ambiguous hero: Hugh Owen and Liberal Wales', in Gwyn A. Williams, *The Welsh in their History* (London, 1982), ch. 6.

14 *Y Cymmrodor*, 3 (1880).

15 Apparently, his ideas about devolved government had been maturing since 1879.

16 'Problems of reconstruction (in 1882)', *THSC 1917–18*, 246–55. Note the significance of the title given it is in relation to post-war Wales.

17 Literally, Future Wales or Wales To Be, but often translated as Young Wales. Parry republished his scheme in his *The Cry of the People* (c. 1906), pp. 139–48.

18 'Cymru'r colegau: Rhydychen, Caergrawnt', *CF*, 2 (1889), 700–3: 'this society is doing excellent work by proffering information about their country's history, and interest in its literature, to the future leaders of Wales'.

19 A Member of the Society, *Home Rule for Wales: What Does It Mean?* (London, c.1890).
20 Ibid.
21 UWB, Coetmor papers 49.
22 A Special Correspondent (J. E. Vincent), *Letters from Wales: A Republication . . . of a Series of Letters dealing with the State of Wales* (1889), ch. 5.
23 *The Scotsman*, 2 January 1890, in Coetmor MS 49.
24 William Hughes Jones, *Wales Drops the Pilots* (London, 1937), pp. 11–12, 29–31.
25 Drawn on the questionnaire organised by the *Carnarvon and Denbigh Herald*, 18 January 1890, seeking 'the views of representative men', in Coetmor MS 49.
26 'Notes – Welsh home rule', *CF*, 3 (1890), 114–15. 'Hasten slowly – little by little a man will go far.'
27 *British Weekly*, 1, 8 February 1890 in ibid.
28 J. Graham Jones, 'Early campaigns to secure a secretary of State for Wales, 1890–1939', *THSC 1988*, 153–5.
29 NLW, J. Herbert Lewis papers C1, Minutes of the Welsh Parliamentary Party, p. 14, dat. 18 February 1890.
30 *The Times*, 3 October 1888.
31 *Westminster Review*, 133:4 (1890), 394–5.
32 51 & 52 Vict. c.41.
33 J. R. Webster, 'Dyheadau'r bedwaredd ganrif ar bymtheg', in Jac L. Williams (ed.), *Ysgrifau ar Addysg* IV: *Addysg i Gymru (Ysgrifau Hanesyddol)* (Caerdydd, 1966), pp. 64–7.
34 J. Herbert Lewis D 9, S. B. Provis of the LGB, 29 June 1889.
35 Printed *Circular* from W. N. Bruce at the Board of Education to all the LEAs in Wales and Monmouthshire, 10 April 1905, in J. Herbert Lewis D9.
36 25 April 1892, J. Herbert Lewis D9.
37 *NWC*, 21 September 1904. Conservatives in Caernarfonshire were equally concerned about southern domination and also, importantly, about the loss of local control to a centralised institution (ibid., 10 December 1904).
38 Kenneth O. Morgan, *Freedom or Sacrilege? A History of the Campaign for Welsh Disestablishment* (Bridgend, 1966), pp. 18–20.
39 J. Graham Jones, 'Lloyd George, *Cymru Fydd* and the Newport meeting of January 1896', *NLWJ*, 29 (1996).
40 J. Herbert Lewis D2, Ellis's report to the Welsh Party, Lloyd George and D. A. Thomas being critical.
41 *Manchester Guardian*, 4 January 1895.
42 John Grigg, *The Young Lloyd George* (London, 1973).
43 J. Herbert Lewis D2, subjects with which the Welsh Party has to deal – Disestablishment and disendowment; temperance reform; a land commission; a chapel sites bill; county court judgeships; a Welsh grand committee; a national council bill; magisterial appointments; a university charter; a Great Forest of Brecknock bill.
44 T. Marchant Williams, *Welsh Members of Parliament, 1894* (Cardiff, 1894), passim; Emyr W. Williams, 'Liberalism in Wales', 200–1.
45 J. Graham Jones, ' "Quietly I hope to push on Welsh questions substantially": Thomas Edward Ellis as second whip', *Journal of the Merioneth Historical and Record Society*, 14 (2004).

46 What appealed about Scotland, in addition to its judicial and ecclesiastical uniqueness, was its success in achieving piecemeal administrative devolution during the course of the century through various boards with delegated powers and a formalising of ministerial oversight with a Secretary of State in 1885 (George S. Pryde, *Central and Local Government in Scotland Since 1707* (London, 1960), pp. 18–20). There was also an interest in Scottish legislation in 1897 which enabled the Scottish Office to vet private bills and the processes of provisional orders in Scotland, witness Vaughan Davies's Private Legislation Procedure (Wales) Bill of 1904 ('Welsh Devolution', *NWC*, 15, 16 July 1904).

47 *Speeches and Addresses by the late Thomas E. Ellis, M.P.* (Wrexham, 1912), esp. pp. 227–41 on Welsh land laws. Their publication in 1912 coincided with a new push to promote Welsh Home Rule.

48 The bill proposed to institute a separate Welsh judicial system to oversee land-lord-tenant relations, which heavily favoured the farmer (*NWC*, 21 May 1887).

49 J. Graham Jones, 'Select committee or royal commission?: Wales and the "land question", 1892', *WHR*, 17 (1994).

50 Richard Lewis, 'The Welsh radical tradition and the ideal of a democratic popular culture', in Eugenio F. Biagini (ed.), *Citizenship and Community: Liberals, radicals and Collective Identities in the British Isles, 1865–1931* (Cambridge, 1996), pp. 325–40.

51 J. Herbert Lewis papers D9.

52 By 1914, Evans became concerned at the future need for Welsh civil servants given the various national bodies which had been created possessing delegated powers from London (*Wales: The National Magazine* [hereinafter *Wales*], 5 (1913–14), 201). Cf. also Thomas Jones, *Welsh Broth* (London, 1951), pp. 135–40. Jones's hostility to John Rowland may not only have been a matter of personality but also one of ideology, with Rowland being seemingly too nationalistic.

53 Percy Watkins, *A Welshman Remembers: An Autobiography* (Cardiff, 1944), pp. 53–6.

54 Leslie Wyn Evans, *Studies in Welsh Education: Welsh Educational Structure and Administration 1880–1925* (Cardiff, 1974).

55 'Our point of view', *The Nationalist: A Non-Political Magazine for Wales*, 1:4 (1907), 5.

56 'Our point of view', ibid., 4:34 (1911), 6, and 4:40 (1912), 6–7.

57 Emlyn Sherrington, 'O.M. Edwards, culture and the industrial classes', *Llafur*, 6:1 (1992), 28–41; Pyrs Gruffudd, 'Yr iaith Gymraeg a'r dychymyg daearyddol 1918–1950', in Geraint H. Jenkins (ed.), *'Eu Hiaith a Gadwant?' Y Gymraeg yn yr Ugeinfed Ganrif* (Caerdydd, 2000), pp. 101–22.

58 'The University of Wales', *The Nationalist*, 1, 4 (1907), 9–11; 'Our point of view', ibid., 1:1 (1907), 7; ibid., 4:40 (1912), 7–9.

59 A Celt, *Cymru Fydd Gymru Rydd* (Carnarvon, 1895), pp. 23–8, including the criticisms of Oxford educated Welshmen, W. Llewelyn Williams and Owen M. Edwards.

60 'Welsh nationality and Welsh patriotism', *Trans. Liverpool Welsh National Society*, 6th Session 1890–1, 13–22.

61 T. Darlington., 'Iaith a chenedlaetholdeb', ibid., 32–43.

62 'Yr hen flwyddyn', *CF*, 4:1 (1891), 3. The Welsh language came into greater prominence in 1890 than ever before. The Government promised to pay

schoolmasters for teaching it in the day schools, the report of the commission investigating the effects of the Sunday Closing Act was published in it, and the agenda of the county councils are also printed in it, despite the spirit of Henry VIII's law [i.e. the language clause of the first act of union, 1536].

63 As the Report on Welsh in Education and Life found in 1927. The Report was a byproduct of the limited administrative devolution given to Wales in education. *Y Gymraeg Mewn Addysg a Bywyd* (Llundain, 1927), Rhan III and cf. a brief account of Davies and the Society on pp. 64–7.

64 D. Myrddin Lloyd (ed.), *Erthyglau Emrys ap Iwan*, vol. I (1937), ch. 3, 'Paham y gorfu'r Undebwyr' (Why should there be Unionists?). The republication of Emrys's essays in three volumes between 1937 and 1940, and their dedication to each of the three nationalists jailed for burning the bombing school at Penyberth, was significant.

65 Mark Ellis Jones, ' "Wales for the Welsh?": the Welsh county court judgeships, c.1868–1900', *WHR*, 19 (1999).

66 Dot Jones, *The Coming of the Railways and Language Change in north Wales 1850–1900* (Aberystwyth, 1985).

67 J. Arthur Price, 'Welsh nationalism and revolutionary politics', *CF*, 2 (1889), esp. 431, 434, 436. Also, J. Arthur Price, 'Welsh education and Welsh public life', ibid., 2 (1889), 593–604. For Price, see Frances Knight, 'Welsh Nationalism and Anglo-Catholicism: the politics and religion of J. Arthur Price (1861–1942)', in Robert Pope (ed.), *Religion and National Identity: Wales and Scotland c. 1700–2000* (Cardiff, 2001), pp. 123–38.

68 *The Times*, 25 September 1890.

69 Rules of Constitution and Byelaws of the North Wales Property Defence Association (4 August 1887), in Parlimentary Papers 1894, C.-7439.-II, *Royal Commission on Land in Wales and Monmouthshire, Minutes of Evidence*, vol. II, 921.

70 Asserted, for example, in J. E. de Hirsch-Davies, *A Popular History of the Church in Wales from the Beginning to the Present Day* (London, 1912), chs. 21–2.

71 For example, 'Mr Lloyd-George, M.P., on Welsh Disestablishment', *North Wales Observer and Express*, 27 April 1894.

72 Henry T. Edwards, *Wales and the Welsh Church: Papers* (1889); David Jones, *The Welsh Church and Welsh Nationality* (n.d., c.1893). The role of Anglican clergymen in the Welsh evangelical (Methodist) revival of the eighteenth century was also highlighted, notably in accounts of Daniel Rowland and Thomas Charles.

73 The *taleithiau* of West Gwynedd; East Gwynedd; Powys; Demetia; Siluria; Glamorgan.

74 Robert Owen, Welshpool, 'A plea for Welsh particularism: vi. Cymru Fydd', *YW*, 5 (1899), 265–73.

75 'The New Round Table, "Home Rule for Wales" ', *Westminster Review*, 133 (1890), 397–400.

76 *Wales: A National Magazine for the English Speaking Parts of Wales*, 1 (1894), iii-iv, Introduction. An attempted counterpart to his *Cymru* for Welsh speakers, it proved less successful.

77 The *Cymru Fydd* journal had made some attempt to combine both Welsh language and English language articles. Its change of editor from the highly politicised radical T. J. Hughes, to O. M. Edwards and the Revd R. H. Morgan had

witnessed some attempt to introduce literary and historical subjects but without apparently encouraging much enthusiasm by the time the journal ceased in 1891.

78 Idris o'r Ynys, 'The national ideal', *The Nationalist*, 1:10 (1907), 7–8.

79 Ibid., 9–10.

81 Ibid., 11.

81 H. Idris Bell, 'Nationality and empire: I', *The Nationalist*, 2:18 (1908), 16–20.

82 Ibid. and H. Idris Bell, 'Nationality and empire: II', *The Nationalist*, 2:19 (1908), 22–4; 'Matthew Arnold on the Eisteddfod and the Welsh Language', ibid., 2:22 (1908), 4.

83 H. Idris Bell, 'An appeal to Welshmen', *The Nationalist*, 4:32 (1910), 47–8.

84 Cf. PP 1917, Cd. 8668, Commission of Inquiry into Industrial Unrest: No. 7 Division. *Report of the Commissioners for Wales, including Monmouthshire*, esp. pp. 11–17; Julie Light, 'The 1917 Commission of Enquiry into Industrial Unrest – a Welsh report', *WHR*, 21 (2003), 704–28. See also Williams below, p. 146.

85 'The month in Wales', *Wales*, 4 (1913), 119.

86 H. Stanley Jevons, 'How to make Wales a nation', *Wales*, 4 (1913), 257–8.

87 Neil Evans, 'The Welsh Victorian city: the middle class and civic and national consciousness in Cardiff, 1850–1914', *WHR*, 12 (1985), 350–87.

88 *The Times*, 19 January 1895.

89 Ibid., 18 January 1895.

90 NLW, J. Herbert Lewis C1, pp. 38–9, 83; and ibid. D9.

91 D. Lloyd-George, 'National self-government for Wales', *YW*, 1 (1895), 231–5, on federalism, and 'Our Round Table Conference', ibid., 235 ff. See also McMahon above for the post-war tensions between Welsh and Irish Home Rulers.

92 D. Lloyd-George, 'The place of national self-government in the next Liberal programme', *YW*, 3 (1897), 11–15; T. Artemus Jones, 'Among the Welsh members: home rule all round', ibid., 4 (1898), 90–2.

93 A federal union 'to give special and fuller effect to the domestic requirement of the several nationalities constituting the United Kingdom' (J. Herbert Lewis D9).

94 NLW, J. Herbert Lewis papers A2/50, Lewis to Lloyd George, 27 January 1911.

95 Edward T. John MP, *Home Rule For Wales: addresses to 'Young Wales'* (Bangor, 1912), pp. vi–viii.

96 John S. Ellis, 'Reconciling the Celt: British national identity, empire, and the 1911 investiture of the Prince of Wales', *JBS*, 37 (1998).

97 'Welsh political notes'. By a Welsh Member, *Wales*, 4 (1913), 176–9.

98 James Evans, ' The future of agriculture in Wales', ibid., 4 (1914), 351–5.

99 Evan R. Davies, 'Administrative Wales', ibid., 6 (1914), 251–2.

100 J. Graham Jones, 'E. T. John and Welsh Home Rule, 1910–1914', *WHR*, 13 (1987).

101 'Wales and its Bill. An interview with the chairman of the Welsh Parliamentary Party', *Wales*, 6 (1914), 177–81.

102 W. Llewelyn Williams, KC, MP, 'The National Needs of Wales I – A Secretary of State', ibid., 6 (1914), 8–11; W. Ormsby-Gore, MP, 'A Secretaryship for Wales', ibid., 189

103 J. Vyrnwy Morgan, *A Study in Nationality* (London, 1911), pp. 427–39. A Welsh Office and Minister was his favoured solution.

5
Welsh national identity and governance, 1918–45

Andrew Edwards and Wil Griffith

Before 1914 the nationalist movement was largely associated with the Liberal Party, even if there were some outside this or who operated in Liberal pressure groups (like Cymru Fydd). After 1918 this changed. As the Liberal Party went into decline, and new issues had to be faced, 'nationalists' began to quarrel more loudly amongst themselves. Supporters of greater Welsh devolution could be found in all parties, albeit to varying degrees. Some ex-Liberals gave up on party politics altogether and put their efforts into governance (many of the 'social liberals' discussed in Chris Williams' chapter fall into this category). Others became increasingly concerned with developing cultural, literary, pan-Celtic or even international organisations. This included the Celtic League (E. T. John's concern from the mid-1920s) the League of Nations (David Davies MP and a host of others) and the Fellowship of Reconciliation (as with the Christian pacifist, George Maitland Lloyd Davies). A small minority – drawn from a range of parties and from none – founded Plaid Genedlaethol Cymru ('the Welsh Nationalist Party', known popularly as 'Plaid' or 'Y Blaid') in 1925.

This chapter looks at the divisions within nationalism, focusing on the way nationalists perceived the Welsh nation – and Welsh governance – in the period from 1918 to the end of the Second World War. The dates are not inconsequential. The chapter begins with the hopes raised by the Speaker's conference on devolution. It ends with attempts to ensure that post-war reconstruction after 1945 addressed the position of Wales more successfully than after the first great conflict. Rather than focus on political campaigns – covered at length elsewhere – it studies what was *behind* these movements. It notes the doubts and concerns over what would happen to the values, traditions – and especially the language – of Wales in a world which was modernising and becoming more evidently 'English'. 'Nationalists', as used here are thus not simply those who formed the Plaid Genedlaethol Cymru, but those who felt that there was a Welsh nation, with a distinctive sense of identity which needed to be fostered and preserved.

It is argued that whilst some of the Liberals' pre-war reforms evidently defused the extent of Home Rule tendencies within Wales, cultural and especially linguistic concerns remained significant. Indeed, the shock to Nonconformist values presented by the war (or at least men's xenophobic commitment to its prosecution) alongside adverse reports on the decline of the Welsh language created something of a backlash. Nonetheless, the first section of this chapter shows how, despite these cross-party cultural interests, the Speaker's Conference witnessed the collapse of a 'nationalist' movement on political and other grounds. The second section indicates that for nationalists working within the existing methods of governing Wales there was still scope for conflict when the nation was 'slighted' by regulations and attitudes which (seemingly) followed English needs. The third section shows how nationalism divided with the formation of a Nationalist party which was at times anti-modernist and anti-English. Its own, often ignored, attempts to address this emphasis were never sufficient to attract mass popular support from Labour voters (although it did attract some ex-Labour activists). Addressing economic concerns was frequently superseded by active campaigning in defence of Welsh language and culture, which sometimes stepped outside the traditions of Welsh liberalism and alienated many potential supporters. The formation of Plaid was thus not a highpoint of a nationalist political movement, but a sign of its disintegration. The fourth section examines the extent to which campaigns for a Secretary of State for Wales during the 1930s crystallised concerns over cultural and linguistic decline augmented by wartime events, providing an opportunity to rekindle a sense of national unity. In the event, the moment passed without any major political shift taking place.

The wartime inheritance

The formation of a coalition government to fight a war against Prussianism naturally pushed party politics underground during the war. Welsh Liberals were perhaps especially responsive to the appeal for unity, since many already felt that politics should be above class and should be concerned with moral regeneration. The voluntaryist effort to sustain, advance or protect social or cultural issues in Wales was kept alive through the continued work of the Welsh School of Social Service. Its progressive concerns included support for the Welsh language and (from the 1920s) for Welsh language broadcasting. It was especially keen for Wales to be seen as a nation committed to the principles of world peace and international security.[1] There was much here that Liberals of many persuasions could accept. Liberals also continued to be concerned with pre-war issues like disestablishment and this was a distinct barrier to non-partisanship. Because the implementation of the Welsh Church Disestablishment Act 1914 was suspended for the duration of the war, some felt that this long-standing Welsh national aim could still be frustrated, particularly when the Conservatives joined the wartime government. Churchmen opposed further 'Home Rule' in the Welsh Department of the Board of Education fearing the consequences for the Church schools.[2] Wartime experiences did, however, wear down the denominational and political rivalries, particularly given the way that disendowment was more sensitively handled. Moreover, the war years allowed Churchmen to prepare for disestablishment and create a suitable constitution for the 'devolved', autonomous Anglican province of the Church in Wales which came into being in 1920.

The church settlement, it would seem, might have permitted a more consensual national politics to have emerged but in fact the war, and its aftermath, were to be unsettling influences. They raised doubts about cultural identities of national groupings and raised questions about the autonomy in governance of national groupings.

The xenophobia and barbarism of war shocked a Welsh language world in which religion and peace were valued aims. The 1921 census – like the 1927 study, *Welsh in Education and Life* – also revealed how far the Welsh language was in decline.[3] Reactions included the formation of literary and academic journals like *Y Llenor*, which became a vehicle for prominent figures from the emergent Nationalist Party, such as W. J. Gruffydd, Ambrose Bebb, Saunders Lewis and Kate Roberts. Other developments included the formation of a Welsh language youth movement (*Urdd Gobaith Cymru*) and the production of patriotic (but not nationalist) histories and other studies of Wales in the Welsh language by university academics. Nor did devolved administration ignore the cultural world. The Welsh Department of the Board of Education produced guidelines encouraging the teaching of Welsh history and the Welsh language in schools and permitting the celebration of St David's Day. Higher education became a topic of national discussion as a result of the crisis of funding in the national federal university. Sir Isambard Owen, vice chancellor of the university, pressed for the establishment of an effective central organisation which could bargain with the Treasury for higher funds and decide on allocations to the respective colleges.[4] Governments in fact steadily permitted concessions to address the concerns and petitions of cultural nationalists. In the 1930s the National Government agreed to support cultural research through the formation of the Board of Celtic Studies, a unit within the national university. Following several years of concerted lobbying – including efforts to get a Welsh speaker on the governing body of the BBC[5] – a separate Welsh Region of the BBC was created in 1937. Its was staffed by Welsh speaking officials, appointed to secure Welsh culture and introduce some

Welsh language broadcasting as well as broadcasting about Wales in English.[6] A department of folk culture was founded at the National Museum in 1936. The Welsh Department of the Board of Education supported the development of Welsh language education and addressed concerns over the invisibility of the Welsh past by reforming the history curriculum.

The Speaker's Conference and its aftermath

All this was not initially sufficient to satisfy Welsh opinion. It did not remedy cultural concerns nor provide a political expression of the Welsh nation. President Wilson's Fourteen Points had seemingly recognised the principle of self-determination.[7] Moreover, in the aftermath of war and in discussions of reconstruction, devolution was seen (both in Wales and in London) as a means of lessening the burden on an already overstretched Westminster.[8] Wales, some argued, should be 'rewarded' with devolution following the nation's war efforts. The point was made quite extensively, notably by the Welsh radicals' journal, the *Welsh Outlook*. The government, it claimed, 'took readily all Wales's services and heavy sacrifices in the war, but it never seems to have given a serious thought for her in its plans of reconstruction'.[9] Wales had too often been slighted: 'the claim of Wales to be anything but thirteen counties of the Kingdom of England is positively denied . . . the government came before the world as the champions of freedom in Bohemia and Poland; to Wales they offer the policies of Edward the first'.[10]

Even before the end of the war in 1918, Welsh MPs and local authority representatives had held preliminary discussions on devolution at a conference in Llandrindod Wells. A year later in 1919, the Speaker's Conference appeared to demonstrate revived interest in London. More meetings and conferences in Wales followed, notably at Llandrindod in 1919 and Shrewsbury in 1921.

As has been suggested elsewhere in this volume, the Speakers' Conference of 1919 was largely ineffective because of a failure to agree between two suggested schemes of devolution, and because it uncovered suppressed doubts over the desirability of devolution.[11] Its proceedings received a mixed reaction in Wales. Many supporters of devolution were critical of the Speakers' Conference and its participants. As one argued, the rationale for devolution for Scotland and Wales was that the 'Imperial' government had served both nations badly. Participants had demonstrated themselves to be 'in the very worst sense, fanatical House of Commons men':

> They are not men who, perhaps, care particularly for the reputation of that discredited assembly . . . [or] perhaps specially anxious to expose or repress the corruption, the jobbery or servility which runs like cankers through the

Parliamentary life of today, but they are devoted to Parliamentary system of centralisation of party funds and bureaucracy.

It was not surprising, therefore, that neither scheme offered a devolved Welsh Parliament substantial powers. Britain had developed in a 'plutocratic' state where:

'Big Businesses' and 'Big Combines' are supreme in the House of Commons, and big businesses and big combines have no intention of tolerating nationalism in their sphere of operations.[12]

The Speaker's scheme for devolution, which consisted of 'Grand Councils' with nominated members selected from the Commons and Lords, simply served to preserve the power of the elite when:

What every Welsh patriot desires is to cut Welsh local affairs away from the corruption and jobbery that are rife in the Palace of Westminster. The Speakers proposal will make this jobbery and corruption worse, for there will be lucrative places going in the Executive Committees, which will act as Ministers of the Grand Council.

Other 'farcical' recommendations and suggestions – in particular that a Welsh Grand Council could sit in London – were treated with contempt, as 'a Council or Parliament that does not sit in its own country can only be an object of ridicule'. The Murray MacDonald scheme was no better received, having failed to give Wales 'the power of the purse' and for making the proposed Assembly 'in every way subordinate to the Westminster Parliament'. However, 'It does give them at least a real Parliament with real Ministries . . . does remove some part of their local affairs away from English control'.

Welsh MPs were no more impressed. J. Huw Edwards (the Liberal MP for Neath) accused the government of 'slighting' his country. 'Wales', he said, 'was a greater nation than Ireland and Scotland' due to the fact that it had its own language. He argued that there were strong national and racial sentiments in Wales, of the level required to 'run Wales properly'.[13] Some went further, arguing that the superior democratic values of the Welsh people were being stifled. Devolution was:

The only possible way in which a nation can make a maximum contribution to the material and spiritual necessities not only of itself, but of the great community which it forms a part . . . [Wales could] . . . give to the world as fine, as rich, as complete an example of a pure democracy as this world has seen.[14]

Nonetheless, neither the shared sense of the 'insult' to Wales, nor the common concern with cultural decline was sufficient to recreate a nationalist 'coalition'. Some were willing to compromise and accept the appointment of a Secretary of State, hence securing parity with Scotland. David Davies, the

MP for Montgomeryshire, saw this as a vital, piecemeal, first step towards self-government:

> It has always appeared to me that the establishment of a Welsh Office was a necessary fore-runner of a Welsh legislature. This has already been the subject of a heated controversy . . . [but] . . . it should be clear that the setting up of a Welsh Office is the most logical line of development. Whether this office is in Wales or in London does not seem to be of supreme importance.[15]

In making his case for a Welsh Secretary, however, Davies highlighted the competing concerns which often divided devolutionists:

> Energies in the past have been often dissipated through lack of unity . . . it is no use saying that we want a Welsh parliament but . . . it must not reside in Cardiff . . . no use saying that there should be a Welsh parliament, but that the preponderating voting power must not be in the hands of any one or two or three counties . . . no use saying that we want a Welsh parliament, but because Mr. So-and-so hopes to become the first P.M. the scheme will not work . . . no use saying that we want a separate administration . . . then turn down the scheme because . . . certain individuals are candidates for the post of Welsh Secretary.[16]

Other concerns expressed were equally pragmatic and perceptive. Labour and Liberals alike feared the prospects of a Conservative at the 'Welsh Office', arguing that 'under Tory administrations, it would be a centre of reaction'.[17] The *Welsh Outlook* questioned whether:

> There is one man living in the world today who is competent to take charge of Welsh Education, Welsh Agriculture, Welsh Licensing, Welsh Health, Welsh Local Government, Welsh Industry and Transport, Welsh Public Works and a score of minor other matters? To ask the question is to answer it.[18]

Similarly, for Home Rulers like E. T. John, calls for the appointment of a Secretary of State were misguided. Yet his alternative plans were also far from popular with nationalists in the north in particular. Some of the more culturally focused nationalists found it difficult to come to terms with the realities of modern Wales, expressing an anti-modernism and anti-industrialism which was to become more apparent in the 1930s. W. Ambrose Bebb (one of the founding members of Plaid) feared that E. T. John's proposed ninety-five member Assembly would result in at least fifty members emanating from the south. This, according to Bebb, 'would put agricultural and pastoral Wales at the mercy of miners'. Bebb's solution was a second, democratically elected chamber, safeguarding the 'poorer parts of Wales' against the 'possible and supposed selfishness of the wealthy south'.[19]

Political tensions between the major parties were also important, with Labour fearing that an Assembly would perpetuate rule by a Liberal (Welsh-speaking, rural) elite. The major devolution conferences at Llandrindod and Shrewsbury were indeed largely organised and run by Welsh Liberals.[20]

Labour had some right to be part of this. In addition to its substantial electoral support in Wales after 1918, theoretically at least it had strong credentials as a Home Rule party. In 1918 the South Wales Labour Federation had
passed a motion in favour of Home Rule and organised a conference in
support of the idea in Cardiff, whilst Labour's national programme had
included a commitment to 'Home Rule All Round'. Yet few Labour representatives were invited to these supposedly cross-party meetings, conferences
and committees. Progressive Liberals regretted this. The *Welsh Outlook* considered Labour's 'absence' at Llandrindod a 'real loss', and attacked those
present who 'did their best to make the cause, and succeeded in making themselves, ridiculous'.[21] The main target here was William George, the Prime
Minister's brother. William George was one of the most vociferous and out-
spoken opponents of the Labour Party. Despite supporting Welsh Home
Rule, George pointed to local 'difficulties' standing in its way, notably 'the
mixture of races in Wales, and because socialism and Labour in industrial
Wales support internationalism'. As the *Welsh Outlook* noted:

> His appearance as a political philosopher and a candid friend of his country was
> at least amusing . . . neither the existence of rival nationalities nor the presence
> of a socialistic party prevented his distinguished brother from conceding absolute
> independence to Bohemia and Poland . . . a Czech or a Pole who damped his
> country's aspirations in such a style, would be promptly set down as a pro-
> German.[22]

Fears that a new Welsh Parliament would be over-run by 'Bolsheviks' – and
south Wales Bolsheviks at that – was a consistent feature of the post-war
conferences.

In the aftermath of the conference, prominent Labour supporters of
devolution – like the miners agent and National Executive Committee (NEC)
member William Harris – eloquently highlighted Labour's doubts and fears
about devolution in an attempt to explain the indifference of his party. Harris
argued that (Liberal) advocates of devolution 'still speak of Wales as if no
change had taken place for 25 years'.[23] The Liberal elite, Harris argued, was
stuck in a time warp, in a Wales where the Welsh language was still dominant
and where trade union aims and aspirations could be ignored. He noted the
urgent need to 'sell' devolution to the 'internationally minded' and 'cosmopolitan' industrial working class in south Wales, criticising a 'nationalist'
mindset intent on winning over only traditionally Welsh speaking and Liberal
supporting voters.[24] The need to dispel the fears – both rational and irrational
– of people living in south Wales was being ignored. This was especially true
of in-migrants, who made up a substantial proportion of the population. The
'new Welsh' living in south Wales but emanating from England had little sympathy for a devolution package sold by 'native Welshmen with capitalist inter-

ests'. Echoing pre-war writers like O. M. Edwards, he complained that no real attempt was made to educate such people so that they understood Welsh hopes, fears and aspirations. On the contrary, the behaviour of Welsh speakers in particular was 'clannish'.

Harris's final point concerned the experience of administrative devolution. Currently, government appointees to devolved boards had no real interest in industrial communities. Jobs went to Welsh-speaking members of the old Welsh nationalist elite. Partly as a result of this perception, Labour in Wales did not warm to proposals for a Secretary of State for Wales. As Harris argued:

> Another suspicion that Labour has is that certain 'Welsh' movements that are now being largely advertised and only intended to secure offices for interested parties.

A Welsh Secretary, he continued, 'would compromise the larger movement', adding that there were 'no Labour organisation[s] in Wales that has shown any anxiety to support this idea of a Secretary for Wales'.[25] The same point was made by others. As the *Welsh Outlook* had noted in 1919, calls for a Welsh Secretary met with 'grave suspicion and mistrust. To its advocates a Secretariat is a halfway house to a Parliament for Wales, a necessary and inevitable preliminary', but, to its opponents, 'a device to postpone the greater reform, if not to place insuperable barriers in its way'.

Labour's beliefs and suspicions concerning the aims of Liberal nationalists were backed by hard evidence. At the Llandrindod conference of 1918, only five Labour representatives were selected to sit on an executive of thirty.[26] There was a long tradition of Liberal magazines celebrating the appointment of 'good Welshmen' to civic posts in Wales. One pre-war journal carried a regular column, 'The sons of Wales', which celebrated the fact that devolved administration created opportunities for 'brilliant young Welshmen' to serve in Welsh public life. It listed the names of those appointed. They were invariably Welsh speaking Liberals.

Deep cracks had thus surfaced in the pro-devolution camp well before the Shrewsbury conference of 1922 which, to all intents and purposes, marked the death of the post-war devolution debate. Its effects were less dramatic than the referendum defeat of 1979, but certainly deflated and demoralised supporters of devolution for a significant period. The aim of the conference had been to allow Welsh MPs and local authority representatives to debate the mechanisations of Welsh devolution. However, the conference served only to highlight differences of opinion of the kind noted above. On the important question of an Assembly's powers there had been 'little discussion', but general agreement that powers over 'public health, liquor licensing, order and good government, poor law, land and agriculture and public education' should be granted.[27] On the question of finance there was again general agreement that 'Home Rule was acceptable only if it could be secured without any additional financial burden on Wales'. The system of electing a putative Welsh Parliament was once again the major stumbling block. Representatives of Welsh rural counties were firmly against representation on the basis of population, which would have given Glamorgan and Monmouth a large majority. Once again the fear of Bolshevism was 'candidly expressed', and 'the only exiting incident of the day arose out of the vigour of that expression and the protest which it evoked from Colonel Watts Morgan and other representatives from South Wales'. In an attempt to break the constitutional deadlock, Welsh MPs suggested that a Welsh parliament consist of two chambers, one 72 member assembly elected by existing parliamentary constituencies and the other 36 member Assembly made up of two representatives from every Welsh county and county borough council. This 'solution' too was 'definitely opposed' by the majority of delegates.[28] Other delegates suggested schemes of proportional representation, although its advocates 'had not come prepared with any detailed scheme' or 'faced the practical difficulties which exist in the way of the adoption of such a scheme'. As Ernest Evans argued, 'the position therefore remains that the difficulties of representation can be met by a bi-cameral system, but that a bi-cameral system is not acceptable'.

Both 'sides' of the conference were blamed for the debacle. Some commentators blamed Welsh MPs for their failure to draft a definite scheme for consideration at the conference; others blamed local authorities for holding narrow and parochial views. As a *Welsh Outlook* editorial noted, Welsh local authorities were:

> Conclaves of reactionaries calling themselves progressives because they know that there are not sufficient reactionary votes in the country to put them in power. And the description is literally true of rural Wales. What then could be expected from the great majority of them but ignorant rhetoric about the Bolshevism of South Wales, empty vapourings about unreal issues, such as the question of the capital of Wales, and whinings about expenditure and cost.[29]

In the face of such realities, interest was waning amongst exactly the people who had to be converted. As Ernest Evans astutely noted:

> I am unduly influenced, not so much by what the conference was, as by the thought of what it might have been, but was not; not so much by the fifty present, as by the hundred and fifty (and more) who were absent. An empty chair can be very eloquent.[30]

All the objections were succinctly put by J. C. Gould MP, whose parliamentary motion in May 1922 effectively kicked Sir R. J. Thomas's Home Rule bill into the long grass. Gould noted that there was no unanimity in Wales, rather there were competing interests, both regional and ideological. There had been little discussion, let alone a mandate for such a bill in the 1918 election; the cost implications had not been thought through. He added that Welsh MPs themselves had changed their minds so much that there was no clear sense even of parliamentary opinion. In addition, opposing such a bill did not imply any less patriotic feeling for Wales. The country might be better served by an alternative form of devolution, such as the appointment of a Welsh Secretary of State.[31]

E. T. John (by now a Labour candidate) made one further attempt to build support among the public (as opposed to MPs). He revived the idea of a National Convention drawn from public and voluntary bodies in Wales, with a view to promoting a Home Rule scheme more radical than that proposed by the Welsh party members – essentially an autonomous assembly with powers such as those given to Ireland in 1921. This received short shrift from J. Herbert Lewis MP and others whom he approached who valued an attachment to the Imperial parliament. The disappointment impelled John along a course in which he sought support for Home Rule through cultural contacts with fellow Celts, especially in Ireland. The Celtic Congress became a vehicle for his aspirations, as he sought to marry national identities forged by language and tradition with a political programme which was as comprehensive as it was ambitious.[32]

Administrative identity

With prospects for Welsh self-government diminishing in the early 1920s, administrative devolution remained at the forefront of delivering good governance. Many of those who had been part of the pre-war Liberal nationalist coalition grew to accept the devolved boards, as Chris Williams shows elsewhere in this volume. Nonetheless, devolved administration could be the site for conflicts with the government as well, indicating that a strong sense of Welsh identity could still be sustained even if Wales did not agree on how the country should be governed. Events at the Welsh Department of the Board of Education provide some evidence of this. When a Welsh minister was in a post it was possible for the Department to have some freedom of action over and above the Board as a whole. Thus Herbert Lewis re-explored the idea of establishing a Welsh National Education Council between 1917 and 1921. Indeed, an internal committee report initiated serious progress, only for the whole business to become entangled in the Home Rule campaigns.[33]

The long drawn out struggle between the Welsh Department in London and the Central Welsh Board in Cardiff over the control of county intermediate schools was a further area for covert 'national' conflict. The two bodies represented two different sorts of administrative devolution, the latter more representative, and two different geographical concepts – whether to be near the people or near to the politicians. It was only in 1926–27 that some common arrangement was forged between the two bodies, but in the process both became tied more closely into Board of Education policy.[34] It was easy to see this as the assertion of 'English' over 'Welsh' interests (and for Welsh administrators to resent this). Indeed, the Permanent Secretary of the Welsh Department, Sir A. T. Davies, had already been shown a clear sense of his subordinate position. Civil servants within the Board were often redirected to other posts 'without any opportunity being afforded one of making any representations on the same subject to the President as regards Wales'.[35]

Former (Liberal) nationalists felt they were making a real contribution through the devolved boards, whatever their limitations. They also felt this was too often derided by critics in Wales. The Coalition Liberal MP Herbert Lewis was a Home Ruler who supported both a federal Britain and a Secretary of State for Wales. He felt that his role in supporting the Fisher Education Act in 1918 was 'real Welsh work', and commented that he was:

> In favour of anything that emphasises the special needs and outlooks of Wales, but I want to hold things in their due proportion and if we can get things in common with England the benefit to Wales is solid and substantial. There are some who attach greater importance to some twopenny-halfpenny thing that accrues to Wales alone than an infinitely greater benefit shared by others, but surely such a frame of mind is both selfish and in the end unpatriotic and unpractical.[36]

Lewis saw the creation of professional Welsh administrators as the bedrock of Welsh devolution, and suggested that all Welsh MPs serve apprenticeships as local councillors before seeking nomination for Westminster.[37]

The perceived value of the devolved administrative system is evident from the way it was defended. On such occasions, the 'nationalism' of some supporters of devolved administration could again become visible. In the late 1920s, the Conservative government tried to reform the devolved administrative system. In Wales they refused to replace the retiring Chair of the Welsh Board of Health, Sir Thomas Hughes, in 1928 on the grounds that the Minister of Health, Neville Chamberlain:

> had considered whether any of the existing members of the Board was suitable for the post of chairman and had come to the conclusion that, for one reason or another, none of them could be so regarded. To have any chance of success in such a position, the man selected must clearly be a Welshman, and a Welsh-speaking Welshman . . . must have a position of standing and authority and possess sufficient character to maintain the necessary order, discipline and authority in the office. Such a man could not have been found without causing inconvenience elsewhere and . . . would have involved an expense which did not seem justified.[38]

Only in 1930 was a new Chairman, John Rowland, appointed, following 'vigorous protests in the Principality' and lobbying by Welsh MPs in the Commons.[39] Welsh MPs led a month long press campaign against what they described as insults to Wales. As Wil John, the Labour MP for the Rhondda, put it, these were the actions of 'the most anti-Welsh government of all time'.[40] In Scotland too, the government tried to reform the system, by merging it with the English civil service. Opposition to this spread across party lines, and was expressed in nationalistic terms. In Scotland, the Labour MP Tom Johnston opposed the 'concentration in Whitehall of the administration of Scottish affairs'. Devolved administration was at least administration by Welsh people, even if they were not chosen by the electorate.

There was comparable outrage when the official BBC handbook for 1929 promised to recognise the distinctive needs of Scotland and Ireland, but made no such claims for Wales. The poor representation of Wales within a variety of official organisations had already been received as an insult. It was reported that the Central Council for School Broadcasting, totalling thirty-six members, had only one Welsh representative.[41] The 'big' Whitehall departments were also attacked on similar lines. Whilst the Department of Education and H. M. Office of Works were both complimented on their readiness to appoint various boards and committees to deal with Welsh issues, the Ministry of Health was attacked for its insensitive handling of Welsh interests. The Central Valuation Committee of the Ministry comprised thirty-two members, but included only three Welshmen, all emanating from Glamorgan, whilst its prestigious 'panel of experts' were all English. There was also agitation over spending. In the late 1920s whilst health insurance committees in Wales (remarkably) had underspent budgets, English committees had overspent. As a result, Whitehall (to the long-term detriment of Wales) pooled the budgets. Welsh commentators believed this was part of a 'deliberate desire to extinguish the national entity of Wales' one that would lead to 'an inevitable reaction' as 'the hands of the extremists are strengthened'.[42]

A distinctive Welsh politics

In 1924, the noted anti-war campaigner, Principal Thomas Rees, in reviewing politics in Wales noted that little or no distinctive Welsh politics had emerged because of the indifference or hostility of the three major (English) parties to Welsh nationhood. He set out an agenda for creating a Welsh politics at the centre of which was the concept of democratically based self-government.[43] In its refined way, it highlighted what were already frustrations among some in Welsh speaking and largely rural Wales at the failure to drive forward the Home Rule debate, a failure which had resulted in the emergence of several more nationalistic and aggressive pressure groups, such as *Y Mudiad Cymreig* which looked to Ireland for inspiration.[44]

The failure of the 'English' government to treat seriously the 'separate' claims of Wales had been a significant factor in the creation of a Nationalist Party in 1925. An early manifesto made clear the party's aim to 'release Wales from the grip of the English . . . we can aim at doing nothing less than to do away with the English language in Wales. We must blot it out from the land'. Each of the three political parties, it claimed, had ignored Wales between 1918 and 1925, thus justifying the creation of Y Blaid. One if its founders, Professor J. E. Daniel, was reported as saying that Wales 'Thrilled with shame and disgust at Mr. MacDonald's blasé and nonchalant non-possumus attitude towards all requests for special Welsh measures'.[45]

Under the influence of Saunders Lewis (the party's first president) Plaid dedicated itself to preserving the Welsh language, culture and way of life – Welsh civilisation – to fighting against the anomic effects and influences of industrialisation and the anglicising forces that accompanied it.[46] Lewis played a prominent role in the development of the party's strategy and politics and was the public face of the party in the inter-war period. One leading Welsh historian describes Lewis as 'a dignified but intransigent figure' who aroused strong feelings, 'hostile as well as admiring'.[47] A Roman Catholic convert with a strong attachment to the pre-modern past, his philosophical ideas were reinforced by studying French neo-fascist writers, whilst his educational ideas were borrowed from Mussolini's Italy.[48] In a speech to his party's Summer School in 1931 he made it clear that his form of nationalism differed in its ideals from the 'older' nationalism of men like W. J. Parry, Tom Ellis and the youthful David Lloyd George. Like other party members, he sought to distance himself from an earlier generation of (Liberal) 'nationalists'. According to Lewis 'older' nationalists would have envisioned a liberal and radical Welsh parliament, which focused on issues such as disestablishment, education and temperance. Echoing Emrys ap Iwan, he argued that such a parliament would have accepted the economic system of Victorian England and its faith in the 'sacred cow' of free trade or – if dominated by the south – it would be the voice of a crude (English) materialism. Lewis's parliament would be different. Lewis attacked the 'imperial', 'English' banking system and towed a hostile anti-establishment line. What the established church was to the older Liberals, the commercial system of the city of London was to Lewis. It was a system which, according to Lewis, 'makes it easier to obtain money for a loan to a foreign state than money to develop a Welsh quarry'. The supremacy of the English Parliament and English bureaucracy made possible the exploitation of Wales. Wales' best hope was to disestablish itself from the London banking and commercial systems.[49] Many nationalists did not accept this, but still agreed with Lewis that Wales had been betrayed by the 'old guard', that the Welsh goal of self-government had been sacrificed on the altar of imperialism and capitalism and that the 'Welshness' and 'nationalism' of supposed supporters of Welsh self-government was phoney. As Lewis argued, Welsh nationalism was:

> The part-time hobby of corpulent and successful men. But we . . . want to expatriate that kind of 'Ardent Welsh Nationalist'. We want to sever the association of the adjective 'ardent' with Welsh nationalism.[50]

And as another edition of the party's newspaper argued:

> The sugary-mouthed Nationalists, the St. David's Day diners, and all quasi-Nationalists of the same kidney, are as powerful enemies to our cause as the arch-imperialists like Winston Churchill and Lloyd George.[51]

Lewis and the Welsh Nationalist Party were deeply critical of the Welsh Parliamentary Party grouping, composed of Welsh MPs at Westminster, arguing that 'they are no party. They are anti-national and only some of them are Welsh'. For Lewis:

> A Welsh Nationalist is one who believes that Wales is a nation and that the Welsh Nation should manfully and delightedly take again the responsibility of building a Welsh civilisation. We are out to put the Dominion of Wales on the map of Europe.[52]

National freedom, individual freedom, opposition to capitalistic imperialism, co-operation between 'free nations', the break-up of Empire, encouragement for the small tradesman and small farmer, the 'smashing-up' of 'Big Trusts and Combines' and the fostering of Welsh culture were all intrinsic aims of the party in 1920s and 30s.[53] In reality, however, cultural and linguistic concerns dominated nationalist thoughts in the early years of the party's development.

Passions were also stirred by the decline of the Welsh language – very apparent following publication of the 1921 census figures – and the decay of Welsh culture. The establishment of the Welsh Nationalist Party followed a period of sustained and intense debate in Welsh language newspapers and journals in the early 1920s over both these issues. For many 'cultural' nationalists, the fundamental justification for devolution rested on its capacity to preserve and develop the Welsh language and Welsh culture, to restore traditional Welsh values and, for some, to return Wales to its pre-industrial past. W. Ambrose Bebb, one of the founding members of Plaid, made the point stridently in 1924 in an article appropriately entitled 'Save the Language: Save Wales'.[54] Others debated the relative merits of culture as opposed to language (and vice versa) but scarcely addressed vital economic issues or problems in their intellectual deliberations.[55]

That said, Lewis denied there was a distinction between the two. He claimed that unlike 'the old-fashioned dilettante "language and literature" nationalism' of Liberal Wales, which separated culture from the political, modern nationalism put the two together. Creating or sustaining Welsh cultural institutions presupposed the desire to have a national existence and thereby 'you are willing the existence of a Welsh nation, and you are therefore willing a Welsh government and political machinery.'[56]

Nonetheless, the claim was scarcely developed. During the inter-war years, Welsh language journals were full of anti-modernist articles which were deeply critical of popular culture and opposed to party politics, which were seen as populistic and devoid of moral values.[57] These sentiments were expressed by the poet, preacher, semi-socialist Christian pacifist, George Maitland Lloyd Davies, in 1927:

> We of this generation are obsessed by the mass mind and its machinery – not only in big business and in politics but in trade unionism and even in the churches . . . the young escape Towyn as from a prison. The old keep shops or let lodgings in the summer and worship the easy affluence and assurance of the Birmingham bourgeois who come. The county school has 400 pupils who pass exams and miss life most conspicuously . . . when they leave school they turn with relief to dances, whist drives and jazz.[58]

The way that English and British influences insinuated themselves in everyday life was also a cause for concern. Anti-English sentiments were regularly expressed in the party's newspapers and other nationalist circles in the inter-war period. Even cultural nationalists such as R. T. Jenkins, who were critical of Lewis's absolutism lamented the loss of traditional Welsh life and values and attacked the anglicisation of Wales and the institution of banal symbols of Englishness. In one article, Jenkins played down the chapel and school as the centre of Welsh rural life, and pointed to the importance of the village shop as the epicentre of the local community. However:

> the shop . . . indoctrinates the whole community with English words and thoughts . . . Silver King, Royal Daylight, Ever-ready, First Grade, Britain's Best and things like that were quietly being pushed into the heads of the locals.[59]

There was also attack on 'modern' trends and values and in particular commercialisation:

> By now the country depends . . . on things that can only come from England, things with English names . . . things that you have to send away for and pay for in English, things that are advertised in English even in our local papers, things in other words that bond English ideas and values.[60]

Others went further. For many, the damage had already been done. As J. Alun Pugh not inaccurately noted:

> It is a matter of laughter that nearly everything on which we unctuously pride ourselves is English . . . for instance, our zeal for teetotalism, our League of Nations Union, our wonderful Sunday, our views on betting, our Sunday School . . . our education, our examination system, our various religious movements and reforms, they all hail from England.[61]

The impact on Wales, and on Welshmen, had been catastrophic:

> The Welshman has, for some time, been little more than an inferior copy of the Englishman: he is fast becoming increasingly unreal. He appears to be incapable of taking any thought for himself, of searching for any way out of his difficulties or even of feeling any sense of shame at the melancholy view his country offers to the eyes of Europe, should those eyes ever bother to rest upon her.[62]

The nature of Welsh education was often blamed for the crisis. The education system allegedly indoctrinated Welsh children with 'English' ideas and values. In the past things had been better. The old elementary education system had served Wales well, allowing school-leavers to take up jobs locally:

> Therefore the best boys and girls of the community were kept in the community, and their Welsh culture penetrated the local area . . . the *gwerin*, that is the workers, were the custodians of Welsh culture.[63]

By the inter-war period this situation had changed:

> Now we have our secondary education and our Universities, the cream [have] turned their backs on working with their hands. As Wales lacks the jobs for the masses who are now leaving University, they are emigrating in droves to England because of the economic order, and Welsh life is all the poorer for their loss.[64]

That pre-war advocate of home rule, E. T. John, in his political sojourn from Liberal to Labour to nationalist fellow traveller, shared these views. By the 1930s he felt that Wales' spiritual (that is, cultural and moral) health, as well as its economic wellbeing, could only come by eschewing English parties and 'English' policies and securing for Wales Plaid's aim of Dominion status.[65]

In building on this view, nationalists developed an imaginary historical and racial Wales which was distinct from England – a past which, if recovered, could allow Wales to return to its true nature.[66] Even for 'scientific' historians like J. E. Lloyd, the Welsh past was defined by the 'unquenchable vigour of (its) national resistance.' Ethnically different from the Teutonic English, the Welsh had preserved their (better) values through their pastoralism, religion, language and through the memory and love of the past. This was embodied in the Welsh passion for music, poetry and stories. As Moses Griffith, a Welsh Nationalist Party founder argued, 'Welsh culture is a rural culture; it has grown from the soil of Wales, and if this culture of ours is to live and thrive, its roots must be nurtured and sheltered.' If Wales achieved freedom, traditional Welsh industries (and a traditional Welsh way of life) would be revived:

> Then the rural craftsmen will slowly return, and the oldest craft in the world – that of tilling the soil – will come into its own once more.[67]

The extremeness of the language deployed, the dismissiveness of pale Liberal or Labour devolutionary ideas, and the authoritarian personality of Saunders Lewis all contributed to limiting the progress of the Nationalist Party, even amongst those who sympathised with elements of their message. The 'world view' of Welsh nationalists in the inter-war period stood in stark contrast to the realities of life in many Welsh communities, particularly in south Wales.

Nonetheless, nationalists did not ignore the economic crisis of the 1930s. On the contrary, the party's propaganda during the period made much of the capitalistic havoc wrought on Wales by an English Imperial government. In the late 1920s and early 1930s attempts were made by members of the party to frame an economic agenda. D. J. Davies was at the forefront of these efforts. A former member of the Labour Party who had attended the 'Marxist' Central Labour College in the early 1920s, Davies had become disillusioned with Labour after the first MacDonald government had failed to pursue a definitive socialist agenda. He was drawn into the ranks of the Nationalist Party whilst a student at University College Aberystwyth from 1924 onwards. Davies produced works concerning the form of Home Rule to be sought and the economic role of the proposed Welsh State. He worked to locate the party's cultural emphasis within a political context. As he argued in 1932:

> Culture without self-government is like a spirit without a body, and a bodiless spirit cannot take its part and express itself in the world of living men . . . [but] . . . those who advocate cultural nationalism without political nationalism are adherents of an out-of-date psychology.[68]

Davies rejected a limited form of devolution as inadequate and argued that Dominion status on the pattern secured by the Irish Free State should be the objective.[69] He advocated nationalisation of the mines and workers control based on 'Guild Socialist' principles.[70] He was also behind ambitious attempts to align the Welsh Nationalist Party with the South Wales Miners Federation. However, in the early 1930s the urgent need to develop Welsh nationalism among non-Welsh speakers led him to establish the party's first English language newspaper, *The Welsh Nationalist*, in 1932, a year after he had been given the task of drawing Plaid's first economic policy under the title *The Economics of Welsh Self-Government*.

In addition to Davies's efforts, 'cultural' nationalists including Saunders Lewis made a (neglected) contribution to economic issues. As the dominant nationalist thinker of the 1930s, Lewis provided eclectic policies for the problems of Welsh unemployment and economic contraction. He advocated planning, public works and statist initiatives such as farming colonies (echoing Italian initiatives). He was dismissive of administrative minds which tolerated depopulation and marginalised Wales in their plans. What Wales wanted and needed, he argued, was the co-ordination of the local authorities, public and devolved administrative bodies under a Welsh National Development Council.[71] However, he was not a detached intellectual. Prompted by Kate Roberts, he regularly addressed meetings of unemployed workers in the 1930s, founded a number of 'Thursday Dinner Clubs' to provide food for unemployed workers and sought to develop the party's economic policy as a result of those contacts.[72] In 1933, a nationalist school to 'counteract depression' in the 'centre of the Anglicised Welsh of south Wales' was opened in Breconshire. However, the emphasis was again on the cultural rather than the political. Based on Danish nationalist co-operative ideas and principles, the school aimed to 're-establish the language, culture and traditions' in a south Wales suffering the ravaging effects of economic depression.

The emphasis on the cultural and social – and on Home Rule or nothing – led Plaid to reject policies which offered economic relief, even though Wales was being ravaged by depression. For example, in 1936 when the National Government considered 'Special Areas' legislation to deal with the ravaging effects of the depression in south Wales, the plans were attacked by Plaid on the grounds they were influenced by 'south Wales socialists', vying with the 'honest supporters of capitalism' to 'bring back to our valleys the nasty capitalists, and to compel them to establish factories amongst us'. The party instead called for a 'national plan' which was different from the government's in several respects. It did not want 'a plan for recovering from the last decade in south Wales', but instead 'a plan [for] recovering from the last century', not to 'restore nineteenth century industrialisation in south Wales', but one which would call 'for the gradual and progressive de-industrialisation of south Wales'. Simply treating the 'cancer' of unemployment was also insufficient. Instead, nationalists believed in 'a plan for changing the principles controlling employment' including 'the social dignity and liberty and property that they had the right to possess here in Wales'.[73]

Plaid's economic policies still suggested a party out of touch with reality and obsessed with romantic images of a bygone age. Davies's more economically focused ideas and aspirations made little headway in the party and he faced a continual battle with the party elite over the emphasis on language and culture as opposed to economic principles and policy. By the late 1930s he had turned his attentions to cultural rather than economic interests.[74]

At the heart of nationalist economic thinking was the need to preserve the Welsh language. Of course, this was also part of a Liberal nationalist tradition. As the *Welsh Outlook* had put it in 1927, 'If Welsh were to disappear Wales as a nation would not exist much longer'. Indeed, it had gone further, placing the Welsh language at the heart of its conception of who should be allowed to govern Wales:

> No man who cannot read, write or speak Welsh fluently has any right to meddle in Welsh affairs at all, for he does more harm than good. Nothing could be more disastrous for us as a nation than for the belief to spread about that it is possible to be a good Welshman and not speak Welsh.[75]

The view was expressed ever more passionately in the 1930s by members of Plaid Cymru. As the poet and social anthropologist Iorwerth C. Peate put it in 1937, the Welsh language was 'the country's only bulwark against extinction. Destroy the Welsh language – and there are many influences tending in that direction – and the whole spiritual culture and national personality of Wales will be undermined'.[76] These fears over the possible extinction of the Welsh language could – and did – lead to direct action. The very public and symbolic burning of the building site of an intended RAF bombing school at Penyberth in north Wales in 1936 by prominent leaders of Plaid Genedlaethol Cymru alienated a number of Liberal nationalists over the means of protest, but not over the motives. Indeed, an emphasis on the importance of preserving Welsh as a living and working language – as a cultured language – was shared by a wider circle of people.[77]

In this respect, the way in which the three perpetrators were tried (in England and in English) induced no little sympathy beyond nationalist ranks and especially among Welsh Liberals, including Lloyd George. It inspired yet another cross-partisan campaign to protect Welsh values, in this instance a mass petition in favour of the right to speak Welsh in court, which reignited the unhappiness about how the legal system operated in Wales. It was also reflected in the creation of *Undeb Cymru Fydd* , which had the restoration of the Welsh language's legal status as one of several cultural aims. This culminated in the wartime concession of limited recognition, through the Welsh Courts Act 1942 – an 'abortion' of an act in the view of Welsh nationalists since it did not give Welsh the same legal status as English. Campaigns for Welsh Language Acts thus became a mainstay of the Nationalist cause after 1945.[78]

Retabling devolution

During the Second World War, widespread concerns over the decline of traditional Welsh life in the face of major social changes suggested that the nationalist coalition evident before 1914 might be recreated. Some members of the Nationalist Party believed that Wales was being 'murdered' by the effects of the war. 'Increased watchfulness' and extra vigilance was required to preserve Welsh life 'since the influence of the military and bureaucratic dictatorial state on the life of Wales [was] increasing'.[79] *Undeb Cymru Fydd* conducted a survey on 'The Condition of Welsh Society' in 1942. The research team was headed by Ithel Davies. Davies had been Labour's candidate for the University of Wales constituency – an unusual seat usually captured by independent and culturally minded figures – in the 1935 election, demonstrating both that 'culture' was not Plaid's preserve but also that cultural nationalists could take an interest in economic issues. [80] The questions devised reveal a plethora of concerns over the future of Wales. Sub-sections of the survey dealt with Education and Youth Movements; Churches and Sunday Schools; Welsh Homes; The Social Life of Wales; Local Government and the Administration of Law. The questions and responses addressed a number of 'old' concerns, but also highlighted anxieties over 'new', modernising influences and concerns. For example, questions relating to the teaching of Welsh in schools addressed typical nationalist concerns – the teaching of Welsh history, Welsh books, the appointment of Welsh speaking teachers etc. – but attention was also paid to the impact and influence of in-migrants (including evacuees) on Welsh school life and on Welsh speaking communities. Concern over the impact of an 'alien' culture was clearly discernible in the replies. War had served to intensify 'negative' changes already taking place in the inter-war period. 'Pub culture', 'young girls smoking', 'whist', 'dancing', 'cinema' (not to mention 'Yanks') all posed new challenges to nationalists desperately seeking to cling to a bygone Welsh cultural age.[81]

For political nationalists, however, the war represented a threat not only to traditional values but to all communities in Wales. The wartime centralisation of powers in London created regional controllers acting at the expense of local government. This further diminished the opportunity for a Welsh voice, or voices, to be heard. Welsh councils – led by Caernarvonshire – voiced their concerns. They were thus capable of returning to a 'nationalist' camp. The industrial transference scheme directing Welsh workers – men and women – out of Wales was also widely condemned. Again, this had a broader resonance. The solution was for Wales' political identity to be recognised by a national policy and by devolved power.[82]

Ironically, wartime centralisation had provided Wales with a new national role. In 1941 a Welsh Survey Board was created, chaired by Sir Percy Watkins. Composed of planning experts like Peter Scott, social improvers like Edgar Chappell and some of the Liberal great and good like Rhys Hopkin Morris, the Board was intended to explore the possibilities of post-war reconstruction for Wales. From the start its membership concluded that planning in an all-Wales context should occur – albeit within the parameters of regional structures and within a reformed local government system.[83]

The regional ideal had partly emanated from the Barlow Commission Report in 1940. The implications were ambiguous. One was that there should be separate planning bodies for south and north Wales. However, an all-Wales perspective developed rapidly. This was in part because local planning structures in Wales were very patchy, as R. David Jones, the Planning Officer for Wales, acknowledged.[84] The debate brought some 'social Liberals' back into the 'national' fold. Edgar Chappell is a good example. Chappell wanted to create thirty-six new and larger local authorities, amalgamating the county councils into regional councils for north and south Wales and with a national administrative council for all-Wales interests. He also advocated the co-ordination of all Whitehall functions relating to Wales in a Welsh Office, headed by a Secretary of State.[85] This was developed into a published programme, *The Government of Wales*, and issued as a popular pamphlet, *Wake Up Wales!*[86]

There was some prospect of creating 'nationalist' unity around such arguments. Campaigns for a Welsh Secretary had been a sporadic feature of the devolution debate in the inter-war period. In 1920 a delegation of Welsh Liberal Coalition MPs sought Lloyd George's support for a Welsh Secretary, but were famously told to 'go for the big thing', namely federal home rule.[87] A further Private Members Bill, calling for a Welsh Secretary of State to be appointed, had failed in 1921.[88] The Conservative Prime Minister Stanley Baldwin refused to consider appointing a Welsh Secretary on three separate occasions in 1928 and turned down a further two requests later.[89] Labour governments were no more sympathetic. In 1930 Ramsay MacDonald rejected calls from the Welsh Labour MP Peter Freeman to appoint a Welsh Secretary. In 1933 and 1934 MacDonald again refused to consider any change to the status quo, arguing that he was not aware of any widespread demand for changes in either the administrative or legislative spheres.[90]

By the later 1930s, though, support for a Secretary of State for Wales (with a seat at the Cabinet table) was gaining ground.[91] In 1937 the Liberal MP Clement Davies presented a Private Members Bill calling for the installation of a Welsh Secretary and a Welsh Office. The proposal was rejected. However, support was also beginning to grow in south Wales' Labour circles. In 1938, Morgan Jones, Labour MP for Caerphilly, met Chamberlain to discuss the issue. In 1942, 1943, 1944 and 1945 the South Wales Regional Council of Labour announced its support for a Welsh Secretary and a Welsh Office. Whilst some notable Welsh Labour figures, including Aneurin Bevan, were to dismiss the idea, others like James Griffiths (MP for Llanelli) were more positive.

Griffiths was one of several Labour figures who argued strongly for this scheme over the next two decades. He asked:

> What kind of Governmental structure should we aim at for Wales in the post-war period? I dismiss political independence, or Dominion status, as an immediate possibility. Even if it were desirable, it is not practicable. The people of Wales have shown no real desire for it. In the field of industry and social services the ties with Britain are too strong, and too deep to be severed. If Wales became politically independent the first consequence would be a reduction in the scope and the level of our social services that our people would not stand for. The Beveridge Plan may be only half-alive in Britain. It would be still-born in a separated Wales.[92]

For Griffiths, the future needs of Wales were best served by extending administrative decentralisation from Whitehall to the regions, especially as 'the necessities of war have accentuated the pace, and widened the scope of this trend to decentralisation'.[93] To ensure greater efficiency and to justify extending administrative devolution, Griffiths called for local government reorganisation which would lead to the creation of larger authorities. These would be equipped to deal with 'larger' issues including water supplies, roads and bridges, electricity and transport and administered by a 'democratically controlled regional authority'. In addition, decentralisation from Whitehall 'should be canalised into the creation of a Welsh Office, with a Secretary of State of Cabinet rank' offering 'real hope for the largest measure of effective self-government in Wales'.[94]

Plaid saw the campaign for a Welsh Secretary as a sign of a Welsh awakening, particularly since the call was coming from the local authorities in Wales and from others as well. However, they had no confidence that the Welsh Parliamentary Party would bring these elements together – and no interest in joining with others to make this happen.[95] Younger nationalists and communists dismissed Griffiths' views. According to Gwynfor Evans, his policy was 'a compromise between the reconstruction of Welsh life on the basis of nationality and the rejection of Wales as an entity of any kind'.[96] Griffiths' plans were treated with equal amounts of cynicism and suspicion:

> Such blind faith in the face of a thousand facts is unlikely to convince a younger generation to whom he appeals. They will see little reason for believing that the government will suddenly feel a tender solicitude for the welfare of Wales . . . Once the master-plan is complete Wales will be as helpless as a fly in a spider's web . . . it is not enough that Wales should be a unit for planning purposes; it must be given full responsibility for planning its own life. No country can be said to be free and responsible unless it can choose its national policy.[97]

The Welsh communist George Woodcock was equally dismissive. He felt a new Welsh Secretary, whether Tory or Labour, would have limited influence in Cabinet the majority of which 'would represent English interests', and would still be crippled by a financial system dominated by Whitehall and the Treasury. Such a Minister – operating away from Wales and unaccountable to it – would inevitably 'sell out' the people. Scotland, even with a Secretary of

State, had suffered from the same depression that had afflicted Wales in the 1930s and from the same process of rural depopulation. A Welsh Secretary was not a cure-all for Welsh problems.[98] Interestingly, however, the Communist Party was officially more supportive of the idea of a Secretary of State – as the first step towards the creation of a Welsh Parliament underpinned by a Welsh polity possessing a more robust socialist ideology.[99]

This resistance to something short of independence did little to create a national coalition. By 1943 Plaid was in disarray. A parliamentary by-election in the University of Wales seat saw Plaid represented by Saunders Lewis. There was a concerted and successful attempt to put up a rival nationalist candidate. Organised by Liberal nationalists like Sir Thomas Artemus Jones, the 'independents' chose Professor W. J. Gruffydd as spokesman for a liberal-minded, culturally driven Wales to stand against the conservative and authoritarian Lewis. Plaid's core beliefs, strategy and tone would have to be reconstructed before it gained any real purchase with the Welsh people.[100]

One possibility was that central government opposition to the idea of a Secretary of State might create some form of national unity. Despite the concession in 1943 of an annual 'Welsh Day' debate in the House of Commons, the wartime coalition government – and Labour's national leadership – remained fundamentally opposed to the demands for a Welsh Secretary. The way in which these rejections were expressed could inflame national sentiments, allowing 'the English' to be seen as aloof and patronising. The Civil Service continually cast doubt on the capacity of Wales to produce an effective administrative class of its own. When Baldwin rejected calls for a Welsh Secretary in 1928, he did so – in part at least – because Whitehall civil servants dismissed Welsh claims as 'sentimental'. When calls for a Welsh Secretary reignited in 1937 and 1938, civil servants were again hostile to change, arguing that no savings would be made by the establishment of a Welsh Office and that strong UK-wide ministries were vital.[101] Other civil servants made the same point, arguing that a Welsh Office would 'still further complicate administration which is already far too complicated'.[102] In June 1942, the Ministry of Reconstruction appointed a Welsh Reconstruction Advisory Council but gave it little autonomy. Whitehall resistance remained intact. Wales was seen as a rural and insular backwater. 'Giving in' to its demands would be 'to encourage parish pump politics' on a national scale.[103] Both Churchill and Attlee dismissed the Secretary of State initiative. As *Y Cymro* opined:

> How can Mr. Attlee be so blind to public opinion as to try and damp the desires of the Welsh members for a Welsh Secretary? Instead of consulting supporters like Sir William Jenkins and Mr. Grenfell, he fell back apparently on those self-satisfied, omniscient mandarins in Whitehall, a few civil servants who are always opposed to any extension of democratic powers.[104]

Pressed by the Labour candidate for Cardiganshire, Attlee defended the wartime government by arguing that no formal representation had been received from the Welsh Parliamentary Party for a Welsh Secretary.[105] That notwithstanding, the official mind was closed to the idea. Further demands from the Welsh Parliamentary Party for a Welsh Secretary were dismissed by civil servants in ways which played up to national stereotypes:

> As cold-blooded and unimaginative Englishmen we find the whole thing rather puerile . . . are there specific instances in which Wales suffers, or think she suffers under the present system, or is it simply vague nationalism or envy of Scotland?[106]

Such sentiments, echoed in various media and different ways, helped create stereotypical depictions of 'the English' which could also reinforce perceived class differences between the 'ordinary' people of Wales and the affluent and superior 'other'.

Whilst the climate in 1945 was thus hardly favourable to devolution, and the discourse of Welsh nationalism did little to sustain an alternative, language, identity and self-perception provided the potential for future campaigns. Yet even if a respect for Welsh tradition and language crossed over into English-speaking Wales, a cultural nationalism was not enough to mobilise mass public opinion. Wales was evidently a part of Britain. Many in Wales saw the political world through the language of Labour. They had faced harsh economic realities. If there were concerns over the preservation of the past, they were perhaps stronger concerns over what lay in the future, and especially over the need to build a more prosperous and secure life. The discourse of Welsh nationalism did not entirely ignore such realities, but they were hardly central and opponents could easily suggest that they were of marginal significance. Welsh Nationalists needed to make a stronger civic case for Welsh devolution – and to overcome the tensions, divisions and doubts which had been apparent since the 1880s. These continued to plague the case for devolved governance, not just after 1945 but for the rest of the century.

Notes

1 Welsh School of Social Service, *Reprint of Report on Mid-Wales*, August 1920; I. G. Jones (ed.), *Gwilym Davies 1879–1935: A Tribute* (Llandysul, 1972).

2 Report dated 11 June 1917, Board of Education MSS TNA ED 24/2052 (TNA).

3 For much of this context see Kenneth O. Morgan, *Rebirth of a Nation: Wales 1880–1980* (Oxford and Cardiff, 1981), pp. 246–53.

4 Sir I. Owen to Board of Education, April 1915, General MSS 6291, 6292 (UWB).

5 Ernest Evans to J. Herbert Lewis, 28 December 1931, J. Herbert Lewis papers, A1/468 (NLW).
6 John Davies, *Broadcasting and the BBC in Wales* (Cardiff, 1994), ch. 2.
7 See Kenneth O. Morgan, *Wales in British Politics 1868–1922* (Cardiff, 2nd edition, 1970), p. 291.
8 *The Times*, 10 February 1919. See also various articles in *WO*, January and February 1919.
9 'The government of Wales', *WO*, March 1919, 55.
10 Ibid.
11 For more on this see Tanner, Chapter 10 below, p. 233.
12 'Welsh self-government and the Speakers' Conference', *WO*, July 1920; Trevor Boyns, 'Rationalisation in the inter-war period: the case of the south Wales steam coal industry', *Business History,* 29 (1987).
13 Hansard, 3 June 1919.
14 Ibid.
15 Major David Davies MP, 'A Welsh Office', *WO*, July 1919, 177.
16 Ibid.
17 'Notes of the Month', ibid., March 1920, 52.
18 Ibid.
19 Letter from W. A. Bebb to the *WO*, May 1919. In John's plans, 37 members were to represent Glamorgan and 13 Monmouthsire. The second assembly was to have three members from each Welsh county.
20 These included Sir Walter Nicholas, Rhys Hopkin Morris, Llywelyn Williams KC, Major David Davies and Ernest Evans.
21 'The Conference and Nationalism', *WO*, July 1919.
22 William Harris, 'Labour and Home Rule for Wales', *WO*, June 1919, 145–7.
23 Ibid.
24 Ibid.
25 Ibid.
26 There were also basic disagreements over the location of an Assembly. Again, assumptions that the Welsh seat of government would be located in Cardiff were deeply resented and resisted by representatives from historically significant towns including Caernarfon (in the north) and Llandrindod in mid Wales. See *The Times,* 4 December 1919.
27 Ernest Evans, 'The Shrewsbury Conference', *WO*, May 1922, 107–9.
28 Two additional seats in the 36 member assembly would also be granted to the University of Wales
29 *WO*, 'Notes of the Month', May 1922, 103.
30 Ibid.
31 *WM*, 5 May 1922.
32 E. T. John correspondence and memoranda, General MSS 20456 (UWB).
33 Report dated 22 August 1921, TNA ED 24/2052.
34 This is based on papers in TNA ED 24/2051. See also Percy Watkins, *A Welshman Remembers* (Cardiff, 1944), pp. 126–70.
35 A. T. Davies to J. Selby-Bigge, Permanent Secretary, 16 January 1919, TNA ED 24/2053.
36 Herbert Lewis to M. R. Evans, 7 January 1921, Herbert Lewis MS A2/60.
37 Ibid.

38 *The Times*, 13 July 1928.

39 *The Times*, 30 April 1930.

40 *WM*, 2 August 1928.

41 Prof. E. Ernest Hughes, 'Wales and the British Broadcasting Corporation', *WO*, August 1929, 230–1.

42 Sylwedydd, 'Wales and Whitehall', *WO*, March 1928, 67.

43 Thomas Rees, *Gwleidyddiaith yng Nghymru: [Traethodau'r Deyrnas 7]* (Wrecsam 1924).

44 D. Hywel Davies, *The Welsh Nationalist Party 1925–1945: A Call to Nationhood* (Cardiff, 1983), ch. 3.

45 Typescript of a speech given by Professor Daniel to a meeting of the Welsh Nationalist Party at the Essex Hall, London (n.d.), General MSS 20428 (UWB).

46 Saunders Lewis, *Egwyddorion Cenedlaetholdeb: [Plaid Genedlaethol Cymru, Pamffledi'r Ysgol Haf, Machynlleth, Rhif 1]* (Machynlleth, 1925).

47 Morgan, *Rebirth of a Nation*, p. 256.

48 Lewis was not the only member of the Welsh Nationalist Party to be intellec-tually attracted to the model of the Italian corporate state. Ambrose Bebb and other prominent nationalists shared these views. On the influence of the French Right on Lewis and Bebb see D. Tecwyn Lloyd, 'Saunders Lewis' and Gareth Miles, 'W. Ambrose Bebb', in Derec Llwyd Morgan (ed.), *Adnabod Deg: Portreadau o Ddeg o Arweinwyr Cynnar y Blaid Genedlaethol* (Dinbych, 1977), pp. 9–30 and 77–95.

49 *WO*, September 1931, 224.

50 Saunders Lewis, 'The New Nationalism in Wales: what it means', *The Welsh Nationalist*, 15 January 1932, 1.

51 *The Welsh Nationalist*, February 1934, 1.

52 Lewis, 'The New Nationalism'.

53 See for example, 'Do you believe in?', *The Welsh Nationalist*, April 1934. R. J. Moore-Colyer, 'Farming in Depression: Wales between the Wars, 1919–39', *Agricultural History Review*, 46 (1998), especially 180–1 for similar non-nationalistic and English sentiments.

54 W. Ambrose Bebb, 'Achub y Gymraeg: Achub Cymru', *Y Geninen*, Mai 1923.

55 See for example, D. Miall Edwads, 'Diwylliant Cymru', *Y Geninen*, Gorffenaf 1923, 168–79; Caradar, 'Addysg Yn Lladd Cenedl', *Y Geninen*, Gorffenaf 1921, 143.

56 Saunders Lewis, *The Banned Wireless Talk on Welsh Nationalism* (Caernarvon, 1931), pp. 5–6.

57 Aled Gwyn Job, 'Agweddau a syniadau cymdeithasol a'r farn gyhoeddus ym Môn rhwng y ddau ryfel byd' (unpublished M. Phil thesis., UWB, 1990).

58 George Maitland Lloyd Davies to Tom Jones, January 1927, Thomas Jones MSS W3 (NLW). For similar sentiments amongst 'social radicals', see Chapter 6 by Williams below, p. 146.

59 R. T. Jenkins, 'Yr Hen Fywyd Cymreig', *Y Llenor*, 6 (1927), 139–48.

60 Ibid. Author's translation.

61 J. Alun Pugh, 'The Making of a True Welshman', *The Welsh Nationalist*, 15 April 1933, 1–2.

62 Ibid.

63 'Nodiadau'r Golygydd', *Y Llenor*, Haf 1927. Author's translation.

64 Ibid.

65 Typescript of speech by E. T. John (n.d. 1929?), General MSS 20428 (UWB).

66 In many respects this was building on the social thinking common throughout Victorian and Edwardian England onto which was grafted a more cynical examination of Wales's relation to England, most notably in the Tudor period and the impact of the union legislation and the Reformation on Wales, mediated by an English nationalism. See Lewis, *Egwyddorion*, pp. 2–4.

67 Moses Griffith, 'Aspects of Welsh Agriculture', *The Welsh Nationalist*, April 1936, 8–9. For Griffith, an agricultural scientist and practical farmer see Llywelyn Phillips, 'Moses Griffith' in *Adnabod Deg*, pp. 96–105.

68 D. J. Davies, 'Self-government our only hope', *The Welsh Nationalist*, April 1932.

69 Emyr W. Williams, 'D. J. Davies: a working class intellectual within Plaid Genedlaethol Cymru 1927–37', *Llafur*, 4:4 (1986), 50–2.

70 Ibid.

71 Saunders Lewis, *The Case for a Welsh National Development Council* (n.d. 1934?), especially pp. 4, 6, 8–12.

72 Saunders Lewis to Kate Roberts, 31 January 1932 file, Kate Roberts MSS File 177 and Saunders Lewis to Kate Roberts, 17 July 1932. See also 'A Candidate for Wales', *The Welsh Nationalist*, December 1942, 3.

73 *Welsh Nationalist*, March, 1936.

74 For more on this see Williams, 'D. J. Davies', 54–6.

75 *WO*, August 1927. See Saunders Lewis, *Is there an Anglo-Welsh literature?* (Cardiff, 1939).

76 Iorwerth C. Peate, 'Threats to Welsh Culture', *WM*, 3 August 1937. Peate, a disillusioned Labour supporter, was founder of the Welsh Folk Museum in 1948 to extol Welsh rural life.

77 Rhys Tudur, '*Y Cymro*, Penyberth a'r ail ryfel byd', *Cof Cenedl*, 17 (2002), 140–6.

78 Mr. Justice Thomas, 'Legal Wales: its modern origins and its role after devolution: National identity, the Welsh language and parochialism', *Welsh Legal History Society*, 1 (2001); *Legal Wales: Its Past, Its Future*, 113–65, esp. 128–49.

79 The Defence of Wales, *Welsh Nationalist*, January 1942, 3.

80 That said, Davies was an unusual character. A farmer's son, he left school at an early age. He became a very young conscientious objector in the First World War before taking a degree at the University College of North Wales, Bangor. A solicitor and WEA lecturer, he was a member of the radical Socialist League and had been Secretary of the University Socialist Federation and active in Swansea Labour politics. (Candidates' biographies, TUC archive, TUC papers 292.715.14, Modern Records Centre, University of Warwick)

81 'Ymchwil Undeb Cymru Fydd i gyflwr bywyd cymdeithasol Cymru', Undeb Cymru Fydd MSS File 165 (NLW).

82 Plaid Genedlaethol Cymru, 'Sut I achub Cymru: adroddiad y flwyddyn', Awst 1943. David Thomas papers Box 2 (UWB).

83 Edgar Chappell papers File E4/1 (NLW).

84 R. David Jones to Edgar Chappell, 15 September 1942, File E4/2.

85 Edgar Chappell, address to Pontypridd Cymmrodorion, 22 October 1942, File E2/7.

86 Chappell papers, Association of Welsh Local Authorities, 28 October 1942 E2/13.

87 James McConnel, ' "Sympathy without relief is rather like mustard without beef": devolution, Plaid Cymru, and the campaign for a secretary of state for Wales, 1937–8', *WHR*, 22 (2005).

88 For more on this see J. Graham Jones, 'Early campaigns to ensure a Welsh Secretary of State, 1890–1939', *THSC* (1988).

89 *Wales – the next step: Devolution, Secretary of State, Parliament for Wales and all that* (1959)

90 Ibid.

91 For more on this see the chapter by Griffith (above) p. 89 and see also J. Graham Jones, 'Early campaigns to secure a Secretary of State for Wales . . .' and McConnel, 'Sympathy without relief'.

92 James Griffiths, 'Wales after the war', *Wales*, 1 (July 1943), 9–10.

93 Ibid.

94 Ibid.

95 Plaid Genedlaethol Cymru, *Adroddiad y flwyddyn* (1943), pp. 9–10.

96 Gwynfor Evans, 'Rebuild the foundations', *Wales*, 2 (October 1943), 19.

97 Ibid, p. 20.

98 Ibid.

99 Welsh Committee for the Communist Party, *The Flame of Welsh Freedom* (1944), foreword by Idris Cox.

100 For more on this see Davies, *Welsh Nationalist Party*, pp. 237–41.

101 McConnel, 'Sympathy without relief'.

102 Ibid., citing TNA, PREM 1/292 Sir James Rae to C. G. L. Syers, 29 June 1938. PRO, PREM 1/292.

103 Handwritten comment on Pepler to Phillips, 4 March 1943, Health and Local Government Office, TNA HLG 71/1123.

104 'Open letter to the Premier', *Y Cymro*, 26 June 1943.

105 Iwan Morgan, *Secretary of State for Wales: Attlee's Reply* (1943). The issue had been raised only by 'questions in the House'.

106 J. A. Barlow to Thomas Jones, 26 April 1944, Thomas Jones MSS, File HHJ (NLW).

6
The dilemmas of nation and class in Wales, 1914–45

Chris Williams[1]

In January 1914 a new political and cultural monthly magazine was launched in Wales. *The Welsh Outlook*, edited initially by Thomas Jones,[2] at that time Secretary to the Welsh Insurance Commissioners, set out its stall in the 'Foreword' of its opening number:

> Welsh nationality is being attacked in a double sense by the economic forces which are everywhere at work breaking down barriers of time and space and race and colour and by the overshadowing presence at our elbow of a social and political power, superior to us in size, in numbers, in wealth.
>
> In the presence of these all-pervasive influences can a small nation of two millions maintain any semblance of its ancient self? Can it absorb into itself the immigrants of the mining valleys and share with them its spiritual heritage? Or must it be transformed out of recognition by its predominant neighbour? In any case is it desirable that its identity should be preserved? These are far-reaching questions which it will be the business of this journal to discuss. For the moment let us anticipate the answer we ourselves shall give. We hold that the assertion and maintenance of our nationality is justified; that our moral and political and social traditions are a precious inheritance the loss of which would impoverish humanity; and that local patriotism is not incompatible with imperial loyalty.[3]

These two paragraphs encapsulate what is termed here the dilemmas of nation and class in Wales, as they confronted progressive intellectuals and social radicals, from the eve of the First World War down to the close of the Second World War. Wales and Welsh nationality were considered to be under threat: from the forces of anglicisation and, indeed, from what later scholars would come to call globalisation. A specific concern was the influence wielded by 'the immigrants of the mining valleys', already by 1914, a cauldron of industrial militancy and political radicalism, who were establishing a predominantly English-speaking and distinctively working-class culture in the south-eastern counties of Glamorgan and Monmouthshire.[4] Yet this concern over the preservation of what was understood as Welshness did not extend to contemplating the dissolution of the United Kingdom: 'local patriotism' was compatible with 'imperial loyalty'.

The motto of *The Welsh Outlook* was 'Where there is no vision the people perish'. In many respects the magazine (which ran until 1933)[5] may be seen as the house journal of a particular branch of the Welsh intelligentsia, which had already exercised a considerable influence over Welsh civil society during the Edwardian era, and which would go on to wield even greater control over a variety of organisations and movements in the 1920s and 1930s. Historians and historical geographers have already noted the importance of prominent individuals such as Thomas Jones, and the involvement of this intellectual elite in spheres including public health,[6] workers' education[7] and town planning.[8] They were at the heart of a series of seminal official reports on the state of labour relations and society in south Wales, including those of the 1917 Commission of Enquiry into Industrial Unrest in Wales and Monmouthshire,[9] and of the 1921 *Regional Survey of South Wales*.[10] They went on to play a key role in the 'social service' response to the problems thrown up by economic depression, widespread unemployment and the poverty brought with it.[11]

This essay concerns itself not with the detail of these initiatives and involvements, but rather with the engagement of these 'liberal-Cambrianists'[12] with the idea of Wales and its political destiny. It draws on the public expressions of this engagement found in influential periodicals such as *The Welsh Outlook*, *The Welsh Housing and Development Year Book* and *The Welsh Review*, as well as in the aforementioned government reports and in pamphlets and books sponsored by organisations such as the Welsh School of Social Service, or published by key members of what has been defined as this 'loosely knit coterie of social radicals'.[13] More private, and fragmentary, indications of their world-view may be found in manuscripts deposited in the National Library of Wales, or in files in The National Archives. Few of these men were elected representatives working in the arenas of local or national government, although they frequently exercised considerable influence in both. The purpose of this chapter is not to provide an overview of what has been termed the 'Second Welsh Home Rule movement'[14] during the years after 1914, nor of the various initiatives brought forward in pursuit of the establishment of a Secretary of State for Wales. Such matters were of concern to the liberal-Cambrianists, but they were rarely the prime movers in these spheres. Rather, it seeks to sketch out the intellectual lineaments and contradictions of their modernistic Welsh nationalism. The contention is that the vision of these social radicals, whilst being far more socially engaged and politically astute than the competing vision that came to be articulated in the 1920s and 1930s by the ideologues of Plaid Genedlaethol Cymru (the Welsh Nationalist Party), at the same time failed to overcome, intellectually and spiritually, the problem posed to their conceptions of Welsh nationhood and culture by the presence, in Wales, of what was perceived to be an alien population.

The chapter thus demonstrates the significance of some of the barriers to a putative national unity that existed in Wales in the inter-war period. As noted in the volume's 'Introduction', identities that are built on linguistic, religious or other 'ethnic' criteria have the potential to alienate as well as to unify, to place individuals and groups outside or beyond the national community rather than to draw them within its bounds. Advocates of devolutionary or nationalist solutions to Welsh political problems have regularly been confronted by this dilemma: that whilst it has been simplest to envisage Welshness and Welsh national identity in essentially ethnic terms, such an imagining has also been corrosive of the coalition of interests necessary for any such project to succeed.

The chapter falls into five distinct parts. Firstly, the personnel and careers of some of the most prominent of the liberal-Cambrianists need elaboration, alongside an assessment of their politics and the political contexts in which they operated. Secondly, their responses to the various Home Rule, devolution or nationalist initiatives of the period will be evaluated. Thirdly, the conundrum of their views on race and nationhood will be explored, before, fourthly, outlining the differences that marked them off from the newer and more aggressive nationalists in Plaid Genedlaethol Cymru. In the concluding section, an assessment will be made of their overall importance to the history of debates about nationality and devolution in modern Wales.

Progressives and their politics

It has already been demonstrated that historians of Edwardian and inter-war Wales have used various labels to describe the particular stratum of the Welsh intelligentsia with which this essay is concerned. 'liberal-Cambrianists', 'social radicals', 'the Cardiff-Barry coterie'[15] (referring to where many of them lived in the years immediately before the First World War), all have their uses and all their pitfalls. Any list of those covered by such tags will, inevitably, be partial and incomplete, more or less appropriate as to time and place. Some were personal friends or close colleagues, others were only acquaintances. There were those at the centre of the grouping, and those on the periphery. Political and career choices took some out of the circle, illness and death terminated the involvement of others. However, three men stand at its centre for virtually all of the period.

Thomas Jones (1870–1955) has been variously described as 'a ubiquitous figure in inter-war Wales',[16] the 'unofficial Prime Minister of Wales',[17] 'a sort of unofficial proconsul for the Principality',[18] and 'a shadowy but very real grey eminence on the borders of the state and society'.[19] Jones, born in

Rhymney and trained in universities at Aberystwyth and Glasgow, had embarked on an academic career before returning to Wales to serve as Secretary to first the Welsh National Memorial Association and then the Welsh National Insurance Commission. In 1916 he was plucked by Lloyd George to join him at the heart of government in Whitehall, becoming first assistant and then deputy secretary to the cabinet, a position which he retained until 1930. Thereafter he acted in many capacities: most importantly as secretary to the Pilgrim Trust (1930–45), as the mastermind behind the establishment of Coleg Harlech in 1927, and as President of the University College of Wales, Aberystwyth (1944–54).

The 'scholar-publicist'[20] Daniel Lleufer Thomas (1863–1940) has been described as the 'most important social thinker' in Wales in the 1910s.[21] Born in Llandeilo, he was educated at Llandovery College and the University of Oxford before training as a barrister.[22] Stipendiary magistrate for Pontypridd from 1909 until 1933, he was appointed Secretary of the Commission of Enquiry into the Land Question in Wales in 1893, and was centrally involved in both the 1917 and 1921 enquiries referred to above. President of the Workers' Educational Association (WEA) from 1911 to 1915, Lleufer Thomas was co-founder and President of the Welsh School of Social Service, and very prominent in the Welsh Housing and Development Association (WHDA) (editing its *Year Book* for a number of years), the National Library of Wales and the University of Wales.[23] He was a founder of the Cardiff Workers' Co-operative Garden Village Society and Vice-President of the Labour Co-Partnership Association. Knighted in 1931, it was the historian David Williams's judgement that 'for fully fifty years he had been active in every important enterprise for the betterment of the people of Wales.'[24]

Edgar Chappell (1879–1949) was born at Ystalyfera and educated at University College, Cardiff. He became a schoolmaster, but developed a strong interest in social issues before the First World War. A Fellow of both the Royal Economic Society and of the Royal Statistical Society, at various times he edited the *Welsh Housing and Development Year Book* and *The Welsh Outlook*. He worked as a special investigator for the Ministry of Agriculture and as an inspector for the Housing Department of the Ministry of Health, and was Secretary to both the 1917 and the 1921 commissions. He was also Secretary to both the WHDA and the South Wales Garden Cities and Town Planning Association (SWGCTPA). Later he established a firm of estate agents in Cardiff, and was an enthusiastic local historian.

In addition to this prominent trio, there were many others with varying degrees of involvement with the organisations and initiatives mentioned thus far. These included E. T. John (1857–1931), industrialist, Liberal MP for East Denbighshire (1910–18) and later Labour parliamentary candidate; the civil servant and public administrator Sir Percy Watkins (1871–1946);[25] William Watkin Davies (1895–1973) whose varied career involved spells as a teacher, a WEA tutor, a barrister, editor of *The Welsh Outlook*, a Nonconformist minister, and a university lecturer;[26] the town planner and architect Thomas Alwyn Lloyd (1881–1960), who served on the 1921 Regional Survey Committee and was a leading light in the Welsh housing reform movement; and the Cardiganshire-born but London-based T. Huws Davies (1882–1940), one-time editor of *The Welsh Outlook* and Secretary of the Welsh Church Commission, a Fabian socialist who later drifted into and back out of Plaid Genedlaethol Cymru. Less obviously involved in most of the organisational activity, but exercising a profound (if not always deliberate) intellectual influence on this group, were academics such as Sir Henry Jones (1852–1922),[27] Sir Alfred Zimmern (1879–1957), Professor H. J. Fleure (1877–1969),[28] Professor Patrick Abercrombie (1879–1957) and Sir Patrick Geddes (1854–1932).[29]

This, then, was a wide swathe of influential and essentially altruistic public servants, spanning the overlapping worlds of government and civil society. Yet many of the organisations or initiatives for or with which these men worked, were supported financially, and sometimes administratively, by the coalowner and politician David Davies (from 1932 Baron Davies of Llandinam). David Davies (1880–1944) was 'a towering figure in the social reform movement in inter-war Wales',[30] a remarkably active, if controversial, philanthropist, sometimes acting in tandem with his sisters, Gwendoline and Margaret Davies, who lived at Gregynog near Newtown. The support of the Davies family ensured that *The Welsh Outlook*, which never broke even, nonetheless continued publication for twenty years, and their money was also critical to initiatives such as the Welsh National Memorial Association, the SWGCTPA and the WHDA. Davies himself was a man of wide interests, concentrated from the late 1920s onwards on the League of Nations Union and the New Commonwealth movement.[31] He served as Liberal, and later Independent MP for Montgomeryshire, from 1906 until 1929, and for a while (1916–17) as Private Secretary to Lloyd George, but became disillusioned with Lloyd George's radicalism in the 1920s.[32]

Politically, where did these social radicals sit in Edwardian and inter-war Wales? Historians have had difficulty placing them accurately. Some were clearly associated with the Liberal Party, or at least with the traditional Welsh Liberal agenda, yet it is more accurate to see them as 'small l' liberals rather than men committed, *sine die*, to the political formation that had been so hegemonic in late Victorian and Edwardian times. Some were, at various points in their lives, avowed socialists, if always of an ethical or Fabian rather than revolutionary or Marxist stamp.[33] Richard Lewis has written of them inhabiting a political middle ground or 'twilight zone' between the traditional 'old' Liberalism characteristic of the Welsh Parliamentary Party in its heyday, and the increasingly aggressive socialism found amongst the burgeoning trade union and labour movement.[34] A good case may be made for seeing the social radicals as championing a Welsh 'New Liberalism'.[35] Modernists, they were conscious that the traditional Welsh Liberal agenda was becoming less and less relevant to the problems facing Wales. They backed the social reform measures introduced by the Liberal governments from 1906, and were proud of the leading role taken by Lloyd George in these developments.

As most were not elected politicians, such flexibility allowed them to work with the grain of the system, exploiting personal connections which could sometimes cross party loyalties. They were 'useful, helpful, constructive Welshmen', in Thomas Jones's words.[36] Yet the absence of any formal, or even sustained personal links with the labour movement in Wales, was to prove a handicap. Their educational backgrounds (most were university graduates) and social position in adult life marked them out as definitely not members of the working class, whatever the nature of their beginnings.[37]

The ambiguities of their political and social status might be one reason why Welsh historians have found them difficult to place accurately. Dai Smith, for example, has seen the social radicals as wedded to an increasingly outmoded 'old liberal-nationalist Wales', unable to comprehend or come to terms with either the rising tide of class awareness so apparent in south Wales or with the appearance 'of a more fiercely intellectual and political nationalism'.[38] Richard Lewis has suggested that they desired 'to engage nationalist sentiment in support of social reform and against class conflict', promoting Welshness 'as a bridge between the social classes'.[39] Certainly many of their acutest concerns related to the rising volume (down to the early 1920s) of industrial unrest and class conflict in the south Wales coalfield. After 1926 the focus of their solicitude shifted towards the amelioration of the social effects of the Depression, and it is true that the class polarisation and economic collapse characteristic of the inter-war decades effectively cut the ground from beneath these advocates of industrial conciliation and social consensus, and drove wedges, on the one hand, between those progressives committed to solving the social and economic problems of the time, and, on the other, those in the labour movement whose focus was instead on battling against non-unionism and fascism. Any assessment of the legacy of David Davies needs to recognise that his Ocean Coal Company pedalled a paternalist authoritarianism that, at the very least, tolerated the South Wales Miners' Industrial Union.[40] Yet to presume that such divisions were implicit in the policies and attitudes of the social radicals from the beginning is to ignore considerable evidence of interest in such policies and sharing of such attitudes from prominent figures within the South Wales Miners' Federation (SWMF) and the Labour Party in Wales. As Julie Light has observed, the social radicals' ideas cannot be seen 'as simply imposed from the top down as some sort of effort at "social control".'[41] Rather than a dichotomy organised on political and class lines, we have here a 'sliding scale' (on some though not all issues) on which individuals took up positions that were only gradually differentiated.

To give one example, that of housing reform, both the SWGCTPA and the WHDA not only included on their governing council prominent Labour leaders such as J. T. Clatworthy, President of the Cardiff Coal-Trimmers' Union, and leading SWMF representatives William Harris, T. I. Mardy Jones, W. H. May and James Winstone (at the time President of the SWMF), they also sought representative members from Labour organisations such as trade unions (including the SWMF, the North Wales Miners' Association, the North Wales Quarrymen's Association, the Steel Smelters' Union, the Sailors and Firemen's Union and the Coaltrimmers' Union), from trades councils, and from labour clubs. SWMF General Secretary Thomas Richards was Deputy President of the WHDA's South Wales Branch in the 1920s and both Vernon Hartshorn and Edward Gill were directors of the Welsh Town-Planning and Housing Trust. Winstone, Richards and Arthur Jenkins all wrote for housing reform publications,[42] Welsh trade unions, co-operative societies and other labour bodies held a housing policy conference in April 1917 at the Cory Hall in Cardiff, chaired by Daniel Lleufer Thomas,[43] and WHDA chairman James Alexander Lovat-Fraser could claim in 1918 that 'no class is more interested in the matter of Education in Town-Planning than the miners'.[44] More broadly, William Jenkins, later to be Labour MP for Neath, served on the 1921 Regional Survey Commission, Vernon Hartshorn served on that of the 1917 Commission of Enquiry into Industrial Unrest, and Frank Hodges published a number of articles in *The Welsh Outlook*.[45] This is not to say that Labour movement figures necessarily shared all the concerns and attitudes of the liberal-Cambrianists, before and after 1926, but it is to suggest that ruling a class divide through the social politics of day may obscure as much as it may illuminate.

Home Rule and devolution

What, then, of the liberal-Cambrianist view of Wales and its political destiny? Broadly speaking, it was a nationalist view in a traditional sense. Some of the coterie, such as Daniel Lleufer Thomas, had been contemporaries of Owen M. Edwards at Oxford, founder members of the Cymdeithas Dafydd ap Gwilym, and had participated in the Cymru Fydd agitation. Others had grown up reading the literature of European nationalism.[46] Most were religious Nonconformists, although some were more pious than others, committed to the principle of disestablishment. Most shared traditional Welsh Liberal views about the desirability of temperance, land and educational reforms. But was this, as Richard Lewis has suggested, 'a rather soft, sentimental, type of nationalism which displayed little or no interest in political autonomy for Wales'?[47] The evidence suggests that, on the contrary, the social radicals had a strong commitment to what they understood as 'Welsh autonomy'.

The Welsh Outlook had been founded to provide what Thomas Jones termed 'an independent national standpoint',[48] and as early as April 1914 had advocated 'Home Rule for Wales', 'quite convinced' that 'decentralisation is essential for the best government of our Country'.[49] The war had necessitated a 'softly, softly' approach on this question in its early stages but, with many in both the Liberal and Labour parties towards the end of the conflict, the liberal-Cambrianists shared a hope that federal Home Rule might shortly be extended to Wales. Various factors appeared to be working in this direction. Firstly, it was anticipated that the solution to the now critical Irish Question could well involve 'Home Rule All Round', establishing subordinate legislatures in Ireland, Scotland and Wales. Secondly, there appeared to be a widespread recognition that one of the guiding principles of the Allies' approach to the war and the impending peace settlement was the right of nations to self-determination, and that Wales had as much right to such a concession as the peoples of the Balkans and Eastern Europe.[50] Thirdly, it was expected that the 'Imperial Parliament' would be faced by such momentous burdens in facing up to reconstruction after the war that the principle of efficiency would demand devolution of much government business. Fourthly, the one-time standard bearer of Cymru Fydd, David Lloyd George, now sat in No. 10 Downing Street. It would take but little effort, on his part, it was assumed, for Wales's destiny to be fulfilled. The long-term objective of many Welsh Liberals, the disestablishment of the Anglican Church, being assured, there was every hope that Lloyd George might prove capable of showing leadership to the majority of Welsh MPs (Liberal and Labour) who were formally committed to the goal of Home Rule.

When, in 1917, Thomas Jones and David Davies both drew up memoranda as to the future direction of the *Outlook*, they agreed that 'Welsh autonomy' should be its 'main cause'.[51] From 1918 until the early 1920s the magazine carried many articles beating the devolutionary drum, including a series by E. T. John himself,[52] and most of the editor's 'Notes of the month' carried at least a column reporting on the latest developments, or lambasting Welsh MPs for their relative inactivity on the issue.

In retrospect, of course, it is easy to understand why Home Rule remained a frustrated ambition of Welsh nationalists. The Irish Question was resolved in ways largely unanticipated, which left no scope for Home Rule All Round.[53] The Speaker's Conference turned out to be a political cul-de-sac. The Home Rule conferences organised at Llandrindod and Shrewsbury ultimately proved futile. Welsh Liberal MPs, divided between the supporters of Lloyd George and those remaining loyal to Asquith, were distracted and ineffective: the most prominent Home Ruler amongst them, E. T. John, lost his parliamentary seat in 1918.[54] Labour MPs had more pressing priorities as the coal industry slid into conflict and chaos. Lloyd George had no time to spare, no political space, perhaps no real interest, in rekindling the fires of his youth.[55] There was no popular movement in favour of Home Rule, nothing even to compare with the limited mobilisation achieved by Cymru Fydd in 1895, and no grass-roots pressure to speak of from within the political parties or from the public at large.[56] The *Outlook* could give the issue all the space it wanted to, but it was read by a small elite of like-minded people, not by the masses. As Kenneth O. Morgan has written, 'opinion in Wales was much more divided by sectional, regional, or class antagonisms than it was unified by the appeal of autonomy.'[57]

It should also be noted that the clarity of the objectives favoured by the devolutionists left much to be desired. For most, the goal was a Welsh legislature that would rule over Welsh domestic affairs. A blueprint for a solution of this kind had been provided in 1914 by E. T. John's Government for Wales Bill, which would allow the Imperial Parliament to retain control of foreign affairs, defence, postal and customs issues, whilst establishing a ninety-strong single-chamber Welsh legislature with widespread domestic responsibilities.[58] But there were at least two other, if lesser, options. One was to press for devolution on a piecemeal and incremental basis. There was already in existence the Welsh Insurance Commission and the Welsh Department of the Board of Education. Pressure could be levelled for a Welsh Board of Health and a Welsh Department of the Board of Agriculture. Although it was acknowledged that such developments were partial and, as a general solution to the problem, unsatisfactory, it was also possible for many to believe that where opportunities for essentially administrative devolution presented themselves, they should not be passed over, but could be regarded as instalments of 'that fuller autonomy, legislative and administrative' which Wales was thought to require.[59] The more substantial but also more problematic alternative to full-scale federal Home Rule was to agitate for a Secretary of State for Wales, in imitation of Scotland. For some, this was a practical first step towards the ultimate objective of a legislative parliament, a firm recognition by central government of the special needs of Wales, but for others there was the concern that such an office might prove ineffective and might thus retard the prospects for more substantial devolution. Why divert energies towards securing a Secretary of State, it could be argued, when the greater prize of Home Rule was apparently within reach?[60] The inability of progressive and nationalist opinion to agree on a single, clear objective hamstrung the devolution campaign and rendered it even more powerless than it might otherwise have been.[61]

Another key factor in explaining the failure of the Home Rulers was their inability to draw in sufficient support from the Labour Party and trade union movement in Wales. One of the reasons why Liberal advocates of Home Rule came to shelve the idea in the 1920s was their realisation that any democratic parliament elected to represent a devolved Wales would, if constituted along similar lines to that of the Westminster Parliament, most probably return a majority of Labour representatives, given the population balance towards the counties of Glamorgan and Monmouth and given the capture of many of their parliamentary constituencies by 1922 by Labour. Long-standing geographical, cultural and political divides in Wales resurfaced. In 1896 Cymru Fydd had foundered on the suspicion of the capitalists and trade unionists of the south that the movement was an attempt by Welsh-speaking Nonconformist Wales to divert the nation away from its profitable engagement with the British Empire.[62] In the 1920s the representatives of that Welsh-speaking Nonconformist Wales feared the 'Bolshevism' and materialism of the mining valleys.[63]

The more politically progressive social radical thinkers acknowledged the force of this argument in dividing opinion that might otherwise be united in support of Home Rule.[64] Their response was to search for a solution that would embody proportional representation,[65] or a geographical weighting of representatives (along the lines, possibly, of the American Senate),[66] or even a geographical expansion of Wales to include Shropshire and Herefordshire[67] to help combat the numerical superiority of the population of south Wales.[68] But it was on this issue that the putative progressive coalition foundered. Labour advocates of Home Rule were not prepared to forswear the likely consequences of what they understood as the appropriate democratic structures of any federal parliament in Wales. If they were the majority in the country, they reasoned, they should be the majority in the federal legislature. Even patriotic Welsh Labour figures such as Dai Grenfell were determined not to put the interests of their class to one side in pursuit of a putative national unity, which might return to the capitalist classes that political representation which had only recently been prised from them.[69] As George Barker, an advocate of a Welsh Parliament, put it, 'Labour can and will look after itself, and will not play second role to anyone.'[70] Class interests would triumph over national allegiances, as David Thomas acknowledged: 'one cannot truthfully say that our national grievances are a burning question with the Welsh rank and file, and you cannot reasonably expect the working-classes of Wales to subordinate the aims which they have in common with their English comrades to such objects as Welsh Home Rule, and a Welsh temperance policy, important though they be.'[71] The clearest articulation of Labour's stance was written for the *Outlook* by William Harris, Secretary of the South Wales Labour Federation and a SWMF political organiser. Harris noted that the 'cosmopolitan' reality of 'the industrial portion of Wales' was 'absolutely ignored by the advocates of Home Rule', who spoke of Wales 'as if no changes had taken place during the last 25 years'. Harris accused 'Welshmen who have occupied and are occupying positions under the State' as having shown 'an utter disregard for the democracy as represented by the industrial element in Wales'. What was needed to 'place the question of Federal Home Rule upon a sound footing at the earliest possible moment' was 'the support of not only patriotic Welshmen, but the support of men and women of other nationalities residing in Wales and Monmouthshire.'[72] Such support was never forthcoming. Not even in the pages of the *Outlook* was there to be any effort to reach out to Wales's considerable immigrant population.

Race and nationhood

In most respects the liberal-Cambrianists appear to have been enlightened, progressive thinkers. Yet on the question of, as they understood it, 'race', their attitudes were regressive, even reactionary.[73] Most of them were Welsh by birth, and by speech, although much of their public work was conducted through the medium of English. They valued the Welsh language for its own sake, but also for the culture and the values that it was held to represent. According to Thomas Jones, the loss of the Welsh language was a process of 'denationalisation' which led to blurred ideals and weakened moral sanctions.[74]

The social radicals worked with a concept of Welsh nationality that was partial and which denied full citizenship to a good number of Welsh voters. As Richard Lewis has noted, in the minds of the social radicals 'blood was thicker than class',[75] but their analysis of blood was considerably more problematic than a common assertion of Welsh nationhood to all resident in Wales. On the contrary, their world-view was one in which somewhat vaguely defined conceptions of racial identity played a major part in delimiting and understanding the nature of 'true Wales'. In this matter, then, they had rather more in common with some of the younger nationalists entering Plaid Genedlaethol Cymru, than has always been appreciated.

This issue has received some passing comment from other historians. Dai Smith has argued that the definition of 'Welsh' used by the 1917 Commissioners was one 'of social behaviour, desired or required, masquerading as a racial characteristic'. Welsh workers embodied what the social radicals viewed as 'the higher values of bourgeois frugality and thoughtfulness', with alien immigrants having a higher propensity to strike.[76] But his brief focus on this is limited to the worries being expressed in the 1910s at the height of industrial militancy. What has not always been appreciated is the extent to which such attitudes persisted for at least another thirty years.

What worried the social radicals was the realisation that, in the industrial districts, especially those of the south, class appeared to have triumphed over nation, giving the south Wales miner a greater affinity with English and Scottish miners than with other Welsh workers. There was little attempt to understand this new culture on its own terms, for not only was its gospel of class conflict very uncomfortable and unwelcome, but it was perceived as having dispensed with the true (spiritual and cultural) values of Wales without having embraced a culture of equal worth. Rather, it had debased itself through a pursuit of materialism, had lost its religiosity, its spirituality, and its Welsh nationality. Its language had been put to one side, and it had sold its soul to Anglo-Americanism. Responsible for much, if not all, of these regrettable tendencies, was inward migration, mainly from England. English migrants were considered to have polluted the coalfield with their alien values. Wales had 'suffered' from urbanisation and from the 'cosmopolitan element' which had a 'constant tendency to herd together'.[77]

These attitudes attained semi-official status in the 1917 Report which depicted north-east and south-east Wales as 'border districts'.[78] Whereas, until the end of the nineteenth century 'the native inhabitants had . . . shown a marked capacity for stamping their own impress on all newcomers, and communicating to them a large measure of their own characteristics', in 'more recent years the process of assimilation has been unable to keep pace with the continuing influx of immigrants.'[79] Such immigration, and its linguistic consequences (the spread of the English language at the expense of the Welsh), was considered to 'present obstacles to the growth of social solidarity':

> Many of the immigrants, cut off from their old religious associations and other restraining influences, drift into indifference, and some flushed, with their larger earnings and freer life, into self-indulgence. Others are attracted by the more idealistic principles of socialism, while not a few of the more active spirits throw all their energy into the work of their trade union, aiming perhaps too exclusively at the merely economic welfare of their own class.[80]

The 1921 Report was informed by similar intellectual imperatives. It observed that whereas the miners of the anthracite coalfield (in western Glamorgan and eastern Carmarthenshire) were 'mostly Welsh-speaking', and 'cling to manners and customs which are characteristic of the Cymric race', the eastern half of the south Wales coalfield had been 'invaded to a very considerable extent by emigrants from all parts of the United Kingdom, with even a sprinkling from beyond the seas.' Such an influx of 'a more or less alien population possibly accounts to some extent for the acceptance by South Wales miners of economic and social theories and policies which would appear to cut across Welsh tradition.'[81] These immigrants, the report considered, were 'often not of a very desirable character. They comprise a considerable proportion of more or less irresponsible people of disorderly habits'.[82]

Various contributors to *The Welsh Outlook* recycled such views of 'those ruined and hideous mis-housed and slavish hordes among the South Wales valleys'.[83] For retired civil servant T. P. Ellis, writing in 1927, migrants had little interest in things that were 'Welsh', instead preaching 'something which is anti-Welsh, that which they call "cosmopolitanism" or "solidarity of the world's proletariat"; a love of other people based on the fundamental assertion that you must hate your own flesh and blood.'[84] This 'racial influx' was 'passionate and unstable', and 'the traditional Welsh country view of things' was at risk of being submerged by 'a sectional industrial view'.[85] Such attitudes also surfaced in the work of William Watkin Davies, who in 1930 lamented the fact that 'the real Wales has of late been largely covered by a veneer of Anglo-Saxondom', simultaneously suffering a 'process of cultural levelling'.[86] Davies reserved his greatest scorn for the south Wales coalfield, 'these awful spots, outposts . . . of hell itself', 'things which in no true sense belong to Wales, but are rather the hideous price which men are paying . . . for an insane lust for gold and power', which he advocated should be visited 'as part of our training in citizenship'.[87] There was an echo here of Patrick Abercrombie's earlier categorisation of the Rhondda as 'the aesthetic climax of what [Geddes] has called the paleotechnic age of industrialism: it is Adam Smith's glorious vision of individualistic success absolutely realised'.[88] Thomas Jones himself endorsed such views in 1929, commenting that industrialism 'has changed our habits of life, our clothes, our food, our sports. It has diluted our population, defaced our land, debased our speech, stratified our society, confused our ideals, and made us mistake comfort for civilisation.'[89]

Such negative opinions of the industrial society of the southern coalfield fed into the voluntary movement in the 1930s. The Reverend Elfan Rees of Cardiff, at conferences staged by the Welsh School of Social Service, claimed that immigrants had 'never shared in the inheritance of Welsh culture and Welsh life', but instead had 'stultified the natural development of native culture', 'strangled our language and scorned our culture' and, in 'dominating

South Wales . . . made it hideous.'[90] The Reverend Selwyn Roberts of Pontypridd, who was associated with the Llanmadoc Religion and Life Fellowship, could argue that Wales had 'suffered from alien accretions', 'the incursion of large elements from outside Wales . . . who neither brought any definite culture of their own nor were able to fit into the culture of the Welsh community'.[91] And these attitudes permeated the views of Welsh civil servants and other public officials, some of whom were associates of the social radicals. Chief Poor Law Inspector for Wales, James Evans, a friend of Thomas Jones, felt in 1928 that he could detect a 'noticeable difference in the character and outlook of the people' between those districts 'where the native Welsh culture most strongly persists' and those 'where the industrial revolution has sub-merged the populace and has introduced an economic doctrine and a philosophy of life', which he felt were 'strange and unsatisfying [and] socially disturbing, to the "Celtic complex".'[92] Dr J. E. Underwood commented in a 1930 Ministry of Health enquiry into the health of school children in the south Wales coalfield that the area contained 'pockets' of a 'migratory community who were attracted . . . by industrial prosperity and high wages'. He went on to state that 'this "foreign" element is socially and industrially inferior to that of the majority of the population', who were of 'old-established Welsh stock' and were 'provident, hardworking, courageous and ready to sacrifice themselves to the welfare of their children.' Underwood argued that the greatest incidence of malnutrition was to be found in schools which drew on the 'socially inefficient communities', as opposed to those which drew from 'the established and permanent type of population'.[93]

It is true to say that the stark and negative attitudes held on the issue of immigration softened over time, perhaps helped by the perceived dimunition of the political and industrial threat of the industrial areas. Gwilym Davies, for instance, called in 1944 for greater mutual understanding between 'Western Wales' and 'Eastern Wales' (synonyms for Welsh-speaking and English-speaking areas), and pointed out that although Eastern Wales was 'mainly English in speech' it was 'not English in thought. Deep down it is Welsh.'[94] Yet even a second-generation migrant such as Edgar Chappell (whose father was from Somerset) could continue to blame the 'immigration of people of alien stock' for the lack of 'national spirit' in Wales.[95] Though a long-term resident and councillor in Cardiff, as late as 1939 Chappell argued that it was 'a cosmopolitan town dominated by English sentiment and inspired by English tradition . . . merely an English city in a Welsh setting', the majority of whose citizens were 'largely indifferent to the forms in which Welsh nationality expresses itself'.[96] By categorising many of the inhabitants of south Wales in such ways, the liberal-Cambrianists were denying their rights to full citizenship in any future Welsh state on the grounds that they were 'non-Welsh'.[97]

The imperatives of democracy were confused and confounded by an anachronistic conception of racial belonging that tended to essentialise Welshness and exclude a good proportion of the people of Wales.

The challenge of Plaid Genedlaethol Cymru

In the wake of the disappointments of the early post-war years a new breed of Welsh nationalist emerged, crystallising, in 1925, in the formation of Plaid Genedlaethol Cymru. To most of the social radicals, this was not a welcome development.[98] On four general issues, the views of the older and newer generations of nationalists diverged starkly.

For a start, the liberal-Cambrianists had a strong attachment to the British State structure, to the British Empire ('a wonderful form of human association, of unity in difference, a partnership in nations'),[99] and to the British Crown, attachments not shared to anything like the same degree by Plaid Cymru, which officially aimed at Dominion status for Wales.[100] The liberal-Cambrianist vision of a future Wales was certainly one which enjoyed greater autonomy in domestic affairs, but one which remained firmly located within a British Commonwealth of Nations. Welsh and British patriotisms were thought to be compatible and complementary.[101] Sir Henry Jones wrote that Wales was 'a partner in all the privileges and responsibilities of the Empire', and asked only for 'room to live within that Empire its own life',[102] whilst Watkin Davies saw Wales's destiny as coming to be 'actively and amicably associated with England' and 'participating to the uttermost in the wider life of the Empire.' For Davies, a 'fairer vision than that of an independent Wales' was that of 'a Commonwealth living a life of ordered prosperity . . . in which Wales, in virtue of its splendid tradition of passionate idealism and of tireless spiritual effort, shall enjoy a foremost place.'[103]

Secondly, the liberal-Cambrianists, though concerned about the influence of England and the English on Wales and on Welsh culture, recognised that it was by no means uniformly negative, and that Wales gained much from a close association with its powerful neighbour.[104] More broadly, they were concerned at the regressive elevation of the 'perils' of 'extreme nationalism' above what they considered to be widespread and progressive trends towards international co-operation and what Thomas Jones called 'the awareness of the unity of mankind'.[105]

Thirdly, the social radicals expressed considerable disquiet over Plaid's authoritarian and anti-democratic tendencies, disquiet heightened by the rise of Fascism and the struggle of the Second World War. Plaid Cymru and particularly its most prominent intellectual, Saunders Lewis, was thought to be out of line with mainstream currents in Welsh thought and culture, and its 'Hitlerian' tendencies and its vision of 'a new Promised Land of Fascism' led to the liberal-Cambrianists making furious attacks on the newer strain of Welsh nationalism.[106] While many had sympathised, up to a point, with the arson of Saunders Lewis, Lewis Valentine and D. J. Williams at Penyberth in 1936, there was much less understanding of Plaid's position of studied neutrality during the Second World War.

Finally, and perhaps most crucially, the social radicals were essentially pragmatic men who realised that their contribution lay most obviously in getting things done. This they did through influence, discussion, persuasion and compromise, working within and managing the existing system as effectively as possible where it was impossible to change it. The apparently idealistic self-conscious purity and other-worldliness of the Plaid's leadership appeared to them grossly misjudged, E. T. John objecting to Saunders Lewis's 'ingrained and intense aestheticism',[107] Edgar Chappell terming Plaid policy 'impossibilist' and 'quite impracticable'.[108]

Hostility to Plaid Genedlaethol Cymru was a motivating factor in edging many of the social radicals away from some of their earlier nationalist objectives. Although Edgar Chappell remained a committed Home Ruler, he carefully distinguished between what he termed 'national or quasi-national' grounds for self-government ('in my judgment they are not the most weighty factors') and what he called 'imperial considerations', 'based on the advantages which would be derived by the United Kingdom and the British Commonwealth as the result of all-round devolution.'[109] Others, such as Thomas Jones and Percy Watkins, in the twilight of their careers, came to resist moves even to establish a Secretary of State for Wales.[110]

In relation to the racial question, the liberal-Cambrian view of Welsh nationality had more than a little in common with that propounded by Plaid Cymru. What marked the social radicals' views out as different, however, was that they placed rather less stress on the Welsh language and none at all on the objective of 'de-industrialisation'. Although valuing the Welsh language, they did not reify it to the extent of envisaging a monoglot Welsh-speaking Wales. They also conceded that it was possible, racially, to be 'Welsh' without necessarily being able to speak Welsh.[111] Although regretting many of the social consequences of industrialisation, they did not think it realistic to plan for a return to a peasant society, or either sensible or sensitive to think in terms of de-industrialisation.[112] Rather they wished to graft the values of the true Welsh culture (though they recognised it might not be possible to graft the Welsh language) onto Wales's industrial settlements.[113] The WEA in Wales, the WHDA, the Welsh School of Social Service, Coleg Harlech: all were initiatives which were marked by this vision.

Conclusion

The importance of the social radicals in contributing to debates about Welsh nationhood has been ignored by some historians, who, from 1925 onwards, give much greater priority to the incipient and largely marginal Plaid Genedlaethol Cymru.[114] Of course, Plaid Cymru has been an important force in Welsh politics since 1966, and some of its earlier leaders have attracted scholarly attention not only for their politics but for their contributions to Welsh literature. The actions of Lewis, Valentine and Williams at Penyberth in 1936, and their subsequent trials and eventual imprisonment, have been seen as a rallying call to a sense of Welsh nationhood. Yet it has to be acknowledged that the ideology, outlook and approach of the social-democratic and even socialist versions of Plaid Cymru that have been in existence for the last half-century bear little relationship to the authoritarian, exclusivist and conservative version that was created in 1925 and which survived until at least 1945. The tenor of today's devolved Wales – operating within the United Kingdom and able to accommodate both Welsh and British identities – has more in common with the nationalism of the liberal-Cambrianists than it does with the nationalism of Saunders Lewis and his friends. More importantly, the liberal-Cambrianists made a difference to the Wales of their day in ways that could not be rivalled by their younger challengers.[115] To see their nationalism as 'soft' and 'sentimental' is surely to take the criticisms levelled at them by Plaid Cymru at face value. Yet on issues of race and class the liberal-Cambrianists were anything but soft. In their hands Welshness and Welsh culture was reduced to certain key components, and the partial and restricted vision that the social radicals had of the appropriate Welsh national community impeded the efficacy of their championing of devolution. For all their vision and energy in so many spheres, they remained unable to reimagine Wales as an open society, and thus contributed to an essentialising discourse that the people of Wales continued to have difficulty escaping from throughout the remainder of the twentieth century.

Notes

1 I am very grateful to Andrew Edwards and to Neil Evans for their help and advice on this subject.
2 For whose career, see E. L. Ellis, *T. J.: A Life of Dr Thomas Jones, CH* (Cardiff, 1992); and Rodney Lowe, 'Jones, Thomas (1870–1955)', *ODNB*.
3 *WO*, January 1914, 1–2.
4 For which, see Dai Smith, *Aneurin Bevan and the World of South Wales* (Cardiff, 1993).

5   For a history of *The Welsh Outlook*, see Gwyn Jenkins, '*The Welsh Outlook*, 1914–33', *NLWJ*, 34 (1986).

6   Pyrs Gruffudd, ' "A crusade against consumption": environment, health and social reform in Wales, 1900–1939', *JHG*, 21 (1995); Linda Bryder, 'The King Edward VII Welsh National Memorial Association and its policy towards tuberculosis, 1910–48', *WHR*, 13, 2 (1986).

7   Richard Lewis, *Leaders and Teachers: Adult Education and the Challenge of Labour in South Wales, 1906–40* (Cardiff, 1993); Peter Stead, *Coleg Harlech* (Cardiff, 1977).

8   Eddie May, 'Coal, community, town planning and the management of labour', *Planning Perspectives*, 11 (1996).

9   For which see, in addition to Smith, 'Deep and narrow valleys', in *Aneurin Bevan*; David Gilbert, 'Community and municipalism: collective identity in late-Victorian and Edwardian mining towns', *JHG*, 17 (1991); and Julie Light, 'The 1917 Commission of Enquiry into Industrial Unrest – a Welsh report', *WHR*, 21 (2003). The original report is Cd.8668 (1917), and papers relating to it can be found in the Edgar Leyshon Chappell papers (NLW).

10 Philip N. Jones, 'The South Wales Regional Survey, 1921', *Cambria*, 8 (1981).

11 Peter Stead, 'The voluntary response to mass unemployment', in Walter E. Minchinton (ed.), *Reactions to Social and Economic Change* (Exeter, 1979); John Davies, 'The communal conscience in Wales in the inter-war years', *THSC 1998*, n.s., 5 (1999); Andrew James Chandler, 'The Re-making of a Working Class: Migration from the South Wales Coalfield to the New Industry Areas of the Midlands, *c.*1920–1940', Ph.D., University of Wales (Cardiff), 1988.

12 The neologism is in Chandler, 'Re-making of a Working Class', p. 37. He argues (p. 43) that whilst 'it would be inaccurate to describe them as a cohesive and well-organised pressure group . . . they were identifiably coherent in ideological terms'.

13 Richard Lewis, 'The Welsh radical tradition and the ideal of a democratic popular culture', in Eugenio F. Biagini (ed.), *Citizenship and Community: Liberals, Radicals and Collective Identities in the British Isles, 1865–1931* (Cambridge, 1996), p. 327.

14 Kenneth O. Morgan, *Wales in British Politics 1868–1922* (Cardiff, 1980), p. 255.

15 Lewis, *Leaders and Teachers*, p. 106.

16 R. Merfyn Jones, 'Wales and British politics, 1900–1939', in Chris Wrigley (ed.), *A Companion to Early Twentieth-Century Britain* (Oxford, 2003), p. 88.

17 David Smith, 'Wales through the looking-glass', in Smith (ed.), *A People and a Proletariat: Essays in the History of Wales 1780–1980* (London, 1980), p. 228.

18 Ellis, *T. J.*, p. 320.

19 Gwyn A. Williams, *When Was Wales? A History of the Welsh* (Harmondsworth, 1985), p. 220.

20 Ibid., p. 229.

21 Stead, *Coleg Harlech*, p. 8. See also the extensive pen-portrait provided by Lewis, *Leaders and Teachers*, pp. 105–8.

22 In the case of many individuals discussed in this essay, I have relied for biographical information on sources including the *Dictionary of Welsh Biography down to 1940* (London, 1959), *Dictionary of Welsh Biography, 1941–70* (London, 2001), and *Who's Who in Wales* (Cardiff, 1921; London, 1933, 1937).

23 See Thomas Jones, 'Sir Daniel Lleufer Thomas', in *Leeks and Daffodils* (Newtown, 1942).

24 David Williams, 'Sir Daniel (Lleufer) Thomas', *DWB*, p. 940.

25 See Kenneth O. Morgan, 'Watkins, Sir Percy Emerson (1871–1946)', *ODNB*; Watkins, *A Welshman Remembers* (Cardiff, 1944).

26 Biographical details gleaned from schedule of W. Watkin Davies papers, NLW.

27 See David Boucher and Andrew Vincent, *A Radical Hegelian: The Political and Social Philosophy of Henry Jones* (Cardiff, 1993).

28 Welsh historical geographers have explored Fleure's legacy. See particularly Pyrs Gruffudd, 'Back to the land: historiography, rurality and the nation in interwar Wales', *Transactions of the Institute of British Geographers*, n.s., 19 (1994).

29 For essays on both Abercrombie and Geddes, see Gordon E. Cherry (ed.), *Pioneers in British Planning* (London, 1981); also Helen Meller, *Patrick Geddes: Social Evolutionist and City Planner* (London and New York, 1990). Abercrombie was not only an intellectual influence, serving on the 1921 Regional Survey Committee.

30 Gruffudd, ' "A crusade against consumption" ', 44.

31 See Paul Rich, 'Reinventing peace: David Davies, Alfred Zimmern and liberal internationalism in interwar Britain', *International Relations*, 16 (2002). Davies occasionally exercised influence over the contents of *The Welsh Outlook*: see T. L. Williams, 'Thomas Jones and *The Welsh Outlook*', *Anglo-Welsh Review*, 64 (1979).

32 Kenneth O. Morgan, 'Davies, David, first Baron Davies (1880–1944)', *ODNB*; J. Graham Jones, 'Montgomeryshire politics: Lloyd George, David Davies and the "Green book" ', *Montgomeryshire Collections*, 72 (1984).

33 Thomas Jones was a Fabian Socialist and a member of the Independent Labour Party, Edgar Chappell Secretary of the West Wales Independent Labour Party, though he was later elected as an Independent for both Cardiff Rural District Council and Glamorgan County Council.

34 'Welsh radical tradition', p. 327.

35 Kenneth O. Morgan, 'The New Liberalism and the challenge of Labour: the Welsh experience, 1885–1929', in *Modern Wales: Politics, Places and People* (Cardiff, 1995); Lewis, *Leaders and Teachers*, p. 39; Light, '1917 Commission of Enquiry', 718–20. J. Graham Jones, 'Wales and "the New Liberalism", 1926–1929', *NLWJ*, 22 (1982), uses the term in a different sense.

36 'Sir Daniel Lleufer Thomas', p. 167.

37 Stead, *Coleg Harlech*, p. 15. Thomas Jones appears to have placed a heavy stress on men of 'quality' being university graduates. See his 'The native never returns' in *The Native Never Returns* (London, 1946), p. 23.

38 'Wales through the looking-glass', p. 233.

39 *Leaders and Teachers*, pp. 40, 41.

40 Hywel Francis and David Smith, *The Fed: A History of the South Wales Miners in the Twentieth Century* (Cardiff, 1998), pp. 40, 90.

41 '1917 Commission of Enquiry', 726.

42 Winstone, 'Miners and the housing question', *WHYB 1916*, 94–6; Richards, 'The improvement of colliery districts', *WHDYB 1917*, 76–80; Jenkins, 'Municipalities and land ownership', *WHDYB 1918*, 58–60.

43 'Welsh labour unions and housing policy', *WHDYB 1918*, 128–30.

44 'The need for education in architecture and town-planning'. *WHDYB 1918*, 56.

45 'Unrest in the South Wales coalfield', *WO*, November 1917, 395–6; 'Adult education in South Wales', *WO*, November 1918, 321–2; 'University reform – Labour must co-operate', *WO*, December 1918, 361.

46 Thomas Jones, 'College memories', in *Leeks and Daffodils*, pp. 70–7.

47 'Welsh radical tradition', p. 332.

48 NLW, Thomas Jones papers, HH1/1.

49 'Notes of the month', *WO*, April 1914, 147.

50 'Notes of the month', *WO*, March 1915, 83; J. Arthur Price, 'State, nationalism and conscience', *WO*, October 1916, 313.

51 NLW, Thomas Jones papers, H4/74, 'Note re: *Welsh Outlook*', p. 4; H4/75, '*Welsh Outlook*: outline of policy'. For Davies's public views see 'Devolution', *WO*, March 1918, 77–8.

52 'Wales: its politics and economics', ran from January to August 1918 and was later issued as a pamphlet.

53 Though note the warning of J. Arthur Price, 'Is Welsh Home Rule coming?', *WO*, July 1917, 247.

54 These developments are traced in Morgan, *Wales in British Politics*, pp. 291–3; D. Hywel Davies, *The Welsh Nationalist Party 1925–1945: A Call to Nationhood* (Cardiff, 1993), chs. 1–2; J. Graham Jones, 'Early campaigns to secure a Secretary of State for Wales, 1890–1939', *THSC 1988*; and J. Graham Jones, 'E. T. John, devolution and democracy, 1917–24', *WHR*, 14 (1989).

55 Kenneth O. Morgan, 'Lloyd George and Welsh Liberalism', in *Modern Wales*, pp. 414–15.

56 A point repeatedly emphasised by Edgar Chappell in his later writings. See his *The Government of Wales* (London, 1943), p. 5; *Wake Up Wales! A Survey of Welsh Home Rule Activities* (London, 1943), pp. 94–5; and 'Back to Cymru Fydd', *The Welsh Review*, 3, 2 (1944), 140.

57 *Wales in British Politics*, p. 259.

58 Ibid. The bill was republished as a *Welsh Outlook* supplement in March 1919.

59 Daniel Lleufer Thomas, *The Welsh Housing & Development Association: Its Record and Its Program* (Cardiff, 1922), p. 8. See also 'Notes of the month', *WO*, June 1917, 203; Thomas to E. T. John, 25 February 1918, E. T. John Papers 1851 (NLW); Edgar L. Chappell, 'A ministry of health', *WHDYB 1918*, 67–8; 'Welsh labour unions and housing policy', 129–30; 'Editorial note', *WHDYB 1919*, 29–30; 'Editorial Note', *WHDYB 1921*, 28.

60 E. T. John to Daniel Lleufer Thomas, 14 February 1919. E. T. John Papers 2086; and unattributed press cutting (probably 1919) in Thomas Jones Papers (NLW), HH5, Item 9.

61 Chappell, *Wake Up Wales!*, p. 97.

62 See Chris Williams, 'Democracy and nationalism in Wales: the Lib-Lab enigma', in David Bates, Scott Newton and Robert Stradling (eds), *Conflict and Coexistence: Nationalism and Democracy in Modern Europe* (Cardiff, 1997).

63 A point clearly expressed by William George, Lloyd George's brother in his speech at the Llandrindod conference, reported in *WM*, 12 June 1919 and in 'The outlook: the conference and nationalism', *WO*, July 1919, 168; by 'The outlook: political futilities', *WO*, October 1919, 248; and by J. M. Howell, 'The future of Liberalism in Wales', *WO*, December 1919, 301.

64 'Notes of the month', *WO*, August 1920, 180; 'Notes of the month', *WO*, May 1922, 104; T. H. Lewis, 'Is Welsh Home Rule doomed?', *WO*, June 1923, 157; J. Emlyn Williams, 'Nationalism as a political creed for Wales', *WO*, June 1924, 149–52.

65 Advocated by E. T. John, 'Wales: its politics and economics', *WO*, January 1918, 15.

66 Ernest Evans, 'The Shrewsbury conference', *WO*, May 1922, 108. Also the view of a certain W. A. Bebb, 'The Welsh Home Rule Bill', *WO*, May 1919, 137.

67 'Notes of the month', *WO*, March 1922, 56.

68 Such views were being expressed in the 1940s by Gwilym Davies. See his 'Wales – western and eastern', *The Welsh Review*, 3, 1 (1944), 55.

69 Grenfell's views may be found in 'Comments of Welsh Labour men and others', *WO*, April 1918, 116.

70 'Views of Welsh leaders of thought', *WO*, March 1918, 83.

71 'The political future of Wales', *WO*, April 1918, 112.

72 'Labour and Home Rule for Wales', *WO*, June 1919, 145–7.

73 Note, 1917 Commission, p. 15, that the term 'racial' was there identified 'as a convenient term to indicate characteristics associated with different counties or provinces of the United Kingdom rather than with distinct races of people.'

74 'Social aspects of trade unionism', in *A Theme With Variations* (Gregynog, 1933), p. 17. It should be noted that there is no trace of this attitude in his much more sympathetic 'What's wrong with South Wales', in *Leeks and Daffodils*.

75 *Leaders and Teachers*, p. 40.

76 'Wales through the looking-glass', p. 232.

77 D. Lleufer Thomas, 'The housing problem in Wales', *WHYB 1916*, 25, 27. See also D. Lleufer Thomas, 'The geography of the coalfield, and its influence on the population', *WHDYB 1921*, 64–5.

78 1917 Report, p. 14.

79 Ibid., p. 15.

80 Ibid., p. 16.

81 1921 Report, p. 11.

82 Ibid., p. 12.

83 'Watchman', *WO*, September 1918, 287. See also 'Notes of the month', *WO*, March 1926, 61.

84 'A constructive policy for Wales', *WO*, April 1927, 92.

85 'A constructive policy for Wales', *WO*, September 1927, 234.

86 *A Wayfarer in Wales* (London, 1930), p. 3.

87 Ibid., p. 199.

88 Lest one mistake the critical nature of these comments, Abercrombie added that no attempt should be made 'to improve the Rhondda – it should be kept, carefully sterilised of human life, as a Museum specimen.' 'Wales: a study in the contrast of country and town', *THSC 1922–23* (1924), 185.

89 'The making of nations', in *WO*, March 1929, 73.

90 'A survey of social tendencies in Wales, 1935–6', *Public Health in Wales* (Llandrindod, 1936), pp. 7, 10; 'The new Wales and the new leisure', in *Wales and the New Leisure* (Llandyssul, 1934).

91 'The devastation of recent years', in Pennar Davies et al., *The Welsh Pattern* (Llanmadoc, 1945), p. 18.

92　'Report on "Conditions in South Wales" ', 24 March 1928, TNA MH57/110A. See similar comments from the Cardiff Divisional Inspector of Schools, Dr Williams, in the notes on the conference that took place at Glamorgan County Council in Cardiff on 20 December 1927 between Drs Eichholz, Underwood and Mr Birch Jones, and HM Inspectors of Schools, contained in TNA MH55/691.

93　'Enquiry into physique, and general health and state of clothing and boots of school children in the South Wales mining districts', TNA MH57/3. For other, very similar comments, see section V, 'General observations', of James Pearse, T. W. Wade, J. Owain Evans and J. E. Underwood, 'Inquiry into the present conditions as regards the effect of continued unemployment on health in certain areas of South Wales and Monmouth', 23 October 1936, TNA MH55/629.

94　'Wales – western and eastern', 55.

95　'Back to Cymru Fydd', 141. See also *Wake Up Wales!*, p. 92. Like Davies, Chappell too worried that any putative Welsh national movement would founder on the fact that 'under any system of democratic government representation must be more or less proportionate to population' (*Government of Wales*, p. 45).

96　*Cardiff Street Names* (Cardiff, 1939), p. 2. See also his view, 'Notes of the month', *WO*, November 1917, 375: 'nationalism does not usually find its best expression in big cities. In Cardiff it manifests itself but faintly'; and 'Notes of the month', *WO*, June 1918, 177: 'the city is thoroughly anti-Welsh in all its attributes . . . that such a town should become the Capital of Wales is unthinkable'.

97　Ellis, 'A constructive policy for Wales', *WO*, March 1928, 70. For this amongst Liberal nationalists, see Chapter 5 by Edwards and Griffith above, p. 118.

98　For early anxieties over Saunders Lewis's brand of nationalism, see 'Notes of the month', *WO*, October 1923, 256–8.

99　'Notes of the month', *WO*, March 1916, 76.

100　Though see W. A. Bebb, 'Wales and the British Empire', *WO*, August 1928, 237–9.

101　T. P. Ellis, 'A constructive policy for Wales', *WO*, February 1928, 42; *WO*, March 1928, 69.

102　Quoted in Boucher and Vincent, *A Radical Hegelian*, pp. 139–40.

103　*Wales* (London and New York, 1924), pp. 244, 245. See also his editor's 'Notes of the Month', in *WO*, March, April, May, July, August 1927.

104　'Notes of the month', *WO*, September 1925, 229. As Jones, 'College Memories', p. 76, put it, 'it was to be left to the nationalists of 1940 to discover that we were writhing in bondage under the heel of England.'

105　'The native never returns', p. 22. Jones (p. 20) viewed the British Commonwealth as 'a stepping stone to world unity and citizenship'. See also T. Alwyn Lloyd, 'Regional surveys and planning in relation to Welsh Home Rule', *WHDYB 1920*, 81.

106　Jones, 'The native never returns', pp. 20, 23.

107　E. T. John to J. Arthur Price, 22 April 1930, E. T. John papers 5200.

108　'Back to Cymru Fydd', 142; *Wake Up Wales!*, pp. 91–2. For the similar reaction of some Liberal nationalists, see Chapter 5 by Edwards and Griffith above p. 118.

109　*Wake Up Wales!*, pp. 4, 6.

110　Watkins, *A Welshman Remembers*, pp. 221–8; Thomas Jones papers HH5/20–1, memorandum dated 6 May 1944.

111 Thomas Jones, 'Welsh character', in Thomas Jones, *Leeks and Daffodils*, p. 193;
    T. P. Ellis, 'Non-co-operation – a reply', *WO*, September 1929, 263.
112 Jones, 'The making of nations', 73.
113 Lewis, *Leaders and Teachers*, pp. 194–5.
114 David L. Adamson, *Class, Ideology and the Nation: A Theory of Welsh
    Nationalism* (Cardiff, 1991); R. Merfyn Jones, 'Beyond identity? The recon-
    struction of the Welsh', *JBS*, 31 (1992); Emyr Wynn Williams, 'The politics of
    Welsh Home Rule 1886–1929: a sociological analysis', PhD, University of
    Wales, 1986.
115 Lewis, 'Welsh radical tradition', p. 340; Chandler, 'Re-making of a Working
    Class', p. 37.

Part III
OPPOSITION AND ALTERNATIVES: BRITAIN, THE EMPIRE AND THE CONSTITUTION

7
Devolution, federalism and imperial circuitry: Ireland, South Africa and India

James McConnel and Matthew Kelly

On the day before the third Home Rule bill was introduced to the imperial parliament at Westminster, the *Daily Chronicle* published messages of support from a distinguished array of Dominion Prime Ministers, statesmen, and public figures. 'These messages', the newspaper confidently asserted, 'show that . . . the voice of the Empire is on the side of Ireland.'[1] This attentiveness to colonial opinion was in fact a novel feature of a debate which by 1912 had endured for a generation. While British and Irish politicians had often framed their arguments about Home Rule in terms of 'Empire' (referencing it variously as a model to follow, a guide for the future, and an ideal to defend) little attention had hitherto been paid to how the hundreds of millions of citizen-subjects who made up Britain's overseas Empire saw the Irish Home Rule question.[2] Yet, even in 1912, the *Chronicle* had merely invited Canadian, Australian, South African, and New Zealand statesmen to endorse Liberal home rule. The newspaper, thereby, effectively manufactured for domestic consumption a homogenised and passive Greater British 'voice' whose function was simply to legitimate Liberal and nationalist assertions that Home Rule had already been successfully road-tested throughout the white empire.

In fact, as will be argued in this chapter, imperial responses to the Irish question were inordinately more complex and nuanced than either UK politicians or the metropolitan press formally acknowledged. As in the 'mother country', from 1886 onwards Britain's dominions, colonies, and dependent territories not only debated the merits of Home Rule, but also the precise linkage between Irish devolution, UK federation, and imperial union. Nor were these purely internal debates: via what Alan Lester has termed 'the circuits of Empire', imperial citizens and subjects 'co-constructed a . . . trans-imperial discourse' through which they communicated both with one another and the imperial centre.[3] Of course, this chapter cannot capture this transglobal debate in its entirety, and so it focuses on South Africa and India in particular. Analysis of these two empire countries together, suggests that colonist and colonised voices did not always fit neatly into British or Irish perceptions of Ireland and Empire.

South African opinion and Irish Home Rule

Although there is a significant and growing literature on the relationship between South Africa and Ireland, it is framed very much in terms of the influence of the sub-continent upon Ireland and its people. Thus, while research has been conducted into South Africa's place within the Irish diaspora,[4] on the military contribution of Ireland to the second South African War,[5] and the political importance of South Africa to late Victorian Irish nationalism,[6] much less is known about how South Africans responded to such encounters or whether events in Ireland aroused colonial interest, comment, or analysis. The discussion which follows seeks to address some of these questions specifically with regard to the debate over Irish Home Rule.

One obvious factor which militated against the development of a critical dialogue was the limited human and cultural exchange between the two countries. The Irish community in South Africa constituted a tiny minority within the small white community, and so Irish influence (and by extension Ireland's profile) was perhaps less than in other parts of Britain's formal and informal Empire.[7] That said, there clearly was some general interest within South Africa for information and news about Ireland (either in its own right or as it affected Britain). The Fenian rising of March 1867, for example, attracted some press attention.[8] However, wider interest in Irish affairs among South Africans probably only emerged between 1877 and 1881, when Irish nationalist criticism of Britain's annexation of the Transvaal, contacts between Irish nationalists and Boer leaders, and the Irish party's obstruction of the South Africa Bill in July 1877 won it some admirers among the Dutch population.[9] However, Natal and Cape newspapers were highly critical of the 'mischievous' and 'mistaken' parliamentary obstruction by Parnell et al. and cynical about Irish professions of concern for South Africa.[10] Doubtless, the vocal support of many Irish nationalists for the Boers during the first South African war also antagonised some colonists.[11]

Arguably, these perceptions and attitudes (augmented by the anti-Irish prejudices of some British immigrants to South Africa) informed colonial responses to Irish Home Rule. Indeed, although Gladstone's first Government of Ireland Bill by no means dominated the South African news agenda in the spring of 1886,[12] it did arouse strong partisan feelings among those who chose to notice it. According to the *Beaufort Courier*, for example, the measure's principal flaw was that it did not challenge the influence over the Irish peasantry exercised by the 'Romish priesthood – [who] by training and inclination [are] foes to the Saxon'.[13] Yet, other South African commentators drew on their colonial experiences to judge the measure more generously. The *Eastern Province Herald*, for instance, claimed that English colonists of the sub-continent took a 'vivid interest' in the success of the bill because having fought 'shoulder to shoulder' with Irish immigrants 'under Imperial suns, labour[ed] . . . together in distant Colonies, [and] wrest[ed] . . . a hard earned living from a Foreign Soil', they had come to recognise the fitness of Irishmen to govern themselves.[14] But perhaps for that reason, the *Natal Mercury* felt that Ireland should reject the bill, since 'had such power been reserved in the case of Canada, Australia, or the Cape [as had been in the Irish Bill], none of these Colonies would have deemed themselves self-governed'.[15]

Evidently, the Empire conditioned how many South Africans viewed Irish Home Rule. Thus, while the *Vryburg Advocate* claimed that the Bill contained 'proposals for disintegrating the Empire',[16] the *Grahamstown Journal* observed that '[t]hough its principles may be ruinous and revolutionary, we ought not to stop at simply denouncing them, but we should endeavour also . . . to consider whether any safe modification of the Home Rule policy can be devised.'[17] As a vocal proponent of imperial federation,[18] the principal revision the paper advocated was the retention of Irish representatives at Westminster.[19] For, as the *Port Elizabeth Telegraph* explained, their retention would serve as a precedent, so that 'the Colonies of England will', eventually, like Ireland, 'find their place by representation in the Great Council of the future.'[20]

Although the Empire federalist debate was near continuous from the mid-eighteenth through to the early twentieth century within Britain,[21] concerted colonial interest in the 'federalisation' of the empire appears only to have developed with the foundation of the Imperial Federation League in 1884.[22] There is certainly little evidence to suggest that South Africans took any particular interest in imperial federation before the 1880s.[23] In fact, even after 1884 (in contrast to elsewhere in the empire) the League made only a modest impression on the sub-continent.[24] But although South Africa possessed only two League branches,[25] the Imperial Federation League (IFL) and closer union did attract some interest among senior political figures and opinion formers,[26] and it was among these men that the Irish question was seen as a possible 'stalking-horse for a scheme of Imperial Federation'.[27]

Of course, South Africa was not the only colony to link Irish self-government with imperial federation,[28] and in Britain politicians of both parties also considered the matter.[29] However, it was an Anglo-South African who ultimately sought to harness the Irish question to the federation cause. Like a number of other senior Cape politicians, Cecil Rhodes was interested in the long-term project of creating an Anglo-Saxon federal union and when he met the Irish nationalist MP J. G. S. MacNeill in 1887 he saw an opportunity to advance this cause. Convinced that the 1886 Bill's exclusion of Irish MPs from Westminster retarded imperial federation, Rhodes proposed that in return for a £10,000 donation the Irish party should commit itself to the retention of Ireland's Westminster representatives when Home Rule next came before parliament.[30] After negotiations in London the following year,[31] Parnell agreed to Rhodes's proposal (though he refused to lobby Gladstone directly) and further agreed to support the insertion of 'a permissive clause . . . providing that any colony which contributes to Imperial defence . . . shall be allowed to send representatives to the Imperial Parliament'.[32] The Rhodes-Parnell correspondence was published and some days later Parnell issued a statement in which he anticipated that though 'a long way off', 'Home Rule All Round' would pave the way for colonial representation in the Imperial parliament.[33]

In England, the response of many of the larger London and national newspapers to the deal was rather muted.[34] This, as one provincial paper commented, may have been due to the media's preoccupation with the ongoing dispute between Parnell and *The Times*.[35] However, some English provincial newspapers were less distracted; irrespective of political affiliation there was a general feeling against associating 'the two problems . . . at the present time.'[36] More interestingly, this was also the position taken by the organ of the IFL, *Imperial Federation*.[37] The correspondence of the League's executive shows that many senior members were extremely concerned that their cause had been linked with such a 'political question' as Irish Home Rule.[38] However, W. M. Ackworth (editor of the IFL's journal) argued forcefully that colonial interest in the question meant it could not be ignored.[39] In fact, although comment in Canada was largely favourable,[40] in South Africa itself the story was either ignored or reported as a curiosity.[41] In nationalist Ireland, meanwhile, the deal was described as being of 'immense importance',[42] but (with the exception of the *Freeman's Journal*)[43] the imperial dimension did not attract comment.[44] Instead, it was only among some English and Irish unionists that the Rhodes-Parnell deal prompted comment and even this revealed only that while all were implacably hostile to home rule, unionists were otherwise divided among themselves as to the merits of imperial federation.[45]

Although in 1893 South Africans expressed general relief at being 'far removed from . . . [the] keenness and party prejudice' of the Home Rule debate,[46] there was still 'a mild feeling of interest about Mr Gladstone's latest Home Rule scheme.'[47] Aware that '[t]here are many men even in Home Rule Colonies who look upon the passing of such a measure as the first step to the disintegration of the Empire,'[48] many South African commentators were reassured that the proposed scheme of Irish self-government bore more than a passing resemblance to existing colonial constitutions.[49] As the *Natal Witness* put it, 'Britain has been learning a lesson from the story of the Greater Britain, which has done so much to broaden the political mind of the older country.'[50]

But South African interest in Ireland's acquisition of institutions apparently analogous to those possessed by the white colonies reflected more than self-satisfaction at the vindication of the Greater British model. For Ireland's membership of the Empire, in combination with its possession of representation at Westminster, appeared finally to establish the principle of colonial membership of the Imperial parliament. Of course, not all commentators welcomed this prospect, but a number of newspapers believed it would bring imperial federation closer. As the *Port Elizabeth Telegraph* put it, the bill 'contain[ed] the germ of a very important development. There is no valid reason why the Colonies should not ask for similar representation'.[51]

The precise importance of the Rhodes-Parnell deal to the retention of Irish MPs is difficult to assess. When Parnell died in October 1891, the South African press did not see his death as a setback for the empire or imperial federation (though some in the Transvaal, whose memories stretched back to the 1870s, apparently mourned his death).[52] Indeed, the *Grahamstown Journal* (which only the week before had restated its faith in imperial union) predicted instead that Parnell's death would accelerate the final demise of home rule which had already been rendered 'unnecessary and impracticable' by unionist 'remedial measures'.[53] According to G. P. Taylor, however, Rhodes did play an 'important part' in securing the retention of Irish MPs at Westminster in the second Home Rule Bill of 1893.[54] For in addition to his donation of 1888, Rhodes had secretly sought to 'square' the Liberals in 1891 by donating £5,000 to the National Liberal Federation (NLF) in return for a pledge on Irish representation at Westminster.[55] Later, in June 1893, the 'sinister Rhodes associate',[56] Rochfort Maguire (who had been elected as a nationalist MP in 1892), wrote an obviously inspired letter to *The Times* reminding Liberals and nationalists of their Rhodesean commitments.[57]

In the two decades between the second and third Home Rule Bills, South African interest in imperial federation waned. In part this reflected a general empire-wide dissipation of interest which had set in even before the IFL imploded in 1893.[58] Despite occasional sympathetic noises,[59] South African delegates (increasingly preoccupied with the closer union movement at home) refused to support proposals advanced at successive colonial conferences for closer union within the Empire.[60] As Botha, writing of the New Zealand proposal at the 1911 imperial conference, told Smuts: 'We easily quashed the Imperial Council of State [plan] . . . I have never heard of a more idiotic proposal.'[61]

But if by 1912 many South Africans no longer saw Irish Home Rule through the lens of imperial union (as in 1886 and 1893), they still took a general interest in Irish Home Rule itself. Indeed, though South Africans were either indifferent or hostile to the Irish Council Bill of 1907, and though a number of Irish nationalists found the political exclusion of the ethnic majority under the Union of South Africa 'ominous',[62] leading South African statesmen were nonetheless willing to publicly express their support for Irish Home Rule in 1912. The endorsement of Boer 'rebels' turned imperial statesmen such as Botha and Smuts was held up by the Liberal press as 'a striking example of the national and imperial effect of Home Rule',[63] though back in South Africa some commentators reproved Botha for 'interfer[ing] . . . with other people's business' and questioned why the local press was so preoccupied with matters so distant from the sub-continent.[64]

But if most South Africans no longer regarded Ireland as a bridgehead for the closer union of the Empire (as evidenced by the fact that Liberal plans for 'Home Rule All Round' while welcomed,[65] prompted some on the sub-continent to wish that the South Africa had been organised as a federation rather than a union),[66] some still believed that the home rule-imperial federation nexus was not fully spent. For another group (which had its origins in post-war South Africa) re-forged the link in the years immediately before the First World War. Formed in 1909, the Round Table movement comprised young men (originally known as 'Milner's Kindergarten') who had served under Lord Milner when he was high commissioner for South Africa and were later involved in the political union of the country. In large part because of their experiences on the sub-continent, Round Table members were committed pan-anglo-saxonists and imperial federationists.[67] Influenced by Earl Grey (who as early as February 1907 had written that 'Ireland may still redeem her past by providing the excuse for Imperial Federation'), several leading Round Table members came to see 'Home Rule All Round' 'as a step, perhaps a necessary one, on the road to imperial unity'.[68] While doubts had begun to emerge in the minds of some Round Table members during 1910 regarding the precise relationship between UK and imperial federation, F. S. Oliver (writing as *Pacificus* in *The Times*) and others sought to convince senior Tories that if the constitutional conference could agree to reconstitute the United Kingdom on federal lines it would benefit both the Irish question and the cause of imperial union.[69] Although in this they were ultimately unsuccessful, the interest shown by some sections of the party contributed to the secret agreement of July 1910 made between the Liberal cabinet and John Redmond to promote federalism as the best means of securing a settlement from the conference.[70] However, uneasiness in Ireland as to whether (to misquote T. P. O'Connor) federalism really was 'Latin for devolution', combined with the collapse of the conference in November 1910 brought these efforts to an end, and though federal proposals for the UK were revived by the Round Table in 1913–14, it was no longer presented in terms of advancing imperial federation.[71]

Indian opinion and Irish Home Rule

> Lord Mayo once remarked to the present writer, when we were waiting in our howdahs for the outburst of a family of tigers, that the problems that he had to solve as Secretary at Dublin and as Governor-General at Calcutta, showed a great mutual resemblance.[72]

So wrote a 'Bengal magistrate' in the *Contemporary Review* in 1890. But, he continued, when considering the political outlook in each country it was more instructive to dwell on difference. Mayo's error was to take isolated incidents indicative of hostility to the Indian Government as reflective of the condition of India as a whole. In reality, he argued, and in contrast to Ireland, the Indian Government was respected as impartial and effective. From the late eighteenth century the authorities had intervened to set fair rents in times of hardship; the magistracy was fair, able, and, above all, not associated with the interests of a particular section of the community. In Ireland the magistracy was obviously partisan, appointments were nepotistic, punishments doled out were severe, and, when faced with talented Home Rule MPs, was horribly out of its depth. Irish land legislation compounded the problem: though radical it was too slow-moving to appease disgruntled tenants, comparing poorly to the pragmatic quick fixes applied locally in India. In short, Irish government was so inadequate it was not surprising the Irish demanded home rule. By contrast, administrative efficiency and fair play in India ensured that even famine did not generate lasting bitterness: the authorities were not regarded as culpable. There was, however, in India the 'hopeful, eager aspiration', 'the fervent prayer' for Imperial Federation centred on Westminster, which, liberated by Irish Home Rule and concerns over Ireland's 'petty domestic matters', could devote time to the concerns of the 'two hundred and fifty millions of Indians'.[73]

Although Bengal magistrates cannot be relied upon to give non-partisan accounts of the functioning of their caste, this was an especially myopic appraisal. It suggested little sensitivity to the politicising processes at work in Ireland and India, and made the classic constructive unionist error that Irish nationalism was merely a symptom of socio-economic grievance. Within a generation, the moderate reformism of the Indian National Congress would be challenged by a popularising, mass-based Indian nationalism that made sense of Indian experiences and unpopular British policies (most notably the 1905 partition of Bengal) through ideas comparable to those radicalising Irish nationalism at the same time. That said, the magistrate was correct to argue that Indian nationalists regarded Irish Home Rule as the necessary prerequisite to imperial federation.

Despite these warnings, leading members of the colonial service replicated Mayo's error, making sense of Indian developments through Irish

example, conscious of the dangers inherent to the Irishisation of Indian politics. S. B. Cook's excellent analysis of the making of the Bengal Tenancy
Act of 1885 has drawn particular attention to this process, demonstrating
how the influence of Irish experience on British policy formation was felt at
all stages in the process.[74] A crucial group of colonial administrators and
governors were experienced in Irish and Indian politics, either because a
posting to Dublin Castle had functioned as a first step toward a glittering
imperial career or because the civil servant was Irish. Lord Morley was the
most prominent example of the former. He was Irish chief secretary (1886,
1892–95), an ardent Gladstonian Home Ruler, and secretary of state for
India (1906–10, 1911). On the latter, Irish peers working in the colonial
service, most importantly Lord Dufferin, brought an Irish perspective, while
Irish Catholics working as colonial administrators saw Indian problems
through Irish eyes.[75] Dufferin's support for the Bengal Tenancy Bill
stemmed in part from his support of Ulster Custom and the influence of
briefing by Anthony MacDonnell, the most prominent Irish pro-*raiyat*
[tenant] in the service; MacDonnell was also heard by the Commons Select
Committee on the bill. The significance of this circuitry, as Cook shows, was
not that the landlord-tenant relationship in Ireland was mirrored by circumstances in India, but that the gradual eroding of the principles of private
property in Ireland, dating from Gladstone's 1870 Land Act, provided an
example of an approach based, in the interests of stability, on customary
rights. MacDonnell was the most significant of a group of influential Irish
administrators whose attitudes were at odds with the conventional thinking
of English, Welsh, and Scottish in the service and on the Indian Council
(Ripon: 'the most Conservative body now existing in Europe').[76] Indeed,
resistance to the bill cohered around the rejection of Ireland as a suitable
analogy for India.[77] And though the bill proved moderate,[78] the Irish experience had whittled away at British confidence that the Empire could be
moulded in its image. As John Stuart Mill argued in *England and Ireland*,
the variety of cultures, customs, and rights characteristic of the empire
ensured that British political economy, exceptional and brilliant though it
was, could not be replicated throughout.[79] Irish men who sought imperial
careers, then, were not necessarily loyal place-hunters, bound by conventional wisdom, but could be men with an agenda shaped by the experience
of social injustice in Ireland. More research is needed to establish whether
this experience propelled individuals into foreign service, for judging by the
periodic liveliness of imperial debate in Irish newspapers this could prove a
valuable line of enquiry.

British politicians were disturbed by how Irish popular agitation had
brought Irish questions to the top of the Westminster agenda. Lord Ripon

(Indian viceroy, 1880–84) saw the wider significance of Irish developments. He told Gladstone in October 1881:

> With regard to Land Tenures we have in many parts of India a state of things to deal with very similar to that which have so long existed in Ireland, except that the landlords here are, I take it, harder and the tenants certainly more patient than they are there. There is therefore all the more need for our interference.[80]

Indian political and associational cultures were not sufficiently developed to produce an agitation comparable to that experienced in Ireland in 1879–82. The Indian National Congress was established in 1885 and until the emergence of the Hinduist movement of national rejuvenation in the 1900s Indian nationalism was a largely urban and middle class affair, with a strongly localised outlook.[81] Its main foci was hostility to the Indian Council and among its principal activities was agitation for an extended and more democratic local self-government, ongoing pressure for the reform of access to the Indian Civil Service, and occasional calls for small but directly elected representation at Westminster. Mainly comprised of the emerging Indian middle classes and *zamindar* (moderatelysized landlords who worked for the state) activists, little expression was given to peasant grievances: indeed, *zamindar* sympathy for Irish Home Rule cooled during the Irish land war.[82] Dufferin warned, however, that the central question the Indian Government faced was 'how long an autocratic Government . . . will be able to stand . . . the importation *en bloc* from England, or rather from Ireland, of the perfected machinery of modern democratic agitation.'[83] As Ripon's advice suggests, the British hoped that timely reform would nip the Irishisation of Indian politics in the bud.

How much significance can be attached to this use of Irish analogy by an Irish peer? That Dufferin would reach for the most immediately available comparison to make sense of his vast new responsibilities is not surprising, and it is clear the pithy ambiguity of the Home Rule phrase was ripe for export. Despite this, Home Rule did not become a popular cry in India until the Great War when it was promoted by Bal Gangadhar Tilak and Annie Besant. Until then, discussion was dominated by the demand for devolved representative government within India and the development of imperial federation. In this regard, India provided a distorted mirror of the Irish. In Ireland some Home Rulers made sense of their demands in terms of the restructuring of the wider governing institutions of the Empire but impatience with the slow emergence of the national demand elsewhere saw them unwilling to make Home Rule conditional on or integral to this process.[84] But, as Dufferin recognised, imperial circuitry carried ideas through the colonial administrations and at a popular political level. The remainder of this essay will explore how Indian nationalists interpreted the Irish Home Rule controversy in relation to the structural development of the British Empire as a whole.

Indian commentary on Gladstone's first Home Rule bill was generally positive, reflecting the favour in which the Liberal Party was held by Indian nationalists. This was reinforced by support for Gladstone personally, which often reached laudatory heights and reflected the increasingly party political flavour of Indian government. Indian nationalists believed this tendency had benefited the Irish. As Surendranath Banerjea told the India Association (a forerunner of Congress) in September 1879, 'Justice was done to Ireland precisely when Irish questions became party questions.'[85] Leading activists like Dadabhai Naoroji consequently believed that Congress should prioritise lobbying at Westminster over building up the grass-roots organisation in India.[86] He was one of several Indian nationalists who helped build strong links with the Liberal Party, flirted with the Irish party, and attempted to have Indian candidates stand for election in British seats with the support of either. Celebrating Gladstone's commitment to Irish Home Rule formed part of this diffuse lobbying culture. Indian commentary on Ireland could be more impatient, suggesting India had a stronger case for self-government because Indian nationalists demanded a smaller degree of self-government and had not indulged in 'terrorist' activities – according to the *Sind Times* ending 'crime and horror' was the primary motivation behind Gladstone's Irish crusade.[87] The *Gujarat Mitra* also supported Irish patriots, but condemned the activities of 'illiterate, murderous and wantonly cruel and rapacious Irishmen'.[88] Such interventions reflected the feeling that Indians were losing out in the competition for British attention. Later radical nationalists urged Indians to emulate more extreme Irish strategies in order to impose their needs on the political agenda. Even the *Times of India*, cynically observing developments in London, reluctantly approved of the first Home Rule bill because it removed Irish MPs from Westminster, thereby creating more space for the consideration of Indian issues.[89] When later bills retained an Irish presence in the Commons, the newspaper, in contrast to Rhodes, judged this their 'crowning defect'. This placed 'Ireland in a position of privilege in comparison with every other part of the Empire, immune against interference in her own affairs, free to interfere in the affairs of the predominant partners, and to use this power for the advancement of her local interests.'[90]

Overall, the tenor of debate reflected the *Hindu*'s conviction that Gladstone's claim that Irish patriotism was compatible with imperial patriotism could be equally applied to India: 'Our Anglo-Indian contemporaries must understand that it is our Indian patriotism which leads us to protest against the unjust and high-handed proceedings of the official class, and fight for our legitimate rights and privileges, and it is our Imperial patriotism that makes us always act loyally to the British Throne, and wish for the permanence of a constitutional British supremacy in India.'[91] The *Times of India* saw the problem through more a pragmatic lens, admitting that the problem 'England's Empire' faced was how to manage the transition of the colonies to 'important and self-dependent nations . . . without [them] ceasing to be loyal units of the Empire.'[92] It was during 1910–14 that the wider significance of Irish Home Rule as a precedent and as a prerequisite for imperial federation became more widely understood. The *Bengalee* saw this in terms of a rolling process of regional devolution and democratic centralisation along national lines:

> British statesmanship has fully realized that the absolute need of Irish Home Rule, as a preliminary to building up first a Federal constitution within the United Kingdom, and next the organization of a real Federation of the Empire. Irish Home Rule will be bound to be followed up by Scottish and Welsh Home Rule; and finally the present English counties also will be organized into an autonomous state with a local Parliament of its own and a local Executive subject to the authority if this Parliament. All these things must be done, before the present British Parliament can be reconstituted into a real Imperial Parliament.[93]

The *Hindoo Patriot* had lamented the defeat of the 1886 bill by 'self-interest', asking whether the British public would 'hail the Irish with the olive branch of peace or villainous gunpowder'? 'As a subject nation themselves', Indians would 'watch the issue with thrilling interest' hoping 'that the cause of justice will prevail.'[94] Such commentary was intensified during the political crisis provoked by the third Home Rule bill. British responses to Carsonism were scrutinised as a measure of the determination of the British parliament to uphold its constitutional rights. This was grave, for the increasingly strong cultural nationalist strands in Indian nationalism (the *Swadeshi* movement) questioned the efficacy of the patriotic reformism that still held sway in Congress. Following the Congress split of 1907, Indian nationalists tended to accept the labels Moderate and Extremist, mirroring the way Irish separatists became more confident promoters of their ideals in this period.

Contesting Moderate assumptions was common among British-based Indian nationalists, such as those associated with the Indian Home Rule Society (established in London, March 1905). One of the society's founder members was Shyamaji Krishnavarma, former Balliol lecturer, educationalist, and disciple of Herbert Spencer. Krishnavarma sporadically linked Irish and Indian politics in his *The Indian Sociologist*,[95] giving space to British and Irish advocates of Indian Home Rule – notably the labour activist H. M. Hyndman and the eccentric former Home Rule MP F. H. O'Donnell – and reproducing sympathetic statements by the *Gaelic American*, a hard-line Irish-American nationalist newspaper.[96] Krishnavarma was eventually prosecuted for sedition and forced to publish from Paris. Citing the *Gaelic American* was particularly aggressive because it insisted on the legitimacy of political violence to further nationalist ends. By quoting the newspaper, Krishnavarma indirectly made the case for terrorist violence as this became a feature of Indian nationalist activism. Another Extremist newspaper conscious of Irish parallels that also drew on the *Gaelic American* was *Bande Mataram*. Associated with Bipin Chandra Pal, author of the classic *Swadeshi* text *The New Spirit* (Calcutta 1907),[97] *Bande Mataram* celebrated the Gaelic League and reported on Irish boycotting and British coercion, publishing suggestive articles like 'Terrorism in Ireland: How the United Irish League Works.'[98] In particular, Extremists urged that Indian Moderates learn from the Irish rejection of the Irish Council Bill in 1907. Inadequate concessions would damage Indian identity and *Bande Mataram* condemned the bill as the product of ' "Liberal" Anglo-Indian' thinking (Anthony MacDonnell was now at Dublin Castle): it was 'a sort of bastard cross between a Colonial Parliament and an Indian Legislative Council'. To have accepted would have meant abandoning Parnellism and the Irish equivalent of *Swadeshi*:

> Instead of a separate nationality with its own culture, language, government [sic] the Irish would have ended up becoming a big English county governed by a magnified and glorified Parish Council. The same kind of bait was offered to the Boers, but that shrewd people resolutely refused to associate themselves with any form of self-government short of absolute colonial Self-Government. The same kind of bait is promised to the Moderates in India by Honest John [Morley] and the honest *Statesman*, if they will only consent to dissociate themselves from the New Spirit and all its works and betray their country. The *Statesman* says that Mr. Redmond has been forced to the refusal by the necessity of deferring to the Sinn Fein-party in Ireland, and hopes that the Indian Moderates will not make the same mistake. Our sapient contemporary opines that the Nationalists in India are not really so strong as they seem and that the Moderate leaders, if they desire to betray their country, can do so with impunity, without losing their position. Well, we shall see.[99]

This tension provided the subtext of Indian coverage of the progress of the third Home Rule bill and the government's handling of 'Carsonism': in essence, the question raised was whether devolution achieved through peaceful means remained a viable political goal in India. Coverage was conditioned by the linkage of the South African problem, the *Swadeshi* movement, and the possibility of imperial federation. In brief, Gandhi's campaign against the ill-treatment of Indian labour in South Africa raised sensitive questions touching on the nature of imperial unity, the free movement of populations within the empire, and the legitimacy of the racial hierarchies the empire appeared to tolerate. The *Bengalee* responded to Asquith's speech introducing the Home Rule bill by noting 'the words "Ireland" and "India" may be interchanged without diminishing the strength of the argument or impairing the accuracy.'[100] Part of a broader argument about the significance of Irish Home

Rule to the Empire as a whole, the newspaper latched onto Asquith's suggestion that any bill must, if demanded, be equally applicable to Wales and
Scotland. Building on the Prime Minister's claim that 'Every year had empha-
sized the imperative need of emancipating the Imperial Parliament from local
cares', the *Bengalee* argued the logic of a wholly federated empire. Problems
of authority would arise, however, if South Africa, Australia, and Canada were
granted representation but not India.[101] Such comments reflected anxieties
created by the widespread notion that India, as a dependency, could not be
governed as the settler colonies were and, in the event of imperial federation,
might even be governed by them.[102] One aspect of this argument – which can
be traced back to the ideas of Dilke and Seeley – was Montagu's notion that
the Dominions, in contrast to India, represented 'the extension of the English
nationality': home rule (i.e. Dominion status), it was understood, had not
created but preserved national unity within the Empire.[103] Indian Extremists
implicitly questioned this distinction, arguing that self-government within the
Empire should not be extended on a racial basis but because a nation had
shown its capacity for self-government. They distinguished their position
from the Old Congress argument that Indians deserved a greater measure of
self-government and democratic devolution simply because they had demonstrated their capacity for it. By contrast, the *Swadeshi* movement, identified as
against 'Anglo-Indian' interests, had elevated the Indian race in the eyes of
the world because it brought about the recovery of their authentic national
identity. 'The world does not and cannot sympathize with slaves who hug
their chains, but it admires all weak nations that aspire towards freedom',
argued *Bande Mataram* in 1909. 'Formerly our place was with the Negroes,
the Malays, the Maoris; now we rank with the Irish, the Poles and the
Russians.'[104] A year later, the newspaper grouped Young Hind with Young
Egypt and Young Ireland.[105] By putting them on a par with the Irish and the
Egyptians, Indian nationalists disputed the legitimacy of imperial federation
proposals based on racial identity. *Swadeshi* ensured what was suitable for the
Gael was suitable for the Indian. Irish parallels highlighted how imperial hierarchies should be determined by the measure of nationalist politicisation
rather than allegedly insurmountable natural or racial conditions. The
Irish example was drawn on to strengthen Indian challenges to the imperial
mentality later analysed as Orientalist.[106]

As indicated, the *Times of India* thought Ireland might be a candidate for
dominion but not exceptional status. Outraged by Carson's defiance of
constitutional politics and the so-called Curragh Mutiny (which threatened a
'military despotism'), the *Times* nonetheless considered the coercion of Ulster
unacceptable: it was incumbent on the politicians to find a peaceful
solution.[107] Indian nationalists tended to be more forceful, arguing that the

unionists did not have a constitutional leg to stand on – the will of parliament must prevail. In 1893 *Gujarat Darpan* had accused the Tories of taking 'up the cause of rowdyism and filibustering',[108] in 1913–14 criticism was much more severe.[109] Indeed, though favourable to the Irish volunteer movements established during the crisis, the *Bengalee* was adamant that the 'pacification of Ulster' was 'the duty of the Government and . . . cannot be relegated to any other authority.'[110] Confidence in constitutional processes and the responsiveness of British politicians to clearly articulated grievances underpinned constitutional nationalism in India and Ireland. Indian Moderates shared the fear of Irish home rulers that unionist defiance would undermine faith in constitutionalism. And while it would be exaggerated to suggest that Indian opinion was directly altered by the Ulster Crisis, it served to justify the politics of non-engagement promoted by the Extremists.

Harry Nevinson's journalistic account of the 'New Spirit in India' jauntily introduced the British to the new developments in Indian nationalism since the turn of the twentieth century. Published in 1908, he described *Swadeshi* as 'the Irish policy of Sinn Fein',[111] a remarkably rapid application of a term that had only recently achieved a high level of recognition in Ireland. Among the political classes, Indian awareness of Sinn Feinism was strong and Nevinson's alertness to new political ideas should not be written off as merely good journalistic instinct. The year before Jawaharlal Nehru wrote to his father from Cambridge comparing Sinn Fein with 'the so-called extremist movement in India' – he had seen Sinn Fein at close hand when in Dublin.[112] A year earlier still, Tilak had privately lamented: 'I don't know when we shall learn to depend on ourselves and ourselves alone'.[113] 'Ourselves alone' was the most common way of translating 'Sinn Fein' into English and there can be little doubt that Tilak picked the phrase up from an Irish source. Tilak's *Amrita Bazar Patrika* urged that Indians emulate Irish nationalists; drawing on the *Gaelic American*, it celebrated Irish defiance of the Irish Council Bill, and asked whether Indians should emulate the Carsonites. To the latter the answer was implicitly no but with the important caveat that only effective political leadership would render constitutional politics sufficiently effective to avoid civil strife.[114] Tilak served a six year prison sentence following a conviction for sedition in 1908 when an article in his *Kesari* was fingered by the authorities as justifying terrorism.[115] Soon after his release in 1914 he lectured on India's future. Seemingly cowed by his prison experiences, he drew on the Irish parallel to demonstrate the moderate nature of his political aspirations:

> I may state once for all that we are trying for India, as the Irish Home Rulers have been doing in Ireland for a reform of the system of administration and not for the overthrow of Government; and I have no hesitation in saying that the acts of violence which have been committed in the different parts of India are not only

repugnant to me, but have, in my opinion, only unfortunately, retarded to a great extent, the pace of our political progress.[116]

Tilak's moderate tone disappointed some Extremists, but in reality the distinction between the Extremists and Moderates had always been ambiguous.[117] Some Extremists, committed to a fully independent India, rooted their defence of political violence in the principles of *Swadeshi*. Others, Extremist in their belief in the efficacy of boycott, regarded *Swadeshi* as compatible with Imperial Federation. Harsh responses by the British to non-constitutional political strategies were liable to blur the distinction between means and ends. Tilak's intervention was an attempt to clarify the problem and it relied on a sleight of hand that any Irish student of Tilak's career would have immediately recognised. Irish Home Rule in late 1914 had entered the most moderate phase of its turbulent history: its ideological differences with Sinn Féin had become fundamental. So, just as the politics of devolution went into terminal decline in Ireland, the popularisation of the Home Rule cry in India gave it a new vitality.[118] But, with regard to the overall political prospects of the Empire, the major outcome of the British failure to reconcile Ireland to the Union was the degradation of the idea of imperial federation.[119] Erskine Childers was an Irish nationalist but, like many liberal imperialists, he argued that imperial federation could be achieved only on a purely voluntary basis: logically enough, national autonomy, achieved through Home Rule, was the necessary prerequisite.[120] With the Irish Free State established in 1921 and Irish nationalists soon fighting a civil war over whether dominion status sufficiently embodied Irish nationhood, a fresh decolonising precedent was established which associated only full independence with the language of finality.[121]

An imperial circuitry?

During the second reading of the first Irish Home Rule bill, an MP questioned whether the unity of the Empire was at stake at all, arguing that the real issue was the unity of the United Kingdom 'of which Ireland should be proud to be a member.'[122] As any consideration of South African and Indian responses to Irish Home Rule suggests, the Irish Question was thought of as an imperial as well as a British Question. And though South African and Indian opinion tended to be favourable to Irish Home Rule, their discussion reflected indigenous agendas that were not deferential to metropolitan or Irish interests. South African attitudes were shaped by the fact that they had already achieved colonial self-government and in some sense they regarded themselves as gate-keepers, able to assess the Irish for membership of this club. Such assessments were predicated on the hope that Irish Home Rule was part of a desired move by the British Government towards imperial federation, which saw them oppose any steps thought inimical or inconsistent with these overall objectives. Consequently, the question of whether Irish MPs would retain seats at Westminster was very significant, potentially marking the beginning of Westminster's transition from being an assembly of national to one of imperial representation. Indian nationalists were less sure of their own right to judge Irish nationalist demands. Their interventions, salted with racial insecurity, revealed the anxieties of spokespersons seeking international recognition of an emergent nation. Over the course of the Home Rule controversy, Britain's treatment of Irish nationalism was regarded as indicative of the imperium's overall responsiveness to legitimate political demands. Celebrating Irish cultural achievement helped Indian nationalists contest the racial assumptions that seemed to underpin imperial government, challenging the distinction between colony and dependency, Anglo-Saxon and the rest. British opinion makers, however, paid little attention to these colonial voices. Where lip-service was paid to imperial attitudes, it was primarily to assert that Irish Home Rule would either strengthen or weaken the Empire, rather than to assess how Irish Home Rule intimated the future government of the empire. Despite the sophistication of much of the discussion, the apparent linkage between Home Rule, UK devolution, and imperial federation was rarely more than a fringe interest in British politics, an ideal that proved forever incompatible with immediate political pressures. There was an imperial circuitry, and the Irish Question could flick its switch, but a good connection was rarely made.

Notes

1 *Daily Chronicle*, 11 April 1912.
2 For an Ulster Unionist view of the empire's stance towards home rule, see Thomas Hennessey, 'Ulster Unionist territorial and national identities, 1886–93: province, island, kingdom, and empire', *Irish Political Studies*, 8 (1993), 33.
3 Alan Lester, 'British settler discourse and the circuits of empire', *HWJ*, 54 (2002), 25.
4 Donal P. McCracken, 'Odd man out: the South African experience', in Andy Bielenberg (ed.), *The Irish Diaspora* (Harlow, 2000), pp. 251–71.
5 Keith Jeffrey, 'The Irish soldier in the Boer War', in John Gooch (ed.), *The Boer War: Direction, Experience and Image* (London and Portland (OR), 2000); Donal P. McCracken, *McBride's Brigade: Irish Commandos in the Anglo-Boer War* (Dublin, 1999).
6 Donal P. McCracken, *The Irish Pro-Boers* (Johannesburg and Cape Town, 1989).

7 McCracken, 'Odd man out', p. 263; T. K. Daniel, 'Faith and stepfatherland: Irish South African networks in Cape Colony and Natal, 1871–1914, and the Home Rule movement in Ireland', in Donal P. McCracken (ed.), *The Irish in Southern Africa, 1795–1910* (Durban, 1992), p. 86.

8 *GJ*, 17 April 1867; *TN*, 17 April 1867; *CA*, 16 April 1867; *EPH*, 23 April 1867.

9 *Parlt. Debs.*, 4th series, vol. ccxxxv, cols. 1768–71 (24 July 1877); *FJ*, 26 July 1877; *Transvaal Advertiser*, 9 October 1891.

10 *NW*, 4 September 1877; *GJ*, 5 September 1877; *EPH*, 1 September 1877; *Eastern Star*, 7 September 1877; *NM*, 6 September 1877. Also see Donal McCracken, 'Parnell and the South African connection', in Donal McCartney (ed.), *Parnell: The Politics of Power* (Dublin, 1991), p. 126.

11 Arthur Davey, *The British Pro-Boers, 1877–1902* (Cape Town, 1978).

12 The *Wynberg Times* and *Natal Witness*, for example, did not comment on the Bill.

13 *Beaufort Courier*, 6 April 1886.

14 *EPH*, 12 April 1886.

15 *NM*, 12 April 1886.

16 *Vryburg Advocate*, 21 May 1886.

17 *Journal*, 12 April 1886.

18 *Journal*, 10 April 1886.

19 *Journal*, 14 April 1886.

20 *PET*, 8 April 1886.

21 Ged Martin, 'The idea of imperial federation', in Ronald Hyam and Ged Martin (eds), *Reappraisals in British Imperial History* (London, 1975), p. 136.

22 M. D. Burgess, 'Lord Rosebery and the Imperial Federation League, 1884–1893', *New Zealand Journal of History*, 13 (1979).

23 For one exception, see Goldwin Smith, *The Empire* (London, 1863), pp. 85–6.

24 C. S. Blackton, 'Australian nationality and nationalism: the Imperial Federationist interlude, 1885–1901', *Historical Studies: Australia and New Zealand*, 7 (1955); Keith Sinclair, *Imperial Federation: A Study of New Zealand Policy and Opinion, 1880–1914* (University of London, Institute of Commonwealth Studies, 2) (1955).

25 *The Times*, 27 February 1885; *IF*, 1 November 1886.

26 *The Times*, 5 December 1884; 16 February 1886.

27 Ibid., 9 July 1888.

28 Blackton, 'Australian nationality and nationalism', 5.

29 *The Times*, 16 October, 24 December 1885; John Kendle, *The Colonial and Imperial Conferences, 1887–1911* (London, 1967), p. 11.

30 G. P. Taylor, 'Cecil Rhodes and the second Home Rule bill', *Historical Journal*, 14 (1971).

31 *The Times*, 9 August 1888.

32 R. Barry O'Brien, *The Life of Charles Stewart Parnell, 1846–1891* (London, 1898), p. 186.

33 *HDC*, 11 July 1888. In 1891 Rhodes offered the by-then isolated Parnell a further £10,000, though this does not appear to have been linked to the imperial federation project. See McCracken, 'Parnell and the South African connection', p. 132.

34 *Daily Telegraph*, 9 July 1888; *Illustrated London News*, 14 July 1888; *DC*, 9 July 1888; *Manchester Guardian*, 9 July 1888; *Morning Post*, 9 July 1888.

35 *Leeds Mercury*, 10 July 1888.
36 Ibid.; *HDC*, 13 July 1888.
37 *IF*, 1 August 1888.
38 See especially Lord Knutsford to Lord Rosebery, 22 July 1888, CUL, RCMS 22/3/16. The League was formally non-political, but many Liberals apparently only joined it to prevent the Tories monopolising the empire as an issue. Kendle, *Colonial and Imperial Conferences*, p. 3.
39 W. M. Ackworth to A. H. Loring, 21 July 1888, CUL, RCMS 22/3/13.
40 *IF*, 1 October 1888.
41 *Transvaal Advertiser, Bedford Enterprise*, and *Wynberg Times* ignored the story. For South African comment, see *CT*, 10 July 1888; *TA*, 9 October 1891.
42 *Cork Express*, 9 July 1888.
43 *FJ*, 9 July 1888.
44 For instance, see *Anglo-Celt*, 14 July 1888; *Kerry Sentinel*, 18 July 1888.
45 *Liberal Unionist*, 1 September 1888; *Irish Times*, 9 July 1888; *The Union*, 23 July, 4, 18, 25 August, 1, 8 September 1888. For the response of the IFL, see *IF*, 1 October 1888.
46 *PET*, 11 February 1893.
47 *TP*, 15 February 1893.
48 *Fort Beaufort Advocate*, 24 February 1893.
49 *CT*, 15 February 1893; *TP*, 15 February 1893; *PET*, 18 February 1893.
50 *NW*, 16 February 1893.
51 *PET*, 18 February 1893. Also see, *NM*, 19 February 1893.
52 *TA*, 9 October 1891.
53 *GJ*, 5, 12 October 1891. In contrast, the Natal press thought Parnell's death would help home rule. *NM*, 9 October 1891; *NW*, 9 October 1891.
54 Taylor, 'Cecil Rhodes', p. 771.
55 Ibid., pp. 777–8.
56 Patrick Maume, *The Long Gestation: Irish Nationalist Life, 1891–1918* (Dublin, 1999), p. 16.
57 *The Times*, 5 June 1893.
58 Kendle, *Colonial and Imperial Conferences*, p. 31; Burgess, 'Lord Rosebery', p. 165.
59 *The Times*, 16 May 1902; Kendle, *Colonial and Imperial Conferences*, p. 164.
60 Kendle, *Colonial and Imperial Conferences*, pp. 26, 94, 96.
61 William Hancock, *Smuts. 1. The Sanguine Years, 1870–1919* (Cambridge, 1962), p. 351.
62 For the Irish Council Bill see *GJ*, 25 May 1907; *TL*, 22, 23 May 1907; *NW*, 22 May 1907; *Mafeking Mail*, 23 May 1907; *EPH*, 22 May 1907; *PN*, 22 May 1907. For Irish responses to the union of South Africa see *FJ*, 17 August 1909; *Irish Independent*, 17, 20 August 1909; *Parlt. Debs.*, 5th series, vol. ix, cols. 1014–16 (16 August 1909). South Africans were unbothered by such 'busybodies', see *GJ*, 21 August 1909; *Transvaal Leader*, 17 August 1909; *PN*, 20 August 1909.
63 *DC*, 12 April 1912. The attitude of the South African press to home rule was also reported in Britain. See *The Times*, 15 April 1912.
64 *PN*, 17 April 1912; *East Rand Express*, 20 April 1912. Botha was reproved by his opponents in the House of Assembly for his action. See HA Debs., 30 April 1912, col. 2304.

65 *Transvaal Leader*, 13 April 1912.

66 *NW*, 13 April 1912.

67 John Kendle, *The Round Table Movement and Imperial Union* (Toronto, 1975), pp. xiii., xv.

68 Ibid., pp. 131–6.

69 Ibid., pp. 136–8. For the conference Neal Blewett, *The Peers, the Parties and the People: The General Elections of 1910* (London, 1972).

70 Michael Wheatley, 'John Redmond and federalism in 1910', *Irish Historical Studies*, 32 (2001). Redmond had received financial assistance from Rhodes in the 1890s and occasionally expressed support for imperial federation in later years, while John Dillon was sympathetic because of the threat posed by 'the Yellow Peril' to the transmarine dominions. McCracken, 'Parnell and the South African connection', p. 134; W. S. Blunt, *My Diaries* (London, 1919), vol. ii, p. 202.

71 Kendle, *Round Table*, p. 154.

72 A Bengal Magistrate, 'The home rule movement in India and in Ireland: a contrast', *Contemporary Review*, 57 (January 1890), 80.

73 Ibid., 97.

74 S. B. Cook, *Imperial Affinities: Nineteenth Century Analogies and Exchanges Between India and Ireland* (London, 1993), p. 18.

75 Cf. Margaret O'Callaghan, ' "With the eyes of another race, of a people once hunted themselves": Casement, colonialism and a remembered past', in D. George Boyce and Alan O'Day (eds), *Ireland in Transition, 1867–1921* (London, 2004).

76 Quoted in Anil Seal, *The Emergence of Indian Nationalism: Competition and Collaboration in the Later Nineteenth Century* (Cambridge, 1971), p. 151.

77 Cook, *Imperial Affinities*, p. 120.

78 Ibid., p. 124.

79 J. S. Mill, *England and Ireland* (London, 1868).

80 Quoted in Cook, *Imperial Affinities*, p. 100.

81 Gordon Johnson, *Provincial Politics and Indian Nationalism: Bombay and the Indian National Congress 1880 to 1915* (Cambridge, 1973).

82 Howard V. Brasted, 'Irish home rule politics and India 1873–1886: Frank Hugh O'Donnell and other Irish "friends of India"', PhD 1974, University of Edinburgh; Howard V. Brasted, 'Indian nationalist development and the influence of Irish Home Rule, 1870–1886', *Modern Asian Studies*, 14 (1980); John R. McLane, 'The early Congress, Hindu populism, and the wider society', in Richard Sisson and Stanley Wolpert (eds), *Congress and Indian Nationalism: The Pre-Independence Phase* (Berkeley, 1988), pp. 47–61.

83 Seal, *Emergence*, pp. 178–9.

84 John Kendle, *Ireland and the Federal Solution: The Debates over the United Kingdom Constitution, 1870–1921* (Kingston and Montreal, 1989), pp. 81–2.

85 Brasted, 'Irish home rule politics', pp. 333–5.

86 Seal, *Emergence*, pp. 282–4.

87 *Sind Times*, 14 April 1886.

88 *Gujarat Mitra*, 11 April 1886.

89 *The Times of India*, 10 April 1886, also *Indian Spectator*, 17 September 1893.

90 *The Times of India*, 13 April 1912.

91 *The Hindu*, 13 May 1886.
92 *The Times of India*, 1 May 1886.
93 *Bengalee*, 16 September 1914.
94 *Hindoo Patriot*, 21 June 1886.
95 Indulal Yajnik, *Shyamaji Krishnavarma: Life and Times of an Indian Revolutionary* (Bombay, 1950).
96 See *The Indian Sociologist*, 1905–10.
97 Pal argued that Indians had replaced their urge to emulate European norms in India, which was 'naturally more destructive than constructive', with the desire to develop India in accordance to 'the actualities of the Indian life and situation'. 'Our old *admiration* for Europe has, thus, been largely supplanted now by an ardent *love* for our own country.' pp. 198–9.
98 *Bande Mataram*, 13, 15 March, 30 May, 21 June 1907.
99 Ibid., 7 March 1907.
100 *Bengalee*, 13 April 1912.
101 Ibid., 16 April 1912.
102 S. R. Mehrota drew attention to this strain of thought in 'Imperial Federation and India, 1868–1917', *Journal of Commonwealth Political Studies*, 1 (1961), 34.
103 Note the imprecision in the use of Home Rule and Dominion status: Ireland was offered Dominion status in 1921, a clear advance over Home Rule. Quoted in 'The Montagu-Chelmsford Scheme. Extracts from a Criticism by a Muhammadan Administrator, with a foreword', published by Indo-British Association, n.d. See Richard Koebner and Helmut Dan Schmidt, *Imperialism: The Story and Significance of a Political Word, 1840–1960* (Cambridge, 1964), pp. 178*ff.*
104 *Bande Mataram*, 10 September 1909.
105 *Bande Mataram* [monthly], November 1910.
106 The classic treatment is Edward Said, *Orientalism* (1978, London, 2003).
107 *The Times of India. Illustrated Weekly*, 1 April 1914.
108 *Gujarat Darpan*, 27 April 1893, quoted in *Indian Spectator & Voice of India*, 28 May 1893.
109 *Bengalee*, 14 February, 12 March, 1 April 1914.
110 Ibid., 14 June 1914.
111 Henry W. Nevinson, *The New Spirit in India* (London, 1908), pp. 221–2.
112 Jawaharlal Nehru to Motilal Nehru, 7 November 1907 in S. Gopal (ed.), *Selected Works of Jawaharlal Nehru* (New Delhi, 1972), vol. 1, pp. 37–8.
113 Quoted in Gordon Johnson, *Provincial Politics and Indian Nationalism: Bombay and the Indian National Congress 1880 to 1915* (Cambridge, 1973), p. 133.
114 *Amrita Bazar Patrika*, 4, 14 November 1905, 24 May 1907, 19 April 1912, 12 November 1913.
115 Johnson, *Provincial Politics*, p. 182.
116 'For Future of India', in *Maratha*, 3 August 1914, reproduced in Ravindra Kumar, *Selected Documents of Lokomanya Bal Gangadhar Tilak (1880–1920)* (New Delhi, 1992), vol. iv, p. 72.
117 For example, see G. A. Natesan (ed.), *Speeches of Gopal Krishna Goknale* (Madras, 1920), p. 305, also Rajat Kanta Ray, 'Moderates, extremists, and revolutionaries: Bengal, 1900–1908', in Sisson and Wolpert (eds), *Congress and Indian Nationalism* (Berkeley, 1988).

118 Brahm Autar Sharma, 'The Home Rule leagues and the Indian National Congress (1914–1919)', *Quarterly Review of Historical Studies*, 26 (April–June 1986).
119 Re. 1886 bill cf. Koebner and Schmidt, *Imperialism*, p. 171.
120 Erskine Childers, *The Framework of Home Rule* (London, 1911), pp. 201–3.
121 Although written from a different perspective, see Partha Chatterjee, *Nationalist Thought and the Colonial World: A Derivative Discourse?* (London, 1986), pp. 131–67.
122 HC, 4th series, vol. ccv, col. 1358 (17 May 1886).

8

Conservatives, 'Englishness' and 'civic nationalism' between the wars

Matthew Cragoe

The inter-war years represented a period of outstanding success for the Conservative Party. They were in power for all but three years, either alone or as the dominant party in coalition government. It was a record that, in 1918, few Conservatives would have dared predict. As David Jarvis has demonstrated, the Conservatives' long-standing anxieties over the likely behaviour of a fully enfranchised working class, which stretched back to the time of the Second Reform Act if not beyond, came to a head with the passing of the Fourth in 1918: 'Class politics seemed finally to have arrived', he writes, 'and with them the day of reckoning for a party long fearful of a democratic assault on their vested interests.'[1] As a consequence, socialism, the storm-bringer of the coming apocalypse, became the focus for Conservative anxiety throughout the inter-war years.[2] It was perhaps the party's primary achievement in the decade after the First World War that they successfully defended the old order against the encroachments of Labour's virile alternative, thereby securing the ground for the fight to defend it against the right-wing assaults of continental Fascism in the 1930s.[3]

Historians have identified a range of political and organisational factors underpinning the Tories' electoral hegemony. The terms of the 1918 Reform Act are considered to have worked in the party's favour, while the removal of the 70 MPs from Southern Ireland after Partition in 1922 certainly strengthened the Conservatives in parliament.[4] Conservative organisation is also held to have been significantly superior to that of the other parties, a political machine which reached right down to the constituencies, serviced by well-trained agents and informed by highly sophisticated and copious propaganda.[5] In addition, the party's ideological appeal was cleverly considered.[6] Ross McKibbin, for example, has emphasised the key role of anti-socialism in their propaganda, arguing that the Conservatives deployed 'ideologically determined class stereotypes' concerning the vicious political tendencies of unionised working men to mobilise support.[7] The initial targets of such propaganda were middle class Liberal voters whose own party was disintegrating, and here the strategy was a great success: whereas in 1924 erstwhile Liberals voted for the Tories over Labour in a ratio of 3:2; in 1931, they did so almost unanimously.[8] As the Conservatives came to realise that the 'working class' was not the homogenous bloc of its darkest imaginings, so the party's strategists broadened their appeal to target other potentially responsive sub-groups such as women and small savers, with the result that by the 1930s its support base was impressively inclusive.[9]

In this paper another angle on the Conservative Party's success in this period will be explored, their appeal to national identity. During the inter-war years, as is well known, the Conservatives deployed a sophisticated rhetoric of English identity. Its prime political exponent was the party's long-time leader, Stanley Baldwin, who became famous for his evocations of an idealised rural England, complete with wood smoke, bird song and contented artisans. His purpose was plain: to sell voters living in a society troubled by class conflict and industrial strife a vision of a better world, where people lived harmoniously in naturally homogenous, hierarchical communities. The attraction of these appeals to the inhabitants of England, particularly the vote-possessing, socialist-fearing inhabitants, is readily comprehensible; but how did this strategy square with the Conservative Party's need to attract support in other parts of the United Kingdom? As the introduction to this volume has commented, the fact that fluid, complex, overlapping, hybrid, multi-layered forms of identity were as common in Britain as elsewhere is now widely recognised. How then was the Conservative Party's 'Englishness' reconciled with Welshness, Scottishness and Britishness?[10]

In this paper, it will be suggested that the Conservative outlook was based on a form of civic nationalism. As Philip Lynch has explained, 'Instead of being defined in ethnic or racial terms, conservative accounts of the nation focus on allegiance to common institutions, a shared history and a political culture which fosters common values.'[11] Thus, for all that they often spoke an apparently 'ethnic' language of 'Englishness', their outlook was not ethnically exclusive.[12] At the heart of their ideological outlook lay a veneration for the political institutions of the state, notably parliament and the Crown. Maintaining the integrity of the territorial boundaries within which parliament's writ ran was always more important to the Conservatives than protecting the boundaries of an 'England' defined in ethnic terms. In effect, the Conservatives governed a state whose major institutions, while identifiably English, possessed a legitimacy that ran the length and breadth of the island. As section one will demonstrate, examining the Conservative Party within the framework of civic nationalism allows the rhetoric of 'Englishness' to be valued at its true weight, as a shorthand for a particular notion of Britishness.

Table 8.1 Proportion of seats won by Conservatives in each of the four countries, 1922–39

	1922	1923	1924	1929	1931	1935	Ave
England	63	46	72	46	82	68	63
Scotland	18	20	51	28	68	49	39
N. Ireland	83	83	100	83	83	83	86
Wales	17	11	26	3	17	17	15

The model of civic nationalism also provides an interesting starting point for an examination of the party's relationships with Wales and Scotland. In these regions of the United Kingdom, as Table 8.1 reveals, the party enjoyed markedly different fortunes in the period after the Great War.

In Scotland, the party held half the seats almost continually from 1924 to 1939, only a disastrous campaign in 1929 spoiling their record. In Wales, by contrast, the party's best performance in 1924 saw them secure only one-quarter of the seats; for the rest of the period they could not even muster one-fifth. Very little has been written about the experience of Conservatism in these two countries, but in the second section, the impact of the party's civic conception of nationalism will be assessed.

'Englishness' and the cultural contours of the Conservatives' civic nationalism

The pastoral impulse embodied in Conservative rhetoric was neither the exclusive preserve of politicians nor a creation of the 1920s. It was deeply embedded in the culture of the mid- and late nineteenth century, as historians such as Alun Howkins make clear.[13] Even if, as more recent scholarship has begun to assert, the English were never really as paralysed by nostalgia as the prevalence of such 'rural' writing might suggest, there is still no doubting the influence such notions had on the way people thought about themselves and the country in which they lived in the inter-war years.[14]

As John Ramsden has remarked, it is possible that had the Liberal Party not collapsed, the responsibility for defining an anti-socialist alliance would potentially have fallen to its share.[15] Had it done so, a very different rhetoric of liberty would have emerged. Whereas late nineteenth-century Conservatism, with its 'civic nationalism', prioritised the territorial integrity of the United Kingdom and opposed all movements for self-government, whether they occurred in Ireland or South Africa, the Liberals offered a different agenda.[16] In power after 1906, they rejected the Tories' Anglo-centric vision and sought to redefine the relationship of British national identity to its ethnic parts, promoting the notion that each territory should be governed in accordance with its own traditions and habits. It was a principle of 'unity in diversity'.[17] A Liberal-led alliance against socialism would thus have been unlikely to choose a mobilising vision with 'Englishness' writ so large upon its banners. The collapse of the Liberals, however, meant that the Conservatives were able to construct their antidote to socialism on their own terms. 'Englishness' thus became a concept laden with political significance, a shorthand for the traditional constitutional freedoms enjoyed by the British people.

No one expressed this more forcefully than the Conservative leader, Stanley Baldwin. As he said in his most quoted speech, delivered on St George's Day, 1924: 'To me England is the country and the country is England. And when I ask myself what I mean by England, when I think of England when I am abroad, England comes to me through my various senses, through the ear, through the eyes, and through certain imperishable senses.'[18] As J. H. Grainger has suggested, Baldwin's vision was predominantly an 'atmosphere', 'an idea of England absorbed into his language through literature, landscape, [and] rural life'.[19] He evoked a series of themes to which he would frequently return over the next decade and a half, and which helped define him in the public imagination as the quintessential Englishman.[20] His was a vision of an essentially pre-industrial English countryside, inhabited by industrious and archetypal Englishmen, such as the blacksmith and the agricultural labourer. The whole vision was clouded in a wistful nostalgia, which celebrated the beauty of everyday things, of ordinary-ness;[21] those things, said Baldwin, which 'seem to touch chords that go back to the beginning of time and the human race'.

Ross McKibbin has cautioned that Baldwin's 'class-harmonious rhetoric' should not be read as being 'at all representative' of contemporary popular Conservatism: at grass-roots level, popular Toryism was imbued with far more negative attitudes regarding the dangers posed by the working class.[22] However, the vision of communal harmony evoked by Baldwin always contained an implicit contrast with the social disharmony that must ensue if the foundations of the current order were upset or overturned. And, indeed, Baldwin did not scruple to make explicit his fears when occasion demanded. Philip Williamson has compiled a mini-anthology of Baldwin's sharper utterances: 'Class consciousness was "class hatred", the General Strike "a Challenge to Parliament and . . . the road to anarchy and ruin". Ostensible generosity towards the Labour Party was interspersed with brutal assaults: in 1924 it expressed "a fantastic heresy of foreign origin", in 1931 "Bolshevism run mad", in 1933 "proletarian Hitlerism".' Baldwin thus never sought to conceal the antipathy to working class militancy that lay beneath the cloak of

'Englishness'. His over-riding concern was to defend the existing order against 'imported ideologies' and prevent his fellow countrymen 'filling their bellies with the east wind of German Socialism and Russian Communism and French Syndicalism'.[23] Socialism, and subsequently Fascism and Communism, he said, were 'foreign' concepts that would ultimately, if allowed to triumph, 'obliterate national traditions, national sentiments, national aspirations, and, with them, national characteristics.'[24] The problem was the more acute since the electorate created in 1918 was full of women and young men whom Baldwin considered uniquely vulnerable to 'the presentation of ideals';[25] it was his achievement, in Williamson's phrase, to 'tame' the democracy by identifying freedom with 'constitutionalism and patriotism'.[26] Baldwin's sense of the 'nation' undoubtedly made the Conservative Party palatable to many not predisposed to think well of it. It was a crucial underpinning of the anti-socialist alliance.

To J. H. Grainger, Baldwin represents 'the only truly successful patriot' among contemporary politicians.[27] His patriotism, however, found a congenial culture in inter-war Britain. Many other writers and artists described England and Englishness in very similar terms: as Raphael Samuel suggests, 'cultural nationalism' was the inescapable sub-text of artistic and intellectual life during the 1930s.[28] The parameters of this cult of Englishness can be traced in various ways; however, it is striking that the idea was rarely deployed in an ethnically exclusive sense. David Cannadine's examination of the writing of history between the wars makes the point well. Discussing Oxford University Press's 'History of England' series, he remarks: 'it cannot be too much stressed that they were all conceived, written and marketed as histories of *England*.'[29] For all that the period 'witnessed the zenith of the British nation-state . . . of the British Empire', it was England whose history was recounted. Scholarship in this period 'celebrated parliamentary government, the Common Law, the Church of England, ordered progress towards democracy, and the avoidance of revolution.' Yet, almost without exception, continues Cannadine, the words 'England' and 'Britain' were used interchangeably, as different names for the same country. Thus for all their 'anglocentric perspective', and their view that 'the history of Britain was merely the history of England as and when it took place elsewhere', they did not define their territory along ethnic lines. It is the very unconsciousness of other 'national' histories beyond that of the dominant English constitutional narrative that is striking to modern eyes, not their wilful suppression.[30]

In broadcasting and the arts a similarly fluid definition of 'England' prevailed, as Andrew Causey has demonstrated. Late in 1933, against a background of economic depression and urban unrest, the BBC aired a series of talks on English character, 'designed to define, and create a historical background to, a concept of national identity'; a few months later, in the spring of 1934, the Royal Academy opened an exhibition of *British Art, c.1000–1860*. Familiar cultural themes permeated both. The BBC talks on 'The National Character' were introduced by no less a personage than Baldwin, and written by one of his own speechwriters, Arthur Bryant, then a lecturer at the Conservative Party's Ashridge College. Unsurprisingly, the content of the broadcasts came straight from the heart of Baldwinite 'Englishness'. 'Irrespective of whether the talks concerned society as a whole, or particular professional and cultural activities such as agriculture, enjoyment of the landscape, or the character of English music', writes Causey, 'the points . . . repeatedly returned to were the importance of the land, the individual character and contribution of the regions, the common interests of all social classes, Britain's moral leadership in the world and a sobriety, reticence and pleasure in nature which were seen as conditioning both the British character and the nation's artistic expression.'[31] The Royal Academy's exhibition, meanwhile, was held at a time when a new wave of scholarship was redating the rise of properly 'English' art from the comparatively recent eighteenth century to a location in the Middle Ages more befitting the self-image of an historic cultural nation.[32] Landscape painting, nevertheless, remained '*the* English contribution'. The author of the exhibition catalogue, W. G. Constable, dwelt upon very similar themes to those highlighted in the BBC's talks, stressing the valuable role in creating the nation's artistic heritage of the island's racial mix in the past, its regionalism, local consciousness and lack of any single centre, such as the Court, providing a narrowing focus for creative energy. In addition, he celebrated the relative weakness in England of those intellectual pacemakers such as the Jesuits and the Church who had had such a profound influence on the continent of Europe. The picture he offered was one of Baldwinite moderation, of popular common sense, and of regional variety contributing to the creation of a wider national artistic tradition.

Thus, historians, broadcasters, and artists alike shared a common pool of cultural ideas in this period. Yet, significantly, their sense of England was not ethnically exclusive. The terms 'English' and 'British' were easily elided, and the cultural qualities associated with one might belong to both. This much, as Rebecca Langlands has written, is implied by the fact that one of the most enduring images of English identity has been Shakespeare's evocation of the 'sceptr'd isle',[33] whose only boundary was the sea. The sceptre itself, of course, remained the greatest of all the unifying symbols available to the state in the inter-war period, and was a potent carrier of this 'Greater Englishness'. Although officially 'above party', moreover, it could generally be identified with the kind of 'one nation' Englishness promoted by the Conservatives.

The monarchy became identified with the Conservative Party in the late nineteenth century. Both Liberals and Conservatives recognised its potential as a unifying force, as Richard Williams points out, but it was under Disraeli that the fusion between the monarchy and patriotism was made, and under Salisbury, when enthusiasm for Empire reached its peak, that the bond was cemented.[34] Thereafter, as Philip Lynch affirms, 'The monarchy became an important element in conservative state patriotism, enhancing themes of trad- ition, a continuous national history and British identity. The popularization of the monarchy promoted deferential acceptance of the conservative polit- ical settlement, its hierarchical social order and pre-democratic institutional framework'.[35] Thus, despite the attempts of Lloyd George to use the investi- ture of the Prince of Wales in 1911 as a vehicle for a rather different kind of patriotism, less obviously Anglo-centric and more celebratory of Britain's 'unity in diversity',[36] the inter-war court remained a stronghold of Tory values. George V's own Conservative sympathies were widely known, and his interventions to ensure Ramsay MacDonald remained in office to lead the National Government, and his congratulations to the members of that Government on their victory in 1931, spoke of the King's anxiety about the direction of the country under socialist rule.[37] As for George VI, as Ross McKibbin remarks, 'The king's relations with Labour leaders were correct, even cordial, but distant; with the older generation of Conservative leaders they were those of intimate acquaintances.' Yet as McKibbin goes on to point out, both men were very careful to patronise the pastimes of all their people, and not those of one section alone. George V, for example, attended soccer's FA Cup Final but not rugby internationals. The monarchy thus repre- sented not just a hierarchic social order, he concludes, 'but a particular, Tory version of it'.[38]

An essentially unitary 'Englishness' thus became an important feature of English culture during the inter-war period. The collapse of Liberalism meant that the task of creating an anti-socialist alliance devolved onto the Conservative Party, who mobilised a rhetoric in which 'Englishness' stood against 'foreignness', 'country' against 'town', and 'parliamentary democ- racy' against Communist or Fascist 'absolutism'. Yet, for all that the Conservatives' 'English' rhetoric played up an apparently 'ethnic' national- ism, it was not exclusive in the way that ethnically defined nationalism can be. As Grainger notes, Baldwin's patriotism was a way of talking about England and Wales and Scotland.[39] Ultimately the party based its championship of freedom not on ethnic but on civic grounds: they, like the inter-war histori- ans of whom David Cannadine writes, conceived of 'Englishness' as bound up with the history of the nation's sovereign institutions. As such it belonged to everyone; it was the history of the people of the 'sceptr'd isle', the people gathered beneath the Crown. The Tories' sense of nationhood stemmed from this, and it was the institution of parliament that truly lay at its heart. How the Conservatives coped in practical terms with the two other nations of the mainland is the subject of the next section.

The Conservatives and the regions, 1922–39

In the late nineteenth century neither Wales nor Scotland had provided congenial territory for the Conservatives. Buoyed by a series of factors – religious dissent, questions over land, and demands for Home Rule – the Liberals became the natural party of government in these regions before the First World War. After the war, however, as the Liberal Party split, the political history of the two countries began to diverge. Wales remained impervious to Tory appeals, the principal beneficiaries of Liberal decline being the Labour Party. In Scotland, however, a more complex situation arose. Middle class disaffection with socialism helped boost Conservatism, but the onset of Depression in the early 1930s stimulated precisely the kind of Home Rule nationalist movement that most offended the Tories' sense of civic nationalism. Philip Lynch has stressed that while political ideas are naturally important to the Conservative Party their primary role has always been to provide a supportive background for its practical exercise of statecraft.[40] In this section, the series of political calculations that the Tories made with regard to the government of Scotland and Wales will be reviewed.

Conservatism flourished in inter-war Scotland. As Table 8.1 demonstrated, they were a highly successful electoral force, and this was based, as in England, on a well developed constituency organisation. Trained agents and large membership lists were as common north of the border as they were south.[41] Moreover, the inter-war years witnessed a period of Scottish domination at the highest levels of the Conservative Party. Following the chairmanship of Sir Arthur Steel-Maitland (1911–17), came George Younger (1917–23), J. C. C. Davidson (1926–30), and John Baird (1931–40). And in addition to furnishing one Conservative Prime Minister (Andrew Bonar Law), Scotland could also boast one Chancellor of the Exchequer (Sir Robert Horne), one Home Secretary (Sir John Gilmour), two Agriculture Ministers (Gilmour and Walter Elliot), and one Health Secretary (Elliot).

The Scots had not always been such willing accomplices. Nineteenth-century Scotland had been secure Liberal territory, though the Tories bore responsibility for the formation of Scotland's distinctive administrative institutions.[42] The proposal to establish the Scottish Office emanated from Gladstone's government, but when his administration fell in 1885, Salisbury allowed it to carry on. How seriously the Tory premier took the notion of devolved administration is questionable: his letter urging the Duke of Richmond and Gordon to become the first Secretary for Scotland suggests he viewed its worth largely in symbolic terms. 'The work is not very heavy', he wrote, '– the dignity (measured by salary) is the same as your present office – but measured by the expectations of the people of Scotland it is approaching the Arch-angelic'. Choosing someone of sufficient weight, however, was key, as otherwise 'The Scotch people would declare we were despising Scotland – and treating her as if she were a West Indian Colony.' 'It really is a matter', concluded Salisbury, 'where the effulgence of two Dukedoms and the best salmon river in Scotland will go a long way.'[43]

For all Salisbury's flippancy, it remains a matter of historical record that, a year before Irish Home Rule altered the political scene for a generation, the Scottish Office had been created, and by Tory hands. By 1900 it had twenty-two employees, including a permanent Under-Secretary and an Assistant Under-Secretary, and was responsible for education, law and order, and (after 1912) agriculture. In the inter-war years, as the activities and functions of local government were modernised, Scotland's distinctive administrative arrangements developed further. As part of the post-war coalition, Conservatives supported the 1919 Scottish Board of Health Act which created a parliamentary Under-Secretary for Scottish health and it was a Conservative administration under Baldwin which (in another largely symbolic act) promoted the Scottish Secretary to the cabinet in 1926. In 1929, the Conservatives met what Sir John Gilmour, the Scottish Secretary, described as the 'clamant need for revision' of the 'creaking machine' of Scottish local government.[44] They proposed a measure akin to that being carried forward simultaneously by Chamberlain in England, though they were able only to carry out a portion of the work at first. After a further investigation in 1937 under Gilmour, however, the local government system was finally overhauled, and, in 1939, the Reorganisation of Offices (Scotland) Act, brought the functions of the Scottish Office together under one roof at St Andrew's House in Edinburgh.[45]

The politics of Scottish Unionism have stimulated greater scholarly attention than has been accorded to the subject in Wales, and several different interpretations exist as to the sense that should be made of the events outlined above. James Mitchell, for example, has suggested that older historiography on the subject, associated with the work of H. J. Hanham, tended to overplay the extent to which the later reforms, particularly, were a nervous reaction by Unionists to the emergence of a new nationalist politics in Scotland.[46] Whilst he admits that, during the early 1930s the Scottish Nationalist Party (SNP) won both public attention (through such incidents as the election of a nationalist as Lord Rector of Glasgow University in 1932) and a growing number of adherents,[47] he argues that traditional accounts underestimate the purely administrative importance of the government's reforms. More recently, Richard Finlay has argued a slightly different case, suggesting that the emergence of nationalism did indeed have a profound impact on the way Conservatives viewed Scotland. He suggests that the emergence of nationalism forced the Tories onto the defensive, obliging them to abandon older notions that Scotland and England enjoyed equal status within the Union in favour of a model which emphasised Scotland's economic dependence on England both for markets and the money to fund social security payments. This policy of highlighting Scottish dependence on England was accompanied by a two-pronged campaign that, while it had no truck with dangerous, potentially separatist nationalism, nevertheless pandered to a sense of Scottish patriotism. First the Tories aimed to ensure that Scotland felt it was not forgotten, suggesting more Royal tours might be organised to emphasise her importance within the United Kingdom. Secondly, the National Government pushed ahead with the Gilmour Committee and the symbolic relocation of the Scottish Government to Edinburgh, a move, says Finlay, designed to convince the Scots that, henceforth, decisions affecting Scotland would be taken 'in Scotland by Scotsmen.'[48]

For all their cogency, neither account places the activities of the Conservative Party into a wider, British context. This, however, is essential if we are to understand the way in which the Conservatives dealt with Scotland in terms of 'practical statecraft'. Where the wider context is employed, it immediately becomes clear how similar Conservative priorities were north and south of the border.[49] Gabrielle Ward-Smith's detailed examination of Stanley Baldwin's relationship with Scotland, for example, is a case in point. She demonstrates that Baldwin enjoyed tremendous popularity in Scotland, and even symbolically faced down a nationalist challenge to secure election as Rector of Glasgow University in 1928. Yet while he deliberately played a Scottish card for Scottish audiences – expressing his deep love of Sir Walter Scott; emphasising the flight of his mother's family, the MacDonalds, from the Isle of Skye for Northern Ireland after the Forty-Five; and delivering trademark appreciations of the Scottish landscape – his central message was no different: 'Your struggle', he told an audience in 1935, 'is now with the Scottish brand of Socialism'.[50] He argued that the 'class hatred' fostered by socialism in Scotland, typified by the industrial militancy in Glasgow in 1915 and 1919, threatened to wrench the Scots from the path of their historic development, which had not been collective but marked by 'an almost divine individualism'.[51] In the face of Socialism, and with Liberalism crumbling, he argued that only Unionism could uphold Scotland's true political and cultural identity.

It was an appeal that was hugely successful throughout the inter-war years. Alarmed by the spectre of 'Red Clydeside', the middle classes flocked to the Conservative colours and gave the Unionists a monopoly over the anti-socialist vote.[52] At key elections, such as 1931, which for Baldwin represented the 'acid test of democracy', candidates pulled out all the stops.[53] As Iain Hutchinson describes, Scottish Unionists stormed home on a wave of alarmist propaganda. Typical were the Unionist candidate at Partick, who criticised both Labour's incompetence and their 'wild extremes of nationalisation and extravagance', and his counterpart in Ayr Burghs, who warned voters that all their 'little investments, our savings, our pensions' were imperilled by social-ism.[54] The election saw 68% of all seats in Scotland fall to the Unionists, the party's best performance not only in the inter-war period, but at any point in the twentieth century. With an apparently sound administrative substructure in place, and a membership that, on paper at least, was numbered in the tens of thousands, the Tories encountered nationalism from a position of some strength in the 1930s.

This is in no way to dispute the alarm experienced by Unionists at the idea of Home Rule sentiment contaminating Tory supporters from the early 1930s on. There were undoubtedly some flutters in the dovecote in 1932 when Kevin Macdowall and a large section of the Glasgow Cathcart Unionist Association came out in open support for Home Rule, but the Party's swift response was well organised and decisive. During October and November three important meetings were held.[55] In the first, under the chairmanship of Sir Robert Horne, MP, the meeting unanimously agreed that no benefit would accrue to Scotland from the establishment of a Scottish parliament which could not equally be achieved by further administrative reforms. A second meeting at the Merchants House in Glasgow in November, attended by 500 representatives of business and public opinion, issued a statement confirming that 'Scotland and England are interdependent and form one unit for all practical and for all national purposes,' and concluding: 'Exaggerated nationalism is the root of the evil of world distress today and should not be introduced into Scotland'. Finally, the Scottish Unionist Annual Meeting in November 1932 accepted a resolution that separate parliaments would be 'gravely injurious both to the economic and cultural life of Great Britain as a whole.'

This was sound party politics, but what of 'practical statecraft'? Although the party lost ground at the general election of 1935 in Scotland, as it did in England, it was Labour, not the SNP that benefited. As a consequence, the Conservatives' top priority remained keeping together the anti-socialist alliance. And since, as several historians have pointed out, Liberalism remained the biggest threat to the Tories throughout the inter-war period in Scotland,[56] if there was an element of political calculation in the Tories' decision two years later to consolidate the administration of Scotland in a relocated Edinburgh Scottish Office, its aim was not simply to pacify a nationalist movement, but to ensure that the key alliance with the Liberals remained strong enough to resist socialism. Equally important, however, as James Mitchell has emphasised, is the idea that such reforms actually made sound administrative sense. They contributed to good government in a way that, in the judgement of the Conservative elite, the grant of administrative devolution to Wales in the same period did not. In the final analysis, the measures taken by the party in relation to Scotland in no way offended their core civic nationalism. Quite the contrary. For, as both Richard Finlay and Gabrielle Ward-Smith recognise, 'In reality, under the guise of giving concessions to Scotland in the face of growing demands for devolution . . . Westminster surreptitiously tightened its embrace over Scotland and greatly (and controversially) reduced the distinctive nature of Scottish local government.'[57] The primacy of English parliamentary institutions remained paramount.

Wales presented the Conservatives with very different challenges. From the time of the general election of 1865 onwards, they remained in a permanent minority in Wales. On occasion the party suffered complete annihilation, as in 1906 when they famously won no seats at all in the principality. Indelibly associated with Englishness, aristocracy and Anglicanism, they never came to terms with the idea of Wales's nationhood.[58] The famous comment of a bishop of St David's in 1880, that Wales was little more than a 'geographical expression' accurately summarised mainstream Conservative opinion on the subject throughout the nineteenth century and beyond.[59] If the Tories were ambivalent about 'Wales', the Welsh were equally ambivalent about 'England'. Although at times of crisis, such as the Boer War, even the most respectably Nonconformist, middle-class, Welsh-speaking, Welshman could describe himself, quite unselfconsciously, as 'English', there is much in John Turner's comment that by the turn of the twentieth century, '[t]here was no necessary incompatibility between being Welsh and being British, but there was a real incompatibility between being Welsh and being English'.[60]

The Conservatives' relationship with Wales in the inter-war years remained highly unsatisfactory. Indeed, as Felix Aubel has pointed out in the only study of Welsh Conservatism in this period, only one of the fifteen Tory MPs returned from Wales in this period, Gwilym Rowlands, a coal merchant (Flint 1935–45), spoke Welsh.[61] Similarly, only once did the Conservatives pick up even a quarter of the Welsh seats, and even then it was not in the party's *annus mirabilis*, 1931, but in an otherwise disappointing year, 1924. For all that the Liberal Party in Wales showed clear signs, particularly in the urban areas, of crumbling as comprehensively as it had elsewhere, it was Labour, not the Conservatives, that benefited. Peripheral to the political life of the principality, Conservatism was relegated to the geographical margins of the country: outside Cardiff and the south-east, only in isolated coastal pockets in the west and north – Pembrokeshire, Flintshire – did it enjoy any visible existence.

It is perhaps indicative of the party's narrow appeal in Wales that Baldwin made few efforts to cultivate a support base there, despite the fact that his family owned important steel works in the principality.[62] His best-remembered speech in the country was delivered at Cardiff, on St David's Day 1925, in the heart of that little island of Tory sentiment that was home to the successful Conservative daily newspaper, the *Western Mail*. It was a very thin effort. He said a little about the culture of the country and then switched back onto more comfortable terrain, waxing lyrical about the Welsh countryside. He remarked that he had recently seen a statue of Hedd Wyn, the famous poet, in a Chelsea studio, and the artist had explained that the sources on which he had drawn for inspiration were Prometheus and the 'Man of Nazareth'. Baldwin said: 'whenever I think of Wales, it is not of her industrial areas, but of the country, and I look upon that figure as a type of what our rural civilisation can produce.'[63] At the time of his death, in 1949, the editor of the *Western Mail* recalled the speech fondly, saying it had 'never been surpassed in felicity of diction or friendly appreciation of Welsh history and people'.[64] The use of the inclusive 'our', however, showed Baldwin was engaged in tying the Welsh countryman into the spiritual vision of England with which he was more commonly associated.

Unfortunately, it was in the industrial areas of Wales that the most visible problems were clustered in the inter-war years, and here that the Labour Party was making headway.[65] After the war, it became a truism that Scotland had benefited during the Depression from having a Secretary of State with a seat in the Cabinet.[66] The range of tactics used by the Tories in 1937–38 to oppose the demand of the Liberal Clement Davies's call for the creation of a Welsh Secretary of State with powers analogous to those of the Scottish Secretary, might at first sight suggest that there were firm ethnic limits to the 'Britishness' of Conservative Party 'Englishness'. The principal opposition, to Davies's Private Member's Bill came from a group of backbench English Tory MPs, led by Herbert Williams and Arthur Reed, who mobilised a rhetoric of 'dependence' remarkably similar to that used by Scottish Unionists earlier in the decade in the face of the Home Rule threat. They declared that the bill was 'calculated to revive unnecessary and undesirable controversy', and went on to express the view that 'the severance of Wales from England will involve great hardship on the unemployed workpeople of Wales, whose benefits are now paid out of funds provided mainly by the inhabitants of England'.[67] Williams and his supporters clearly saw the Bill as a separatist 'Trojan horse' and in response pointedly sought to remind the Welsh of the economic realities underlying Anglo-Welsh relations.

Yet as the campaign launched by Davies wore on, it became clear that the Government was acting not simply from a desire to block the legitimate expression of regional patriotism; rather, its primary duty was the promotion of good government. Following the defeat of his bill, Davies successfully sought a meeting with Chamberlain to discuss the issue further. The tone of the meeting on 30 June 1938 was agreeably positive; Chamberlain's final response, however, was predictably negative. For all that he claimed not to be 'lacking in sympathy for the argument from national sentiment', he rejected outright the claim that 'the administration of Welsh affairs should . . . be concentrated in a single department'. Instead, he asserted that in matters of administration Wales was already receiving 'special treatment', and that he could not endorse the 'considerable expense' entailed in establishing a separate Welsh Office.[68]

As James McConnel has shown, Chamberlain was careful to weigh the evidence in this matter carefully before coming to his conclusions.[69] Upon agreeing to meet the Welsh deputation, the Prime Minister had asked his private secretary, C. G. L. Syers,[70] to establish whether an official answer given by the Home Office to a parliamentary question on the same matter, dating from 1928, still held good.[71] At that time the Home Office had advised the government, 'there is no evidence of any general demand for the change; it would serve no practical object, and is obviously desired for purely sentimental reasons; and it would involve considerable expense in increased staff and administration.'[72] The Home Office responded that not only did it stand by its 1928 statement but added that it had consulted the Welsh department of the Board of Education, the Welsh Board of Health, the Welsh department of the Ministry of Agriculture, and the Board of Control, all of whom had emphasised that no savings would be effected by the establishment of a Welsh Office.[73] Sir James Rae at the Treasury was also consulted and told Syers that a 'separate administration for Wales would still further complicate administration which is already far too complicated. It would moreover lead to a good deal of additional expenditure. I cannot see in what practical field Wales would benefit.'[74]

The level of expenditure and the administrative efficiency of the state, therefore, would seem to have been at the heart of Chamberlain's decision to turn down the request for a Welsh Secretary in 1938. The unlikelihood of there being any electoral dividend for the Conservatives in Wales following the establishment of the Secretaryship seems to have been a rather less important factor.[75] Ultimately, the point of view adopted by Chamberlain seems to have rested on the simple concerns of 'practical governance'.

Conclusion

In a penetrating discussion of the twentieth-century Conservative Party, Harriet Jones remarked: 'Conservatism has adopted as a central goal the defence and justification of an economic system which is based on economic inequality in an age in which the Party has depended for permission to rule upon the votes of the earners as well as the owners.'[76] This is doubtless true, but we perhaps need to recognise that a major factor in the Tories' appeal has been to offset financial inequality with an offer to the people of equality in a somewhat different sphere, national identity. It has been the suggestion of this chapter that, for all the pronounced 'Englishness' of Tory Party rhetoric in the inter-war years, its import was ultimately inclusive. It referred to a kind of civic 'Englishness'; its qualities were held to run to the boundaries not just of England, but of the area governed by those institutions which defined the identity of the nation for Conservatives, parliament and the Crown. It was, in effect, 'Britishness'. Tories were quite happy to celebrate the several patriotisms within the United Kingdom: indeed, the party had always had a strong localist appeal. What they would not tolerate, however, was separatist or Home Rule movements, and in this respect it is interesting to reflect that Baldwin's rise to the head of the Conservative Party occurred within a few months of the final settlement of the Irish Question in 1922. Not only did this take seventy hostile MPs out of parliament, it also removed the most persistent challenge to the Tories' notions of civic nationalism. With that problem solved, the Tories could turn their attention fully to the new focus of their 'fear and loathing',[77] socialism, and set about constructing an anti-socialist alliance on a thoroughly Conservative basis. Its appeal was undoubtedly to the spirit of the nation, and a nation defined by its English institutions. However, viewed within the civic nationalist paradigm, there was no contradiction here. For as Stanley Baldwin himself once put it: it was 'perfectly possible and to-day natural for us to feel proud of being Scotch or Welsh and intensely British at the same time.'[78]

Notes

1 David Jarvis, 'British conservatism and class politics in the 1920s', *EHR*, 111 (1996), 83.

2 John Turner, 'Letting go: the Conservative Party and the end of the Union with Ireland', in Alexander Grant and Keith J. Stringer (eds), *Uniting the Kingdom? The Making of British History* (London, 1995), p. 270.

3 Philip Williamson, 'The doctrinal politics of Stanley Baldwin', in Michael Bentley (ed.), *Public and Private Doctrine. Essays in British History Presented to Maurice Cowling* (Cambridge, 1993), pp. 185–6.

4 Kenneth Wald, *Crosses on the Ballot* (Princeton, 1983); William Miller, *Electoral Dynamics in Britain since 1918* (London, 1977).

5 John Ramsden, *Politics in the Age of Balfour and Baldwin, 1902–1940* (London, 1978) offers the classic account. The significance of organisation has been questioned by various scholars: I. G. C. Hutchinson, 'Scottish Unionism between the two world wars', in Catriona M. MacDonald, *Unionist Scotland, 1800–1997* (Edinburgh, 1998), pp. 80–3; for a slightly later period, Janet Johnson, 'Did organization really matter? Party organization and Conservative electoral recovery, 1945–59', *Twentieth Century British History*, 14 (2003).

6 David Jarvis, 'The shaping of Conservative electoral hegemony, 1918–39', in Jon Lawrence and Miles Taylor (eds), *Party, State and Society: Electoral Behaviour in Britain since 1820* (Aldershot, 1997), pp. 132–6.

7 Ross McKibbin, 'Class and conventional wisdom: the Conservative Party and the "public" in inter-war Britain', in Ross McKibbin, *The Ideologies of Class: Social Relations in Britain, 1880–1950* (Oxford, 1990), p. 270.

8 Ibid.

9 Jarvis, 'British conservatism and class politics', 80.

10 Gabrielle Ward-Smith, 'Baldwin and Scotland: more than Englishness', *Contemporary British History*, 15 (2001), 66.

11 Philip Lynch, *The Politics of Nationhood: Sovereignty, Britishness and Conservative Politics* (Macmillan, 1999), p. 5.

12 Rebecca Langlands, 'Britishness or Englishness? The historical problem of national identity', *Nations and Nationalism*, 5 (1999), for the notion that 'Englishness' itself was a somewhat mongrel concoction drawing freely on Celtic myths.

13 Alun Howkins, 'The discovery of rural England', in Robert Colls and Philip Dodd (eds), *Englishness: Politics and Culture, 1880–1920* (London, 1986); J. H. Grainger, *Patriotisms, 1900–1939* (London, 1986), pp. 86–103; Paul Street, 'Painting deepest England: the late landscapes of John Linnell and the uses of nostalgia', in Christopher Shaw and Malcolm Chase (eds), *The Imagined Past: History and Nostalgia* (Manchester, 1989); John Lucas, *England and Englishness: Ideas of Nationhood in English Poetry, 1688–1900* (London, 1990).

14 Peter Mandler, 'Against "Englishness": English culture and the limits to rural nostalgia, 1850–1940', *TRHS*, 6th series, 7 (1997); John Baxendale, ' "I had seen a lot of Englands": J. B. Priestley, Englishness and the people', *HWJ*, 51 (2001).

15 John Ramsden, *An Appetite for Power: A History of the Conservative Party since 1830* (London, 1998), p. 247.

16 Lynch, *Politics of Nationhood*, p. 9.

17 Ibid., p. 17; John S. Ellis, 'Reconciling the Celt: British national identity, empire, and the 1911 investiture of the Prince of Wales', *JBS*, 37 (1998), makes this point well.

18 Stanley Baldwin, *On England* (London, 1938), p. 5; Williamson, 'Doctrinal politics', 191.

19 Grainger, *Patriotisms*, pp. 318, 328.

20 Ward-Smith, 'Baldwin and Scotland', 67.

21 For Baldwin's ordinariness, see Ramsden, *Age of Balfour and Baldwin*, pp. 208–10.

22 Grainger, *Patriotisms*, p. 358; McKibbin, 'Class and conventional wisdom', pp. 292–3.

23 Grainger, *Patriotisms*, p. 359.
24 Quoted in Ward-Smith, 'Baldwin and Scotland', 67.
25 Quoted in Ramsden, *Age of Balfour and Baldwin*, p. 209.
26 Williamson, 'Doctrinal politics', p. 191.
27 Grainger, *Patriotisms*, p. 358.
28 Raphael Samuel, 'Introduction: exciting to be English' in Raphael Samuel (ed.), *Patriotism: The Making and Unmaking of British National Identity*, volume 1: *History and Politics* (London, 1989), p. xxiii; see for example, Malcolm Chase, 'This is no claptrap: this is our heritage', in *The Imagined Past*; Philip Dodd, 'Englishness and the national culture', in Robert Colls and Philip Dodd (eds), *Englishness: Politics and Culture, 1880–1920* (London, 1986); Catherine Brace, 'Looking back: the Cotswolds and English identity, c. 1890–1950', *Journal of Historical Geography*, 25 (1999).
29 David Cannadine, 'British history as a "new subject"' in Alexander Grant and Keith J. Stringer (eds), *Uniting the Kingdom? The Making of British History* (London, 1995), p. 16.
30 Writers of history in this period were disadvantaged by the poverty of studies in the regions. The history of Wales was in many respects a creation of the post-1945 period: Matthew Cragoe, 'Wales', in Chris Williams (ed.), *A Companion to Nineteenth-Century Britain* (Oxford, 2004); the history of Scotland was only taught in schools north of the border as 'local history' in the inter-war years: Richard J. Finlay, 'National identity in crisis: politics, intellectuals and the "end of Scotland", 1920–1939', *History*, 79 (1994), 250.
31 Andrew Causey, 'English art and "the national character", 1933–34', in David Peters Corbet, Ysanne Holt and Fiona Russell (eds), *The Geographies of Englishness: Landscape and the National Past, 1880–1940* (New Haven, 2002), p. 275.
32 For the theme of timelessness and identity in inter-war Scottish landscape painting, Duncan Macmillan, *Scottish Art in the 20th Century, 1890–2001* (Edinburgh, 2001), pp. 64–5.
33 Langlands, 'Britishness or Englishness?', 57–60.
34 Richard Williams, *The Contentious Crown: Public Discussion of the British Monarchy in the Reign of Queen Victoria* (Aldershot, 1997), p. 174.
35 Lynch, *Politics of Nationhood*, pp. 8–10.
36 Ellis, 'Reconciling the Celt'.
37 Andrew Thorpe, *The British General Election of 1931* (Oxford, 1991), pp. 83–90, 120–2.
38 McKibbin, *Classes and Cultures: England 1918–1951* (Oxford, 1998), pp. 5–6.
39 Grainger, *Patriotisms*, p. 359.
40 Lynch, *Politics of Nationhood*, pp. 9–10.
41 Hutchinson, 'Scottish Unionism', pp. 74–80.
42 For reflections on 'civic' and 'ethnic' nationalism in Scotland at the start of this period, Graeme Morton 'What if? The significance of Scotland's missing nationalism in the nineteenth century', in Dauvit Brown et al. (eds), *Image and Identity: The Making and Re-Making of Scotland Through the Ages* (Edinburgh, 1998).
43 Quoted in James Mitchell, *Conservatives and the Union: A Study of Conservative Party Attitudes to Scotland* (Edinburgh, 1990), p. 19, on which the following paragraphs draw.

44 *The Times*, 12 March 1929.
45 James Kellas, 'The Party in Scotland', in Anthony Seldon and Stuart Bell (eds), *Conservative Century. The Conservative Party since 1900* (Oxford, 1994), p. 684.
46 Mitchell, *Conservatives and the Union*, p. 25.
47 Coupland, *Welsh and Scottish Nationalism*; Christopher Harvie, *Scotland and Nationalism: Scottish Society and Politics, 1707–1977* (London, 1977), p. 51.
48 Finlay, *A Partnership for Good?*, pp. 102–13.
49 This paragraph draws freely on Ward-Smith, 'Baldwin and Scotland'.
50 *The Times*, 30 November 1935.
51 Ibid.
52 Key Scottish supporters also played precisely the same 'rural' cards as Baldwin: J. C. C. Davidson, for example, regularly reiterated that his people were country folk, and dwelt on his dislike of London. J. C. C. Davidson, *Memoirs of a Conservative. J. C. C. Davidson's Diaries and Papers* (London, 1967), p. 111.
53 Thorpe, *British General Election*, p. 222.
54 Hutchinson, 'Scottish Unionism', pp. 83–5.
55 Mitchell, *Conservatives and the Union*, pp. 45–8.
56 Hence the large number of men with very advanced opinions, notably John Buchan, William Elliot, and Bob Boothby; J. P. Parry, 'From the Thirty-Nine Articles to the Thirty-Nine Steps: reflections on the thought of John Buchan', in Bentley (ed.), *Public and Private Doctrine*, pp. 225–8.
57 Ward-Smith, 'Baldwin and Scotland', 65.
58 Matthew Cragoe, *Culture, Politics and National Identity in Wales, 1832–86* (Oxford, 2004); Kenneth O. Morgan, *Rebirth of a Nation: Wales 1880–1980* (Oxford and Cardiff, 1981).
59 Morgan, *Rebirth*, p. 57.
60 Matthew Cragoe, '"Brimful of Patriotism": Welsh Conservatives, the South African War and the "Khaki" Election of 1900', in Matthew Cragoe and Chris Williams (eds), *Wales and War: Society, Politics and Religion in the Nineteenth and Twentieth Centuries* (Cardiff, 2007); Turner, 'Letting go', p. 257.
61 Felix Aubel, 'The Conservatives in Wales, 1880–1935', in Martin Francis and Ina Zweiniger-Bargielowska (eds), *The Conservatives and British Society, 1880–1990* (Cardiff, 1996), pp. 105–8.
62 Ward-Smith. 'Baldwin and Scotland', 69.
63 Baldwin, *On England*, pp. 251–2; he expressed similar sentiments to the Honourable Society of Cymmrodorion at a dinner in Mayfair: *The Times*, 8 April 1933.
64 *WM*, 15 December 1947.
65 Morgan, *Rebirth*, pp. 272–303; Duncan Tanner, 'The pattern of Labour politics, 1918–1939', in Duncan Tanner et al. (eds), *The Labour Party in Wales 1900–2000* (Cardiff, 2000).
66 *WM*, 18 August 1945; R. H. Campbell, 'The Scottish Office and the Special Areas in the 1930s', *Historical Journal*, 22 (1979).
67 *The Times*, 24 November 1937.
68 TNA, Neville Chamberlain to Morgan Jones, 27 July 1938, PREM 1/292.
69 James McConnel, ' "Sympathy without relief is rather like mustard without beef": devolution, Plaid Cymru, and the campaign for a secretary of state for Wales, 1937–8', *WHR*, 22 (2005).

70 TNA, C. G. L. Syers to William John, 24 June 1938, PREM 1/292.
71 TNA, C. G. L. Syers to A. S. Hutchinson, 24 June 1938, PREM 1/292.
72 TNA, F. A. Newman to Miss Watson, 29 June 1928, PREM 1/292.
73 TNA, A. S. Hutchinson to C. G. L. Syers, 28 June 1938, PREM 1/292.
74 TNA, Sir James Rae to C. G. L. Syers, 29 June 1938, PREM 1/292.
75 *WM*, 30 July 1938: shortly after refusing the Welsh case, Chamberlain agreed to
    further administrative devolution for Scotland. The *Western Mail* fulminated
    against this 'further insult' to Welsh sensibilities, but again, it created few polit-
    ical ripples in the principality.
76 Harriet Jones, 'A bloodless counter-revolution: the Conservative Party and the
    defence of inequality, 1945–51', in Harriet Jones and M. Kandiah (eds), *The Myth
    of Consensus: New Views on British History, 1945–64* (London, 1996), pp. 3–4.
77 Turner, 'Letting Go', p. 270.
78 Ward-Smith, 'Baldwin and Scotland', 77.

9
The government of London

John Davis

There was a point, soon after the overhaul of London government in 1888–89, when it was possible to believe that the capital's citizens could speak with one voice. Previously a combination of the scale of the London problem and the reluctance of the powerful City Corporation to be absorbed into any new metropolitan municipality had denied London the usual benefits of municipal incorporation. In consequence it had failed to share in the Victorian civic revolution, by which Britain's larger provincial cities had gained both self-government and the control of key local services like gas, water and tramways from the mid-nineteenth century. The reform movement of the 1880s had claimed to speak for a London population deprived of standard civic utilities by, in their view, a malevolent combination of interest groups – jobbing vestrymen, City Corporators, bloated ground landlords and public utility monopolists.

London patriotism: ambiguity and ambivalence

When many of the municipal reformers gained power on the newly minted London County Council (LCC) in 1889, they saw civic consciousness-raising as one of their principal tasks. This took many forms. The ruling Progressive (Radical Liberal) Party inaugurated in the early 1890s a series of annual 'Citizen Sundays', at which county councillors and – mostly Nonconformist – clergymen sought to rally the London citizenry in support of the council's civic gospel. In 1892 a Progressive member of the first LCC, William Saunders, published a near-verbatim summary of the council's principal debates. In the following year a group of London Liberals created a municipal weekly newspaper, tellingly entitled *London. A Journal of Civic and Social Progress*. It aimed to be 'the Hansard of the County Council'[1] and, beyond that, to educate the London public in municipal affairs, both in Britain and abroad.[2] On the strength of the paper's first issue, a sympathetic Radical journalist enthused to its promoter, Robert Donald, that 'you have produced [a paper] that will interest the ordinary citizen – the apathetic Londoner – and satisfy him that there is a great future for him and his city, such as was undreamed of in the bad old days . . . when the land speculator and the jerrybuilder ruled over us.'[3] That was certainly the paper's intention. The core of the progressive philosophy in the 1890s was that London's previous civic fragmentation and backwardness had resulted in the metropolis being badly governed, that 'the absence of civic control of the common necessities of light, water, food and carriage, means imperfect service and high prices'[4] and that municipal intervention on the part of an activist local authority could remedy those problems. From the start the rejuvenation of civic spirit was associated with the promise of municipal empowerment through the control of essential public services.

Progressive attempts to galvanise London's civic patriotism were not entirely futile. They presumably contributed to the impressive turnouts at LCC elections in the period. They doubtless helped generate the elevated sense of public duty evident in the council's high-calibre staff. Ultimately, though, there were serious obstacles facing any attempt to generate a London-wide civic consciousness. In its early days, the Progressive LCC had benefited from a near consensual acceptance of the evidence of London poverty produced by Charles Booth in 1889 and a widespread belief that municipal agencies should address the problem. Later the Progressives' advocacy of municipal control of public services attracted naturally Conservative suburban voters eager to secure a better tram service or lower water bills. Such factors helped secure the Progressives' eighteen-year tenure of power in a city that was predominantly Conservative in parliamentary elections, but they could not indefinitely conceal the divisions inevitably present within metropolitan society.

Those living in a city the size of London inevitably felt some ambiguity as to whether they considered themselves Londoners first or residents of Hampstead, Hackney or wherever. A deeper difference of outlook between suburban and inner-city dwellers was reinforced by the inadequacy of the county boundary, devised in 1855 on the basis of the Registrar-General's definition of London, which even by 1900 excluded much of the built-up area north of the river and in the south west. Many of those living in Greater London and working in the centre were therefore beyond the reaches of the LCC, in Middlesex, Essex, Surrey or Kent, enjoying the lower rates of those county councils. Many of them also appreciated the Conservative complexion of those counties, in contrast to the often militant Radicalism of the early LCC – a reminder that as local politics became more concerned with social issues and more explicitly ideological, it was bound to intensify political differences within the metropolis.

National politicians dealing with London lobbies therefore seldom felt themselves to be under pressure from an emphatic and undivided metropolitan opinion. The contrast with later devolution movements in Scotland and Wales is instructive. From the late 1960s to the late 1990s, central government was bound to acknowledge a politically organised and ostensibly united nationalism, whatever differences actually existed within Scottish and Welsh society. Nationalism in Scotland and Wales gained strength from its ability to appeal across the ideological spectrum and to affect detachment from traditional party politics. London never possessed that influence. In dealing with Scotland and Wales, central government was mindful of a nationalist rhetoric which depicted Whitehall as a quasi-colonial occupier of the Celtic nations. By contrast, those living in the nation's administrative centre did not naturally think of Whitehall and Westminster as alien powers. London's politicians, it is true, were given to grumbling almost from the birth of the social service state in the late nineteenth century that the capital contributed far more to the Exchequer than it got back, but the issues at stake in this discussion remained technical, lacking the political punch of, for example, the 'it's Scotland's oil' campaign of the 1970s. Whatever the state of relations between Whitehall and County Hall, the language of London politics never contained the metaphors of occupation, even colonialism, to be found in nationalist debate.

There was, in short, little political incentive at any point in our period for central Government to appease or encourage London 'Nationalism.' The pressure for change in London government derived instead from popular dissatisfaction with the state of local public services. It was at its strongest when, as in the 1880s or the 1990s, it was augmented by a loss of public confidence in the administrative system then in place, but at all times the main justification for overhauling London government would be to provide better services. The principal object of devolution proposals in the 1970s and the 1990s was to create national assemblies: administrative transfers were a secondary consideration. In London, by contrast, the strongest arguments for reform were normally administrative ones, and national politicians pressed to overhaul London's representative institutions inevitably questioned whether the administrative gains anticipated would justify the likely political furore. This administrative localism was weakened by its failure to cut across conventional political divisions. With day-to-day municipal politics in London, as elsewhere, revolving around service provision, it became more difficult to separate issues of London government reform from routine party politics. In principle, of course, the goal of improved services was a shared aim, and there were times – most obviously in the post-First World War period, when politicians of all colours sought to build a 'land fit for heroes' – when municipal modernisation appeared genuinely consensual. Generally, though, the politics of London reform were divisive. London government reform was sometimes advanced as a precondition for 'municipal socialism.' It was frequently coupled with proposals for equalisation of the burdens of local taxation, to remedy a situation in which the poor east end paid higher poundage rates than the west end or the suburbs. It inevitably implied a challenge to the status quo and frequently a threat to private industries supplying local services. It was therefore generally associated with the left in London politics, with the Progressives before 1914 and the Labour Party from the early 1920s. This association was not inevitable: the Conservative leadership of the LCC pressed for structural change after the First World War, as will be seen, but for most of our period London reform was a left-of-centre concern, and attempts to conjure up the image of a united citizenry conflicted with this reality.

This inherent partisanship was sharpened by the boundary question. Discussion of Scottish and Welsh devolution could, of course, proceed on the assumption that national boundaries were given. London's service-based localism was, though, inescapably associated with the question of London's appropriate municipal boundary. The 1855 metropolitan area differed substantially from the much larger Metropolitan Police area of 1829, and bore no relation to the 'natural' or legal areas for local services such as water supply or fire prevention, which in turn bore no necessary relation to one another. Those eager to modernise London government generally advocated a substantially larger metropolitan area for several reasons. First, before the implementation of green belt legislation in the 1940s, there was no obvious end point to London's outward expansion, and an ambitious definition of London's outer boundary appeared to offer a safeguard against repeating the mistake of 1855 and excluding tracts of suburbia from the county area. Secondly, several of the municipal functions which reformers sought to confer upon a metropolitan authority – most obviously water supply and, later, transport planning powers – required large service areas. Thirdly, the development of planning theory from the 1900s onwards placed ever greater emphasis upon the inter-relationship of the town and its immediate rural hinterland.

Thus from the 1900s, when the end of Progressive control of the LCC prompted new thinking about the future development of London government, consideration of the London question tended to imply reconsideration of the county boundary. Such thinking, though, tended to treat London's fringe as if it remained under the unreformed Victorian regime of the county justices. In fact the cautious but comprehensive county government reform of 1888, which had established the LCC as a democratic authority, had also created elected county councils for Middlesex, Kent, Surrey Hertfordshire and Essex and provided a mechanism by which built-up suburban areas could attain county borough status. The suburban counties and all the county boroughs except for the east end authority of West Ham carried lower social burdens than London itself, and consequently taxed their residents more lightly. Incorporation into an enlarged London authority carried the threat that their rates would rise to London levels. The probable ideological objections of these predominantly Conservative areas to any metropolitan super-authority were thus reinforced by a substantial material incentive to retain their independence, and the politics of metropolitan reform gained a sharper edge.

Municipal reform in the late nineteenth and early twentieth centuries

The first point to make about proposals for London municipal reform throughout this period is that they entailed little actual devolution proper, that is, the transfer of power downwards from central government to local or regional bodies. The one central government power consistently sought by the municipal left, from the London Municipal Reform League in the 1880s to Ken Livingstone's Greater London Council (GLC) a century later – control over the Metropolitan Police – remained firmly in the Home Office's grip until the qualified transfer of 1999. For most of this period, and particularly during the years of local fiscal crisis before the First World War, London's local authorities, believing that the capital gained less than its fair share of central government subsidy, were more concerned by new powers being thrust upon the local government system as a whole than they were anxious to secure further devolution.[5] A putative reformed metropolitan authority, at any point in this period, was therefore likely to gain most of its powers through 'horizontal' transfers from other local authorities – perhaps including the anomalous but powerful Corporation of London – and from private-sector utility companies, rather than from Whitehall. Thus the London reform movement of the 1870s and 1880s, inspired by Joseph Firth's monumental *Municipal London* of 1876 and achieving partial fulfilment in the creation of the LCC in 1889, fused a traditional Liberal reformist concern to root out vested interests and occasional corruption in the existing system with a powerful consumerist drive to take expensive and often inefficient utilities – principally gas and water – into public hands. The London Municipal Reform League, cast in the image of single-issue Radical pressure groups on its foundation in 1881, emerged as a vocal and by no means ineffective lobby, which persuaded the second Gladstone government to add London municipal reform to its lengthy wish-list. Unsuccessful legislation of 1884 attempted to create a single metropolitan authority (with district councils exercising delegated powers) within the 1855 area, replacing the Metropolitan Board of Works, the City Corporation and the local parish vestries.[6] The eventual creation of the London County Council under the 1888 legislation nonetheless owed less to pressure-group lobbying than to contingency, in particular to the conjunction of the corruption scandal (over speculation in land acquired for street improvements) which discredited the indirectly elected Metropolitan Board of Works in the late 1880s with the various political pressures bringing about the reform of county government in England and Wales in 1888.

The powers of the new council were little larger than those of the old Metropolitan Board, and much of the political energy of the Progressive group which controlled the authority until 1907 was spent in pressing for the further empowerment of the LCC. With London's water, gas, markets and docks in private hands, the LCC felt itself to fall short of those dominant provincial authorities which had set the pace of municipal enterprise earlier in the nineteenth century. Its energetic and often politically provocative use of the powers that it did possess in such areas as housing and tramways, its close relationship with London trade unionism and its enthusiasm for direct labour operations meant, however, that the Progressive Council gained little sympathy from the Conservative governments which dominated its eighteen years and from whom alone new powers could come. 'The way the Government regarded the London County Council,' claimed the Progressive leader Sir William Collins towards the end of the long period of Tory ascendancy in 1905, 'was that of the mother who said, "Go and see what the children are doing at home and tell them they mustn't." '[7] Indeed in two council elections, in 1895 and 1898, the Prime Minister Lord Salisbury and the Conservative opposition on the LCC flirted with proposals for the council's dismemberment, distributing its powers to enlarged local bodies.[8] These failed, but although the LCC escaped the threat of dismemberment when the Conservatives settled for relatively weak second-tier authorities in 1899, it rapidly faced a more substantial threat to the Progressive ideal of municipal empowerment.

This threat lay in proposals for non-democratic authorities to control those local services which required administration beyond the limited area of the 1855 administrative county. Perhaps the greatest blow to Progressive ambitions came with the creation of a quango, the Metropolitan Water Board, to settle the politically sensitive water issue in 1902. Water control had been the means by which the great provincial municipalities had 'come of age' in the nineteenth century. London's private supply had proved expensive and, during the droughts of the late 1890s, inadequate. The denial of water control not merely to the LCC but to any popularly elected authority was deeply damaging to Progressive municipal aspirations. Doubtless a degree of political vindictiveness lay behind the rejection of the LCC's claim, but there remained an objective justification that the 'natural' water area and the area covered by the private water companies stretched far beyond the administrative county boundary. The Royal Commission investigating the water question in 1899 had rejected LCC control on the principal ground that all but one of the home counties sought control of their water supply, and indulging them would imply a fragmented control which was 'open to so much objection as to be practicably inadmissable.' Significantly reflecting the national efficiency tone of the times, the Commission's arguments for 'a permanent and not a fluctuating body', whose members were 'selected on account of their business capacity and, if possible, their knowledge of matters connected with water supply' made it clear that a nominated body was not a second best solution in their eyes.[9] In the event the Board created in 1902 was complex in constitution, with each of the home county councils, the Corporation and all the new Metropolitan Boroughs represented, along with the boroughs and urban district councils outside the LCC area and the Thames and Lea Conservancy Boards. The LCC itself was given only ten members out of sixty-seven.[10] A similar outcome to the question of traffic control was threatened by the report of the Royal Commission on London Traffic in 1905, which considered it 'impossible to bestow upon any existing authority, or any combination of existing authorities, the power of controlling locomotion and transport and carrying out the necessary works over the entire area of "Greater London"', and called for a nominated Traffic Board for London.[11]

At a time when national policy appeared to be moving away from ad hoc bodies in local government, with the abolition of the School Boards in 1902 and the obvious threat to the survival of the Poor Law guardians with the appointment of the Royal Commission on the Poor Law in 1905, London was being threatened with the proliferation of ad hoc bodies. Worse, the authorities proposed would either be indirectly elected or simply nominated bodies. It was against this threat to municipal democracy that the LCC Progressives envisaged the enlargement of the London county area to create a plausible Greater London authority, despite the apparent political dangers of bringing the conservative suburbs into the administrative county. Rumours that the LCC was looking at boundary extension first surfaced in October 1903, at around the time that H. G. Wells called in a Fabian Society address for the adoption of 'scientific' local government areas.[12] Wells's Fabian antagonist, Sidney Webb, who was, unlike Wells, a Progressive county councillor, argued three years later for an enlarged London body, as a component of the solution to the question of Poor Law reform then exercising him, and suggested that 'West Ham, East Ham, Tottenham, Walthamstow, Willesden, Richmond and other districts must come under the central authority.'[13] A similar scheme was promoted by the Liberal Progressive, Fitzroy Hemphill in 1906 and again, slightly amended, in 1907. Hemphill was moved by the threat of the proliferation of ad hoc bodies in the manner of the Water Board and the projected traffic board: 'the true remedy is not to multiply the central bodies, but to enlarge the area of local government.' He was impressed, on an LCC visit to foreign ports, by the independence enjoyed by the Hansestadt Hamburg, which, 'as a free state, has full powers of local government, there being no body between it and the Imperial Government.'[14] By this point the Progressives had lost power at County Hall, permanently, as it would turn out, but the Liberals were in office at Westminster. The Liberal President of the Local Government Board, John Burns, himself a former LCC Progressive, was believed to be working on proposals for the enlargement of the London county, entailing the transfer of water control, in 1907, but no scheme was forthcoming, and the only significant London measure produced by the Liberal Government turned out to be the creation in 1908 of another quango, the Port of London Authority, in response to the long-running problem of management of the docks. As if to underline Hemphill's contrast with Hamburg, the LCC gained only a very limited presence on London's port authority, nominating four members out of twenty-eight.[15]

The Progressive arguments for municipal boundary extension were straightforward: that the existing state of affairs was inefficient, that it entailed wasteful duplication of staff and that it weakened London's claim for democratic control of services extending beyond the existing county boundary. The arguments of the outer suburbs against extension were no less direct. 'We don't want anything from London and London should not want anything from us except what it has now', Alderman Burt of Richmond told the *Morning Post* in 1907. London offered them little: 'we have our own gas company, our own electric light company, and, in connection with Barnes, our own system of drainage . . . Part of our supply of water comes from the Metropolitan Water Board, but it is water which in fact comes from our own river. We also have our own hospital.' Alderman Sloper, the Mayor of Hornsey, believed that 'if we were to come into the general body . . . our assets would be wanted to cover up the wildcat finance and corruption which have been going on in some other parts of London', a view encouraged by the Progressives' tendency to link extension with rate equalisation within London. Hornsey, like Wimbledon and other outer areas, aspired to county borough status to safeguard its autonomy; it welcomed the prospect of 'a ring of county boroughs . . . around London, with possibly some common body to which matters of transit, such as through tramways, main roads, and so on could be referred, so that they might be dealt with on a comprehensive plan.'[16]

Arguments along these lines took place in and around several of the larger English towns and cities from the 1900s to the 1920s, as urban authorities sought to modernise their Victorian boundaries.[17] The London dispute remained academic before the First World War, but became pressing immediately after the armistice, when politicians of all colours looked to public agencies to promote social reconstruction. By that stage the case for extension had impressed itself upon the previously minimalist Conservative majority on the LCC. Calls for greater co-ordination in London government had become almost cacophonous. The far-reaching Kemp Departmental Committee Report on Local Taxation in 1914 had approved the extension of local areas to enable local government to cope with what it called semi-national services, suggesting a national Commission 'to inquire into the circumstances of individual areas with a view to making proposals for extensions or amalgamations.'[18] In 1918 the Town Planning Institute and the London Society appointed a joint committee to flesh out the Society's proposals for a greater London traffic and housing authority.[19] The 1919 Select Committee on Transport called – in bold type – for 'the immediate creation by Parliament of a London Traffic Authority' to remedy a problem which 'has reached the dimensions of a public scandal'.[20] A conference of the 122 London local authorities interested in the housing question in October 1918 called for London's housing authorities to 'work together in carrying out as a co-ordinated whole' their new schemes.[21] Neville Chamberlain's committee on the unhealthy areas of Britain's cities called in 1920 for a unitary plan for the capital's reconstruction. Finally, in 1920 the Advisory Committee on London Traffic renewed the 1905 Commission's call for a London Traffic Authority.[22]

The case made for reconsideration of metropolitan government by the Clerk of the LCC, James Bird, in June 1919,[23] therefore already enjoyed a fair wind. It also enjoyed near-unanimous support on the council itself. The dwindling Progressive group remained loyal to their pre-war policies. The young London Labour Party (LLP) deployed at this point a line on London government largely indistinguishable from pre-war Progressivism. The Labour programme for the 1919 council elections called for 'a parliament for greater London for purely London affairs' along with district councils dealing with local issues, while the LLP secretary, Herbert Morrison, told the 1919 Select Committee on Transport that 'the area of the LCC should be considerably enlarged' to allow it to take over the tube.[24] The Municipal Reform (i.e. Conservative) leadership of the council tended rather to emphasise the benefits of administrative rationalisation of a system now prone to ad hocery, but they too reached the conclusion that the LCC's area 'was too restricted to enable certain powers which they already possessed to be efficiently exercised.'[25] As J. W. Gilbert, Chairman of the Council, told the Prime Minister David Lloyd George in December 1920, the fact that the operation of education, public health, main drainage and transport services extended beyond the existing administrative county meant that 'in arranging for their organisation, the Council has to enter into relations with a large number of authorities both within and without the present county area.' This might mean the buying or selling of services between authorities, the creation of separate rating authorities as with water, or the separation of control and administration as with the fire service.[26] Further, although the council's Conservative leadership remained less eager than their opponents to extend the Council's range of services, the national post-war drive for reconstruction often meant that they had no choice: 'day after day, almost, certainly week after week, Parliament is throwing new and important duties upon us, which frighten me sometimes', pleaded the chairman of the Local Government Committee, R. C. Norman, 'and you cannot expect that we can efficiently carry them through if we have only antiquated tools to work with; it is not fair.'[27]

The danger was, now, that the administrative modernisation generally agreed to be required to cope with reconstruction would be entrusted to yet more ad hoc bodies. The democratic deficit inherent in such a solution alarmed G. H. Hume, leader of the majority Conservatives on the LCC, who believed that 'in time this undue multiplication of ad hoc bodies will become intolerable. I think it was the reaction against such a state of things that swept away the old Metropolitan Board of Works.'[28] The east end Progressive Councillor H. H. Gordon pointed to the paradox that the authorities exercising larger powers would be unelected 'while those whose work is less important are still to be subject to popular will.'[29] Both men, along with many of their LCC colleagues, identified something of a crisis for urban local government in this period, as outdated systems struggled to cope with the consequences of suburban expansion.

The intellectual case against the mushrooming of quangoes was hard to refute. Indeed, the LCC could reasonably expect to be pushing at an open door in its dealings with central government. The 1918 housing conference, which had demonstrated the fragmentation of the existing system, had been suggested by the Local Government Board (LGB). Even before the War, the LGB had 'safeguarded' the possibility of London enlargement by endorsing the application of East Ham for county borough status only on condition that its new status should not provide grounds for opposing future metropolitan expansion. Whatever the level of enthusiasm in Whitehall, though, the political difficulties involved in coercing the suburban authorities into amalgamation remained. The suburban gloss on the LCC's actions was expressed crisply by the Middlesex County Council's Parliamentary Committee:

> although no attack is made upon local administration outside London the condition inside London is admittedly unsatisfactory . . . but the remedy [proposed] is not that the London County Council put their own house in order, but extend the obsolescent machinery to the districts outside[30]

Suburban authorities anticipated being asked to underwrite 'the enormous amount of out relief that is now being given in the East End of London', culminating in the gesture politics of Poplarism.[31] However clear the case for rationalising London government, it was by no means evident that it implied the enlargement of the LCC. Lloyd George's laconic response to the LCC deputation in 1920 emphasised 'how very tremendous the difficulties always are' surrounding boundary extension, praising Norman for the skill with which he 'evaded giving me any idea as to how it was to be done!' The Prime Minister's assertion that 'anything in the nature of annexation . . . would be an impossible scheme from a practical point of view'[32] made it clear that it would not be done at all, making the subsequent appointment of the Royal Commission on London Government, under the Conservative Viscount Ullswater, something of an empty exercise.

The Ullswater Commission was never likely to endorse the LCC proposals – even had most of its members not sympathised with the suburbs' desire for autonomy, the clear signs from Lloyd George that he had no interest in bullying the suburbs into annexation ensured that the LCC proposals were destined for the long grass. Early in the Commission's private deliberations:

> The Chairman indicated that in his personal opinion the extension of the area of the administrative county, even if desirable, was not practicable in view of the opposition to any such proposal which had been manifested by local authorities in their evidence. At the same time he was himself of opinion that a moral responsibility rested upon the inhabitants of districts adjoining the county to contribute to reduce the financial burdens which fall upon the poorer districts in respect of certain services.[33]

Rate equalisation was therefore promoted as an alternative to expansion of the administrative county; the suburbs would find their 'moral responsibility' less daunting once the Commission's investigations had demonstrated that their rate equalisation proposals would actually benefit all but the City and the west end.[34] An elaborate equalisation scheme, later ignored, became the main constructive proposal of an otherwise negative and conservative report.[35] The Commission's respect for the historical status quo in local government induced it, as the dissident authors of the Minority Report argued, to turn a blind eye to the implications of 'the unguided growth of London', with the result that its detailed rebuttal of the council's administrative case for enlargement was unaffected by the wider municipal issues.[36] In an echo of pre-war Progressivism, the dissidents, Robert Donald and Stephen Walsh, included a section on 'Civic Patriotism', which attacked the Commission's deference to suburban particularism. They stressed that civic patriotism was not the monopoly of 'the smaller authorities in outer London' and argued that 'it is quite possible to belong to the capital by interest, society and habits, and yet to dwell in a rural suburb.'[37]

The Ullswater inquiry was a loaded investigation, and has not had a good press, but whatever its overall value, the Commission did make clear the complexity of the question, and illustrated a number of weaknesses in the LCC position. Suburban areas were not, in the 1920s, mere dormitories. Sir Albert Gray, one of the Commissioners argued that the highest proportion of any suburb's residents working in the LCC area was Wimbledon's at 30%: 'this class are still a minority.'[38] More damagingly, the Commission cast serious doubt on the council's by now somewhat formulaic arguments for the municipalisation of public services. If any one issue had driven the movement for a new municipal reform it was transport. The Commission found unanimity amongst its witnesses on the need for a Greater London transport body, but it was not clear that municipalisation was the preferred solution. The LCC tended to treat all public utility issues as analogous to the water question in the late nineteenth century, when an irreplaceable commodity had fallen into monopolistic private control and municipalisation apparently offered unequivocal benefits to the consumer. The variety of modes of transport available, and competition between private operators meant, though, that such a situation did not prevail in transport, and the council's position as tramway monopolist within the administrative county weakened its ability to present itself as an honest broker. A bullish LCC Highways Committee report of April 1922 had endorsed the 1919 Select Committee's call for a single London traffic authority, while rejecting the Committee's specific suggestion of another quango. The LCC Committee hinted strongly that the new authority should be an enlarged LCC and 'much deprecate[d] any action that would have the effect of adding another *permanent ad hoc* authority to those already existing.' It was moved by the fear that the 'Combine' of private tube railway operators aspired to gain monopoly powers, and the belief that buses were competing with the council trams without paying their share of the costs of road maintenance and improvement.[39] Nonetheless, its report appeared to outsiders to have been designed to protect the council's tramway interests, which lost £88,000 that year.[40] In the view of E. E. Hiley, the Ullswater Commission's transport expert, 'the convenience of the travelling public appears a secondary consideration and the policy is actually suggested of forcing the passengers to use the Municipal Tramways by the withdrawal of the Buses (a more popular form of travel) from the popular routes.'[41] Certainly it was a remarkable stance for the once minimalist LCC Tories to adopt.

With grassroots Tory fundamentalism growing after the sharp economic downturn of 1920, the position of a Conservative authority which sought to extend municipalisation and which threatened suburban independence was always likely to be questionable. The message was driven home in 1922 when the London Municipal Society, the Tory umbrella organisation in London, rejected the proposals put to the Ullswater Commission by the Tory LCC.[42] Fundamental reform of London government was effectively off the agenda by the time that the Ullswater Commission Report heaped its own disapproval on the LCC proposals in 1923. The Commission's attitude reflected the general rejection of urban boundary extension in the 1920s, as the nation's governors remained true to the historic county boundaries lovingly preserved in 1888.

Politics and planning in Depression and war

The capture of the LCC by Herbert Morrison's Labour Party in 1934 focused the council's activities upon the inner city and on its existing housing and health powers. Early in his municipal career Morrison had been entirely loyal to the Progressive and Labour policy of enlargement. Campaigning for North Southwark in an LCC by-election in 1920 he had called for popular control of transport by a single authority – 'not by a Trust but by the LCC.'[43] Morrison being, almost from the start, the pre-eminent architect of London Labour policy, 'Home Rule for London' was the dominant note of London Labour's programme in the early 1920s.[44] Morrison's position – and that of his party – shifted, though, during the 1920s, as the London traffic question sharpened into a clear choice between public and private monopoly.[45] By 1928 the Conservative majority on the LCC had moved from their earlier attempts to protect their own tramway operations from private competition to a policy of disposing of the municipal tramways to the private 'Combine', which operated the underground railways and the bulk of the capital's bus services. The election of the second Labour Government in 1929, with Morrison as Minister of Transport, meant that that manoeuvre could be blocked, but in the process of devising legislation for the public control of London's local transport, Morrison accepted what had been clear since the Ullswater Commission reported – that the necessary consolidation of transport control could not wait upon the creation of a Greater London authority. He concluded 'that municipalisation was impracticable, as there was no one local authority covering the London traffic area . . . and that management by a joint authority of the local bodies had nothing to commend it from the point of view of democracy and could not be relied upon for efficiency.'[46] This realisation led him towards the conclusion that the ad hoc public corporation was the appropriate agency to run public services, and away from any interest in municipal enlargement. The London Passenger Transport Board, which came into existence in 1933,[47] therefore added another unelected, single-purpose authority to the complex pattern of London government. The fact that what was essentially Morrison's bill could be passed largely intact by the Conservative-dominated National Government demonstrated that the advance of the quango no longer provoked political debate.

The LCC consequently played little part in 1930s discussions of regionalism, and the issue of London government reform became, literally, an academic question, most obviously in the work of the Webbs' protégé W. A. Robson at the London School of Economics. Robson's *chef d'oeuvre* of 1939, *The Government and Misgovernment of London*, founded the case for a London regional body upon the evident threat to democracy 'in a world of competing creeds and hostile authoritarian doctrines.'[48] In a work more polemical than profound, Robson ascribed London's municipal backwardness to the failure properly to overhaul the jumbled collection of vested interests which had constituted its Victorian local administration, exacerbated by the proliferation of county boroughs in outer London between the wars.[49] The want of a recognisable London authority had produced such anomalies as the Metropolitan Water Board ('from the point of view of administrative efficiency, a paid commissioner would probably do the work better', while 'the democratic element in the Board's constitution is very small: it is no more than a name to the mass of Londoners'[50]) and similar quangoes. Still more seriously, the capital's municipal shortcomings explained 'more than any other single cause both the absence of a strong or effective regional patriotism and also the indifference of Londoners to the monstrous growth and misdevelopment of the region.'[51] London's existing government did not adequately either govern or represent London, in other words, causing a civic disengagement that was worrying in the context of the spread of totalitarianism abroad. The work's tepid reception in the LLP literature ('while we may not agree with Mr Robson in detail, we are sure that at some time Government . . . will have to tackle the problem from the regional angle') suggested that regionalism was not high amongst the party's concerns.[52] It took the Second World War to push London regionalism up the agenda. The London blitz obviously made the case for holistic renewal, and the Regional Commissioners created to co-ordinate local government in wartime exemplified the possibility of cutting through existing jurisdictions to 'get things done.' More specifically, war brought Morrison's absorption into the Churchill coalition and his replacement as LCC leader by Charles (later Lord) Latham. Latham combined an interest in town planning theory with a belief that only a metropolitan super-authority could implement the post-war regeneration of greater London. He believed that previous town planning had been unambitious, 'regulative, not creative', and that the planning of the future London should be considered 'as an integral part of the orderly arrangement of its communal life, in which public interests must be paramount, and as a section of a complete structure which will include the provision of transport, public services, social services.'[53] Ambitiously, he saw the Metropolitan Traffic Area, embracing Hertfordshire, Surrey, a third of Essex, a quarter of Kent and parts of Bedfordshire, Buckinghamshire, Berkshire and Sussex as providing 'sufficient room for long-term planning.'[54] In the revivalist language of wartime, Latham envisaged a new conception of local government. Whereas the social problems of the 1930s had reduced municipal services to 'a series of aids to the "down and outs"', post-war renewal would allow local government to raise its sights:

> Planning, housing, roads, must have as their object the creation of the 'city beau-tiful'; education must aim to bring knowledge and culture to all; hospital and medical services to prevent and relieve suffering wherever it may be; open spaces, lidos, open-air theatres, playing fields must be regarded as places where *all* can relax, rest and enjoy their leisure.[55]

The conjunction of planning vision and municipal authority was crucial to his proposals: 'there must be a master-plan covering the determined area', he wrote at the beginning of 1941, 'which must be settled by and carried out by a local government unit having jurisdiction over that area.'[56] This was the background to the LCC's sponsorship of the 1943 *County of London Plan*, produced by the LCC's County Architect J. H. Forshaw and Sir Patrick Abercrombie, the leading light of British town planning theory, which led in turn to Abercrombie's *The Greater London Plan 1944* (published in 1945).

Abercrombie's London plans have spawned a substantial cottage indus-try of planning history in recent years. That they did not, in fact, greatly influ-ence the rebuilding of London owed much to the non-appearance of the super-authority intended by Latham to put them into effect. From the start it was clear that 'a serious difference of opinion existed' on the London Labour Party Executive over Latham's proposals.[57] The chief substantive problem lay in the movement of national Labour policy towards nationalisa-tion, which would affect the public utilities and other local services, and which was generally inconsistent with Latham's regionalism. Beyond that lay a polit-ical objection expressed by the Executive in somewhat mechanical terms, that the size of the new authority might mean that 'the individual elector found himself or herself increasingly remote from the centre of municipal activity.'[58] Whether this concern should be taken literally is unclear, but it is doubtless significant that Labour had captured the LCC only nine years earlier after twenty-seven years of Tory control. The danger that a Greater London body consisting largely of suburban seats would revert permanently to the Conservatives cannot have been far from the Labour Executive's mind.

Whatever the theoretical appeal of Abercrombian planning doctrines to the post-war Labour Party, the Attlee governments did little to implement them and nothing to change the structure of local government. At the same time the nationalisation programme deprived local government of its public utility powers. To Labour eyes, whatever attractions the possibility of a Greater London authority had once possessed now dwindled. 'Practically all of the large-scale services which might have given ground for such an extension [of the LCC] have been taken over by Public Boards sponsored by the Government', the party's regional conference concluded when it revisited the issue in the 1950s, 'and . . . there is no practical possibility of such services coming over to local government.'[59] With the administrative case thus diminished, the political objections assumed still greater clarity: 'would Labour have a secure majority on such a body?' Morrison asked rhetorically in 1953.[60] Politics dictated that an enlarged London Council could only be created by a Conservative government eager to end Labour's hegemony at County Hall, and that a Conservative creation would not be greatly empowered. So it was, by legislation of 1963, that a Greater London Council was created by the Macmillan Government, with the safeguard that it possessed only nebulous 'strategic' powers, insufficiently substantial to shield it from abolition in 1986.

The institutional inertia of the LCC

The 1963 reform was one of four substantial measures of metropolitan reform in the modern period. The other three all followed the collapse of unrepresentative structures unable to command public confidence: the 1855 legislation was prompted by the fall of Chadwick's nominated Metropolitan Commission of Sewers; the 1888 Act in part by the disgrace of the Metropolitan Board of Works; and the 1999 Act by loss of faith in the Byzantine expedients devised to replace the GLC.[61] Throughout the period covered here, though, the whole of greater London, outside the square mile of the City, was governed by regular directly elected local authorities. The Act which created the LCC gave a similar structure and accountability to local government on the county fringe, and the 1888 pattern, once set, was very hard to alter. However irrational the system might have appeared in its structure, however awkward the arrangements for inter-authority co-operation over shared services, the mere existence of anomalies did not in itself make the case for root-and-branch reform. It was always easier to deal with a problematic issue like water supply by creating a quango or, later, by nationalisation. In the absence of any significant 'Home Rule for London' movement, the political complications of reform would always appear daunting – Conservatives might anticipate controlling a greater London body but were protective of suburban independence and ideologically suspicious of any super-authority; Labour was in principle more sympathetic to the planning ethos and its attendant big local government, but found it hard to reconcile that aspiration with its national-isation plans, and feared losing the political bastion that it had gained in the LCC. The result, in London as in other large cities, was that the local government system remained essentially Victorian, failing to adapt, either in areas or in powers, to twentieth-century urban life. This weakness was partially con-cealed by the growth of the social service state during the twentieth century, with local government assigned a significant role as the agent of welfarism, centred on 'Victorian' powers over housing, health and education. This role was eagerly adopted by the Labour LCC: the encomia produced under the Labour regime to celebrate the LCC's fiftieth anniversary in 1938 and to com-memorate its passing in 1965 inevitably stressed its social policy record.[62] Significantly, this was a role which could be largely confined to the inner city and was not greatly impaired by the failure to embrace outer London. The London Labour Executive's rebuttal of Latham in 1943 suggested that the state of the suburbs was not Labour's concern:

> We have further considered that while the municipal structure of Greater London, regarded as a whole, may reasonably be said to be untidy, the reproach is one that applies more completely to some of the areas beyond the County boundary than to the County itself. Within the present County of London there is but one authority for education, town planning (except for the City of London), hospitals, large-scale housing, main drainage, and social welfare.

In essence, the London Labour Party was acknowledging that metropolitan opinion was fragmented and that Labour's concern was for the inner city which it dominated rather than for the wider metropolis which was poten-tially hostile. The early Progressives had advocated municipal expansion despite the apparent threat to their political position. The post-1918 LCC Conservatives had pressed the administrative case for enlargement against the wishes of their suburban Tory colleagues. Labour would not make the same mistake. The Progressive attempt to found civic identity upon the communal control of essential services across the built-up area was effectively abandoned. Civic identity was appropriated by Labour's 'people' in its inner-city heart-land and the council's aspirations narrowed accordingly.

Conclusion

The nineteenth-century municipal system, allowing individual communities to petition for incorporation according to a standard 'template', had proved a flexible and efficient means of building localism into British government.

In the twentieth century, though, the 'hardening' of the system, as individual authorities developed their own corporate identities and guarded their boundaries, made institutional change more difficult, while the politicisation of local government tended to make reform proposals controversial, however strong their administrative rationale. Nowhere was this more true than in London. Self-evidently, the capital was large enough and prosperous enough to support a more ambitious local government organisation than it was allowed to possess in this period, but it proved politically and institutionally impossible to modernise the London system, or even to extend the existing system to cover the enlarged built-up area. In consequence, far from offering any sort of platform for municipal development, London retained much of the backwardness of which the Victorian reformers had complained.

The Progressives on the early LCC had sought to mobilise metropolitan opinion behind their own activist vision of local autonomy. There was, though, not one London voice but several, and the absence of any plausible and coherent 'London opinion' became the fundamental obstacle to any regional devolution. Whatever the divisions and differences within Scottish and Welsh society at the time of the devolution debates from the 1960s onwards, the nationalist parties presented a sufficiently united front to convince central government that their demands required attention. In the 1970s, in particular, they could play a pivotal role at Westminster, whereas parliament in our period was seldom much more than a battleground for competing London interests, public and private, right and left, inner-city and sub-urban – a frequent but neither an efficient nor an accountable arbiter of London questions. In consequence there was seldom any need to address London government issues comprehensively, and the capital's administrative evolution was therefore a haphazard one. By the close of our period the Greater London region was governed by six county councils and 106 directly elected local authorities in all, in addition to the various indirectly elected and ad hoc bodies.[63] The police, local transport, the ambulance service, water, gas and electricity supplies and the docks were all beyond direct popular control. How much this mattered is impossible to say. The rococo structure of London's government and services doubtless sapped that civic sense to which the Progressives had once appealed. How much practical damage it did is harder to assess. Anomalies were unavoidable in such a complicated system, and it was hard to defend a situation in which the LCC was unable to move the slum-dwellers of East and West Ham into their cottage estate at Becontree, a few miles down the District Railway, because they were not residents of the administrative county.[64] How much deeper structural damage was done is anybody's guess. The LCC Progressive W. H. Dickinson argued in 1913 that the eighteen years of parliamentary indecision between 1890, when London's ship-owners had first raised the condition of the Port, and 1908, when the Port of London Authority (PLA) was finally created, had seen the capital lose ground to Harwich, Southampton, Antwerp, Hamburg and other rivals, but the PLA, once up and running, was apparently a well run agency.[65] Similarly, the quango management of London Transport in its early years after 1933 aroused far less controversy than would the GLC-controlled London Transport from 1969 to 1984.[66] What was undeniably lost by the proliferation of ad hoc solutions to London's municipal problems, though, was the scope to manage each function with reference to the rest, and to secure the kind of comprehensive local management that Abercrombie and the planners envisaged in the 1940s. In the definitive study of the 1999 reform, suggestively sub-titled 'Governing an Ungovernable City', Tony Travers suggests that 'Londoners continue to survive despite their government, rather than because of it.'[67] That was as true in the first half of the twentieth century as it is now.

Notes

1 Prospectus for 'London', 2 January 1893, Robert Donald Papers, House of Lords Record Office, D/3/2.
2 See, e.g., the articles in *London* on Nottingham (17 October 1895), Liverpool (7 November 1895), Southampton (5 December 1895), Plymouth (6 February 1896), Wolverhampton and Edinburgh (7 May 1896), Glasgow (five parts, 23 July to 20 August 1896), Huddersfield (16 July 1896), Berlin (23 January 1896), Brussels (20 February 1896) and Budapest (9 April 1896).
3 E. Parker to Robert Donald, 2 February 1893, Robert Donald Papers, D/3/10.
4 Editorial 'Our Programme and Principles', *London*, 2 February 1893.
5 See the Report of the LCC Finance Committee, 'Summary of London's Financial Grievances Against the Exchequer', 22 June 1910, in London County Council *Minutes*, 28 June 1910 and reprinted in the Report of the Departmental Committee on Local Taxation, England and Wales (Cd. 7315), pp. 83–8, *Parliamentary Papers* 1914 XL.
6 John Davis, *Reforming London: The London Government Problem, 1855–1900* (Oxford, 1988), pp. 77ff.
7 Quoted *Municipal Journal*, 3 February 1905.
8 Davis, *Reforming London*, pp. 202–3, 227ff. In the event, the Salisbury government shied away from creating powerful second-tier authorities under the legislation of 1899, which defined 28 Metropolitan Boroughs, many of them too limited in area and tax base to be plausible recipients of devolved powers from the LCC. The Corporation of London was largely untouched by this legislation. As a result, the relationship between the two tiers within the administrative county and the position of the City Corporation largely disappeared from subsequent discussion of the London reform question, which is why this essay is largely concerned with the greater London issue.

9 Final Report of the Royal Commission on Water Supply within the Limits of the Metropolitan Water Companies (Cd.25), *Parliamentary Papers* 1900 XXXVIII, Part 1, pp. 59, 60.

10 Metropolitan Water Board, *London's Water Supply, 1903–53: A Review of the Work of the Metropolitan Water Board* (London, 1953), pp. 12–13.

11 Report of the Royal Commission on the Means of Locomotion and Transport in London (Cd.2597), *Parliamentary Papers* 1905 XXX, p. 97.

12 For the rumours, see *Municipal Journal*, 16 October 1903; for Wells, Ken Young and Patricia L. Garside, *Metropolitan London: Politics and Urban Change 1837–1981* (London, 1982) pp. 109ff.

13 Quoted in *Municipal Journal*, 12 October 1906. The districts mentioned by Webb were all built-up areas lying outside the county boundary.

14 'The London County Council and Outside Areas', interview with Hemphill in *Morning Post*, 19 November 1907.

15 J. G. Broodbank, *History of the Port of London* (London, 1921), II, p. 340, and see generally vol. 2, ch. 30 for the difficult road to legislation.

16 These quotations from the responses to Hemphill in *Morning Post*, 21 November 1907.

17 John Davis, 'Central government and the towns', in Martin Daunton (ed.), *The Cambridge Urban History of Britain*, volume 3: *1840–1950* (Cambridge, 2000), pp. 275–8.

18 Report of the Departmental Committee on Local Taxation, England and Wales (Cd.7315), *Parliamentary Papers* 1914 XL, p. 95.

19 *The Times*, 1 March 1919. The report was published as Royal Town Planning Institute, *The London and Home Counties Authority: Memorandum on a Bill for the Establishment of a Development, Housing and Traffic Authority for London and the Home Counties* (London, 1919).

20 Report from the Select Committee on Transport (Metropolitan Area) (147), iii, *Parliamentary Papers* 1919, VII.

21 Report of the Housing of the Working Classes Committee, 6 November 1918, in London County Council Minutes, 12 November 1918.

22 Report of the Advisory Committee on London Traffic (Cmd.636), *Parliamentary Papers* 1920 XXI, p. 12.

23 Report by the Clerk of the Council on the Local Government of London, LCC Local Government Committee presented papers, 27 June 1919, LMA LCC/MIN/8274.

24 *London Labour Chronicle*, March, August 1919.

25 From the summary of the LCC's case in the Report of the Royal Commission on London Government (Cmd.1830), *Parliamentary Papers* 1923, XII, p. 7.

26 London County Council. 'Notes of Proceedings on 9 December 1920 at No.10 Downing Street, SW, of a Deputation to the Prime Minister . . .', pp. 1–2, in TNA, HLG 9/3.

27 R. C. Norman, in LCC, 'Notes of Proceedings on 9 December 1920 . . .', p. 4.

28 'Problems of greater London', interview in *Surrey Comet*, 9 August 1919.

29 'Greater London Council. Need of Body Popularly Elected', interview with H. H. Gordon, LCC, *Daily News*, 18 February 1919.

30 Report of Parliamentary Committee, 9 February 1922, in Middlesex County Council, Royal Commission on London Government, 1919–1923:

Reports to and Decisions of Committee (Parliamentary), LMA MCC/CL/ CC/3/262.

31 'A Member', quoted in transcription of the Report on the Council's Local Government Committee, 24 January 1922, p. 21 of the transcription in TNA HLG 9/3.

32 LCC, 'Notes of Proceedings on 9 December 1920', in TNA HLG 9/3, p. 7.

33 Royal Commission on London Government, 'Minutes of a Meeting held on the 14th June 1922 at the Ministry of Health', in TNA HLG 9/9, pp. 1–2.

34 'Effect of Proposed Equalisation Scheme', Report of the Royal Commission on London Government, Appendix IV, pp. 125–9.

35 Royal Commission on London Government, Report, pp. 82–113.

36 Royal Commission on London Government, Report by Mr Donald and Mr Walsh, p. 148, and for the detailed criticism of the LCC's administrative case, see the main Report, pp. 59–67.

37 Ibid., Report by Mr Donald and Mr Walsh, pp. 196–7.

38 Royal Commission on London Government, 'Personal Impressions, Notes and Memoranda', Sir Albert Gray, circulated 8 June 1922, in TNA HLG 9/44.

39 Report of the Highways Committee: 'London Traffic Arrangements', 6 April 1922, (emphasis as in original) in London County Council *Minutes*, 9 May 1922.

40 Report of Highways Committee, 22 June 1922, (emphasis as in original.) London County Council Minutes, 27 June 1922.

41 Royal Commission on London Government, 'Personal Impressions, Notes and Memoranda', 'Notes by Mr Hiley with Regard to a Central Traffic Authority', 24 July 1922, in TNA HLG 9/44.

42 London Municipal Society, Executive Committee Minutes, 23 March, 4 October 1922, Guildhall Library MS 19528/2.

43 Herbert Morrison, election address, North Southwark, 13 May 1920, Herbert Morrison Papers, Nuffield College, Oxford, D/2.

44 James Gillespie, 'Municipalism, monopoly and management: the demise of "socialism in one county", 1918–1933', in Andrew Saint (ed.), *Politics and the People of London: The London County Council, 1889–1965* (London, 1989), p. 109.

45 Ibid., pp. 120ff.

46 Herbert Morrison, *Socialisation and Transport* (London, 1933), p. 149.

47 T. C. Barker and M. Robbins, *A History of London Transport, II, The Twentieth Century to 1970* (London, 1974), ch. 15.

48 W. A. Robson, *The Government and Misgovernment of London* (London, 1948 edition), p. 349.

49 Thirty-four such incorporations were authorised between 1921 and 1938, Robson, *Government and Misgovernment*, p. 326.

50 Ibid., p. 339.

51 Ibid., p. 324.

52 Review of Robson by D. H. D[aines], *London News: Monthly Publication of the London Labour Party*, April 1939.

53 C. Latham, 'Replanning for Living', *London News*, January/February 1941.

54 C. L[atham], 'Notes on the Replanning and Reorganisation of Greater London', 6 December 1940, with London Labour Party, Joint Sub-Committee on the Reform of London Government, 1950– , LMA Acc/2417/J/9.

55 C. Latham, 'A New Conception of Local Government?', *London News*, November 1941.
56 Latham, 'Replanning for Living'.
57 London Labour Party Executive Committee Minutes, 26 November 1942, LMA Acc/2417/A/3.
58 Summary of the LLP Executive and LCC Labour Party joint report on The Reform of London Local Government, *London News*, April 1943.
59 LLP, *The Work of the London Labour Party, 1950* (1951), p. 12.
60 'Notes of a Meeting of the London Labour Party Sub-Committee on the Reform of London Government', 13 March 1953, LMA Acc/2417/J/9.
61 The post-1986 system is incomprehensible without recourse to M. Hebbert and T. Travers (eds), *The London Government Handbook* (London, 1988).
62 Sir G. Gibbon and R. W. Bell, *History of the London County Council, 1889–1939* (London, 1939); W. E. Jackson, *Achievement: A Short History of the London County Council* (London, 1965).
63 Herbert Morrison, *How London is Governed* (revised edition, 1949), pp. 5–6.
64 An anomaly pointed out by C. Waley Cohen of the Mansion House Council, as a member of the London Council of Social Service's deputation to Baldwin and Neville Chamberlain in November 1927, *A Royal Commission on the Housing of the Poor and the Regional Planning of London: A Request to His Majesty's Government to Institute an Authoritative Enquiry into the Problem* (London, 1927), p. 13.
65 See the draft article entitled 'The Problem of London Government' or alternatively 'The Emancipation of Local Government', ?1913, in the W. H. Dickinson papers, LMA, F/DCK/23/003.
66 Horace Cutler, *The Cutler Files* (London, 1982) ch. 9; Paul E. Garbutt, *London Transport and the Politicians* (London, 1985), ch. 5.
67 Tony Travers, *The Politics of London: Governing an Ungovernable City* (Basingstoke, 2004), p. 210.

10

How devolution died: the British Labour Party's constitutional agenda, 1900–45

Duncan Tanner[1]

Before 1914, 'Home Rule All Round' – the establishment of devolved governance in Ireland, Scotland and Wales, and possibly England – was seriously debated, even if it never became government policy.[2] It was supported by a curious alliance of opposition Conservatives anxious to keep Ireland within the Union and prevent the disintegration of Empire, and by Scottish and Welsh devolutionists (Liberals and Labour) who had very different motives. The idea was revived in 1917–18. The establishment of a Speaker's Conference on Devolution in 1919 induced some optimism: a similar mechanism had been used to counter objections to women's suffrage and secure the 'Fourth' Reform Act.[3] However, Irish civil war and the spur to Imperial rebellion which it encouraged was an unfortunate context in which to raise devolution more generally. Whilst the Speaker's Conference disagreed on which form of devolution to adopt, deeper and hitherto suppressed doubts about its desirability came to the surface. The Coalition government ignored the report. Thereafter, the Conservative Party's largely pragmatic interest waned as Irish Home Rule was addressed by other means. The Liberals' decline as a political force meant that the prospect of obtaining devolution rested with Labour. Supporters of change had some right to be hopeful. Before 1914, there was considerable support for some form of devolution amongst Socialists in Scotland and Wales. Labour MPs (in the main) supported Irish Home Rule – and with it 'Home Rule All Round'. The Labour movement's own constitutional traditions encouraged doubts about centralised decision-making procedures. In 1918 'Home Rule All Round', like proportional representation, was included in Labour's programme for government, and party leaders backed some form of devolution during the Speaker's Conference. However, it was not even a serious contender for consideration when Labour took office in 1924. Despite (some) pressure from within Scotland and Wales, 'Home Rule All Round' had slipped off the agenda. Although enthusiasts continued to campaign, devolved governance only re-emerged as a serious issue in the later 1930s. However, by then

Labour refused even to support the appointment of a Secretary of State for Wales with powers comparable to the Secretary of State for Scotland. By 1945 devolution was dead.

Few have tried to explain this process. The only study of the Speaker's Conference in 1919–20 claims that disagreements between supporters of devolution 'removed the issue from any further practical consideration', making no attempt to explain the Labour leadership's subsequent position.[4] Labour attitudes are given scant attention in general works and in accounts by political scientists.[5] There is good work on Welsh and Scottish Labour attitudes to devolution, but little on the national leadership's reactions to these pressures.[6] This is partially because influential scholars have argued that Labour had few constitutional interests.[7] Although Miles Taylor has recently demonstrated that Labour was far more concerned with constitutional issues than has generally been assumed,[8] he provides no analysis of the three occasions in the century when devolved 'parliaments' became a central political issue and passes over the various campaigns in favour of a Secretary of State for Wales or for strengthening Scottish devolution. This Anglo-centric emphasis is reinforced by a literature on cultural influences which suggests that conceptions of Englishness and Britishness permeated elite political attitudes (and hence may have marginalised devolution) and by a post-colonial literature which claims that 'English' ideas helped structure 'Celtic' political horizons - and hence limited thoughts of an 'independent' way forward.

Whilst this chapter builds on this recent work and these conceptual approaches, it also challenges some of their assumptions with both fresh ideas and new research. The first section below reviews the literature on Englishness and Britishness and its influence on opinions. It suggests that whilst pre-existing cultural orientations can have a strong influence on policy, they do not necessarily suggest a single policy orientation. Moreover, political actors at times choose to support policies which do not conform to their own cultural inclinations. Hence ascribing an (assumed) political attitude to an (assumed) cultural orientation is doubly dangerous. Section two focuses on the role of Englishness in constructing Labour's own policy orientations. Whilst Labour was hardly immune from the influence of an established cultural orientation, the chapter notes frictions between languages and symbols of Engishness/ Britishness which were in common currency and (some) Labour figures' reinterpretation of those symbols. The chapter also notes the influence of a Labour/Socialist culture of dissident and of the 'Celtic' cultures which influenced several early Labour leaders.[9] The third section discusses the influence of this mixed intellectual/cultural climate on Labour's constitutional orientation before 1914, suggesting that devolution was part of a party 'programme' which had points of contact with 'English' societal cultures *and* points of difference. The fourth section shows how this evolved into Labour's agenda for the modernisation of British governance after 1918. Finally, the chapter examines how Labour's constitutional attitudes evolved in the 1930s, when the party's thinking was much influenced by the emergence of mass unemployment and the growth of fascism. It is argued that these new issues provided a fresh rationale for older orientations; and pushed the party further away from devolution. Hence, to see policy as an attachment to symbols of English/British rule is to simplify a complex process and pass over the influence of a popular radical tradition, which saw constitutional reform as a means of limiting the influence of entrenched elite hierarchies, rather than replicating their ideals.[10]

Culture and politics: Englishness and Britishness

McKibbin's and Taylor's accounts of how Labour constitutional attitudes were constructed are conceptually quite simple. Other works find assumptions about race, gender and ethnicity permeating constitutional discussions in 1867.[11] Likewise, debates over the governance of Ireland and the enfranchisement of women in 1916–22 apparently reflected ideas on the nature of the British Imperial State and of what constituted citizenship.[12] It *may* be that Labour's cultural Britishness allowed it little space to support separate identities within the UK, or saw constitutional representations of this difference as unhelpful, although the case has not been made in these terms. Certainly an explosion of work on English and British cultural identity has provided the basis for such an argument. In addition, writers influenced by post-colonial theory have suggested that cultural imperialism limited the capacity of those in the 'Celtic fringe' to see the world through their own national eyes, whilst those in England viewed Celtic countries in the same way as the colonies.[13] Attempts to reinterpret dominant English/British values within Wales produced scarcely different practices. There was a 'profound resignation' to a dominant (alien) culture. British identities were forged across the UK from English traditions. This included a belief in the superior (i.e. rational, calm, moderate) governing spirit of an English ruling elite, especially when compared with the emotional radicalism and passion of the Celts. For such people, British political institutions were symbolic representations of a British national identity and of Britain's imperial mission.[14] To question those institutions was to question Britain's imperial role. To base nations on 'dialects' or race would, as Salisbury put it, 'undo the work of civilisation.'[15]

Yet there are problems in assuming that English/British cultural attitudes were uniformly received within England, let alone uniformly received by

'Celts'. Englishness was a contested term. The Englishness constructed and described in many recent texts was based on rural values, was socially and politically Conservative and resonated with class-based assumptions.[16] It is difficult to see this being accepted across working class Britain. Indeed, rather different conceptions of an English identity were generated in northern England and of Britishness in Cornwall. We need to study which elements of this contested discourse had the greater purchase in constructing attitudes within England. Equally, we need to ask whether the existence of multiple discourses of Englishness and Britishness allowed 'Celts' to negotiate forms of British identity which were compatible with their own traditions.

For example, some Idealists were keen *not* to promote a single and all-dominant English/British set of values, seeing Britain's diversity as its strength. This could embrace support for devolved governance, especially if the Imperial parliament was left free to concentrate on substantive (i.e. imperial) issues as a result.[17] Idealists could support Celtic languages and cultures as an example of that productive diversity or as a means of protecting a rural way of life. This mixture of support for indigenous cultures within a framework of subordination could be quite cleverly integrated into public ritual, as Jon Ellis has shown through his incisive study of the Investiture of a new Prince of Wales in 1911.[18] Nonetheless, the state's intent as expressed in a single ceremony and the co-existence of some shared cultural reference points in England and the Celtic fringe is hardly evidence of a shared and (effectively) identical British identity. People in Wales, Scotland and Ireland did not necessarily see shared reference points as a commitment to Englishness. As historians of Victorian England demonstrated decades ago, and historians of Black Africa have shown more recently, people who faced and interacted with dominant cultures were not necessarily subsumed within them.[19] The assumption that people are discursive sponges devalues the efforts which those people made to maintain and reforge their own identity and values, even whilst using a discourse associated with English/British beliefs (or conducted in English).[20]

So far as the Labour Party is concerned, the hold of an English/British identity reinforced by elite educational and cultural traditions is less apparent than assumptions of cultural uniformity would suggest. Most obviously, many early Labour leaders had their roots within Scottish, and to a lesser degree Welsh, culture. Their Britishness was tinged with other allegiances. Even where this was not the case, Labour politicians were elective members of a dissenting political culture. Their political self-identity was based on an often belligerent opposition to the 'establishment' – and especially to that establishment's ideas on how Britain should be governed (i.e. by them). This was not a socialist institutional culture which insulated activists from broader societal values, as people once argued; but peoples' self-identification could still push them towards questioning, interpreting or partially challenging ideas which were themselves part of a fractured tradition.

Moreover, the conceptual literature assumes that cultural identities would necessarily construct political approaches – it ignores human agency and political calculation. The world of politics is concerned with priorities and calculations. During the First World War, politicians pragmatically accepted women's suffrage without changing their culturally constructed views of gender roles. Whilst cultural studies have established the case for societal culture as a political force – and a preference for 'British' solutions could be part of this – we need more evidence of its influences on the world of elite decision-making.

Labour cultural perspectives before 1914

Discussion of Labour's relationship with dominant cultural, religious and political traditions goes back to W. T. Stead's study of the 'books that made the Labour Party' in 1906. Labour MPs were invariably Nonconformists in background or allegiance and part of a British Protestant tradition often seen as one of the main generators of a British identity.[21] Many of them respected elite literature, music and learning.[22] Many felt close to nature, like other Victorians. Like upper and middle class Victorian public servants, their own testimonies and self-images describe a motivation to serve their people, out of a duty which the strong should perform for the weak.[23] Much of this reads like some academics' conceptions of 'Englishness'.

However, Labour made its own use of these shared values. Its sentiments on the delights of rural Britain are a good example. It is the descriptions by non-Labour writers which have attracted much historical attention. In these, nature was a symbol of the past and its splendours. The white cliffs of Dover, for example, were to be preserved as 'a symbol of the island home which an Englishman loves so well'. Nature was often part of a less corrupt, less sullied, past. Appreciating it would 'engender a patriotic pride', raising awareness of times 'in which great things were done' and a landscape in which 'generation after generation have lived their unrecorded lives'. If there was also some enthusiasm for the tough mountainous landscapes of Wales and Scotland (and for their separate rural cultures) it was often the 'yeoman'-like characteristics of the people living in these areas which was attractive.[24]

By contrast, Labour figures were often concerned with access to beauty, cleanliness and the freedom of the countryside. Hardie and others idealised a rural past – but it was a 'Merrie England' characterised by what Snowden termed 'tribal communism', where 'people were more equal and free'.[25] The writings of Cole, the Hammonds and others stressed (English) rural struggles against the establishment. This literature was a key element of Labour's educational culture. In Labour's hands, the *Scottish* land clearances (for example) were part of a *class* experience, which enthusiasts for rural tranquility reportedly ignored. This conception of the past provided little support for a distinctly Scottish or Welsh sense of national oppression by English invaders:

> Just as in Yorkshire 200 years earlier arable land was formed into sheep farms, so in the Highlands of Scotland in much more recent days – in the memory of our farmers – the land and the hill pasture, and even the right to the rivers and the sea – were taken away'.[26]

Nor was Labour's attitude to English national character identical to that generated by inter-war writers such as Ernest Barker, A. G. McDonnell and Arthur Bryant. Their Englishness was personified by the gentleman-governor, an amateur who ruled nation and Empire in a disinterested way, free from passions and extremes. The association between such values and the ethos of the public schools excluded most Labour activists from a role within the governing class – and from this form of Englishness.[27] In return, Labour pioneers proposed not rule by English 'gentlemen' but a very different governing ethic. Socialism was to create 'a man of ideals, of historical spirit, the man in whose intelligence, religion and sense of what is good report will have a dominating influence, the generous and ungrudging co-operator with his fellows'.[28] Labour intellectuals attacked notions of gentility and amateurism which rationalised government by an inexpert elite. Objectively, they may have shared some values; but they *felt* as if they were very different people.[29]

Many expressions of Englishness included a superior attitude to the Celtic fringe, alienating at least some Labour figures. For Matthew Arnold in the 1860s, Celts contributed sentimentality, lyricism, music, passion to the British State, but not the values enshrined within governing institutions. 'Balance, measure and patience, these are the eternal conditions of high success; and balance, measure and patience are just what the Celt has never had'.[30] For J. S. Mill, just as the French State had absorbed the Breton and Basque into its system of governance, so British institutions had to spread across the UK, absorbing and dominating sub-cultures. It was better, Mill wrote, to be part of the French State than to be:

> the half-savage relic of past times, revolving in his own little mental orbit, without participation or interest in the general movement of the world. The same applies to the Welshman or the Scottish Highlander as members of the British nation.[31]

Reflecting this in the 1920s, the former Liberal Education Minister H. A. L. Fisher felt that 'provincial tongues' like Welsh should be allowed to wither. The USA wisely imposed on its heterogeneous immigrants 'the standards and ideals of English Law and of Anglo-Saxon liberty'. Liberals could not justify forceful removal of the 'self-imposed linguistic handicap of a nation or race', but his sympathies were clear.[32] Unsurprisingly, in parts of the 'Celtic fringe' such attitudes could turn 'England' into an alien 'other' and turn 'Englishness' into a synonym for arrogance. Whilst racial characterisations were hardly unknown within contemporary socialist writings, the racial inferiority of 'Celts' seems a less common theme within Labour rhetoric.[33]

Wales and Scotland produced their own rival and racially defined conceptions of national identity, which described their ethnic inheritance as superior to that of the English. There were pale reflections of this in some Labour writings. MacDonald and Hardie drew on their Scottish backgrounds to suggest that Labour espoused a 'Celtic' Britishness. MacDonald commented that seeing the Welsh mountains and people made him feel 'I was at home in Scotland. The imagination of your people, their love of liberty, their lyrics are characteristic of my own people'. Moreover, the Welsh desire for a simple and free religion 'unhampered by State regulations and unobscured by elaborate ritual' was part of a broader *Labour* sentiment, with purchase across the UK: 'The Labour Party has shown itself to be inspired by everything that is essential to the spirit of a simple religion. Its politics expresses the mind of the common man who believes; it hates everything which makes for the subordination of one man to another.'[34] In addition to the importance of Catholicism in some Labour backgrounds, the distinctive Welsh and Scottish forms of Nonconformity in which some Labour pioneers developed perhaps placed them partially outside a Protestant Britishness.[35]

Of course, not all forms of Englishness stressed racial superiority. Community or civic pride, a historic attachment to an area and its achievements, could be part of a national patriotism in which the locality became a microcosm of the nation.[36] What one was proud of locally became 'Englishness'. Comparable developments were probably evident within Wales, where 'Welshness' was seen very differently in different parts of the country.[37] However, in Labour's hands local pride could also elide into praise for the people's 'spirit.'[38] Such sentiments were expressed in Labour events like the Durham Miners' Gala or May Day marches, in the same way that the Investiture in 1911 may have presented the Liberal government's conception of the appropriate relationship between England and Wales.[39] Labour's 'Britishness' intersected with dominant values; it did not replicate them. Moreover, whilst Labour proclaimed the value of Britain (and Empire) those who set its agenda did not generally subscribe to a discourse of forced national unity, nor one of cultural homogenisation.

Socialist intellectuals and the British constitution

For writers like Bagehot and Dicey, British governing institutions were a symbol of Britain's national character. They were an 'English' antecedent of the British State. The values they encouraged were England's contribution to the British mix. Labour's ideological inheritance made some activists suspicious of the political authority enshrined within these institutions. From the Chartists onwards, the governing elite had been portrayed not as the embodiment of England, but as peddlers of hypocrisy. Parliament was not a symbol of British identity, but the home of numerous betrayals and part of a feudal system of domination.[40] This critique of the existing political system made some socialists positively enthusiastic about constitutional change,[41] including universal suffrage, abolition of the House of Lords, devolution, proportional representation, the referendum and other reforms. Labour intellectuals displayed a good deal of interest in other countries and their constitutional procedures.[42] Some working class party members from the left were not far behind. Lansbury supported a range of constitutional innovations, including the referendum, as late as 1912 (even though this was becoming the Conservatives' pet device for resisting change).[43]

Yet many socialist radicals also felt that the party had betrayed this tradition and accepted dominant values and political arguments as it developed as a political force. MacDonald was their favourite target. To some extent this is understandable. Like many Conservatives, MacDonald felt the constitution was legitimated by age and tradition: 'The fabric of this organization has been built of the stuff of which honour, good sense, reverence, respect, consist'.[44] The implication was hardly radical: 'To degrade in the imagination of the people even a bad House of Commons is a crime.' When the rebel socialist Victor Grayson seized the Speaker's mace, and Ben Tillett attacked parliamentary procedures as bourgeois and hierarchical, they were shunned by Labour MPs.[45] For some, reaching the Commons was an expression of their acceptance into a venerated elite. Others – like Philip Snowden – felt a bond with the financial world and its institutions, in part because they were less critical and more appreciative of his talents than his own party.[46]

Despite this, Labour MPs' actions and policy statements do not suggest subservience to establishment values. Keir Hardie's decision to wear working men's clothing to Parliament (and to present this as his normal behaviour) was a symbolic rejection of conventional values. Moreover, Labour's respect for procedures and rules had its roots in the traditions of the labour movement. Respect for the rule book was a feature of trade union and socialist organisation, since rules prevented elites abusing their power. Mastery of parliamentary rules also reflected working class pride at conquering an 'upper class' domain. Democracy – and the rules needed to run it – was the mechanism for making governance the will of the majority. Good governance was dependent on institutions functioning effectively. Showing respect for parliament (which most Labour MPs certainly felt was appropriate) was also showing respect for Labour's own political culture.

Labour's acceptance of the adversarial Westminster system also had 'labour' roots. Left wing MPs (and constitutional reformers) like George Lansbury and Fred Jowett wanted a more consensual 'cabinet' system of governing, akin to that operating in municipal councils. However, an adversarial system was in some ways closer to the background of working class MPs. Hardened political campaigners, they had joined labour organisations to fight and to lead. Labour leaders' own personal narratives – and the party's collective 'foundation myths' – regularly describe their struggle against popular indifference.[47] Critical and constructive debate, often using rationality (and especially statistical evidence) to destroy the opposition was a way to affirm working-class intelligence and construct a critical body of citizens. Making parliament a place of critique was entirely consistent with a Labour culture which placed unsentimental 'realism' and 'practicality' high up in its hierarchy of values. For such people the organisation imposed by the party system was not a problem. 'Democracy without a party', MacDonald wrote, 'would be a crowd without a purpose'.[48] UK-wide organisation – of trade unions as well as political groups – meant collective strength. Nationwide politics, organised and with clear rules, was the means by which the relatively powerless could challenge the huge power of wealthy elites.

Labour's apparent support for the monarchy has also been used to suggest it was closely integrated into a dominant British culture. Once again, however, the position is more complicated. Keir Hardie for one identified the peoples' 'superstitious reverence' for the monarch as an opiate – and highlighted the excesses which surrounded royal rule to demystify the institution:

> Besides the royal residences, the royal yachts, the royal staghounds, and the royal rat-catchers, there are officials innumerable who draw fat salaries as one of the indisputable adjuncts of the Throne.[49]

MacDonald's line was more pragmatic, but fell far short of simple acceptance. Whilst the monarchy did not interfere with politics, the political reformer could 'pass it by without notice', or accept that it avoided the problem of electing a President. Yet in line with the party's radical inheritance, MacDonald disliked the association of royalty with the 'court', the haunt of 'gilded worthless people', which encouraged 'vulgar displays of wealth' especially by the *nouveau riche*. Deference to the monarchy was discouraged. MacDonald praised the USA and 'the pride of the citizen who calls himself a citizen of his State and not a subject of his monarch'.[50] When the King held a convention in July 1914 to try and resolve the Ulster problem, the party bemoaned this 'undue interference on the part of the crown'.[51] Labour MPs could be attracted to royal ceremony; but they did not necessarily accept the monarchy, or the landed elite, as symbols of their Britishness.

The most obvious example of Labour's attitude to constitutional privilege was its stance on the House of Lords. During the constitutional crisis in 1910–11, the party's view was emphatic:

> That the destruction of the Finance Bill by the House of Lords is a breach of the Constitution and a usurpation of the rights of the House of Commons ; that it creates a menace to the liberties of the people and that those liberties can only be secured by the total abolition of the House of Lords.[52]

The 1910 manifesto was more succinct: 'The Lords must go'.[53] Labour had no interest in preserving institutionalised (and unearned) privilege. This was the party's dominant constitutional attitude. Whilst for some academics the party's support for adult as opposed to female suffrage marks it as a male-centred institution (which it was), nonetheless universal suffrage was both party policy and a long-standing radical demand.[54]

Similarly, Labour inherited a tradition of doubts over the way that foreign and military policies were created and controlled by an aristocratic elite. For MacDonald and Snowden the diplomatic and military elite was distant from the people. It made policy decisions away from the scrutiny of the peoples' representatives and in ways that were frequently detrimental to their lives. On this issue – as with others identified above – many Liberals were equally vociferous. Edwardian attacks on the assumed alliance between armaments manufacturers, military leaders, imperial interests and members of the Foreign Office were led by radical Liberals such as Noel Brailsford, Norman Angell and J. A. Hobson (all of whom worked with the Labour Party after 1918). However, Labour leaders made a substantial contribution. For Snowden, the international companies promoting the arms race were 'the most up-to-date and complete form of capitalistic organization the world has ever seen'.[55] MacDonald attacked the 'altogether deplorable' way that decisions on foreign policy were taken secretly within Whitehall. He attacked sensationalism, xenophobia and an English/British nationalism (as in the naval scare of 1909) because it generated antagonism to others.[56] National pride, he argued, should not be turned into nationalism by militarists.[57] This stress on internationalism was as much a 'Socialist' as it was a 'Liberal' stance and had strong popular radical antecedents.

Labour's solutions to the way that a 'gentlemanly class' promoted war included the abolition of 'secret diplomacy'. Discussion in the open would make agreements between diplomatic/military elites impossible. The Civil

Service and especially the Foreign Office (which was recruited from within this elite) should be democratised. Foreign policy, MacDonald wrote on the outbreak of war, was dominated by 'a handful of men drawn from the aristocratic and plutocratic classes'. Militarism rested on their 'class diplomacy'.[58] Whilst MacDonald's opposition to war meant he was no longer representative of the party leadership, his analysis had been shared by many leading Labour figures across the previous decade.

The party's official statements on Irish Home Rule were equally and emphatically in favour of democratisation. This was hardly surprising. Irish and British radicalism had been linked since the 1880s. Ireland was as much a moral crusade for socialists as it had been for Gladstonian Liberals. A whole series of English Labour MPs proclaimed their adherence to the cause in 1910, following this with impassioned support when Irish Home Rule was debated in Parliament.[59] After 1910, Irish Home Rule became subsumed within Labour's support for 'Home Rule All Round', meaning the decentralisation of governance within Ireland, Scotland and Wales. This was also the stated policy of the Independent Labour Party. Nonetheless, reform of local government attracted far more attention than devolution.[60]

Devolution, then, was just one element in a package of constitutional interests, designed to give power to ordinary people. MacDonald's case for devolved governance, argued in *Socialism and Government* and in *Parliament and Democracy* (1920), was the most articulate. Democracy, he wrote, had to be expanded and enriched so that the nation – and humanity – benefited. Parliament should become a democratic reality, chosen by reflective citizens. Devolution would contribute to this. His argument was not primarily focused on the need to generate parliamentary time (as many Liberals argued). Like the 'nationalist claim for liberty' this was 'but a small part of the case':

> Devolution is required in order that the citizen may keep in touch with his Government and may feel, through a graduation of widening groups, an identity with his Government.[61]

Other forms of identity were important in this. Britain was just a geographical name. 'The Scottish Briton or the Welsh Briton requires Scotland and Wales through which to function.' He ceased to be a real person 'when he is policed or "educated" out of his political individuality.' Devolution was required to 're-establish the social contacts which men make in communities with their distinctive traditions'. Artificial homogeneity was a construct: 'At the root of it all is Capitalism with its fatal allurements of materialist gains and organisation for materialist efficiency'. The destruction of diversity was a fatal mistake:

> What have we not lost by diverting Scottish education, Scottish conceptions of land ownership and holding, Scottish literature, Scottish society, because Scottish

nationality has been sunk in the political organisation of British nationality, a nationality as artificial as Esperanto or Urdu vocabularies? The same is true of Wales and of Ireland. And the devastation has been made complete by the destruction or suppression of true local government.[62]

The second consequence of artificial British nation-building was a people:

possessed by such ideas as geographical expansion, military might – the amalgamation of those appetites of possession and authority known as Imperialism. A people become Imperialist by the sacrifice of the qualities that alone enable it to fulfill its Imperial destinies.

In darker moods, MacDonald felt that the materialism of the trade union movement made it especially vulnerable to imperialist arguments. Yet he also seemed to suggest that 'Englishmen' (as opposed to Celts) were equally at risk.[63]

Since the weakness of British democracy was the position and power of the British establishment, altering governing structures whilst preserving that establishment was inadequate. Without an attack on establishment power, new institutions would simply preserve old problems. Consequently, even for MacDonald and Hardie devolution was less important than other reforms. For other Labour leaders, capturing the municipality, School Board or Poor Law Union was more productive as a means of challenging the establishment's hold over peoples' conception of 'fitness to rule'. Support for democratised, Labour-controlled, local government was often a higher priority than national devolution.[64] Indeed, devolution could be seen as privileging the Scottish, Irish and Welsh and ignoring the broader problem.

Of course, the appeal of an English/British nationalism as an influence on the fate of devolution cannot be ignored. In 1914, many labour leaders rallied unquestionably to the flag. However, even here the language of patriotism took many forms. There are innumerable instances of Britishness being defined in relation to a Germanic 'other' in 1914, with Labour (and Liberal) advocates of intervention powerfully contrasting a 'British' belief in liberty with the authoritarian militarism of the 'Prussian Junkers'.[65] This even permeated the language of those opposed to war. For MacDonald, Britain was 'the great liberal land where exiles came.' In trying to maintain Labour hostility to militarism and conscription, Bruce Glasier stirred the embers of an earlier radical patriotism:

Now may the workers of Great Britain run up the Red Flag and the Union Jack side by side! Now may the beacon fires of public opinion be lighted from town to town and the old Magna Carta and Habeas Corpus which our fathers won for us with their blood be unrolled once more . . .[66]

Labour's support for 'Britishness' could also include support for Empire, although this did not necessarily involve absorbing elite attitudes. For

MacDonald, Britain's imperial mission was to make its democratic principles and traditions more widespread:

> 'British' justice, 'British' honour, 'British' administration, carry to our minds certain qualities of justice, honour, and administration, and our imperial policy has always been commended to our people at home – whenever they troubled their heads about it – on these moral or qualitative grounds . . . Now the task of the democratic parties of the Empire is to establish guarantees that this moral quality will be preserved untainted.[67]

MacDonald's views, in this and other respects, are often misunderstood. He could be quite authoritarian. He is often seen as little more than a Liberal, influenced by Idealism, who dressed this up in a mixture of Darwinian ideas and stolen socialist rhetoric. His commitment to the idea of a national will – a general will which bound the people to the state – might indeed seem to sit uneasily with his support for devolution and a union of separate peoples.[68] Yet his commitment to simple socialist 'truths' and the influence of his Scottish background help to explain this apparent conundrum. For MacDonald national identity was a positive thing; but it had to both preserve a heritage and sustain progress. 'Nationality', he wrote, 'contained in itself the best of conservatism and the wisest that was in revolution'.[69] Capitalism had imposed a deadening uniformity on people; socialism (and the British Socialist State) would reawaken a positive diversity.[70] Of course, many of MacDonald's colleagues were less pluralistic. For some, Britain's imperial greatness gave it a global strength which should not be diluted through internal division within the UK. At the end of the war, these competing tendencies were tested in a series of discussions on Britain's constitutional future.

Devolution and the reform of governance 1918–24

After 1918 Labour needed policies on the economic and social problems which gripped the country – but also on constitutional reform. Irish unrest meant Home Rule was at the top of the political agenda. The extension of the franchise, proportional representation, reform of the machinery of government and of the Lords – like devolution – were all referred to commissions and special conferences by the coalition government between 1916 and 1920.

Competing strands within Labour's approach to constitutional change were evident when the party established policy advisory committees in 1918. Responsibility was divided. The Machinery of Government Sub-Committee's remit included parliamentary procedure, electoral reform and devolution, plus the 'theory and practice of the various revolutionary movements', and the position and status of civil servants and public employees. The Local

Government Committee was to address municipal governance, including the size and power of local/regional authorities.[71] A Scottish Labour Party was formed, although there was no Welsh equivalent. Despite proclaiming the value of this structure for developing policy ideas, both the NEC and the TUC tried to limit the role of these committees and groups, fearing challenges to their authority from 'intellectuals' and 'sectional interests'.[72] Corporatism, not pluralism, was at the heart of the party's governing mentality.

So far as devolution was concerned, there was a real object to consider. The Speaker's Conference on Devolution was established by a Commons' vote in June 1919. As with the other constitutional reforms addressed by commissions between 1916 and 1920, it was viewed through Edwardian eyes. Austen Chamberlain saw federal home rule as 'the only scheme which would make Irish Home Rule safe and the union of Ireland possible'. The Conference was asked to investigate devolution as a means of creating time for the Imperial Parliament to discuss Imperial issues, another Edwardian (but not uniquely Conservative) conception.[73] Liberal representatives on the committee were generally supportive of devolution. Labour gave support too, now on the grounds that the Imperial Parliament was overloaded. Perhaps surprisingly, the Conference agreed on the principle of devolution. However, there was no agreement over the form and remit of the 'federal' assemblies to be established. As chair of the Conference, the Speaker (Viscount Ullswater) put forward a moderate proposal. It included a (possibly bi-cameral system) of Parliaments for England, Scotland, Ireland and (possibly) Wales, with limited devolved powers. The assemblies were to consist of Westminster representatives, whilst Parliament would have power to block legislative proposals even in devolved areas. The assemblies would control limited portions of existing taxes rather than raise their own funds. The Conference divided over the relative merits of an English Parliament as opposed to regional English bodies, although the latter attracted broader support – regional assemblies within England meant that there could be two assemblies within Ireland, and hence no 'national' Irish solution. A rival scheme proposed by the Scottish Liberal MP Murray MacDonald involved elected parliaments in Ireland and Scotland. This was contested by Welsh representatives on the grounds that Wales, with its own language, was even more of a nation than the others. However, Conservatives argued that 'nationality' should not decide this or the structure of devolution more generally.[74] The Conference accepted the Speaker's scheme by just one vote.

Nonetheless, devolution was not undermined simply because its supporters disagreed over the merits of competing schemes. The opposition of leading government figures – including Lloyd George, Balfour and Curzon – meant the conference never had a chance.[75] *The Times* had noted that those appointed to the Conference were 'undistinguished and unrepresentative', and hence unlikely to force government action. *The New Statesman* made a similar point. The Conference included no heavy weight English representation, no prominent Labour figures, a disproportionate number of Liberals (with no influence over the coalition Government) and a large helping of Ulster Protestants. As Lord Brassey (a supporter of devolution) noted, it was as if the Government wanted the conference to fail. As Lord Birkenhead perceptively added, once it was decided to address the Irish problem by other means, the Conference was 'doomed to failure'. A Federal solution was unnecessary and lacked popular support.[76] The Conference report, published in 1920, scarcely registered in UK political debate. Thereafter, and with the Liberals a declining force, the hopes of devolutionists rested on the Labour Party.

In 1918–19 the Labour Party seemed concerned with other matters. Like the government, Labour's constitutional concerns focused on Ireland. The NEC supported self-determination and 'redress for all persons who have suffered oppression' – but the oppressed were felt to live in Ireland and the Empire, not in Scotland and Wales. It did not help that of the party's main enthusiasts for devolution, Hardie was dead and MacDonald discredited. Doubts which had been masked before 1914 more easily came to the fore. In 1918, devolution was delegated to a sub-group of the Machinery of Government Advisory Committee. By contrast, a special conference of the NEC, the Parliamentary Labour Party and TUC was called to discuss the Irish situation.[77]

By 1921, support for devolution was slipping away even in Scotland and Wales. Liberals in Wales were presenting devolution as a way of preserving their hold over the nation's governance and values. Even for Welsh Labour devolutionists, bad, elitist, governance by the establishment (even if Welsh) was no real improvement over (bad) governance by a British Parliament. In Scotland, what had been a central and accepted part of the Labour programme in 1918–19 was being contested by 1923, with growing support for more clearly separate Scottish policies, but within the existing British economic framework.[78] Economic and social concerns were increasingly dominating party debate – in Wales and Scotland, and even more so at UK level. The housing and industrial crises demanded and received attention. The party's emphasis on the state as a means of delivering economic and social benefits meant decentralisation was not a natural priority. Since the market was the cause of excess competition, restructuring the market and industry via direct state intervention was a core party aim.

The clearest evidence of this lukewarm attitude to devolution comes from the party's intellectuals. Labour's constitutional theorists – Sidney Webb, Harold Laski and G. D. H. Cole – were far less attached to 'Home

Rule All Round' than Hardie and MacDonald. On constitutional issues (as in economics) Labour intellectuals were not immune to a dominant cultural/intellectual orthodoxy. The imprint of Figgis, Maitland and Ernest Barker is clearly evident in the early work of Cole and Laski. At this time, Laski regularly cited the Liberals Mill and Graham Wallas in his writings, whilst his views on decentralisation and liberty were also clearly influenced by a Liberal tradition. Nonetheless, socialists' ideas before 1914 were developed within a 'socialist' framework marked by attacks on the 'Servile (Liberal) State'. After 1918, the failure of capitalist systems to provide for workers' representation within the state, and the Labour/Fabian reaction to that challenge, provided the context in which they debated collectivism, democratisation and decentralisation.[79]

The Webbs almost entirely ignored 'Celtic' sentiments in their constitutional analysis. They rejected the establishment of 'a litter of subordinate legislative assemblies for particular parts of Great Britain'.[80] In a country 'so homogenous and closely knit', they argued, any division of services extending throughout the whole island 'both impairs efficiency and increases cost'. A whole range of state functions – defence, taxation, justice and nationalised industries – could not be subdivided. Moreover, any divergence from state guidelines on welfare benefits, health, safety legislation for industry and minimum wage rates stemming from the creation of devolved assemblies would destroy their idea of a National Minimum standard of life. If this was to be avoided, the powers which could be devolved would have to be severely restricted. Reasonable decentralisation of this kind could be achieved by creating larger local authorities with bigger boundaries. They made a single concession in a single footnote: 'On the other hand, national feeling may be so intense as to require the sacrifice of a division of administration as well as of legislation'. Whether or not people read these works, the sentiments expressed resounded throughout the labour movement.

Labour thinkers were not indifferent to constitutional issues. They simply supported constitutional changes which did not include devolution, because their primary aim was improving the quality of *British* governance. The Webbs' now neglected *Socialist Commonwealth* was in fact a detailed constitutional prospectus for Britain. It was based around elected Parliaments of Consumers and Producers.[81] They wanted a functional democracy which took economic needs seriously, including a 'social parliament' to ensure that the civic will of the people regulated any economic selfishness from producers. They felt that Parliament as constituted was undemocratic. There was only a 'small degree of correspondence between the institution and the work that it has to perform,' because its members did not prioritise the economic condition of the people.[82] The Second Chamber – a bastion of privilege – did not act as a revising mechanism. MPs did not scrutinise legislation and hold the executive to account. Government was conducted by Ministers and officials, who collaborated with the 'powerful interests' affected by policy. The result was at best Cabinet, at worst Prime Ministerial rule 'exercised through a subservient party majority of more or less tied members, and an obedient official hierarchy of unparalleled magnitude.'[83] The Civil Service had insufficient expertise to sustain good governance, so could not counter these problems. As a result of these weaknesses, government was a dictatorship tempered by popular revolt and the need to placate capitalist interests.[84]

Cole was for much of this period a Guild Socialist, concerned primarily with industrial democracy. Like Laski he had strong libertarian credentials and disagreed with the Webbs on a variety of topics. Yet the idea of constructing a functional democracy which took workers' economic needs as its focus was ingrained in the work of all three. For Cole, there should be decentralised regional economic 'parliaments,' with an enhanced role for a co-ordinating economic organisation at the centre. Laski felt that centralised authority often made the wrong decisions, was 'narrow and despotic and over-formal,' whilst centralisation created the 'decay of local energy.' [85] However, neither Cole nor Laski saw 'territorial' devolution as the answer. Indeed, Laski added a detailed critique of the case for devolution as advanced by Murray MacDonald. The dependence of devolved bodies on block grants from central government would mean the system was not really independent at all. Disagreements over money would absorb much parliamentary time. Hence time saved from the parliamentary agenda by devolving 'local' issues to assemblies would be lost in other ways. The machinery of governance would not become more efficient. Better results could be obtained by giving greater powers to local government (on German lines) 'without the creation of a vast and expensive new structure'.[86]

These intellectuals worked with local government practitioners in Labour's Machinery of Government sub-committee and on the devolution sub-group chaired by the MP Willie Graham. The latter included two recent (English) recruits to the party, alongside experts like Herman Finer and authorities on Wales and Scotland.[87] Their discussions reflected the intellectuals' doubts. It was suggested that devolution needed careful definition; that separate proposals should be put forward for Scotland, Ireland and Wales; that devolution by subject matter and not by 'geography' should be addressed alongside the reorganisation of local government areas. The addition of the Coles and Page Arnot to the committee ensured that industrial democracy received growing attention.

Rooted assumptions were also evident. In the opinion of one committee member (Lionel Curtis of the Round Table movement) devolution should *only* be considered on the grounds that it would give the Imperial Parliament time to do its work: 'It was necessary to get rid of the demands for powers resting merely upon the 'amour propre' and 'particularism' of the constituent nations of the United Kingdom'.[88] Such sentiments – examples perhaps of an established culture permeating Labour politics – were not unusual amongst those English socialists recruited to left wing causes. The Marxist Walton Newbould was one of many who felt the Welsh were best kept under the tutelage of paternalistic English rationality:

> The Welsh are a queer lot – all Celts are – McLeans, McDonalds and Welshmen – to the Sassenach a mystery. They make up the British nation and have to be understood and explained to and co-operated with. The Welsh – perhaps they have less Northman blood in the veins – are not so steady. They jump up and down. They are suspicious, seem untrustworthy. But are not bad – when understood.[89]

Alternatives to devolution also emerged from within the Local Government Committee. Whilst the committee's primary concern was municipal policy (and especially housing) the size and powers of local authorities was part of their agenda. 'Regionalism' was proposed as an alternative to devolution.[90] Cole, C. M. Lloyd and Clement Attlee were the major advocates, whilst Herbert Morrison proposed something similar in evidence to the Royal Commission on London Government.[91] Larger regional units were supported on various grounds: Parliament was not dealing with local matters; 'real' local government was only possible if units were large enough for financial autonomy; major initiatives in town planning, transport and other areas were already being organised through unelected bodies because they had to be co-ordinated across local authority boundaries. Only regional government could ensure local needs were addressed effectively whilst also ensuring accountability. Finally, extending boundaries would enable rural and urban areas to be recombined, with 'good' urban policies being extended into less well-governed rural areas.[92] Regionalists rejected devolution for Scotland and Wales as 'lip-service to the principle of devolution. The right way is for Parliament to devolve as many of its functions as possible to the local authorities.' Even socialised industries were seen as part of their remit.[93]

Regionalism had powerful supporters (including Attlee and Morrison). However, like devolution it did not fit well with party culture. Opponents felt it was just another layer of local government. Party officials were concerned that any major decentralisation would lead to the construction of separate Labour organisations, which would run separate (and possibly contradictory) Labour policies. Labour officials resisted this development when the structure of the party was debated during the war. The TUC also wanted power concentrated at the centre where it could influence events through institutionalised Labour consultation procedures. Individual unions wanted to negotiate uniform national conditions with a single national body and felt devolution would divide their strength. If devolution had to occur, they argued, conditions of labour should be reserved for the Imperial Parliament.[94]

Unsurprisingly, there was no official devolution bill during the 1924 Labour government – and no attempt to create elected regional assemblies. Despite (some) pressure from Wales and Scotland, the party rejected devolution within the state and within the party – even the formation of a Welsh Advisory Committee was rejected.[95] A few enthusiasts struggled to keep devolution on the Labour agenda in the 1920s. Some amongst a newer generation supported it in the 1930s; but the moment had passed.[96]

The demise of devolution

As Labour moved closer to government, attention switched to other constitutional changes. The reform of central government was a particular emphasis. Initially, Labour intellectuals focused on the Civil Service and its potential role in *supporting* a Labour government. This reflected the tenor of the wartime Haldane Committee report on the Machinery of Government (Haldane attended Labour's Advisory Committee; Sidney Webb was one of Haldane's team).[97] Over time, a curious alliance of older socialists and newly recruited intellectuals redefined the problem in ways which were more clearly related to pre-war Labour sentiments. They saw the Civil Service not as an asset but as a mechanism for blunting the party's radicalism. They wanted Ministers to counter this by drawing on ideas from within the party's policy apparatus. As the party's research secretary reported in 1924:[98]

> It is most desirable that the Labour Ministers should be, to some extent at least, independent of their Departmental advisors – or, at any rate, should not be helplessly in the hands of these – and that they should have automatically brought to their notice information and suggestions relating to their official functions by which they may, if they like, supplement or check what will be brought before them in their offices.

The NEC and TUC were uninterested. To the disquiet of party intellectuals, they restricted direct contact between Ministers and party advisory committees and filtered out advisory committee policy documents which they opposed.[99] To the annoyance of Laski, Snowden stacked a government committee established to investigate the Civil Service with conservatives. For Snowden and MacDonald, experience of office in 1924 suggested that the Civil Service was not an obstacle to the creation of 'sound' policies: the problem was party members with unrealistic ideas.[100] This gap between party leaders and party activists/intellectuals became more pronounced over time.

Following the experience of 1924, TUC opinion shifted. Leading officials expressed concern over the potential influence of government officials as Labour entered office in 1929. After the government fell, Citrine argued that the party's effectiveness had been undermined 'because of the influence of the Civil Service'.[101]

Labour's long-standing concern over the power of the establishment – and its commitment to address this via constitutional changes – was enhanced by the cathartic shock of 1931. This produced a partial and temporary alliance between trade unionists and party intellectuals on the need for changes in the machinery of governance which went beyond addressing the role of civil servants. A new and radical version of this older discourse was given theoretical sharpness by Laski. Democratic systems, he argued, were teetering on the edge of an abyss. The government had been undone in 1931 by a social elite because it threatened their position. This interpretation was given mythical status when Attlee, Morrison, Laski and Webb reconstructed the events of 1931 in ways that justified their new political aims.[102] The Lords, City, Bankers, and Civil Service were cast as conspirators against the party and the people. Popular deference to the monarchy, the Lords and to 'gentlemen' politicians, Laski wrote, was symbolic of the peoples' 'collective inferiority complex'. Deferential traditions had accustomed the prisoners to their chains. Chains had to be broken. Cole, Laski, Attlee and Cripps drew up a party programme which had constitutional change at its core. *For Socialism and Peace* (1934) included a raft of constitutional changes, including abolition of the House of Lords, reform of the Civil Service and army, changes in parliamentary procedure, reforms of Cabinet governance and the nationalisation of the banking system (since the financial elite's capacity to undermine change had been amply demonstrated by the constructed crisis of 1931). Devolution was conspicuously absent from this list.[103] The emphasis was on changes which would limit the powers of a metropolitan elite and allow the party to introduce socialist policies.

Support for these dramatic changes in the machinery of government was reinforced by the radicalisation of the party and by an enhanced commitment to centralisation and state direction in economic affairs. Nationalisation became a stronger element in the party programme. Economic 'planning' provided a fresh rhetoric to justify a deep if vague Labour belief in using the power of the state to address Britain's problems.[104] Centralisation had become an unchallengeable feature of the party programme. The decimating impact of the slump on working class living standards had also created an urgent need for a radical economic action plan. The planned reform of central government machinery was part of this. Giving Scotland and Wales an assembly would make these countries dependent on their own resources and *prevent* them from addressing economic challenges: their 'economies' (which were in any case closely integrated with the rest of the UK) could not sustain services at the current national standard, let alone at a higher level.

There was no Labour indifference to the economic problems of Scotland, Ireland and Wales. On the contrary, there is evidence that 'Celtic' areas were developing an heroic identity. Wales was 'discovered' by social investigators as London had been fifty years earlier. In 1933–34 special correspondents for Labour newspapers filed numerous reports on their tours through the coalfield or trips to the slate quarries, praising the 'spirit' displayed by industrial Wales.[105] Labour's Special Areas Commission under Hugh Dalton looked in detail at Wales and Scotland. It concluded that the market would not solve their problems. Central government would have to force 'English' industries to relocate. Gaitskell argued 'it is of great importance that the new investment should be concentrated in the depressed areas.'[106] Dalton's commitment to regional economic policies was carried over into his post-war position as Labour's Chancellor.[107] Nor did 'Celtic' Labour necessarily disagree with this emphasis. MPs schooled through the National Council of Labour Colleges (especially strong in Scotland and Wales) saw issues in socialist and internationalist terms.[108] Others from within these areas pragmatically concluded that industrial diversification was essential and that this needed central government support.

At the same time, there was growing support for devolved governance short of outright devolution at UK level. The National Government made cosmetic changes, hoping to appease a sentimental and cultural nationalism before it developed in political directions. Some sections of the Labour Party in Scotland and Wales, and a larger element of the Liberal Party, were pushing for more. However, the emphasis of such pressures had changed, focusing less on 'Home Rule' than on extended powers for the Secretary of State for Scotland and the establishment of a Secretary of State for Wales. In part this reflected a concern that traditional values and cultures were being destroyed by homogenisation and economic decline. However, in Wales calls for the appointment of a Secretary of State drew increasingly on concerns over the collapse of staple industries and hence the whole economy of south Wales.

A second factor in Labour's growing hostility to devolved government during the 1930s (and after 1945) was its view of nationalism. In 1929, the secretary of Labour's International Committee, Leonard Woolf, proposed that the party should launch an 'attack upon nationalism', a 'disease' so 'formidable as to threaten the security of the world'. Nationalists, he argued, had no respect for reason and human brotherhood. They exploited suffering to create antagonism between peoples.[109] For Laski, nationalist rivalries had created the First World War. Like Strachey, he felt nationalism had promoted imperialism, fascism and xenophobia.[110] Such sentiments turned normally unemotional men like Hugh Gaitskell into 'warlike' opponents of continental dictators and caused them to exaggerate the threat from fascist/nationalist movements within the UK. In Gaitskell's case, these views stemmed from direct contact with events in continental Europe.[111] Few English Labour figures highlighted the influence of French fascism on the founding father of Welsh nationalism, Saunders Lewis – few even knew of him. Nor were right wing Scottish nationalists the cause for much concern. However, that did not prevent Labour seeing Welsh and Scottish nationalism as part of a European-wide movement with demonic potential.

The experience of war and the circumstances of post-war Britain had a mixed impact. Wartime propaganda promoted a sense of British identity – in part by recognising the contribution of all four nations.[112] Intellectuals – from painters to planners – praised Britain's diversity and argued for its preservation. Some English Labour figures readily accepted this. Attlee and others enjoyed Welsh rural life and praised (and exaggerated) a distinctive Welsh rural spirit.[113] Even Laski – who argued that 'economic equality is the effective condition of democratic government' – still allowed for and encouraged cultural difference. Self-determination could 'liberate a spiritual energy' and add to the general 'happiness of mankind'. The things that marked Wales as different were to be encouraged. 'We would gain nothing – and we should lose much', Laski wrote, 'by the forcible suppression of the Welsh language in Schools'.[114]

However, Labour leaders did not think that devolution was necessary in order to address such issues, nor to resolve the Welsh economic problem. There was some divergence of opinion here between the London leadership and some (but not all) Welsh Labour MPs. By 1945, the appointment of a Secretary of State for Wales received support from a majority of the Welsh Parliamentary Party. Wartime economic problems had reinforced the view that the economic needs of south Wales were best addressed through direct representation in Cabinet.[115] By contrast, Herbert Morrison, who was in charge of constitutional issues, paid more attention to the comments of (Welsh) civil servants. They were concerned that appointing a Secretary of State for Wales would lead to less efficient government of both Wales and of Britain. A long memorandum on these lines in 1943 was favourably received by Morgan Phillips (General Secretary of the Labour Party) and Morrison.[116] Morgan Phillips separately highlighted the party's belief that the existence of a separate Secretary of State for Scotland had delayed decision-making during the war – to the detriment of the people. He also felt Welsh economic problems needed British support. 'Coal', he wrote, 'must be dealt with on a national basis. What is true of coal is equally true of many other problems affecting the life of Wales'.[117] Attlee made much the same point:

> This Government will not forget . . . the shameful economic evils which afflicted Wales between the wars. . . . But I do not disguise from you our belief that it would be a mistake to think that Wales can achieve economic well-being altogether apart from consideration of policy for Britain as a whole; nor do I accept the view that the appointment of a Secretary of State would solve the economic problem.[118]

For UK Labour leaders (and many in Wales and Scotland) both Britishness and the need for a state-wide approach to economic policy had been reinforced by the experience of war and the challenge of post-war reconstruction. This was hardly the time to question a role for the monarchy or the Lords – or to propose a Welsh or Scottish Parliament. However, Labour's continuing emphasis on reforming central government led to an official review of the Machinery of Government, established by Attlee and Cripps and chaired by Sir John Anderson. English socialists who had supported reforming the machinery of central government and sustaining local government had moved up through the ranks and were now in leading party and government posts.[119]

It could be argued that Labour had imbibed an 'Imperial' emphasis from a dominant English culture, and that the policy of English (and 'Celtic') Labour reflected 'English' cultural orientations. The UK Labour Party's never pronounced interest in devolution had certainly been influenced by the 'Imperial crisis' which surrounded the Speaker's Conference in 1919–20 and the establishment of an Irish Free State in 1921. Before 1945, party figures had at times voiced an English/British conception of 'the Celts,' seeing them as emotional, radical, homely – and in need of some 'English' rationality and governing capacity. The rejection of a Secretary of State for Wales in 1945 coincided with further imperial problems. However, to describe the dominant thrust of Labour policy as the consequence of a post-imperial mindset would be a vulgar characterisation of a complex process. There was no organic relationship between Imperial attitudes and attitudes to devolution. In the earlier period, some Labour *supporters* of devolution were also advocates of Empire. In 1945 some of the most active opponents of devolution were the most committed anti-imperialists. More important was the way that Labour's own cultural and political imperatives had hardened over time and pushed the party away from devolution. Initially, Labour wanted political changes which would curtail the power of an 'establishment' which kept economic injustice off the political agenda, diverting people with other issues. This had included 'Celtic' issues like disestablishment, temperance and Home Rule and a British nationalism which induced a xenophobic militarism. Since economic justice was Labour's key aim, the constitutional changes necessary to limit the establishment's power were its priority. The cultural identities of peoples within the UK were not insignificant – but could be addressed by other means. 'Celtic' concerns were largely part of a broader problem. Mass (regional) unemployment and the rise of nationalism/fascism made it seem that democracy itself was on trial. By 1945 Labour rejected even limited devolved control because in its view the key problems were economic not cultural, whilst anything that encouraged nationalism was to be resisted at all costs. Economic problems required concerted state action, not the division of Britain and the pretence that this could somehow solve the difficulties. Hence devolution died, not through neglect, nor through the triumph of an 'English' culture, but through the development of alternative (and popular) Labour perspectives on the best way forward for ordinary British people.

Notes

1 I am grateful to Michael Freeden for his perceptive comments on an earlier version of this chapter.

2 Pat Jalland, 'United Kingdom devolution 1910–14: political panacea or tactical diversion', *EHR*, 94 (1979).

3 John D. Fair, *British Inter-party Conferences: A Study of the Procedure of Conciliation in British Party Politics 1867–1921* (Oxford, 1980) especially ch. 11; Martin Pugh, *Electoral Reform in War and Peace 1906–18* (London, 1978).

4 Fair, *British Inter-party Conferences*, p. 225. There is one concluding reference to a deeper cause (imperial federation and the greatness of Britain) but the point is not amplified.

5 David Powell, *Nationhood and Identity: The British State since 1800* (London, 2002); Vernon Bogdanor, *Devolution in the United Kingdom* (Oxford, 1999); Brigid Hadfield, 'The United Kingdom as a territorial state', in Vernon Bogdanor (ed.), *The British Constitution in the Twentieth Century* (Oxford, 2003), pp. 591–604, 611–14.

6 For informed overviews see Kenneth O. Morgan, *Rebirth of a Nation: Wales 1880–1980* (Oxford and Cardiff, 1981) and Richard Finlay, *A Partnership for Good? Scottish Politics and the Union since 1880* (Edinburgh, 1999).

7 Ross McKibbin, 'Why was there no Marxism in Britain?', *EHR*, 99 (1984).

8 Miles Taylor, 'Labour and the constitution', in Duncan Tanner et al. (eds), *Labour's First Century* (Cambridge, 2000).

9 Ramsay MacDonald, Keir Hardie, Robert Smillie and other significant figures had Scottish roots. For the Welsh, see Kenneth O. Morgan, *Wales in British Politics 1868–1922* (Cardiff, 2nd edn, 1970).

10 For the importance of this tradition, see Eugenio Biagini and Alistair Reid (eds), *Currents of Radicalism* (Cambridge, 1991).

11 Catherine Hall, Keith McClelland and Jane Rendall, *Defining the Victorian Nation: Class, Race, Gender and the British Reform Act of 1867* (Cambridge, 2000).

12 Nichola Gullace *'The Blood of our Sons': Men, Women, and the Renegotiation of British Citizenship during the Great War* (London, 2002). See also McMahon above for the Irish/Imperial dimension.

13 E.g. Stephen Knight, *A Hundred Years of Fiction: Writing Wales in English* (Cardiff, 2004) and for a review of the extensive Scottish material, Liam Connell, 'Scottish nationalism and the colonial vision of Scotland', *Interventions: International Journal of Postcolonial Studies*, 6 (2004).

14 Robert Colls, *Identity of England* (Oxford, 2002), especially ch. 17; Ben Wellings, 'Empire-nation: national and imperial discourses in England', *Nations and Nationalism*, 8 (2002); Christopher Bryant, 'These Englands, or where does devolution leave the English?', *Nations and Nationalism*, 9 (2003).

15 Cited in Peter Mandler, ' "Race" and "nation" in Victorian political thought', in Stefan Collini (ed.), *History, Religion and Culture* (Cambridge, 2000), pp. 230–1.

16 David Lowenthal, 'British national identity and the English landscape', *Rural History*, 2 (1991); Julia Stapleton, *Englishness and the Study of Politics: The Social and Political Thought of Ernest Barker* (Cambridge, 1994) and Julia Stapleton, *Political Intellectuals and Public Identities in Britain since 1850* (Manchester, 2001).

17 See e.g. Henry Maine, *Popular Government* (London, 3rd edn, 1886), Sidney Low, *The Governance of England* (London, 1904).

18 John S. Ellis, 'Reconciling the Celt: British national identity, empire, and the 1911 Investiture of the Prince of Wales', *JBS*, 37 (1998), 394.

19 See e.g. Geoffrey Crossick, *An Artisan Elite in Victorian London* (London, 1978); R. Q. Gray, *The Labour Aristocracy in Victorian Edinburgh* (Oxford, 1976). For imperial reinterpretations of British values, see e.g. Philip D. Morgan and Sean Hawkins (eds), *Black Experience and the Empire* (Oxford, 2004).

20 Raymond Williams, cited in Jane Aaron, 'Postcolonial change', *New Welsh Review*, 67 (2005), 34.

21 W. T. Stead, 'The Labour Party and the books that helped to make it', *Review of Reviews* (1906).

22 Chris Waters, *British Socialists and the Politics of Popular Culture, 1884–1914* (Manchester, 1990).

23 Duncan Tanner, 'Ideological debate in Edwardian Labour politics: radicalism, revisionism and socialism', in Biagini and Reid, *Currents of Radicalism*, p. 291; Peter C. Gould, *Early Green Politics: Back to Nature, Back to the Land and Socialism in Britain, 1880–1900* (Brighton, 1988).

24 David Matless, *Landscape and Englishness* (London, 1998), p. 19.

25 Clare Griffiths, 'Labour and the countryside: rural strands in the British Labour movement, 1900–1939', Oxford D.Phil. thesis 1996, p. 39.

26 Cited in ibid, p. 44.

27 Stapleton, *Political Intellectuals*. See also Andrew Causey, 'English art and "the national character" 1933–4', in David Peters Corbett et al. (eds), *The Geographies of Englishness: Landscape and the National Past 1880–1940* (New Haven and London, 2002).

28 James Ramsay MacDonald, *Socialism and Government* (London, 1908), p. xxviii. For the rather different Fabian view, see e.g. H. H. Schloesser, 'The place of the expert under socialism', *Socialist Review*, November 1908.

29 See above, p. 252.

30 Colls, *Identity of England*, p. 282.

31 Wellings, 'Empire-nation', p. 104.

32 Alfred Zimmern, summarising Fisher, *Nation & Athenaeum*, 15 March 1924, and Fisher's response, 29 March 1924.

33 Murray G. H. Pittock, *Scottish Nationality* (Basingstoke, 2001), pp. 98–9, and Huw Pryce, 'Modern nationality and the medieval past: the Wales of John Edward Lloyd', in Rees Davies and Geraint Jenkins (eds), *From Medieval to Modern Wales: Historical Essays in Honour of Kenneth O. Morgan and Ralph A. Griffiths* (Cardiff, 2004).

34 J. Hugh Edwards, 'As others see us: an interview with Mr J. Ramsay MacDonald, MP', *Wales: The National Magazine*, 6 (1914), 126–8.

35 For this in Glasgow, Ian Wood, *John Wheatley* (Manchester, 1990), ch. 2. The idea that Welsh Nonconformity (the 'national religion') sustained respect for the rights of small nations (like Ireland) is a myth – but one which helped sustain a sense of Welsh distinctiveness. If Scottish Presbyterians could be active Protestants, they were nonetheless discernibly separate from English churches.

36 Paul Readman, 'The place of the past in English culture', *Past and Present*, 186 (2005).

37 R. Merfyn Jones, 'Beyond identity? The reconstruction of the Welsh', *JBS*, 31 (1992).

38 See Neville Kirk (ed.), *Northern Identities: Historical Interpretations of 'The North' and 'Northernness'* (Aldershot, 2000); Steve Caunce et al. (eds), *Relocating Britishness* (Manchester, 2004).

39 For Durham, Huw Beynon and Terry Austrin, *Masters and Servants: Class and Patronage in the Making of a Labour Organisation: the Durham Miners and the English Political Tradition* (London, 1994), ch. 9.

40 Eugenio Biagini, *Liberty, Retrenchment and Reform: Popular Liberalism in the Age of Gladstone, 1860–1880* (Cambridge, 1992), ch. 1.

41 Logie Barrow and Ian Bullock, *Democratic Ideas and the British Labour Movement 1880–1914* (Cambridge, 1996).

42 See e.g. H. D. Lloyd on Swiss democracy, *Labour Leader*, 6 March 1908. The ILP's 'Revisionist' journal, the *Socialist Review*, paid considerable attention to Socialist politics outside Britain, including the constitutional systems in which they operated.

43 See the *Daily Herald*, 20 December 1912. Many of the left placed their faith in proportional representation, seen as a means to allow socialists to espouse socialism (see e.g. *Clarion*, 15 December 1913).

44 Cited in Michael Freeden, *Liberal Languages: Ideological imaginations and Twentieth Century Progressive Thought* (Princeton, 2005), p. 84.

45 Paul Ward, *Red Flag and Union Jack. Englishness, Patriotism and the British Left, 1881–1924* (Woodbridge, 1998), p. 83; David Clark, *Victor Grayson: Labour's Lost Leader* (London, 1985). For further examples of MacDonald's respectful views, see Freeden, *Liberal Languages*, p. 84.

46 McKibbin, 'Why was there no Marxism in Britain', 314–15; Duncan Tanner, 'Philip Snowden', *ODNB* (Oxford, 2004), vol. 51, p. 502.

47 Jon Lawrence, 'Labour – the myths that it has lived by', in Tanner et al., *Labour's First Century*, pp. 344–7.

48 MacDonald, *Socialism and Government*, p. 13.
49 Neville Kirk, 'The conditions of royal rule: Australian and British socialist and labour attitudes to the monarchy, 1901–11', *Social History*, 30 (2005), 80–1. For Tawney's attack on the 'Mumbo-Jumbo' and 'mystification' associated with aristocracy, Ross Terrill, *R. H. Tawney and his times* (Cambridge MA, 1973), p. 184.
50 MacDonald, *Socialism and Government*, pp. 43–4.
51 D. McDermott, 'Labour and Ireland', in Brown, *First Labour Party*, p. 263.
52 Labour Party *Quarterly Circular*, July 1909.
53 Labour Party manifesto January 1910, in F. W. S. Craig, *British General Election Manifestos 1900–1974* (London, 1975), p. 20.
54 Sandra Stanley Holton, *Feminism and Democracy: Women's Suffrage and Reform Politics in Britain 1900–18* (Cambridge, 1986), ch. 3.
55 Cited in Clive Trebilcock, 'Radicalism and the Armament Trust', in A. J. A. Morris (ed.), *Edwardian Radicalism* (London, 1974), p. 196.
56 MacDonald, *Socialism and Government*, p. 36, and David Marquand, *Ramsay MacDonald* (London, 1977), p. 165.
57 Edwards, 'An interview with Ramsay MacDonald', 128.
58 Cited in Marquand, *Ramsay MacDonald*, p. 183.
59 McDermot, 'Labour and Ireland', pp. 260–3.
60 Devolution was scarcely debated at either the annual conference or in the party's policy discussion forum, the *Socialist Review*. Extended powers for local government attracted more attention. See e.g. William Leach, 'The Municipal Socialist: a plea for a Socialist Municipal Bureau', *Socialist Review*, August 1910.
61 The following is based on MacDonald's *Parliament and Democracy* (London, 1920), pp. 70–5.
62 Ibid., p. 74. MacDonald made this point explicitly in a speech at Cardiff in 1924 – 'there is nothing more hopeful for Wales than that Welsh education is based upon Welsh foundations' (*WM*, 15 March 1924).
63 Ramsay MacDonald diary, 1 October 1914, MacDonald papers, TNA JRM 30/69/1753.
64 Tanner, 'Radicalism, Revisionism and socialism', p. 285.
65 Summarised in Duncan Tanner, *Political Change and the Labour Party* (Cambridge, 1990), pp. 361–73.
66 Ibid., p. 140.
67 Cited in Ward, *Red Flag*, p. 70, and see also p. 137.
68 Freeden, *Liberal Languages*, p. 87. Here my interpretation differs from James Meadowcroft in his *Conceptualizing the State: Innovation and Dispute in British Political Thought, 1880–1914* (Oxford, 1995).
69 *WM*, 15 March 1924.
70 Cited in Freeden, *Liberal Languages*, p. 178. MacDonald's commitment to the idea of a national will, embodied in the state, was modified by his belief that the state was dominated by inherited position, and was part of a system which imposed uniformity.
71 Minutes of the Advisory Committee on the Machinery of Government, 19 November 1918; Memorandum by the Secretary of the further work of the Advisory Committee on Local Government', n.d. Labour Party archives, JSM/LG/43.

72 McKibbin, *Evolution of the Labour Party*, pp. 163–77, 206–21. This is argued more fully in Duncan Tanner, *The Political Anatomy of the Labour Party* (Oxford, forthcoming).

73 Speaker's Conference on Devolution (1920) Cmd.692, xiii, 1151.

74 HC, 3 June 1919 c. 2028 (Clynes for Labour). On Wales, R. J. Thomas c. 1948, T. A. Lewis c. 2080–4 and J. Hugh Edwards, c. 2122. For opposition to devolution based on nationality, see Edward Carson, c. 1825, Walter Long c. 1904. The only Conservative who dissented from this view was Captain Ormsby-Gore. See Griffith above p. 89 for his pre-war interest in Welsh devolution.

75 Fair, *Inter-party Conferences*, pp. 227, 229.

76 Ibid., pp. 231, 233.

77 NEC Mins, 19 May and 18 October 1920.

78 LPA, Labour Party Scottish Council, 7 October 1922. For Wales, Edwards and Griffith, above, pp. 124–5.

79 Cecile Laborde, *Pluralist Thought and the State in Britain and France, 1900–25* (Oxford, 2000), p. 83, and Michael Freeden, *Liberalism Divided: A Study in British Political Thought 1914–1939* (Oxford, 1986), pp. 295–312. For Laski and democracy, H. J. Laski, 'Democracy at the cross-roads', *Yale Review* (July 1920), 780–90, 801. Marc Stears, *Progressives, Pluralists and the Problems of the State* (Oxford, 2002), pp. 104–21 considers Cole, Laski and democracy, but not their views on devolved governance.

80 The following is based on Sidney and Beatrice Webb, *A Constitution for the Socialist Commonwealth of Great Britain* (London, 1920), pp. 121–3, 131–4. See also *New Statesman*, 15, 22, 29 November 1919.

81 Brian Lee Crowley, *The Self, the Individual and the Community: Liberalism in the Political Thought of F. A. Hayek and Sidney and Beatrice Webb* (Oxford, 1987). The following draws on pp. 157–73.

82 Webb, *Socialist Constitution*, p. 59.

83 Ibid., p. 72.

84 See his support for the *Report of the Machinery of Government Committee to the Minister of Reconstruction* cited ibid., p. 120. Webb was a member of the committee.

85 Laborde, *Pluralist Thought*, pp. 87–8; H. J. Laski, *Authority in the Modern State* (New Haven, 1919), p. 78.

86 A point made generally in *The Foundation of Sovereignty* (London, 1922). The comments here are from a review of work on devolution and from his work with J. S. Henderson. See *American Political Science Review*, 20 (1926), 883–4.

87 LPA, Machinery of Government Committee Mins, 26 November, 17 December 1919, and addition, 27 January 1920, JSM/MG/8, 12, 14.

88 LPA, Sub-committee on devolution, 6 February 1920, Machinery of Government Committee JSM/MG/16.

89 Ramsay MacDonald papers, J. Walton Newbold to J. R. MacDonald, 13 August 1919, 30/69/1163.

90 C. R. Attlee, G. D. H. Cole and C. M. Lloyd, *Labour Party Bulletin*, 19 (1921); G. D. H. Cole, *The Future of Local Government* (London, 1921); C. M. Lloyd, 'The re-organisation of Local Government areas', January 1925, JSM/LG/131.

91 Davis, above, p.231–3.

92   LPA, 'Draft pamphlet on the reform of Local Government areas', 10 December 1920, JSM/LG/58.

93   Lloyd, 'Reorganisation of Local government'; Morrison, 'Notes on report of Sub-Committee on Ports', 13 October 1920, JSM/LG/55.

94   McKibbin, *Evolution of the Labour Party*; NEC Mins, 12 November 1919.

95   MacDonald papers E. P. Wake to J. R. MacDonald, 21 May 1924, 30/69/174.

96   See pp. 35, 133–6, 138.

97   Minutes of the sub-committee on the adaptation of the Civil Service to new functions, 14 May 1919, JSM/MG/23.

98   Joint Research and Information dept. memo, January 1924, TUC papers 292.30/7 (Modern Records Office, University of Warwick).

99   George Young, 'The Foreign Office and Labour Governments', January 1925, Joint (TUC/Labour) International Department Memorandum, TUC papers 711/5; Labour Party Education Advisory Committee Mins, 22 January 1924. For the TUC, W. Milne Bailey to Fred Bramley, 26 May 1924, TUC papers 292.30/7.

100 H. J. Laski to F. Laski, 12 April 1924, Laski MS DLA 38 (University of Hull).

101 TUC GC Mins, 26 June 1929; Citrine memo, 12 January 1935, TUC MSS 292.750.1/10.

102 H. J. Laski, *Democracy in Crisis* (London, 1933), p. 9 and his *The Danger of Being a Gentleman and Other Essays* (London, 1939), pp. 27–8, citing an essay first published in 1932. For 1931, Lawrence, 'Labour – the myths that it has lived by', pp. 351–2, and Laski, 'The lessons of 1931', *New Clarion*, 29 October 1932.

103 Taylor, 'Labour and the Constitution', p. 160. The TUC also reasserted its right to influence Labour policy formation in the early 1930s by working within centralised party structures. Devolution and decentralisation were not part of its mindset.

104 Dan Ritschel, *The Politics of Planning: The Debate on Economic Planning in Britain in the 1930s* (Oxford, 1997); Richard Toye, *The Labour Party and the Planned Economy, 1931–51* (Woodbridge, 2003).

105 See e.g. *New Clarion*, 29 July, 19 August, 2, 9 September 1933, 24 February 1934.

106 H. Gaitskell and D. Jay memorandum (n.d., 1936), Gaitskell papers C2 (University College, London), p. 17.

107 Ben Pimlott, *Hugh Dalton* (London, 1985), pp. 402–7, 456–7. For the shared British/Welsh perspectives, Ted Rowlands, *'Something Must Be Done': South Wales v. Whitehall 1921–1951* (Merthyr Tydfil, 2000), pp. 115–17.

108 W. W. Knox and Alan MacKinlay, 'The remaking of Scottish Labour in the 1930s', *Twentieth Century British History*, 16 (1995). For Wales, Dai Smith, *Aneurin Bevan and the World of South Wales* (Cardiff, 1993), pp. 200–5.

109 Leonard Woolf, 'Memorandum on the work of the International Group, n.d. but 1929, Mitrany papers Box 4, BLPES.

110 Ibid., pp. 22–4 and his foreword to Robert A. Brady, *The Spirit and Structure of German Fascism* (London, 1937). For Strachey's influence, Hugh Thomas, *John Strachey* (London, 1972), ch. 9.

111 Evan Durbin to Hugh Gaitskell, 31 January 1939, suggesting the latter was 'a bit cracked about fascism in this country', Durbin papers 3/10, BLPES.

112 See e.g. Sonya O. Rose, *Which People's War? National Identity and Citizenship in Wartime Britain* (Oxford, 2003), pp. 218–38.

113 Attlee wrote regular letters from his (repeated) holidays in north-west Wales in the 1930s, which he saw far more favourably than the urban north-west of England. The Labour peer Lord Sankey was another enthusiast. This reflected a long tradition of socialist visitors to rural Wales, stretching back to and including pre-war Fabian summer schools.

114 H. J. Laski, *Nationalism and the Future of Civilization* (London, 1932), p. 50.

115 R. Merfyn Jones and Ioan Rhys Jones, 'Labour and the nation', in Duncan Tanner et al. (eds), *The Labour Party in Wales, 1900–2000* (Cardiff, 2000), pp. 247–50. For Labour in Scotland and Liberal nationalists in Wales see Finlay above, p. 27 and James McConnel, ' "Sympathy without relief is rather like mustard without beef": devolution, Plaid Cymru, and the campaign for a Secretary of State for Wales, 1937–38', *WHR*, 22 (2005).

116 LPA, 'Memorandum on the proposed appointment of a Secretary of State for Wales', n.d. February 1943, Morgan Phillips papers GS/WAL/8.

117 LPA, Morgan Phillips to Miss E. M.Jones, 15 June 1945, Morgan Phillips papers GS/WAL/4.

118 C. R. Attlee to Dai Grenfell, 5 September 1946, Grenfell papers d207/1/ Box 9, West Glamorgan Record Office.

119 J. M. Lee, *Reviewing the Machinery of Government 1942–52* (London, 1977). For the role of Morrison in this, Taylor, 'Labour and the constitution', p. 162.

Index